Dancing in the Heart of Life
Jane O'Brien

Copyright © 2015 Jane O'Brien

All rights reserved. This book or any portion thereof may not be reproduced or used in any manner whatsoever without the express written permission of the author except for the use of brief quotations in a book review.

First published in 2015 by Heart of Life Books
BM Jane O'Brien, London, WC1N 3XX
www.heartoflife.net

Distributed by Lightning Source UK Ltd
Chapter House, Pitfield, Kiln Farm, Milton Keynes, MK11 3LW

A catalogue record for this book is available from the British Library.

ISBN: 978-0-9931238-0-1

Edited by
Rebecca Wood, Freelance Editor, Twickenham
and
Marjohn Pourtabib

Cover design and illustration by Jeremy Scott - glimmerdigital.com

I have changed some names in the text to respect the privacy of the individuals concerned.

You would know the secret of death.

But how shall you find it unless you seek it in the heart of life?

The owl whose night-bound eyes are blind unto
the day cannot unveil the mystery of light.

If you would indeed behold the spirit of death,
open your heart wide unto the body of life.

For life and death are one,
even as the river and the sea are one.

Khalil Gibran

Contents

Foreword vii
Acknowledgements ix
Introduction xi
1. In the Beginning 1
2. Dances with Death 16
3. And This is My Beloved 29
4. So Now What? 53
5. Pioneering Spirit 76
6. Flew Away 98
7. A New Beginning 116
8. Growing and Glowing 121
9. More Things in Heaven and Earth 143
10. Growing Up 164
11. Psycho What? 173
12. Transformation 204
13. The Good Doctor 219
14. Breaking Through 225
15. Look Out London, Here We Come! 234
16. Sex! 251
17. Darkest Night 274
18. A Crown of Jewels 300
19. Typhoid Janie? 322
20. Rags, Riches, Rags… 331
21. I Still Remember the Smell of the Lilacs 355
22. Epilogue: The Conclusion is not The End! 370
Appendix A - Prayer of Bahá'u'lláh – Tablet of Ahmad 375
Appendix B - Prayer of Bahá'u'lláh – From the Sweet-Scented Streams... 377

Foreword

In 1968, I met this quiet, dark-haired American woman, the young and to me slightly hippy-looking wife of the producer of our show. Her accent, her clothes, the things she spoke about, the way she dealt with her children, one of whom was the same age as mine, all proclaimed her as other, novel and different. This was an Ireland before television, before blockbusters, an Ireland where the Catholic Church ruled most aspects of our lives, where books and films were censored and a very conservative government had been in power almost since the creation of the state. An Ireland that appeared unchanged for centuries, unimaginably distant from the roar of the Celtic tiger, where Women's Lib was a ludicrous notion referred to in scoffing derision by both sexes, and most women automatically cooked and ran their homes as their mothers had before them.

Who ever heard of Brown Rice? Rice pudding, *white and luxuriously creamy, with raspberry jam and thick almost-yellow cream on top*, yes. But brown and served for dinner? This was patently eccentric and obviously disgusting. And a fridge the size of a pantry – who needed that? Most Irish homes were cold enough not to need a fridge at all in our opinion. And breastfeeding a child who was walking around? That was nearly indecent. And then rebuilding your house and taking down most of the interior walls – they'd definitely freeze without doors to keep the heat in. We presumed Jane O'Brien would eventually adapt, lose her mad American ways, settle in, become like the rest of us.

I'm eternally grateful she never did. She crept into our midst, but she was, like in the children's story, the Mouse That Roared. Philip, Jane's actor/producer husband, was larger than life and much more visible than his wife, and we thought Jane was quiet and shy. Philip would tell us of Jane's latest exploration, from grinding her own corn to making clothes to running cookery classes and opening a wholefood shop. It gradually became apparent that Jane may have been quiet and self contained in the company of a group of theatre people, but it was also apparent that she was anything but uninteresting. She knew about things we had never thought of, never heard of, things we realized we wanted to know more about.

Jane has always been the person ahead of me on the road, the one who carries the lamp and tells me what she sees, who has the nerve to be the first. Because of her a contingent of young Irish people working in theatre discovered wholefood eating, enthusiastically embraced non-chemical organic and sustainable living in so far as it was possible, and raised children by these principles at a time when these were very far from being the mainstream notions they are today. Now the third generation is following in the same footsteps.

Jane was the first person I knew to discover Psychosynthesis. I can still remember the day she told me about it, my immediate response being that I definitely wanted to explore it. Just as switching to the wholefood diet she practiced changed my body and health immeasurably, so my lifelong adherence to psychosynthesis changed my mind and spirit. I didn't realize until I began to write this, but Jane is the person who has influenced my life the most. In her quiet, non-proselytizing way, by example, she has pointed me towards those things that have had the most profound effect on my life and the way I live.

I have been awed by the strength of Jane's faith during her times of greatest tribulation. Although I do not share her religious beliefs, I learned as always by observing her. She knows that Life is the great teacher, and is always striving to understand and grow through the highs and lows of the experiences life has brought her. Life is the classroom and these are her lessons. I am constantly moved and touched by her struggles to make sense of it all, her willingness and humility in acceptance.

Maybe there are people who know they are teachers, and people who are teachers but don't know it. Jane O'Brien is one of the latter. She has had times of great joy and great sadness, of plenty and of want, like many of her age, but it's her way of dealing with what life has sent her that teaches those of us who know her. She shows the rest of us how it can be, how we can be. I hope the stories in this book have the same effect on a wider audience, and that Jane's life, and the wisdom and awareness she has harvested, enrich many more lives in the way she has enriched those of us who love and value her.

Dearbhla Molloy, Actor

Acknowledgements

I am grateful to so many for help in this project that it would seem impossible to list them all, but I shall mention a few. In terms of professional help I appreciated all the time that I spent with my therapist, Stacey Millichamp, helping me to trust myself enough to express myself authentically. She patiently encouraged me to be honest and forthright and to share the depths of my feelings. Thanks to Rebecca Wood for editing the book which helped the narrative flow better. Thank you to Marjohn Pourtabib for the additional editing to get the book ready for publication. I thank Jeremy Scott for his work preparing the photos for publication but more importantly for the wonderful book cover that he designed.

I thank the late Dr Elisabeth Kübler-Ross whose work I admired greatly. She read a version of my book several years before her death and enthusiastically gave me a quote to recommend it. She said, "I love it. I really love it. I love your faith and courage and your work with holistic health. Everyone should read this book." I am grateful for the encouragement from Elisabeth and from her son, Ken Ross, who founded the EKR Foundation which continues his mother's work. I thank Bob Proctor, author and philosopher for his supportive comments about my book. Also I appreciate my friend and colleague, John Harricharan, author of *When You Can Walk on Water, Take the Boat* and *Morning Has Been All Night Coming*, for his support. My thanks go to Pam Tyler who has been a very valuable catalyst in my life and has shared some of her wonderful material for this book. I really appreciate the Foreword that Dearbhla Molloy, dear family friend and actor, has written which so moved me that I could barely speak after I read it. I thank Annabel Knight, dear friend, writer, actor and drama coach, who took my breath away with the blurb she wrote for my book; it is so honouring of me and my life. I thank Philip's niece, Becky, for permission to quote her letter and Ron Berglas, actor, for permission to quote his material. Much appreciation goes to Sylvia Birrane, Dawn Brown, Keith Casburn, Susanna Copelli, Sarla Danak, Sonia

Fitton, Irene Gloux, Carol Hammond, Leslie Higgins, Suzy Kamada Ward, Nicki Kefalas, Monica Manunza and Gerrie March, Arthur Molinary, the late Ivy Northage, Owen Potts, Joyce Sack, Angela Shaw, Ayla Shekvet, Donna Stewart, Jeremy Turner-Welch, Sarah Tyler-Walters, Becky Walsh and many others for their wisdom and guidance over the years. I thank Holly Rodgers of Stuart-Rodgers Photography in Chicago, Evanston and Highland Park, Illinois who kindly gave me permission to use wedding photos taken by her father, Buck Rodgers

In connection with obtaining permission to quote pieces from other books and websites I thank the following people: Nick Duffell and Helena Løvendal-Duffell, authors of *Sex, Love and the Dangers of Intimacy*, Rachel Hayward of Beyond Words Publishing, Ernest Hecht, Managing Director of Souvenir Press Ltd., Anthony A Lee of Kalimat Press, Bob Moore - Historian with the Jefferson National Expansion Memorial in St Louis, Missouri, Klaus Ottmann, Ph.D., Editor and Chief, Spring Publications, Robert P. Vivian, Marshall of the Baronial Order of Magna Charta.

I thank Ted Slawski at the Synthesis Center in Massachusetts and Nigel Peace of Local Legend Publishing. My special appreciation also goes to Jack and Ginny Acker, Bev Breeze, Kitty Bryant, Lilian and Robert Chambers, Morgan Deare and Mary Healey, Rosaleen Doyle, Karen Dubois, Carole and Trevor Flatt, Mandy Flatt and Mike Carr, Geoff Foster, Amanda Freeman, Gayle Green, Carmen Henry, Ian Holder, Noah Karrasch, Michael Kaufmann, Martin Logue, Eleanor Mazidian, Shona Mc Stravick, Dominick Mereworth, Lynn Orschel, Maliheh Pourtabib, Hoda Rushdy, Norma Scott, Anna Sedgwick, Cynthia Town and Robert Lee Walker, Sculptor, for their continued support and encouragement. Also I add special thanks to my youngest son for editing, formatting and tech support. I include my deep appreciation of my family, friends, colleagues and the many people who have helped me along my way.

Introduction

I have written my story as a celebration of my life, which has been enormously dramatic and challenging. I hope that by reading about my experiences, you might realise that I have faced similar issues to the ones that you might be facing right now so you are not alone. I have always most enjoyed finding a little piece of wisdom and sharing it with others in hopes that it will help them. That is why I enjoy reading autobiographies because usually I can pick up some little gems to help me in my struggles.

What are the types of situations that I have encountered? I had a life threatening illness at age 14 that left me with after effects that I addressed through dietary change and psychology because doctors didn't have answers. I became a Bahá'í and met the love of my life at age 19. Being a Bahá'í inspired me to live the best life I possibly could, to listen to that still small voice within me and to value myself as a human being even when I had lost confidence and felt worthless. I married my husband, American actor, Philip O'Brien, once in 1965, divorced him in 1987, and married him again in 1998. I wouldn't have married him once never mind twice if he hadn't really been the love of my life! I had five children, four live births, and tragically one baby who died at four weeks, and one miscarriage. I raised three children to adulthood.

I inherited money from my mother and grandmother, first at age 21 and in various amounts for about 10 years after that. Then in 1979 I received approximately a million and a half dollars as a windfall from an investment that suddenly became much more valuable than it had been. Ten years later I was on a slippery slope of financial loss until I eventually lost my home. Shortly thereafter I experienced the deaths of three of the closest men in my life, my eldest son who committed suicide, my husband who died of cancer, and my father who died in his 91st year from pneumonia following Parkinson's disease. I didn't know how or if I would come back from all that or even if I cared that I did. I didn't then. I do now. I studied health and healing, counselling and psychotherapy, and after not having ever needed to work for a living before, I trained as a counsellor and began to build a part-time private practice in counselling, showing that it can be done even later on in life. Later I got my Masters Degree as a psychotherapist. I have lived in four different cultures and six American states, which means that I don't have a regional accent that people can identify. That adds to a sense of mystery about me that I enjoy.

That is just an appetiser, a kind of taster of what is ahead of you in my story. There is much, much more to it than that. I hope you enjoy and benefit from reading my story. I love both the highs and the lows of my life. I have learned so much, and have been privileged to experience such a wide variety of events and emotions that even the enormous pain and despair of some of the hard times have opened in me greater depth and understanding. Whatever we do, life passes by in an instant, and what then? Therefore I suggest that one of the most important things that we can ever do in our life is to decide how we are going to live, what we want to do, and how we would like to be remembered, so that despite our inevitable mistakes, we may make choices that reflect our values and make our life meaningful to us.

CHAPTER 1

In the Beginning

Life was very different growing up in the 1940s and 1950s. I was born in St Louis Missouri, USA. My mother was 34 when she married my father which in those days was considered quite late. She fell pregnant with me very soon after the wedding. My father, who was about a year younger than she, had been married before, but his wife had died tragically, leaving him with a little girl of about five years old who was also part of our household. My father changed jobs frequently, which meant that I moved around a lot as a child. He worked for Montgomery Ward, Ford Motor Company, RCA Victor in Canada, to name a few, and we lived in St Louis, Chicago, Detroit, New York, New Jersey, and Montreal, Canada. Once when I questioned him about his work, he said that he always moved from one job to a better one, so I guess that made it worthwhile to move so frequently.

I remember when I was about five or six we lived in Montclair, New Jersey. My sister, Marianne, was a bit of a rebel, and I idolised her, but I also fought with her and blamed her for any trouble when I could! I didn't get into trouble much, probably because I was the baby, and I would have been seen by the adults to be copying her behaviour at times. There were long periods of time when I was on my own with my parents because Marianne sometimes went away to boarding school. I missed her when she was gone. I didn't really understand why she went, but now, as I look back, I think it must have had to do with her having a difficult relationship with my mother. I don't think that my mother had a clue about how to deal with a child who was not her own and perhaps even found the demands of her own child to be a bit too much. My mother was 35 years old when she had me, so I imagine that she was in shock having found herself the carer for two children so soon after marriage. As the only girl in her family, with three brothers, she had been the darling. One of her brothers was killed in a bicycle accident when he was 14, and so she had to deal with that loss as well as stand up to her two other brothers – an older one and a younger one.

My sister and I both liked reading. There was no television in those days, precious little radio, and certainly no computers, so we entertained ourselves from a very young age with books from the library. My mother would put us to bed, each in our own rooms, listen to our prayers and call for lights out. Once she left the room, I reached for my torch, got down way under the covers toward the bottom of the bed, making sure that the covers would hide my head and the light, then I would start to read and I would enter my own magical world of heroes, heroines, villains, demons both real and imaginary, from my borrowed books. I read Bible stories and ordinary children's stories. My mother caught me from time to time and would take away my torch. After a designated period of time the torch would be returned to me, and the whole procedure would begin again.

In school although I was shy and quite timid in front of my classmates, I had determination and a real desire to do what I wanted to do. One day a storm had blown down a tree in the playground, so it was possible to climb on the trunk of it because it was lying across the ground. The only problem was that there were oceans and oceans of water around and under the tree trunk because of all the rain. The teacher said nobody was to climb that tree. Well, I didn't see it like that! I felt that a person had to climb a tree that has fallen on the ground. How many opportunities would a person get to do that? So I climbed over the trunk, delighting in the freedom of doing so, but I also fell into the water! My clothes were all wet that afternoon, and the teacher was not pleased with me!

Peter, a neighbour and one of my best friends, had a back garden with a great climbing frame that I loved using. He had a loose floorboard in his room under which he kept all his treasures, like special pebbles, a deck of cards, and a water pistol. He showed them to me, and he didn't show them to anyone else. I felt really special.

One Halloween, I went out early in the afternoon calling "trick or treat" at each door with Shirley, another neighbour and good friend. I was dressed up as an elephant and Shirley was a dancer or something. One man didn't respond to our ringing the bell, but we knew he was home. After all, we had said trick or treat, so we rubbed a dry bar of soap on his screen door as our trick. It isn't easy to get bits of embedded soap off a screen door like it is off a window. Shirley and I had just soaped some of the screen when he came to the door. We felt mortified and apologised profusely, but the man was really nice. He accepted our apology and laughed to himself.

Peter, Shirley and I and a few others would stand on the side of the road, and we would watch the cars driving by. When there was a break in the traffic, which happened often because there weren't many cars, we would stretch a thread from a tree on one side of the street to a tree on the other. Then we would hang leaves and branches on the thread. We would stand on the path looking and laughing because the drivers who came after that would slow down, look and wonder at the branches hanging in mid-air across the street. Finally, they would slowly drive through, break the thread, and the leaves and branches would fall to the ground. We lived in a very quiet neighbourhood, so it was easy for us to hang more thread and leaves and wait for the next cars to come along.

Autumn in New Jersey was my favourite time of the year. I loved the leaves changing colour. Whenever my dad raked them in the garden, Marianne and I would jump in them, fall in them and play in them. I loved that special smell which only autumn leaves have, and the crispy crunchy dryness of them. I loved the cooler air, knowing that winter was coming, and that meant snow and sleds. Oh how I loved snow. I ate it, I rubbed it on my face, and of course I threw the occasional snowball, but not to hurt anyone. We would even pour hot maple syrup on to the snow and eat the crystallised syrup-snow. It was wonderful. What I loved to do more than almost anything else was to make a snowman in the garden. It felt so good after working hard outside in the cold to go in and have my dinner all ready for me and still hot.

I didn't eat much at all as a child, and I was very fussy about what I did eat. I got so involved in my activities that I forgot about food and often wasn't really interested. My mother thought I should eat lots of different things. Well that didn't suit me. We used to go to a restaurant called Bonds where they sold "Awful Awfuls", which were huge milkshakes. My dad could finish one, and I could finish about a half of one or not even that much, and do you know what, if you drank three Awful Awfuls, you would get a prize, and do you know what the prize was? It was another Awful Awful. I always wanted to win that prize, but I could never even finish one. I liked a cheeseburger but only with ketchup, no lettuce, no tomato, just plain. I loved fillet of sole, and I could eat it daily, but nobody would let me have it daily. So if I didn't like what was for dinner, I would just do without and get on with the important things I had to do.

Often in the evenings when we were having dinner, my mother and father would be arguing and arguing. Well even for the little that I ate, I liked to have a bit of peace, so I simply said: "bicker, bicker, bicker". You'd think I had said the worst words in the world. They shouted at me and I got sent to my room. My room was nice, and it was mine. I had my bed, a little table by my bed, and my Bible stories and some other books and a lamp. At the advanced age of 6, I didn't really have dolls anymore because there were other things that interested me at that time. There was a closet and a chest of drawers with a mirror over it, where my clean clothes regularly appeared in the drawers as if by magic. To this day I have no memory of my mother ever washing clothes, and yet I am sure that she did. I could sit in my room and look out the window or read. Even if I might have been crying when I came up, but once I was in my room, I felt safe, and I would calm down. I liked the silence and the stillness of my room. There I would dream and dream and dream. I loved daydreaming, but in school my teachers always told me to stop dreaming. I would rather have drifted away at times than listen to their voices droning on in my ear. I heard them anyway. They didn't realise that I heard them better when I was daydreaming, and it was a lot more fun because I went to places and did things in my daydreams that felt like real adventures.

Another thing my teachers would say is "Janie is very careless in her work. She has to be more careful. She would do a lot better if she paid more attention to her work and was less careless." I felt I needed to be outside in the wilds of the neighbourhood, learning about life from the trees and the animals, the birds and the bees, and the wind, the sun, the rain, earth and snow. I knew they would never understand me. I believed that it was by experience that we learn, not by some teacher standing there in front of us acting like they knew it all and just talking to us and telling us things. I liked the stories they told, but I also liked to write my own stories. I wanted to be an author when I grew up.

On days at home in the bad weather when we couldn't play outside, Marianne and I would set up card tables and chairs in the living room and cover them with blankets, so we could have some tunnels to crawl through. We could pretend all kinds of things in those tunnels except one day I was shocked by the visit of one of my mother's friends, so the game got forgotten. The lady came in to see my mother, and I looked at her from the safety of our newly constructed tunnel, so she didn't exactly see me but I saw her. Her stomach was huge, not just a little fat or big, but really huge. I had never seen anything like it in my life, and I was very observant, or so they said. I liked to observe people. Because my sister, Marianne, was older than me, I felt I ought to ask her because sometimes she had a better idea than I did. I did ask her, and she said to me that the lady hadn't breathed properly as a child, and you would get a huge stomach if you didn't breathe properly. That was enough to terrify me. I was particularly aware that when I read under my covers at night while hiding, breathing was not my strong point. I knew I had to do something. I sat in the tunnel, and I breathed so deeply it felt as if my breath came from my toenails. I concentrated breathing in and out, in and out, in a very careful way because I didn't want that to happen to me when I grew up. I knew things were going to change, and I was going to get bigger and other things too, but I couldn't leave my house ever if I looked like that. Oh it was horrible. I was a skinny little kid at that time. It was only much later that I realised that the lady had been pregnant, and her large stomach had nothing to do with the quality of her breathing!

I worried about the little wild animals and their food in the winter. I used to go out in front of my house on days when I had no school or in the afternoons, and I would sit quietly and wait. A little squirrel would come down the tree, and it would take a peanut from my hand. Then I would get out another peanut, and I would sit quietly again. The same squirrel would do the same thing. It kept eating from my hand. I loved animals, and the crisp cold weather, and the clear wind dancing through my hair. I loved the rain pouring down while I walked along, and I loved the sun beating down on me.

I loved having pets. I longed for a dog, but my mother said, no! One day my father said he would take Marianne and me out to see some rabbits. My mother said "Go to see them, but under no circumstances bring any home!" Of course we saw these wonderful white furry rabbits, and came back home with a cage and two rabbits. My father fixed the cage to the side of the garage. I am sure that Marianne and I were supposed to care for them and feed them, and I am equally sure that when we were at school, the job became one for my mother. She was not pleased about that, and one day there were simply no more rabbits at our home, and I leave you to guess who got rid of them!

My mother and father both said that once I got an idea in my head, I wouldn't stop until I had gotten what I wanted. They didn't, however, praise me for that quality or help me to realise how it could really serve me later on in my life. They also did not notice the patience that I developed as I pursued my goal. I longed for a dog throughout my childhood. I had one as a very young child, which my mother gave away, and as a teenager, I finally persuaded my mother to let me have a dog again. This time I took full responsibility for my dog until I became very seriously ill and was hospitalised for six weeks. My mother was working and visiting me in hospital, and again she gave my dog away. It wasn't until years later, shortly after I was married, that I finally got a dog that was not given away. My husband and I both loved dogs, so we got a miniature dachshund, and we named him "Irving Katz". That was just the beginning of a series of dogs, and I have always had a dog since then.

One summer day, my father tried to get Marianne and me to help in the garden, so we sat in the garden while he was planting tomato seeds. We would have helped, but it was hot, and we were hungry, and we had a box of Cheesits, which were cheese crackers. It was nice out in the garden, but in the heat all we could really manage was to finish that box of Cheesits. What did we know about tomatoes and gardens anyway? By the time we finished the box of Cheesits, Dad had already put the tomato seeds in the ground. He wasn't so happy with us.

One of my favourite things to do with my father was to play chess. He had started teaching me the game when I was about five years old. Nobody else in our family played and he was very good at it. For those of you who know the game, he would relinquish his queen and two castles - or rooks - at the start of the game, and he would still beat me. Sometimes to encourage me, he would let me win. Gradually I became better until eventually I could occasionally beat him at a game even when he didn't relinquish any of his pieces. That was a real triumph and he was always encouraging my progress even when I beat him. When I got a little older, and played chess with boys of my own age, I always had to ask the question, will they still be interested in me if I can beat them at chess? Usually I did beat them. Playing chess allowed me to begin to understand that my actions caused consequences and to learn to take responsibility for what I did. Whenever I had a major decision to make, I would look at my choices and consider all the options.

My father never went to church because he didn't believe that a priest or a minister truly represented God. My father was a really good man. He was kind, fair and honest. He was fun and more cuddly than my mother was. He was strict too, and he sometimes got angry with Marianne and me. I really liked Sunday School because all of the stories were so exciting. One spring Sunday my mother was taking me to church, and I was all dressed up in my new Mary Janes, which were black shoes with a strap across them. They looked great with my lacy white socks and I had a new dress on that I loved. It was yellow with a white collar, and the colour was lovely on me with my dark hair hanging down and my pale skin. Everybody always said I was so pale! I thought I was fine, but that didn't stop them. Anyway on the way to church, I said to my mother, "When Jesus Christ comes again, can we go to see Him?" She said yes, and I thought that would be a dream come true. Off we would go in a plane to the place where He was, and we could see and hear Him. I was over the moon. I could see that my mother, in her wisdom, realised the importance of that, and so I rested content. I hadn't expected her to say yes because I didn't think such a thing mattered as much to her as it did to me. After all, she had so much to do and to worry about, but I was thrilled when she agreed. I could never figure out why everyone wasn't looking all the time for Jesus to come again like He said He would. He was pretty good the first time around, and I thought He would be great when He came back because He would have had so much experience, and people would be more able to understand Him this time. I was sure that they wouldn't send Him to the lions or crucify Him the second time like people did when He first came.

I really thought my sister, Marianne, was great. She loved horses and she could draw them much better than I could. I looked up to her and wanted to be just like her. I loved the times when we played together, but we didn't have much time because school kept us so busy. I went to four or five different schools before I was eight years old because we all moved about once a year as my dad kept getting new and better jobs. I remember when he worked for Ford Motor Company we had one of the first Fords with a windscreen wiper. That was really exciting. Later we had to move to Montreal because he got a new job in RCA Victor in Canada. He became a vice president of the company. It was a company that made records, televisions and record players and it handled some very popular recording artists. I'll never forget what happened when we drove from New Jersey to Canada to start living there. My sister and I had turtles that we had to take in the car with us because they couldn't be put into moving vans without food or light. They needed our care. We stayed in a hotel for a few days before moving into our new flat. While we were in the hotel, we kept the turtles in the bathtub to give them a little more room than they had in their little bowls. We really had a lovely time there, and we were sure that our turtles were very happy. Goodness knows what the maid thought when she came to clean our rooms in the mornings!

We went to our new flat when it was ready and our belongings had been delivered. We were thrilled to have a home again, and we got very excited just putting our things into our new rooms. Then suddenly we realised that we didn't have our turtles. We had left the turtles in the bathtub of our room in the hotel! We were so scared that we had lost them. My father had to phone the hotel to find out if they were still there. The people in the hotel had kept them, so he had to arrange to get them. He was not amused! Marianne and I on the other hand really were amused! After my father left to collect our turtles, we couldn't stop laughing. Of course, when he came home, we had to be very serious and show him that we could admit our mistake.

I loved living in Montreal. Our apartment overlooked a playing field. In the winter, part of it was flooded and turned into an ice skating rink. I really enjoyed ice skating, and I couldn't believe my luck to have an outdoor skating rink just across the road from where I lived. Our milk was delivered daily by a man driving a horse cart. He let all the local children get up on the cart and travel a short distance between apartment buildings. It was great fun, and we all clamoured to get onto the cart. There were two languages in Montreal, French and English, so I got more French in school than I had ever had in the USA. I made good friends, and even though I loved living there. Because my parents still weren't getting along well, my mother decided to leave my father for good. One day she had arranged to have our possessions packed up and shipped to St Louis, and after that was done, we just left. My dad and Marianne came home to an empty flat, and we had gone. I am sure such a decision took a lot of courage in those days. Separation and divorce were seen as barely acceptable and "not the done thing". There was a terrible stigma attached to being a divorced woman with a child.

I was seven years old when my mother and I went back to St Louis to live with my grandmother. At first I thought it was a temporary visit, but actually it was another two years before I even saw my father again. I missed my dad and my sister, Marianne, a lot during that time. I was so excited one weekend because my dad was coming to see us in St Louis. It was great to be with him again. Then after his visit, as he was getting ready to leave and go back to Canada, my mother and father both told me that they were never going to live together anymore. I was devastated. I ran to my bed and cried, wondering what I had done wrong, and what I could do. Gradually I realised that there was nothing I could do. Even so, I couldn't help but think that I was partly to blame. The arrangement was that I could go to visit my father for five weeks each year, and that usually happened in the summer time when I had a holiday from school. I was also unable to see Marianne except during my holiday visits to my dad because she lived with him, so I went from being a little girl with a big sister and living with my family, to living as an only child with my mother and grandmother. It certainly wasn't as much fun, and I felt lonely.

It was only on rare occasions that I would get to talk to my dad and to Marianne because telephone conversations were expensive and they didn't happen often. We could never talk for long. I wrote letters to him, and he wrote letters to me, but Marianne and I didn't write to each other. Some of my best times were during my visits to him. One summer I went to Montreal for my annual visit and it happened that Perry Como, a popular showman of the time, was going to be in town for a visit. Because RCA Victor handled his music, Dad was designated to entertain him, his wife and a few other members of his family. Marianne and I longed to be allowed to meet them, and we begged Dad to please let us do so. We waited as patiently as we could for what seemed like a long time. Finally Dad said that he was going out to dinner with Perry Como and his family, and after dinner he would phone us so that we could then join them all at the restaurant for dessert. We were thrilled. In those days, we didn't have an ordinary telephone line but we had a "party line", which meant that two households used the same number, so it often happened that a member of the other household was using the phone when we wanted to make a call. Naturally we were so afraid of missing my father's call that we watched the phone like hawks and occasionally picked it up to see if it was free. Once when I picked it up, somebody else was on the line. I said that we were waiting for a very important phone call, and if they didn't mind, would they please get off the phone and make their call later. They did, and eventually my dad phoned and said we could go. We got a taxi to take us to the restaurant. Marianne and I went to meet Perry Como and his family, dressed in our best clothes, and we had a wonderful time being allowed to participate in such an exciting occasion. Later that evening my Dad said that he was very proud of us, so we were delighted.

When I was 15 years old, I went on a school trip with about 10 other students. My English teacher and his wife, who later became lifelong friends of our family, supervised our group. My dad arranged for all of us to go to the Perry Como Show, and I really enjoyed meeting Perry Como a second time. Dad also invited us to have afternoon tea at Peacock Alley, which was part of the Waldorf Astoria Hotel. All of these things made Dad my hero. I loved my visits with him because I could really talk with him about anything. It was a great relief for me to be with him because I felt respected by him and treated like an intelligent human being. I felt like my mother and her family treated me like a child. I also worried about my dad, so each time I would join him on a visit, my first question would be, "Are you happy?" When he said, yes, I felt better and could relax.

RCA Victor also handled Elvis Presley, and I really would love to have met him too, but it never happened. Dad once said to me that he thought he would grow his hair long and style it like Elvis's hair. I knew he was kidding but I just replied "you don't have enough hair to do that!", and we all had a laugh.

I loved my mother and my family in St Louis, but living there without my dad was so hard. I noticed it especially when I was in secondary school. Each autumn there would be a special fathers' day when fathers would attend classes to find out more about what their children were doing in school. I always had to find an uncle or a friend of my mom's to go with me. I remember feeling so lost. I longed to have my father magically turn up at my school on fathers' day as a surprise, but it never happened. This experience of being raised without my father made me feel as if I didn't quite fit in or belong. I knew of nobody else in my class or even in my school whose father wasn't around.

For six years I lived in a household with my mother, my grandmother, and my grandmother's housekeeper. Living in a household of older women with no neighbourhood children around was a big contrast to my life in Montreal where I had been part of a real family and had plenty of children nearby. My mother asked my grandmother if we could move back to St Louis and live with her. My grandmother replied, "you would be as welcome as the flowers in spring." I certainly didn't feel very welcome in her home. My grandmother loved me underneath it all, but she didn't know how to show it to me. She was not the typically American home-made apple pie and lots of hugs grandmother I might have expected. My grandmother was a strong and principled woman. Although I have to admire her for her values and her sense of honour, I found her strict and aloof. I felt like the child who could do nothing right. My cousin, who was just about a year older than me, seemed to be her favourite, but she didn't live with my grandmother. She only appeared occasionally for short periods of time when she was on good behaviour. My grandmother often praised her and wondered why I couldn't be more like her. I lived in my grandmother's home 24 hours a day, and I couldn't behave as an adult all the time. I did try, but I often felt like a born troublemaker who was usually in the way of the adults around me.

Much later, when I was at the University of Illinois I returned home to visit my grandmother who was ill and confined to bed. It was about a year before she died. She told me that she was disappointed in her children because she felt that they hadn't lived "meaningful" lives. I told her that I was going to live a life that was meaningful to me. She asked what I was going to do, and I replied that I didn't know, but maybe I would write a book. I was shocked and pleasantly surprised that she trusted me enough to tell me about being disappointed in her children. She was a proud woman, and I knew she would not have admitted such a thing to many people. That was a real gift to me because it showed me that she really did love me. I hadn't been very sure of her love for me before that conversation.

In retrospect I imagine that it must have been quite hard for my grandmother to suddenly have a young child in her home. She had already raised her four children. She and my mother had remained extremely close. After having moved from her big family home to an apartment and losing her husband, she must have grown used to her peaceful existence. Actually we were probably all in shock, me for not having my father and my sister around, my mother for having chosen to leave her husband, and my grandmother for having her home invaded by me and my mother.

After living with my grandmother for six years, my mother and I moved to our own apartment. It was great for me because I was much nearer to my secondary school, and I was freer to be myself and to do the things I liked to do like listen to my music. I was considerate of my mother and her wishes, and yet I could relax in a way I hadn't been able to do in my grandmother's home. One of the things I really enjoyed was sitting watching television with my mother in the evenings. I was not popular at school, and I didn't go out much and certainly never on a school night. I found myself able to do some kinds of homework like maths, which was my best subject, in front of the television. My mother used to say to me, "You will remember these times when we watched television together years later when you have your own life." She was right. Television was live in those days. It was a fairly new medium. We loved courtroom dramas like Perry Mason, Westerns like Have Gun, Will Travel, and The Lone Ranger. Speaking of that, one time my dad took me to Madison Square Garden to see the Lone Ranger. Dad took me backstage to meet the Lone Ranger afterwards, and he gave me one of his silver bullets! I was thrilled.

When my mother and I had our own apartment I could finally have girl friends over to visit or spend the night. My mother was great. She participated in my life, but she didn't force me to be someone I wasn't. She always told me that I should think what I wanted and do what I believed was right, but not talk about it. She realised that my thoughts were often misunderstood by those around us. My mother worked in the lumber business that her father had started and made successful. My two uncles ran it, and she didn't seem to have an equal partnership in it, so she was a secretary/receptionist. I don't know if she was consulted about major decisions to do with the business. I do know that it was not easy for her to work there. I didn't like the attitude in the family that my mother was "poor Alice" the single parent. I longed to grow up so I could take responsibility for myself and create a different life for us without having to rely on people who pitied us.

On Reflection

Remembering how I was as a child reminds me of that tender innocence and simplicity that I can so easily forget in the rush of adult life. Some of us are so eager to grow up and be independent that we run away from anything that we consider 'childish'. In attempting to declare our own independence we may also run away from feeling frightened, sad or vulnerable and imagine that if we deny those feelings, we can remain strong. However if we actually acknowledge that child within we may be able to reawaken our ability to deal with fears, grief and anxieties and also learn to play again and be spontaneous in a way we may have forgotten because of carrying so many responsibilities. The child in us may be closer than we imagine.

Part of the problem is our elementary idea of what it means to grow and develop through our lives. We often think of growth as a straight line from birth until death, and that makes it look like it is necessary to leave the child further and further behind as we grow up. However, another way of looking at growth is to think of it like the rings of a tree, which means that each age is ever present. In the case of a tree, each year a new layer of sapwood is added around an existing core and a new ring forms. So with human growth; each year a new ring forms in our psyche, which includes all the previous ones, and so in a way as adults we are like the trunk of a tree with the child at our core.

I frequently tell my clients that one of the most important things we can do as adults is to reacquaint ourselves with our inner child. Sometimes people reject that idea because it feels like hard work to suddenly be aware of and even look after the little vulnerable part of ourselves. However, we are the only ones who can respond to the child within us in a healthy and loving way because only we can discover what we really wanted and needed as a child and therefore what that little child might want and need now. Very often the child within us feels frightened, lost, hurt, and abandoned, and when we are able to pay attention to the vulnerable feelings of the child inside us, we feel much stronger and healthier. When we deny our vulnerability and feeling lost, frightened or hurt, even to ourselves, we live a fragmented and less secure life. When we are feeling fragmented and insecure we are not as flexible and spontaneous as we are when we can soothe ourselves or ask for help in our vulnerable times. What could be more refreshing in our daily adult lives than to be able to enjoy the playfulness and spontaneity of childish behaviour at times as a relaxing refreshment in the midst of our 'grown up' responsibilities?

I have often worked with performers. They come to me when they have a problem with stage fright or audition nerves. Part of the problem is that they try to fight their fear and deny it, which only makes things worse. I encourage them to treat the fear as they would a frightened child who is standing beside them and say to that child, "I am with you, and we are going to do this together". When they are able to do that, and imagine themselves taking the child by the hand and together facing the audience or the casting people in an audition, they are much more at ease. The child really loves to perform, but when he or she is frightened it is paralysing and the adult is unable to function adequately.

In my own life, I remember a time when I couldn't speak in front of an audience because I was terrified to do so. Gradually after having resolved a lot of the childhood pain I had experienced I got to the point when I was at ease standing in front of an audience. One evening I had been asked to read a prayer in front of several hundred people. I stood up to do so, looked at an audience that was expectant and waiting for me to read a prayer and I suddenly imagined that I had my little inner child in my arms dressed in a black witch costume, laughing and looking out at the audience. I was touched and very amused by my image, wondering what my audience might have thought if they had really seen me holding a delighted child in a witch costume in my arms as I was about to read a prayer. My amusement and delight in the childish image immediately relaxed me enabling me to read the prayer with reverence and respect and the pure joy of that delightful child.

Another area of difficulty if we are not taking care of our own inner child is in relationship. Often we expect our partner to always be there to comfort us when we are hurt and generally look after us, and for a time that may work well. However, our partners are not always necessarily available for us, and if we cannot manage our vulnerable feelings ourselves, or are unwilling to do so, we may put too much strain on our relationship. Relationship is about being responsive to the needs of the other, but if there is too much expected, as would be the case if we have not learned to care for ourselves, we may be severely disappointed. Then we might think the relationship is at fault when it may be simply that we need to be more responsible for our own self-care.

We can contribute a great deal to the smooth running of a healthy relationship if first we have a clear relationship with our own needs as well as that of our partnership, and we are able to look after ourselves and each other in a balanced way.

If you want to regain your feeling of joy and wonder and delight, begin to take care of yourself when you feel frightened, confused or lost as if those feelings are coming from a child within you. It does make an enormous difference. Then gradually you will really appreciate the pleasure you get from just imagining that little child, who is the core of who you are, joining and participating in your life.

Chapter 2

Dances with Death

For some people death is still something of a taboo which can make it difficult to think about or discuss. Death is inevitable so it may be useful to have some understanding of its impact. Death is as primal as birth and yet in many ways more mysterious, sometimes as urgent and compelling, and also beyond anyone's control. Death reminds me of my human fragility and of my necessary dependence on forces beyond me. It enhances my sense of purposefulness and compels me to make my life meaningful. If there were no death, and the panorama of my life stretched out endlessly into the future, I might not feel a sense of urgency to set goals and achieve the things that are important to me.

We learn about death in so many ways, by reading from the world's great spiritual traditions, by being with loved ones as they approach death or when they die, by reading the many popular writings about near death experiences or death itself. I have had many times when I felt as if I were about to die: times when I was seriously ill, hurt, disappointed in life, or feeling despair and helplessness. Sometimes I actually wanted to die just to escape some dreadful experiences. Other times I was frightened that I would no longer have the chance to do everything I wanted to do, and I was afraid of the process of dying.

I will share with you some of my own early experiences of death that impressed upon me the fact that my life is preciously short, and I could never know how long I might have to live it. At birth, both my mother's life and mine were threatened because she had toxaemia and pre-eclampsia, serious complications of pregnancy that forced the doctor to deliver me by emergency Caesarean. I came into this world a month premature, weighing only 4 lbs. My mother was released from the hospital two weeks before I was, so I was temporarily abandoned at that very early stage in my life. I was told that my mother was afraid to touch me because I was so tiny, delicate and fragile. Sometimes my aunt, an experienced mother of two baby boys, came to help by holding me and feeding me. She was not afraid I'd break! Years later my mother would tell me how frightened she had been of losing me and of losing her own life at the time of my birth. She would always say "You were cute then!" I questioned her "then" because I wanted to be cute still. She never reassured me, so I would sarcastically say, "Thanks!" like the rebellious, defensive teenager that I was.

My earliest memory is that of my grandfather's death. I must have been about a year old. My mother and I were staying with my grandparents because my grandfather was dying. My mom took me with her when she went to help with my grandfather, but my dad and half sister stayed at home in Chicago at that time because my dad had to work. I remember being in a cot in a small room in my grandmother's apartment. There were a lot of noises at that time: people moving back and forth in the hall next to my room. I was left alone in the room and I have a feeling even now that I was aware of the commotion and that something important was going on outside my little room. Responding to the feelings outside my door, I stood up, held on to the railings of the cot and cried. I recall that my mother came in to settle me down, but she wouldn't lift me up and take me out to be with the other people. I just never saw my grandfather again. I remember that time so clearly for someone so young.

At age five, when I was living in Montclair, New Jersey, with my mom, dad and older half sister, Marianne, I became ill with a fever and very sore throat. The doctor had come to see me several times but it didn't help and I just grew sicker, and my fever rose. In panic, my father rushed me to the hospital because he was not happy with the doctor's judgement. As soon as I got to the hospital, I was diagnosed with acute tonsillitis, and had an emergency tonsillectomy, without which the toxins in my body from the overworked tonsils would have killed me. I remember going under the anaesthetic, even though I didn't really understand what was going to happen. I lay on the operating table, and I was asked to close my eyes. The anaesthetist promised me a treat if I closed my eyes and went to sleep. I obediently closed my eyes and the darkness enveloped me as I went to sleep in that cold operating room. I felt a bit better after the operation despite a very sore throat, and I was delighted to be given ice cream. That was all that concerned me at the time! Only my parents really knew how close they had come to losing me then.

When I was 13 years old, I was living with my mom in a small apartment in St Louis, Missouri. We hadn't been there very long, having recently moved out of my grandmother's apartment. I had been so excited to have my own room again instead of sharing a room with my mother as I had done at my grandmother's. It was a lovely room, painted robin's egg blue with three big windows in it. I had thoroughly enjoyed the chaos of moving in, even getting our furniture and some of my old toys out of storage from when we had left Montreal. Of course those toys meant nothing to me six years later. I was certainly too grown up for them.

My excitement at bringing order to our new home was cut short, however, when I came down with a seemingly relentless fever, cold and severe coughing and I went through about 10 large boxes of tissues in only a couple of weeks! I was used to colds and some sinus problems, but that was a real record to use that many tissues in such a short time. I was so uncomfortable and could hardly sleep because of the extreme coughing fits. I felt so awful that I prayed for some kind of relief or release. I did recover slowly, but I was extremely sick with what turned out to be a heavy dose of bronchitis.

A year later, when I was 14 I was still living in the apartment with my mom, and had spent a few weeks getting back into the school routine after the summer holidays. It seemed as if life was just getting started when I came down with another high fever. I had a severe pain in my back when I tried to walk, and I could barely manage to get up to use the toilet. I wasn't in any condition to walk anywhere else. My mother was beside herself with worry as this illness went on for several days without any relief, and I was certainly not getting any better. My fever was high, about 104 degrees farenheit, and the pain in my back was most unusual. My mother finally took me into Barnes Children's Hospital in St Louis. When I arrived, they gave me a spinal tap, and determined that I had encephalitis, which is an inflammation of the spinal cord and the base of the brain. I was put into an isolation ward because I was severely ill.

On the first day lying in the dark in that hospital room, I was not allowed to leave the bed at all, which meant that I had to use a bedpan rather than the toilet. That dreadful bedpan was so cold, and I was so embarrassed about the thought of using it that I waited for an exceptionally long time without using it at all. I held on as long as I could, however I was finally unable to do anything else, so I used it and felt demoralised and dehumanised because I was given no other option. I got really angry about the lack of privacy and refinement. I didn't understand how sick I actually was, and I hated my condition. The room was very small and dark, and I felt as if nobody cared and they had just thrown me in what seemed like a closet because they didn't know what to do with me.

The sheets seemed to lie over some kind of plastic or rubber mattress cover, which made them rather clammy and uncomfortable especially because my body felt so hot. I was mostly left on my own in the room, and although my mother visited me as often as she could, much of the time I was in pain and just lay still staring at the ceiling. My head hurt too much to read as I normally might have done. The nurses were not particularly chatty. They came in and checked my temperature, but I was feeling so miserable, hurt and angry at my poor body that there was very little interaction at all.

A few days later I was moved to a room on the main ward, and the room was lighter and more pleasant. There were even some open windows to let in fresh air. I didn't feel quite so isolated. I was still very feverish, but I decided that I would get up to go to the toilet when necessary rather than using that dreadful bedpan. I really wanted to regain a sense of control and dignity. I had no idea how weak I was. The hospital bed was higher than my bed at home. Instead of sitting up and jumping down off the bed as I would ordinarily have done, I attempted to slide, almost slither on my back like a snake, down from the high bed onto the floor. I don't know why I did that, but I guess the burning fever affected my judgement. I was just sliding off the bed, when my mother appeared at the doorway and saw me. She shouted for the doctor, and just as I was reaching the floor, he came in and scooped me up. I hadn't realised that when my feet hit the floor, there would be no strength in my legs to hold me up. Fortunately the doctor caught me just in time to prevent me from ending up collapsed in a heap on the floor.

I still remember that doctor's name. It was Doctor Spitz, and I thought he was really handsome. I considered him a good friend while I was in the hospital. After that experience, I knew that I had to stay in bed and use the bedpan, so although I resigned myself to it, I continued to hate it. I hadn't known that I couldn't walk because my legs were too weak to hold my weight. I was really terrified that I would never be able to walk again. It didn't help that the doctors and nurses didn't really tell me much about what was going on for me in the way of diagnosis. They tried to placate me with kind but empty words saying only "you will be fine". However, I knew that my legs wouldn't hold me up, and how could that ever become fine? I had no idea what kind of life I had ahead of me.

Another affront was the hospital food. Obviously when I was really ill with a very high fever I wasn't hungry, so the food didn't matter, but when I began to feel a little better and got even a little hungry, the food was just awful. Fortunately some of my relatives would bring me food especially on weekends when they weren't working, but much of the time I could barely eat what the hospital served. I still remember how delighted I was when I saw my aunt and uncle come in with various food parcels because I knew then that I could enjoy a meal again. At that stage of my life, one of my favourite foods was vichyssoise, that lovely potato and leek soup that is eaten cold. Soup wasn't the easiest thing to take into the hospital, but they did it, and I was delighted. It really tasted good especially after having eaten so little for so long.

I remained on my back in the bed in my feverish state eating very little and being watched by nurses and doctors. My fever rose even higher. I think it must have reached 106 or 107. Whatever it was, the nurses knew that if it went any higher, I would definitely die, so they took rather drastic measures to save me. I was dimly aware that nurses were giving me an iced-alcohol bath to bring down my temperature. That was horrible because the sponge bath on my burning body was so cold that it felt excruciating. I went into a kind of dreamy state and then had what I later came to understand as a near death experience. I saw a large lake with a lot of people on the other side of the lake looking at me. I felt a sense of love coming from them that I can barely describe. It was so powerful. I felt as if I had come home. I felt no pain at all, just an enormous sense of relief.

Then I was asked if I wanted to stay there or go back to my body and continue my life. I didn't really know where "there" was, but wherever it was, it felt just great, no pain and a sense of love and acceptance that I could hardly imagine existed. I don't know if it was a voice or a force that I felt. I said that I wanted to live for two reasons: 1) I knew if I died then, it would devastate my mother because we had such a good time in our little life together. 2) I really wanted to experience the love of a man as an adult and to have children before leaving my life. I was told that my life would be difficult, but that it would be worth it in the end if I chose to carry on with it.

I then woke up, feeling cooler, and as if I was just beginning to get better. I remained in the hospital for six weeks, and gradually the fever subsided. I was given regular physiotherapy to rebuild the strength in my legs. I grew an inch to my final height of 5 foot 9 inches, and I lost 20 lbs in those six weeks. When I went home, it was with a wheelchair, with the knowledge that I wouldn't always need it but would need it for a while if my legs got tired. I felt vulnerable, weak and was more susceptible to illness much of the time. I also found that I had become a very light sleeper. I hadn't been that way before, but for a long time after the illness, the slightest noise in the night would waken me. That was especially difficult because the man in the apartment below ours, whose bed was in the room under my room, snored very loudly which would wake me up.

I was happiest during the summer when I had an air conditioner humming in my room and blocking out other noises.

I was also left with bladder urgency and frequency, and I seemed to get cystitis every time I overly exerted myself. I came down with every cold and flu that was around, but the most difficult thing was the bladder urgency. When I was an older teenager and went on a date, I would have to excuse myself to go the "ladies room" more times than I care to remember. It was so embarrassing when I was trying to impress my dates. The doctors said that I would be back to normal in five years, but it wasn't as simple as that.

It was only many years later that I was able to call my experience in the hospital a near-death experience. I wouldn't have known how to describe it at all, but after having read numerous accounts of near death experiences, I felt that must have been what happened to me on that day in the hospital. I do know that I felt that the fact I had survived meant there was a purpose in my continuing to live even if I didn't know then exactly what that purpose was. It just felt important to me to know that there was a reason for me to be alive because it felt like I was worth something. I had been rather marginalized because my parents had been divorced at a time when divorce was extremely rare. Their divorce made me feel different and odd and therefore perhaps not very acceptable or valuable. Even in my school, I knew of no other student living with only one parent. So I came out of that severe illness with a sense of worth and value that felt very deep and real. I felt that I wanted to live as fully as I could because I didn't know how long I might have.

I didn't talk to anyone about my near death experience at the time because I intuitively felt that at best I would be misunderstood; at worst people would think that I had gone mad and hospitalise me not just for a physical illness but for a mental illness. I sometimes wondered myself if I had gone mad because I never heard anyone else talk about such an experience. Indeed a year later a friend of mine told me that the doctors were waiting for six months to determine whether or not my mind had been damaged by the illness. The doctors had decided that my mind was fine. Still the thought that there might be something wrong with me because of the illness continued to haunt me.

I knew that time in my life when I nearly died was important and I really wanted to understand it better so much later I asked a wise and intuitive person about its meaning. His interpretation was that it was as if my life had been going in the wrong direction, and I had to be taken out and reprogrammed. That was done during my near-death experience. I appreciated that interpretation which made sense to me and gave me a different way of looking at the experience.

In the summer of 1961, just a few short years after my illness, I had just graduated from secondary school and had been due to go away to university that September. My mother had been ill for some years with a degenerative illness, arteriosclerosis that was diagnosed not long after I had recovered from encephalitis. It was so difficult to watch. She was having trouble walking, and her mind was affected so that she often became confused and didn't remember things, which was most unlike her. After my graduation, I went to spend six weeks in Switzerland visiting my dad, his new wife and their young daughter, my younger half sister. By then, my older half sister had grown up and was living elsewhere. I came back home and found that my mother had become worse. She needed constant care. Thereafter a carer stayed with her whenever I was away. I was coming home from Switzerland to prepare to go away to university. Her condition was beyond my capacity at 17. I felt terrible about that, but it was the truth of the matter. I so wanted to make her better. It was hugely painful to watch the deterioration of her body and her mind as a result of that dreadful illness.

After I had been home for a few weeks, my uncle took me out to lunch and informed me that I would not going away to university. Instead I was going to stay in St Louis to attend Washington University, and also look after my mom. It was August and too late to apply to Washington University for that September. I was shocked and frightened. It felt as if my whole life was about to be destroyed, but he was her brother, and seemed to have authority. I told him that I couldn't look after her, and he replied that of course I could. I was devastated. I felt like my life and future going down the drain, and I wasn't even qualified to care for somebody as ill as my mom was at that time.

I got home and wrote to my dad, who was on a business trip to New York City at the time, telling him what my uncle had said. A few days later I got a shocking phone call from my dad. He said: "I am willing to go to court to get custody of you, but if I do spend the energy and money on a court case, I need to know that if custody is changed, you will come with me?" I was stunned. He asked me: "Will you come with me, if I am given custody?" I said I don't want to hurt anyone here. My mom was sitting in the living room near to me as I spoke on the phone. He said: "If you stay there and look after your mother, you will end up just like her." I had to admit that he was probably right, but what a decision to have to make in an instant on a long distance phone call! Long distance phone calls were very expensive in those days, and therefore they rarely happened, so even hearing from my dad by phone from New York was a complete surprise, never mind the challenge of his message. I said to him that I would go with him if it came to that, even though it hurt me a great deal to admit that for fear of how it would affect my mother. He told me he would phone my uncle and let me know what happens. He phoned my uncle and told him that he would take it to court if anyone attempted to prevent me from going away to university. That ended the conflict, and I went away, but carrying with me huge worry and guilt for failing in my responsibilities as a good daughter. Whenever I was away from her and St Louis, I continued to worry about my mom. I felt so helpless. Despite that feeling my father reassured me telling me that I had to live my own life. How I wished that my mom and dad were still married to each other and living together. Then I wouldn't have been so alone, and she would have had care.

My mother died three years later in February 1964, after that long and ruthless illness had destroyed her, and then my grandmother (her mother) died in June of that year. My grandmother and I had had our differences, but there was no doubt that we loved each other. After her death I was even more determined to fulfil her wish for me to live a meaningful life. She helped me enormously in many ways to have the courage of my convictions.

Losing my grandmother and my mother within months of each other was a profound loss to me. Suddenly at age 20 my maternal line had gone, and although my father was still alive, I felt terribly alone. After all, he lived a quarter of the world away from me in Switzerland with his wife and daughter. I just had to get on with my life, which I did, but I really missed my mother and grandmother. I had been advised not to see my mother's body after her death. While I understand that advice had been an effort to protect me, I found it very hard to believe she was indeed dead. My experience of my grandmother's death was far better. There was a reception at the funeral home, and people came to pay their respects and view the body, which was well presented. I felt that it looked like a wax figure, but still I saw her body, and it was really dead, so there was no question in my mind that she had died. died. Looking back I wish I had seen my mother's body because I think it would have made it easier to accept her death.

Something happened at that reception while I was there talking to people who came to pay their respects. Suddenly a man with silver-grey hair came in who reminded me in some way of my father. I had no idea who he was, but there was something about him that felt familiar. He came over to me to introduce himself, and he was Dan Hundley, my father's cousin who lived in St Louis, and who had come to see me and pay his respects to my family. I was so pleased that he had done that. It was as if there were a hint of my dad standing beside me, and I could really have done with my dad's support at the time.

His visit to the funeral parlor was the start of a long friendship. He sent me photos of my ancestors, information about the family history, and I saw him and his wife occasionally after that. I was deeply touched that he would come to my grandmother's funeral. He clearly knew the family and knew that my father, Tom who was his cousin, had a daughter, me, who would be there.

Although it felt as if I was on my own to face the world, I had several saving graces. One was that I had already become a Bahá'í in August of 1963, just about six months before my mother's death, which gave me a channel for my spiritual life, a community, and a sense of meaning and purpose. And I had already met the man who was to become my husband, to whom I got engaged just one year to the day after my mother's death. I will say more about that in the next chapters.

Another saving grace was that my mother left me money, about $50,000, which I would get when I was 21. Because my grandmother had died after my mother, I took over my mother's share in my grandmother's estate. My grandmother wanted to be sure that I was cared for. After my mom's death, she arranged that I should have one third of her estate alongside her two sons. My grandfather had been a very successful businessman in St Louis with his own lumber business, so there would be some money coming to me through my grandmother. My uncle said to me that I ought to use his lawyer to help to process my share of the two wills, my mom's and my grandmother's. That didn't feel right to me, but I sought my father's authority again on that point.

My father suggested I go to see his very good friend and lawyer, Norrie Allen, which I did. Norrie was a sharp and very bright man. He looked at the two wills, and said that he didn't see any problem, and he would be happy to represent me. He did so, and my mother's will was simple and straightforward because I was the only beneficiary. The process of sorting out the two wills was very complex and ended up taking ten years to resolve. I was eternally grateful for Norrie's help throughout that long and arduous process. I felt a sense of responsibility to use the money well. I used to say that my mother and my grandmother loved me, because even though they died and left me, they left me money.

That money really felt like a vote of confidence and gave me a sense that I wanted to do right by my mother and grandmother by taking good care of it. My belief that my mom and grandmother had faith in me that I would use the money wisely gave me trust in myself. Each time I made a decision about what to do with some of that money, I remembered them and was grateful to them and hoped that they would approve of what I was doing with the money that they had so generously given to me. I often felt that they were right beside me supporting me because they had given me the means to look after myself in a very practical way. In a way it was as if I hadn't lost them. I never forgot that I had the freedom and support in my life that money gives because of my family's generosity and not because of my own efforts. I carried with me a degree of guilt as well as a sense of purpose because of having been left money.

By 17, I had left St Louis and would never live there again. I had a determination to live a meaningful life and to fulfil my purpose in whatever way I felt that to be, and to create a new life for myself. My father's intervention, which enabled me to go away to university, profoundly changed and dramatically improved the course of my life. As painful as it was, even considering the thought of leaving my mom to join him when she was terminally ill, my father rescued me and threatened my uncle ensuring that I would be able to attend university away from St Louis, as had been planned.

Because I had experienced life-threatening illnesses that had left me with debilitating after-effects, I could have become a sickly person like my mother. I could have been stuck as an invalid looking after an invalid mother and never had a life of my own. Instead I was able to use my own life-threatening experience as the impetus to grab life with a keen sense of urgency, when my father in his wisdom offered me the chance to do so. Tragedy, whether it is serious illness or death, contains both options for us. We can either allow it to define and limit us, giving us an identity of victim, or with support, we can use it to propel us with a sense of urgency and hunger for life. I am sure that I sometimes did feel like a victim, yet in my stronger moments I acted decisively knowing that I had been given a chance to live my life as I wanted to do, which I grasped with both hands.

On Reflection

This chapter illustrates how unexpectedly we can find ourselves in the midst of dealing with serious illness and death. Do you have an understanding of what death means to you? Do you believe that your existence on earth is simply physical or do you believe that you are a spiritual being having a physical experience? Does your belief affect how you live your day to day life?

No matter what you believe, losing loved ones when they die is really painful, and there are some deaths that we don't 'get over' but that we learn to live with for the rest of our lives.

What do you believe happens after death? Might there be some form of life ahead? Do you look forward to ongoing relationships with those whom you love after you pass away into a 'next life'? How does knowing that you will die impact your life here on earth?

Death is not simply about physical death, but also about endings. This moment dies to the next. Anything in which we are involved has an ending, whether it is a course or a project or a relationship or anything else you might consider. How do you deal with endings? Many people find endings painful and hard to manage even if we may realise that the ending of one thing signals a new beginning.

What do you want to achieve in the time you have here on earth? Do you judge yourself and your choices by your own values and standards or do you fear some external judgement from God or some other authority?

When you are faced with your own mortality, will you call on anyone? Will you regret the things you did or didn't do? How frightened will you be? Do you imagine that you will die alone, or that you may be met by loved ones who have died before? I remember Dr Elisabeth Kübler-Ross saying that we are always met by those whom we love who have gone before, but what do we actually believe about that?

Although it is perhaps frightening to think about it now, voicing and naming the fear rather than allowing it to fester inside is very healthy. Sometimes we feel that it is easier to think we will cross that bridge when we come to it. However, considering these big questions now may affect the rest of your life and shape the way you see death whenever it touches you.

Chapter 3
And This is My Beloved

In my second year at university, my life was about to change considerably in a way that I would never have dreamed possible. I was 19 years old returning to the University of Illinois from a trip to Florida for Easter vacation with some of my friends. As we drove back, I noticed a configuration in the clouds that looked to me like Jesus Christ with his arms outstretched coming to embrace me. I wasn't a religious person in the conventional sense, but I did hold spiritual values that I considered important. I valued honesty, truthfulness, caring, helpfulness, selflessness, devotion, and loyalty. I spoke to my friends about what I saw and what it meant to me, but there wasn't much discussion of it. Nevertheless, the image in the cloud felt like a good omen to me.

For the next few weeks I went about my business, doing my usual studying and attending classes. One day in May, I drove to Chicago to get my hair cut at a hairdresser recommended to me by a family friend who was an agent in the entertainment industry and represented models, actors and actresses. This was a journey of about 150 miles, but I thought the recommendation was worth the trip. It didn't seem like a long journey because I had often driven back and forth between St Louis and Chicago and really enjoyed driving. I also wanted a day out away from the campus where I was just coming to exam time. I had been studying a lot and needed a break.

I got to the hairdresser, and there was a real buzz in the atmosphere. People were very busy, and hairdressers were flying around the place. The clients looked as if they had good reason to have their hair done by experts like these. They might have all been actors or models. These were the physically beautiful people of Chicago who went to great pains to make sure that they looked beautiful at all times. There was a level of professionalism, and I had the feeling that the hairdressers here were experts in their field. The man who was going to style my hair was called John. He was an extremely energetic and enthusiastic man of about 25, so not much older than me. He was rather slim and short but attractive and he just had a nice quality about him. There was something about his energy, enthusiasm and character that made me trust him and feel interested in what he had to say. As he was cutting my hair, we got through the small talk fairly quickly and began to speak of our deeply held beliefs.

I told him that I had been raised as what I called a "lukewarm Presbyterian". I used that expression because my mother was the only parent who was religious and took me to the Presbyterian Church. My father had studied religion and found that he didn't agree with a number of things that most religions taught. I loved going to church at one time, but later I became more like my father and appreciated his views. Like him, I didn't think that I needed a priest or minister to intercede between God and me because I felt I could develop my own direct relationship with God. I also felt I didn't need to go to church because I could pray anywhere and at any time. Often on Sunday afternoons my grandmother would ask me, "Did you go to church today?" I would reply, "No I didn't go to church, and I don't have to go to church to prove that I am religious. I can pray wherever I want". I also told John that I didn't like the prejudice that I witnessed in churches where diversity was not allowed or accepted. I felt that Christ gave us a message of love without saying that we needed to love only people of a similar colour to ourselves.

John exclaimed that what I was saying was just what the Bahá'ís believed. I said doubtfully, "There is nothing that goes along with me". I had, in my own way while growing up, attempted to understand something about several different religious beliefs, and I didn't think I would ever find a religion that truly expressed what was in my heart. I was thrilled, however, to hear that there was a Faith that might be aligned with my beliefs, as much as I doubted that it would be possible. I was also thrilled to have heard the word Bahá'í mentioned because I had seen the Bahá'í House of Worship on the North Shore of Lake Michigan in Chicago. I had been travelling in a taxi one day from Lake Forest College to Chicago, and I had passed a most beautiful building on Sheridan Drive beside Lake Michigan that looked as if it were in the wrong history book. I was stunned when I saw it and asked the taxi driver what it was. He said that it was the Bahá'í Temple. I asked, "What is that?" He said he didn't know, and that was the end of the conversation. My mind had been filled with questions, and at the time there was no way to get the answers that I sought.

Those were the days when women spent hours in hairdressers under massive hairdryers. I hadn't brought a book with me, so John gave me a book called *The Hidden Words* by Bahá'u'lláh who was the Founder of the Bahá'í Faith. I opened the book and read first:

HE IS THE GLORY OF GLORIES!
This is that which hath descended from the realm of glory, uttered by the tongue of power and might, and revealed unto the Prophets of old. We have taken the inner essence thereof and clothed it in the garment of brevity, as a token of grace unto the righteous, that they may stand faithful unto the Covenant of God, may fulfill in their lives His trust, and in the realm of spirit obtain the gem of divine virtue. (Bahá'u'lláh, 1975, p.5)

I was already attracted by that. I didn't consider myself to be righteous, but I could see that there were connections with the Prophets of old, but that it was a new statement in short paragraphs that I might enjoy.

Then I read:

O SON OF SPIRIT!
My first counsel is this: Possess a pure, kindly and radiant heart, that thine may be a sovereignty ancient, imperishable and everlasting. (Bahá'u'lláh, 1975, p.5)

I was gripped by what I read, and I felt an energy that I can only describe as higher than that to which I was accustomed. I felt as if some part of me that hadn't received nourishment in this form before was now being fed very gently and very thoroughly. That part was really hungry for what it was receiving because I read that book in its entirety with much joy, and then I asked John if he had anything else for me to read.

John gave me another book by Bahá'u'lláh, *The Seven Valleys and The Four Valleys*. As before I felt a new energy as I read this book and digested what I could from it. Again, I read it in its entirety. It is a very mystical book.

One story from the book is about a lover who had been separated from his beloved. He was in a terrible state through the anguish of separation, and doctors could do nothing for him. Finally one day he was in the depths of despair, and he could live no more, so he left his house and went towards a marketplace. Suddenly a watchman followed him and frightened him, so he ran and ran. Then other watchmen began to follow as well. Finally in the most difficult circumstances, he scaled a high garden wall, which was his only and last hope of escape. He was so afraid of the watchmen. When he reached the top of the wall, he just threw himself down into the garden below caring little whether he lived or died. There he found his beloved with a lamp in her hand searching for a ring she had lost. He raised his hands in prayer on behalf of these watchmen who had frightened him so…

> …for he had found many a secret justice in this seeming tyranny of the watchman, and seen how many a mercy lay hid behind the veil. Out of wrath, the guard had led him who was athirst in love's desert to the sea of his loved one, and lit up the dark night of absence with the light of reunion. He had driven one who was afar, into the garden of nearness, had guided an ailing soul to the heart's physician.
>
> Now if the lover could have looked ahead, he would have blessed the watchman at the start, and prayed on his behalf, and he would have seen that tyranny as justice; but since the end was veiled to him, he moaned and made his plaint in the beginning. Yet those who journey in the garden land of knowledge, because they see the end in the beginning, see peace in war and friendliness in anger. (Bahá'u'lláh, 1991b, pp.14-15)

This story reminded me of many times when I have thought that life was just awful. I have found out sometimes much later that what I thought was awful, was in fact, a real turning point and blessing, which set me in a much more rewarding direction. I really took the point of attempting to see the end in the beginning. That concept also reminded me of my favourite game at the time, which was chess. One of the keys to winning the game is to check out all the possible results of any move that I might make before making it, thus attempting to "see the end in the beginning".

By then surely my hair was dry, and John came to comb out my new coif! I was delighted in so many ways, both with the haircut and with my reading. John offered me the two books, and I said that I would be in Chicago during the summer and would return them to him then. I drove back home quite changed: very pleased that I would have some time to read the books again and again.

The days went by, and exams grew closer and closer. As they did so, I slept less and less. I often found it impossible to get to sleep. I tried counting sheep that I imagined jumping over a fence. That certainly didn't work. Smoking sometimes helped but at that time it didn't. I had a new ally however, and I saw that after I read the books by Bahá'u'lláh, I was able to go to sleep without any difficulty. I guess it was to do with a kind of relaxation that came from the nourishment that I was receiving in some way from those books. I didn't understand it, but I was very grateful because after I slept well, I could take my exams in much more comfort.

After the exams were over, and I had been to St Louis to see my mom and other relatives, I drove to Chicago and stayed in a motel near Skokie on the north side of Chicago. I had a job starting soon in a department store called Carson, Pirie Scott which was nearby. I stayed in the motel for a few days while I found a place to live. I remember feeling so terribly lonely and thinking to myself that I could have gone back to St Louis to be with my relatives and find work there, but something was driving me to stay in Chicago on my own. My mom was ill and barely recognised me, and the other relatives were aunts, uncles and cousins. My parents had been divorced for some time and my father lived in Switzerland with his wife and daughter. I had visited them during the previous two summers, and I felt I ought to work this summer. I really felt nearly like an orphan, I was so lost and lonely.

During that evening when I felt such extreme loneliness, I wondered seriously what I was doing, and yet part of me knew I had to do it. I didn't know why, but staying with my decision to work in Chicago for the summer seemed to be one of the most important choices I would be making in my life, and indeed I feel it was.. It was the beginning of a lifetime of joyful service, adventure and support in which I would be meeting people from all over the world whom I never would have met in any other way. This was the most important turning point in my life, and I nearly gave up before I even started. But I didn't give up. I stayed the course, and I held my lost and lonely feeling and kept on keeping on.

I found myself living in an apartment in Evanston, a suburb, north of Chicago. I had three flatmates, but I had my own room. I only ever saw one of the flatmates because the other two were always out or away. I began my job at the department store and was settling into my new life. One day in

July, a dear friend of mine from college got married. I attended the wedding and went on from there to get my hair cut in the same shop by the same hairdresser, John. This was the first time we had met since that eventful day when he gave me the Bahá'í books.

Again we talked about life and beliefs and thoughts and things that were important. John invited me to go with him and his fiancé to a Bahá'í fireside the following evening. A fireside is a meeting held in someone's home where the matter of Bahá'í is discussed, and people are given the opportunity to learn more and ask questions. I accepted readily. That began an intense two-week period during which time we met almost every night to go to Bahá'í meetings. I wanted to know everything and to read everything. I loved several things that I heard about the teachings of Bahá'u'lláh. One was that we had to investigate truth for ourselves. I had never heard of a Faith in which the followers were advised to think for themselves.

Another teaching was that we needed to eliminate any and every kind of prejudice from our lives. The one with which I had been most familiar was racial prejudice. I didn't understand racial prejudice because I felt that all human beings are children of the same God, so how could one be better than another? I discovered that other prejudices arose about people either with or without money or education or endless other things that really don't make one better than another. I came to understand that we all had different or varying capacities. Some might have a thimbleful and some a bucketful, but what was important was how we filled those receptacles and developed our capacities in this life. Surely the person who fills his or her thimbleful has lived a more meaningful life than the one who has put a few drops into his bucketful, even though the person with the bucketful may have had more capacity in the beginning?

The Bahá'í teachings said that everyone deserved an education. Bahá'u'lláh had written the equivalent of over one hundred volumes of material to guide us both personally and globally into a harmonious time of the Kingdom of God on Earth. This promised Kingdom of God on Earth was at least implicit in the teachings of all the Divine Educators. I so longed for peace and harmony among the people of different nations. I valued the contributions that people of different cultures had made to the world. I remember having visited the United Nations headquarters in New York City some years before, and I loved seeing examples of the crafts and products from different nations.

A Bahá'í principle called Progressive Revelation means that religion is like a school and that from age to age a new Divine Educator comes to teach the people, like Moses, Krishna, Buddha, Jesus Christ, Zoroaster, and Muhammad, to name a few. Bahá'u'lláh explained that there are and will be many more Divine Educators, and no group of people on Earth would ever be left without divine guidance. He suggested that these Divine Educators come to restate the same spiritual truths like love, justice, compassion, brotherhood and to bring new social laws that are appropriate for the level of people's understanding at the time. The Bahá'í teachings explained that humanity as a whole grows and develops just like an individual, and that is why there is periodically a need for new social laws to come about. What people understood at the time of Moses and Jesus Christ, for instance, would have been more limited than what people understand now.

The Bahá'í teachings said that humanity had been through its adolescence and was now entering the very first stages of maturity. I felt that to be true. It made sense, and it also gave hope for the eventual world peace that has been promised down through the ages. The Bahá'í Faith is a very optimistic Faith that promotes a sense of personal and collective welfare. I felt that Bahá'u'lláh brought a feeling of unconditional love, in which He told us how we could look after ourselves by cultivating certain attributes and developing good qualities in ourselves. He also gave us the promise of continued guidance for the future of humanity.

I lived very near the Bahá'í House of Worship in Wilmette. I went there and bought books and devoured them. I loved them. I was still hesitant, however, about diving into the lifestyle. I am not a joiner. I don't join clubs, organisations, religions etc. So I tried really hard to knock holes in the argument. I was particularly interested in the fact that Bahá'u'lláh said that at this time in the world, people should not consume alcohol. I considered this, and because I didn't drink much, I preferred to make my own decisions about how much alcohol to drink. I didn't even like alcohol that much. In hindsight, I can see that I was very afraid of being deluded into buying a Faith or a belief system that might not have been grounded in reality. Like most people, I was afraid of being brainwashed and of joining something that turned out to be other than I thought it was. So I went through a significant period of testing and questioning, as I would suggest anybody do before they choose a Faith for themselves. It is a bit like getting married, and I would hope that people don't get married before getting to know their potential partner well enough to make such a decision. I feel that the choice of a Faith is a very important one to make, and it deserves consideration.

Gradually I began to see the importance of not drinking alcohol because it does have a strong effect on our personalities. At the moment in our culture, it is the cause of a lot of violence and the breakdown of family units. People, sometimes, are negatively affected by alcohol. Therefore I could see that it was important to take quite a strong stand on it. Although I might be able to be moderate in my drinking, that wouldn't be of help to the person who couldn't be moderate. The Faith seemed to promote a model of life that builds on the positive qualities that we all have and moves away from things that tend to bring out the negative qualities in people. Drinking may not be all that harmful for some people, but when it is harmful, it can be very harmful indeed. It can encourage judgement, criticism, warfare, and prejudice. I began to see how practical the Faith was in saying don't do the things that promote the less helpful parts of yourself and do instead the things that promote the healthy parts of yourself.

As I began to understand the reason for Bahá'u'lláh's prohibition against drinking alcohol, I accepted that I could change my habits and adapt for the sake of a more harmonious world for all. I had been around people drinking, and I found such a range of reactions in people. Some people became relaxed, cheerful and merry, while others grew more tedious, boring, repetitive and nonsensical, and still others became argumentative, downright rude, ugly and violent. I certainly didn't want to change my consciousness, and alcohol does that. I have never in my life regretted my early decision not to drink alcohol. In fact I have celebrated that decision.

One of the most damaging things that we do, according to Bahá'u'lláh, is backbiting. He said that backbiting quenches the light of the heart and extinguishes the life of the soul. That is pretty weighty if you ask me. I never liked talking about others behind their backs, and I was glad for that admonishment because it would save a lot of hurt feelings. Backbiting has a very insidious way of harming other people's view of the person discussed. It can travel large distances and can be very damaging whether or not it is true. It is what sometimes happens in the media when people suffer a form of trial by media in place of the legal system.

I remember feeling uncomfortable - kind of dirty or ashamed - if I spoke badly about somebody. Equally I feel very uncomfortable when I am around someone else who is doing so. I have spoken up, in those circumstances, saying that I feel very uncomfortable and that I don't want to hear what is being said. One of the worst things about backbiting is that it doesn't go away. If I have heard something unkind about someone, I cannot necessarily forget what I have heard, and as a result, it can colour the way I am with the person. Therefore it changes my relationship with the person and with others who interact with that person.

Bahá'u'lláh also made it very, very clear that women and men are equal. What He said was wonderful, and I had no doubt that I was equally valued and welcomed as a human being. This was exceptionally important to me because I was born at a time when women usually seemed to be an adjunct to their husbands, somehow just that bit secondary. They wielded power but subtly and in very manipulative ways. I knew that one of the ways in which women did so was to make sure that every idea became their husband's idea, and then they would get what they wanted. What a round about way to get something done! I didn't like that. I wanted my ideas to be valued regardless of my gender.

I met Bahá'ís in many different areas of Chicago and one day we even went to a fireside in Milwaukee. It was fabulous. I found them to be special. They seemed very gentle, good and concerned with life, people, the world and the improvement of all of the above! I found new energy in myself and a new kind of peace, joy and happiness.

I worked in my job during the day and read whenever I had spare time. I asked my many questions and continued to explore this phenomenon known as The Bahá'í Faith, the newest of the world's independent religions, that began in Iran in 1844. The Bahá'í Faith has a similar relationship to the previous religions as Christianity has to Judaism. It arose out of them and values them while at the same time having its own independent status. I have mentioned only a few of the well documented religions known to us, but I realise that there are many religions about which we don't know, and yet they exist and are valid.

The founder of the Bahá'í Faith is "Bahá'u'lláh" whose title means The Glory of God and "Bahá'í" means follower of Bahá'u'lláh. The Bahá'í Faith is a faith of unity. This theme of unity starts with a belief in one God for all people. There is one God, one Creator of the universe, and this Supreme Creator is in many ways unknown to me. The way that our Creator can reveal to us what is necessary is through Divine Educators such as Abraham, Moses, Jesus Christ and Bahá'u'lláh. We can understand them because they are human like ourselves as well as divine in the sense of being representatives of God on Earth. Bahá'ís accept the founders of the world's religions and the word that came through them as the word of God. The scriptures of the world's great religions are sacred because they come from one source. Thus it could be said that there is one God and one religion that is expressed in many different ways, different times and different localities through different Divine Educators.

The last level of unity in the Bahá'í Faith is that of humanity and the rest of creation, like the minerals, vegetables and animals, the universes and the planets in their spheres. People the world over, no matter what colour or what creed, no matter what language they speak or beliefs they hold are all creations of that one God. Despite the seemingly ever present conflict between various peoples, the task now would seem to be to learn to appreciate unity in diversity, and that means embracing our differences as well as our similarities. That is a difficult task for people in the world today because there is such a degree of fear of the unknown and desire for power over others. The relationship of people to nature and the rest of creation is important for the wise and respectful care of our mutual home, planet Earth.

So in the Bahá'í Faith there is one God, who speaks to humanity through a series of Divine Educators or Messengers who arise from age to age to inspire us and move us forward in an ever-advancing civilisation. Today we seem to be reaching toward global unity whereas in the time of Moses, there was the development of tribal unity. In the time of Christ, unity extended further to the city state, and Muhammad was able to unify a nation of tribes.

When I thought of these ideas, they made so much sense to me. I could imagine that humanity as a whole would develop similarly to an individual because I saw that when I was a young child, God was to me someone like my father or Santa Claus, whereas when I got older, I couldn't imagine God in a human form, but something far beyond that. I used to think of God as something like energy or electricity or the atoms and molecules in the universe, but more than and different from all of that. I loved the inclusion of all the faiths in a way that was filled with appreciation and respect. I felt the unity which had been described in the Bahá'í teachings whenever I attended a Bahá'í meeting.

I was already beginning to fall in love with Bahá'u'lláh and the Bahá'í teachings, so I continued to seek to learn more. I found that similar to other faiths, there are Holy Days and a new calendar. The Bahá'í calendar consists of 19 months of 19 days each. Also at the beginning of each Bahá'í month, there is what is called a 19 Day Feast where the Bahá'ís gather together to read prayers and writings, to discuss community business and socialise. The Bahá'í day starts at sunset, so the Feast is held after sunset on the first day of the month.

I was relieved that there is no clergy in the Faith; that each Bahá'í is on the same level. I really valued that because I never believed that the clergy had more access than I had to the same God I loved and to whom I prayed. With the principle of universal education, people would be able to read the sacred scriptures of all faiths themselves. There is no proselytising and even children who grow up as Bahá'ís are free to make their own choice when they come of age. There was so much to learn and to read and to absorb. I felt as if I had just been shown the ocean and was enthralled, wanting to drink it all in. There was never enough time in the day and night to learn it all.

I was really excited by the principles of the Bahá'í Faith that I hadn't seen expressed quite so clearly anywhere else, such things as the elimination of all forms of prejudice, the equal rights and opportunities for men and women, the understanding that religious truth is unified in the sense of all coming from the one source and relative to the time and the place where a religion originated, the aim to reduce the extremes of wealth and poverty in the world, the encouragement of education for everyone, the responsibility of each person to investigate truth for him or her self, the establishment of a world governing system, and the recognition that science and religion are in harmony.

Time seemed to stand still as I was learning and absorbing so much in those few days I spent with John and met so many wonderful people. Then at the end of the two weeks he left Chicago because he was going out to work with Native Americans in Arizona, and he was going to marry his fiancée when he arrived there. I will be eternally grateful for John and his gift to me. He had shown me the way to my soul's desire. He had set me on the path, and introduced me to numerous people. It was up to me now to continue or not as I chose.

John left on a Saturday. On the Sunday afternoon I went to my first worship service at the Bahá'í Temple in Wilmette. It started at 3pm and I went into the glorious auditorium in the building that looks like concrete lace with nine doors. Because the doors were made of glass alongside many big windows, I could see outside as far as Lake Michigan, which was across Sheridan Road and a little distance from there. I could also see the lovely gardens with pools of water that were visible on all sides from the auditorium. It was uplifting to have such a view and be in the midst of an auditorium filled with people with one thing in mind, and that one thing was the worship of God. It was like being in a dream of how life could truly be, and I longed to see our world become such a harmonious and glorious expression of love and unity. All of this was in the suburbs of one of the biggest cities in America.

I looked around the room at the people gathered, and I saw people of varying colours and age groups, all sitting there gathered together in worship. I had never seen such a mixed group of people in any church service that I had attended. I could tell by the kind of clothes that people wore that some people were wealthy and others were living on a more meagre income. By listening to the people around me in the audience I could tell that there were people of various national and educational backgrounds. I felt completely at home, comfortable and filled with the joy of such a spiritual meeting. In the half-hour service, there were readings from the Koran, the Old Testament, the New Testament and the Bahá'í writings. There was no clergyman telling us anything about how to live our lives or what anything means. There were two hymns sung by an a cappella choir. We couldn't see the choir because it was on the first balcony and quite high up in the dome, so we just heard the voices. It was magic. In the centre of the dome was a stunningly beautiful gold engraved symbol which means "God is Most Glorious".

I was surprised that there wasn't a collection for money at any time in this service. In the Bahá'í Faith, the only contributors are the Bahá'ís themselves. Money is not accepted from people who are not Bahá'ís. I was over the moon about that. It was so different in this way from any other religious organisation in which I had participated even briefly. I appreciated the principle that only Bahá'ís may contribute to the Bahá'í fund because it felt like Bahá'ís were taking personal responsibility for what was theirs. They were not expecting other people to finance their faith. I was delighted to learn that there are no collections or charges at public Bahá'í events. I had been so used to payments for weddings, funerals, and various services offered by churches. Sometimes those requirements for payments seemed inappropriate or unfair. If there is a Bahá'í wedding, there is no charge for that, nor is there a charge for funeral services. The Bahá'í Houses of Worship and any Bahá'í services are gifts from the Bahá'ís to the people of the world.

I felt that the Bahá'í Faith expressed all that was important to me personally as well as my hopes for the world. After that first meeting, I went home and telephoned John's fiancée and told her that I wanted to be a Bahá'í. She suggested that I write to the Secretary of the Spiritual Assembly of the Bahá'ís of Evanston, where I was living. I did just that. The secretary lived on the same street as I did at the time.

It was suggested that I study with a member of the community for a little while, to help me know for sure if I really wanted to be a Bahá'í. I was thrilled to do that because I was able to learn more and ask more questions. There is no longer such a requirement to study and becoming a Bahá'í is a much simpler process now.

The relationship of the Bahá'í Faith to money continued to delight me because it felt so different to what I had experienced in many other contexts in my life. Within the Bahá'í community there is a level of respect and understanding when it comes to contributing money. Bahá'ís are not asked how much they give nor are they embarrassed into giving money to the Bahá'í fund. There is no pressure. Bahá'ís are informed about the financial situation in their communities, and then it is their own choice about what they contribute. I remember a lovely story about someone who used to contribute to the Bahá'í fund. Each month, a woman would gather up what little she could manage in coins, put them into an envelope and post the envelope to the Bahá'í Centre. She was unable to afford enough postage, so the people at the Bahá'í Centre would have to pay the postage. In the end, her very sincere and generous contribution, which was a sacrifice for her, cost the Bahá'í fund more than was received. Nevertheless, I feel sure that her attitude and her desire to contribute to the fund she loved so dearly became an inspiration to those of us who can contribute with greater ease.

I have a lovely story about that attitude towards giving from the time when my children were young. At one time my two older children were saving money for wristwatches, and that was quite a job in those days because they got pocket money according to their ages. For instance, when they were five, they got five pence a week. Anyway, they had saved about half of what they needed when we received information that the Bahá'í fund was in crisis. My husband Philip and I were discussing the situation at the dinner table, and the children heard us. A few days later, they had decided that they wanted to give their saved money to the fund and forget about buying watches. They did so, and a few weeks later, an American relative was visiting, and she spent a day in Dublin visiting the shops. She came home with gifts for everyone. To my children's surprise she had bought watches for them that were far better and nicer than they would have been able to afford with the money they planned to save. They never forgot that and nor did I. We all learned how sometimes what seems like a sacrifice in the short term, becomes a portal for something even better to happen in the long term. It showed us all that we never really know what might happen as a result of an action that we take in an effort to be of service and to do something for someone or some cause other than ourselves.

I felt that because they were children, they had a pure spirit. They certainly did not give their savings to the Bahá'í fund because they were expecting to be rewarded for what they did. They gave out of childlike purity of heart and intention. Then when later they received the gifts, it was as if life's synchronicity had shown them how good it is to give selflessly.

When I go on pilgrimage and visit the Bahá'í World Centre, in Haifa, Israel, I am thrilled when I realise that the little money that I have contributed has, along with contributions from Bahá'ís all over the world, joined together to enable such a centre to exist. Just as when I went to New York in 1992 to attend a Bahá'í World Congress, I was very moved to know that the little bit of work that I do for the Faith and the small contributions that I have made have helped to make such an event happen. I was part of a group of 30,000 Bahá'ís from all over the world. We were a small representation of the worldwide Bahá'í Community, and it was an overwhelming experience to be present. The previous Bahá'í World Congress had occurred in 1963 in London at the Royal Albert Hall. I was not a Bahá'í at the time, although I became a Bahá'í just a few months later.

Without clergy, I wondered how the Faith was administered. I learned that there were Spiritual Assemblies consisting of nine members elected annually in local and national communities. The international governing body of the Bahá'í Faith is called the Universal House of Justice and also consists of nine members which are elected every five years and reside at the Bahá'í World Centre. I thought that sounded very fair to have elected representatives take care of the business of running the Faith in any locality.

One of the most important principles of Bahá'í Spiritual Assemblies was that there is no electioneering among Bahá'ís in voting for members of those Assemblies. In other words, there are no election campaigns because nobody is actively trying to get elected to an Assembly. It is seen as part of the service of being a Bahá'í to respond to the request when someone is elected to an Assembly. One of the outcomes of responding to this call to service, rather than engaging in an election campaign, is that the members of Assemblies are not answerable to those who elect them but rather to the principles of the Bahá'í teachings.

The Bahá'í elections take place in an atmosphere of prayer and devotion and this emphasises their devotion to service and being called to serve. Bahá'ís are asked to consider:

> ...without the least trace of passion and prejudice, and irrespective of any material consideration, the names of only those who can best combine the necessary qualities of unquestioned loyalty, of selfless devotion, of a well-trained mind, of recognised ability and mature experience. (Shoghi Effendi, 1968, p.88)

That may seem like a tall order, and it is one that requires serious thought. The Assemblies exist to do what is best for the community in a spirit of truth and obedience to the teachings of Bahá'u'lláh. There are appropriate checks and balances in place to deal with an Assembly that is not managing its work in accordance with the Bahá'í teachings, but no Assembly member can promise another individual in the community to do anything. That was a real shock to my system and a most welcome one.

Around this time I also discovered that it is possible to get married in a Bahá'í service and I became very excited by the notion. Each marriage ceremony is unique: the couple chooses prayers and readings according to their tastes. They choose the place, music, what they wish to wear, and a reception if they wish. A Bahá'í marriage is free and must be witnessed by two people approved by the Assembly in the area where the marriage is being held. Each partner has to say, "We will all, verily, abide by the will of God". That is a pretty good promise to make, in my view.

I knew I wanted to get married one day, and I wanted to have a Bahá'í wedding, so I was glad to know that there was a concept of marriage in the Bahá'í Faith. Another thing I loved about Bahá'í marriage was that people of any religion could have a Bahá'í ceremony at no cost. In those days it sometimes happened that if the couple getting married were of different religions, neither of their respective religious groups would be willing to perform the ceremony because they were marrying outside their religion. There was no concern about marrying outside the religion if a Bahá'í married someone who wasn't a Bahá'í, so the Bahá'í marriage was open to all.

Of course, with my mother who was so very ill with arteriosclerosis, I was curious about the Bahá'í view of life after death. Bahá'u'lláh spoke glowingly of life after death in many writings. I had always believed that there had to be more to life than that which I experienced on a daily basis so it wouldn't make sense to me if there weren't a life beyond this one, so I was happy to see that confirmed within the Bahá'í writings. He said:

O SON OF THE SUPREME!
I have made death a messenger of joy to thee. Wherefore dost thou grieve? I have made the light to shine on thee its splendor. Why dost thou veil thyself therefrom? (Bahá'u'lláh, 1975, p.12)

Bahá'u'lláh said that we need to say obligatory prayers, and He gives us a choice of three. There is one short one called "the noonday prayer", a beautiful long one that can be said at any time in the 24 hours, and there is one that is to be said three times a day.

Here is the noonday prayer that seems to say it all:

> I bear witness, O my God, that Thou hast created me to know Thee and to worship Thee. I testify, at this moment, to my powerlessness and to Thy might, to my poverty and to Thy wealth. There is none other God but Thee, the Help in Peril, the Self-Subsisting. (Bahá'u'lláh, 1991a, p.4)

I really enjoy the long one, and some days I only manage the noonday prayer. At that time I wasn't used to the idea of saying prayers at all. I must say though, it didn't take me long to become accustomed to it because His prayers are so beautiful.

Here is a short excerpt from the Long Obligatory Prayer:

> Whoso wisheth to recite this prayer, let him stand up and turn unto God, and, as he standeth in his place, let him gaze to the right and to the left, as if awaiting the mercy of his Lord, the Most Merciful, the Compassionate. Then let him say:
>
> O Thou Who art the Lord of all names and the Maker of the heavens! I beseech Thee by them Who are the Daysprings of Thine invisible Essence, the Most Exalted, the All-Glorious, to make of my prayer a fire that will burn away the veils which have shut me out from Thy beauty, and a light that will lead me unto the ocean of Thy Presence.
>
> Let him then raise his hands in supplication toward God—blessed and exalted be He—and say:
>
> O Thou the Desire of the world and the Beloved of the nations! Thou seest me turning toward Thee, and rid of all attachment to anyone save Thyself, and clinging to Thy cord, through whose movement the whole creation hath been stirred up. I am Thy servant, O my Lord, and the son of Thy servant. Behold me standing ready to do Thy will and Thy desire, and wishing naught else except Thy good pleasure. I implore Thee by the Ocean of Thy mercy and the Daystar of Thy grace to do with Thy servant as Thou willest and pleasest. By Thy might which is far above all mention and praise! Whatsoever is revealed by Thee is the desire of my heart and the beloved of my soul. O God, my God! Look not upon my hopes and my doings, nay rather look upon Thy will that hath encompassed the heavens and the earth. By Thy Most Great Name, O Thou Lord of all nations! I have desired only

what Thou didst desire, and love only what Thou dost love. (Bahá'u'lláh, 1991a, pp.7-9)

Bahá'u'lláh also said that we needed to read the Holy writings morning and evening because that helps us to keep our contact with God alive. As He said:

O SON OF BEING!
Love Me that I may love thee. If thou lovest Me not, My love can in no wise reach thee. Know this, O servant. (Bahá'u'lláh, 1975, p.6)

I had no idea at that time how important prayer would become to me. The longer I live, the more evidence I see of the value of reading prayers. Growing up, I was taught to say prayers, and I would always say a prayer before bed, but I became aware that people most often used prayers when they were in real trouble. I found that I could become high just on reading prayers, and that there were so many more reasons for saying or reading prayers than I could have imagined before.

There are prayers for healing or for those who have passed on, or just to be in communication with God, or to help a friend. There has even been a great deal of research done on how effective prayer can be for people who are ill. If you feel so inclined, have a look at Larry Dossey's *Healing Words*. (1993.) It is a very interesting book on that subject.

This is a very interesting concept to me because reading the revealed writings of the Divine Educators seems to have a different effect on me than reading any other kind of material. It seems to inspire me, to put me into communication with God and my soul or self and to help me to align myself with that which is best in me. I feel that as time goes on, I will see more and more reasons why the regular reading of the Holy writings helps me to live more deeply, profoundly and to bring out the best in me.

The Bahá'í Holy writings and prayers include writings by Bahá'u'lláh, the Báb, who was His Forerunner, and His son, 'Abdu'l-Bahá. They each write in very different styles, and together they have created a formidable volume of writings from which to choose. I spent a great deal of time reading these, which gave me a feeling of being held within an ordered creation, which exists for the purpose of carrying forward an evolving civilisation. I knew how important it was for me to really tune in to that level of intelligence at the

Source of creation. Reading the Bahá'í writings educated me in a belief system that sees the world as deeply meaningful, intentional, intelligent and evolving rather than the apparent meaningless, mundane, chaotic surface of life that we often see or with which we often must engage. I saw a hopeful and very exciting vision about the future of the planet and of the human race when I read:

> The gift of God to this enlightened age is the knowledge of the oneness of mankind and of the fundamental oneness of religion. War shall cease between nations, and by the will of God the Most Great Peace shall come; the world will be seen as a new world, and all men will live as brothers. ('Abdu'l-Bahá, 1982, pp.19-20)

That sounded to me like the Kingdom of God on Earth that had been promised by Jesus Christ. I believed what Christ had said, but again, I didn't see much evidence of it in daily life, where I was often more aware of the petty concerns, arguments and hypocrisy that was present in human interactions. I grew to more easily accept and understand that the human condition included an enormous range of behaviour, and I was heartened by realising that despite our foibles, we were moving towards a bright and glorious future. With hope for the future, I felt that my life and my efforts were more meaningful. There were inevitably some things which I only dimly understood in the Bahá'í writings, but even with those, I was willing to defer to their authority, trusting it as more accurate than any other I had known.

My desire to be a Bahá'í grew, and after meeting my tutor a few times and studying the book, *Bahá'u'lláh and the New Era* by John Esslemont (2006), my tutor told me that she thought I understood enough about the Faith to become a Bahá'í. Then I met with the Local Assembly at their next meeting which was 27th of August, 1963. There were nine people present, and they spoke to me about what I understood of the Faith. I told them that I was deeply committed to it. We spoke for about an hour and a half. Then I was sent home not really knowing what had happened and certainly not feeling that I had been accepted to become a Bahá'í. My flatmate asked how it went and I said: I don't know if they want me!

Suddenly the phone rang, and it was a member of the Assembly asking me to come back. What I didn't understand was that they needed time to consult together on whether they felt that I did understand what I was accepting in becoming a Baháʼí, whether they thought I should study more or if they felt I was ready. I nearly ran down the sidewalk to get back to the Secretary's apartment, and when I went in they welcomed me with open arms and gave me tea and cakes.

I was over the moon, and I think that I must have floated back to my home that evening. I remember waking up the next morning and many mornings after that looking in the bathroom mirror and saying to my reflection, "You are a Baháʼí!"

That was just the beginning. I had decided to visit California with my flatmate shortly after that. We were both adventurous, and I felt that I needed to see California then for fear that I might never again get such an opportunity. And so, I wrote to my father. I told him that I was becoming a Baháʼí, and asked him to please read the enclosed leaflets. I added that I was going to travel to California in my car with my flatmate from England instead of returning to my course at the University of Illinois. That last declaration is not the kind of thing that is designed to thrill fathers! However, I assured him that I would return to the University after Christmas for the spring term.

Well, my father looked at my letter and responded: "You're crazy, but God bless you!" I then wrote to him and said that he couldn't have read the material on the Faith that I had sent because he would have seen how reasonable it was if he had done so. He wrote again saying that I was right and that he hadn't read it. When he did, he described the principles of the Faith as "most admirable". I was relieved to have his support because the reaction from other members of my family had been rather more circumspect. Because my father validated my choice of Faith, I was able to withstand some of the other objections.

When I again saw my mother, on my way to California, I told her I had become a Baháʼí, and she was lucid enough that she exclaimed, "What you? Religious?" I certainly hadn't been consciously looking for religion. I wasn't known for my devotion in the traditional sense at all, but I had a profound sense of spirituality, of God as an unknowable force, and of life after death. That was a surprisingly good reaction from my mother, who was so ill that she didn't remember or register much of what I said to her. Other family members were suspicious that it might be somewhat Communist, and I assured them that it wasn't. This was around the time of the McCarthy trials, and everyone feared Communism.

When I arrived in Los Angeles with my friend, I contacted the Bahá'ís immediately and became involved with activities and began to meet people and make friends. It was wonderful. I stayed there for just about two months before I returned to Chicago to work again at Carson, Pirie Scott near Skokie, Illinois. Once again I found a place to live – a little one room flat with a Murphy bed that resides in the wall in the daytime! It was great fun.

I had been to see my mother several times, and I had a feeling that shortly after I returned to my course at the University of Illinois that she would die. That was correct. She waited till I was having lunch with a dear cousin whom I hadn't seen for years due to disagreements in the family between our parents. Once there had been that symbolic reunion with the two opposing sides of the family, she passed away. I was not there with her, and I never saw her body. That made it very difficult for my mind to take in the fact of her passing. At one level I knew it was so, and relatives advised me not to see her body. As a result, I now make it a point to see the body of loved ones who have died, because it is easier for me to relate to their deaths when I have seen the evidence. I find that viewing the body of a loved person is sacred and a privilege that I greatly appreciate.

I had a bit of an argument with the minister whose duty it was to lead my mother's funeral. He refused to read my favourite Bahá'í prayer: *"From the Sweet Scented Streams"*.[1] I absolutely loved that prayer, and it was very significant and pertinent for use at my mother's funeral. I really felt that as my mother's only child, a simple request to have my favourite prayer read at her funeral could have been honoured by a man whose duty it was to conduct the funeral and offer some pastoral care to me in my loss. I was so distressed by that because I was truly her closest relative especially considering that she had been divorced from my father for such a long time. That minister's refusal lived with me for many years. Much later, and in the company of some Catholic friends and a priest who held a small memorial service for several of us during a summer school workshop in psychosynthesis, I was able to read that prayer aloud with others in her memory which helped to redeem and

---

1   See Appendix B

heal the hurt that minister caused me with his lack of cooperation and caring at my mother's funeral.

And so, as Kahlil Gibran (1992, p.101) says in *The Prophet*:

You would know the secret of death.
But how shall you find it unless you seek it in the heart of life?
The owl whose night-bound eyes are blind unto
the day cannot unveil the mystery of light.
If you would indeed behold the spirit of death,
open your heart wide unto the body of life.
For life and death are one,
even as the river and the sea are one.

And so I found my Beloved, my Heart's Desire. I had become a Bahá'í: a decision that changed my life unbelievably from the day I made it. It has taken me to live in other countries, to develop friendships with a wide range of people, to live as part of a worldwide community that supports, encourages and loves me. Becoming a Bahá'í was the first step. When 'Abdu'l-Bahá was asked how do we become Bahá'ís, he said, "little by little". I knew it would be a gradual process, but I was impatient with myself. I longed to improve myself and become a better person through learning more about the Bahá'í teachings. I looked back at my life and began to be grateful for both the good times and the difficult times because I felt that all my experience had enabled me to find this Faith in which I could truly believe.

On Reflection

Our experience of religion has a huge impact on our lives, how we see ourselves, what our values are and what relationship, if any, we have with our creator. Some of us may not believe there is a creator at all and may feel that life is the result of some random series of events in the universe, which is without order and without meaning. Even if we have not been raised with a particular faith, the culture that we are born into will have views and values based on some religious perspectives that affect us unconsciously even if we don't realise it or believe in it.

We can go along and accept the ideas and culture into which we have been born, or we can begin to forge our own viewpoint and in doing so live more truly according to our own determined beliefs. Some people have had horrendous experiences of religion or faith. Others have been very nurtured by their experiences. Whichever direction we find religion pulls us, we are affected by it in some way. Our cultural and religious background informs our ideas about all aspects of life and of death. Therefore it is important to think about and reflect on conscious and unconscious beliefs that might underpin the details of our lives.

I am going to suggest some short exercises to help you to begin to understand what you may be carrying on a subconscious level that may be affecting your thoughts and feelings even now. Take your time to relax and enjoy reflecting on your experiences. You may choose to reflect in one sitting or over a period of time.

Consider what values have been present in your culture and what is the predominant faith or faiths in your culture. How closely aligned with the faith are those cultural values? How strict or lax are those values now? Write down your thoughts and feelings as you consider these questions.

1. What is the faith background of your parents?

Even if they are not practising now, how do their values reflect the values of their faith background? Have they delved deeper into their faith or have they rejected it and reacted against it? Write down your thoughts and feelings about these issues.

2. What has been your personal experience of religion or faith?

Spend some time with this question, noticing your thoughts and feelings as they come up. Write down whatever ideas and feelings emerge.

3. What have been the important rules and laws within your family?

How do those rules and laws relate to your parent's faith background and the faith background of your culture? Make a list of these rules and laws.

Do you agree or disagree with each of these rules and laws? Notice your feelings as you consider this question, and write down your impressions.

4. See if you can recall some events or actions in which you have participated and about which you have felt a sense of shame or guilt.

Compare these events and actions with the rules and laws within your family to help you see if your shame or guilt might be due to an inherited moral code that belongs to your family or culture. If you have transgressed your own personal set of values, you certainly might feel your own shame or guilt. If you are reacting to an inherited moral code that you don't share, your guilt and shame are also inherited.

As you look back over these thoughts and reflections, you may have a clearer sense of what values you have chosen and what values you have inherited. When you really understand your own personal values, you can be more true to your own code of conduct and not respond to a socially-accepted rule book that is not your own. When you have completed these exercises do something to celebrate and reward yourself because these are important questions, and they do take some hard inner searching to answer honestly and from the heart.

Chapter 4
So Now What?

Having embraced the Bahá'í Faith, I found my life began to change very rapidly. My previous experience of different faiths had never challenged me in the way that I was challenged after I chose to become a Bahá'í. I certainly have felt inspired or uplifted by other faiths, but almost immediately upon becoming a Bahá'í I felt like I had begun an initiation. This initiation seemed to cause me to question everything that I had thought, felt and concluded. I sometimes experienced feelings like immense joy and gratitude but also anger, grief or hatred. I didn't understand those feelings at the time. They seemed to arise only since having become a Bahá'í, and they didn't seem to be connected to any other current events in my life. I could only conclude that my emotions were going through changes caused by my growing faith, and I actually welcomed those feelings because they indicated to me that there were profound changes happening within me even if I didn't understand them all. It was rather uncanny, but I could feel the aliveness of my faith, which seemed to be working through me rather than being just a set of structures on the outside. It was an exhilarating and exciting time, but it was also sometimes exhausting and confusing because I was looking at everything in a new way. My love of the Faith and of Bahá'u'lláh's magnificent writings held me steady, and I found my way through.

I was assured by the Bahá'í writings that I was loved by God. I remembered the hymn: *"Jesus loves me this I know, for the Bible tells me so"*. As a young child I had felt that God loved me. I certainly knew that I loved God, and I loved the story of the birth of Jesus Christ in Bethlehem. However in the intervening years, I had lost touch with that feeling in some measure. When I began reading Bahá'u'lláh's words, I felt reassured of God's love for me. This was a different experience of feeling loved and accepted than I had ever had from a human being. It gave me the desire to do my best work and be the best kind of person that I could be.

So Now What?

As a new Bahá'í I began to read prayers daily. I hadn't said prayers regularly since my mother insisted that before bed I said: "Now I lay me down to sleep, I pray the Lord my soul to keep. If I should die before I wake, I pray the Lord my soul to take. God bless Mommy, Daddy and everyone and everything. God Bless me. Amen."

As a child I didn't need mother to remind me to say prayers each night because I loved the feeling I got whenever I said them. I loved the story of Jesus Christ and I had the feeling that He loved me. That feeling really touched my heart because it seemed that most adults I knew thought that children were troublesome. I was often reminded that children should be seen and not heard. I always imagined that Jesus would have listened to me and taken me seriously. My mother also talked about being protected by guardian angels and I felt that my prayers encouraged the angels to pay attention to me.

I was delighted to reclaim my regular connection with God. I learned to say prayers that connected me with a sense of love, protection, and wisdom. I found prayers that I chose to say daily and ones that were for particular occasions. Up until this time, I would speak to God in my own way, which I continued to do at times, but I also enjoyed being able to use the prayers of Bahá'u'lláh and 'Abdu'l-Bahá and the Báb that were so stunningly beautiful. I often kept a card with names of people for whom I prayed regularly written on it, and I would read their names daily when I said my prayers.

As a Bahá'í I had a new set of principles by which to judge myself, circumstances, and situations that occurred. For instance, as a child I had observed that women were not treated as equals to men, and that worried me because I couldn't see why gender would make any one human inferior or superior to another. The Bahá'í writings assured me of gender equality; likening men and women to the two wings of a bird that would enable humanity to soar. I loved that analogy. There is a word that was used in the past: "helpmate". In the Bahá'í Faith husbands and wives were considered helpmates to each other, just like the two wings of a bird, each contributing complementary strengths to enable their union to flourish.

But it wasn't all clear blue skies. My aunt and uncle were suspicious of my choice, and certainly more so than my father had been. All in all, I felt that something I cherished deeply, which I had chosen because it felt true for me was being criticised by my family. I felt shattered and lost. For support, I decided to go to a small dress shop that my mother and I had frequented for many years, which was run by three sisters whom I had liked. I went in and told them enthusiastically of my newfound faith, explaining that my father had given me his approval and sharing with them how carefully I had investigated its claims and found it exactly what I was seeking. I said that I had met many of its followers, and that they were wonderful people.

I liked these women and felt sure they would be there to give me the reassurance that I needed in the face of the criticism from my extended family. So I asked them if it seemed right to join a faith after I had seriously investigated it and gotten the approval of my father, even though some members of my mother's family didn't agree. I was shocked when they replied: "You must always do what your mother wants you to do." I felt deeply disappointed. They knew that my mother was ill and nearly dying in a nursing home and unable to advise me on anything. They knew that my father was half the world away, and even though he agreed with my choice, he wasn't here today to support me.

I was so hurt, angry and shocked that I left that shop, got into my car, drove away and never went there again. Although this was a very painful time for me, looking back on it I can see that it was the beginning of me striking out on my own path and breaking away from the approval of my culture and childhood community.

In my heart I knew that I had made the right decision to become a Bahá'í, and I had my father's blessing. I also knew that if my mother had been well, she would have enjoyed hearing about the Faith and would have respected and appreciated my decision. But for all of that I was really on my own feeling very much abandoned by my family and feeling out in the cold then. I was most hurt because my aunt and uncle showed me that they didn't trust my intelligent discrimination. At 19, I felt old enough to be able to use my own judgement and I longed for their approval to add to my father's. I also just wanted to please my family members and make them proud of me.

Of course, looking back now I can understand that I was not as old and adult as I thought I was. I could have been wrong, so I feel sure that they just wanted to protect me from possible harm, but I didn't feel that then. I felt so utterly disappointed with them. I couldn't wait to leave St Louis and get back to Chicago where I felt at home.

So Now What?

Bahá'u'lláh says:

> The best beloved of all things in My sight is Justice... By its aid thou shalt see with thine own eyes and not through the eyes of others, and shalt know of thine own knowledge and not through the knowledge of thy neighbour. (Bahá'u'lláh, 1975, pp.5-6)

I took that to mean that I was my own judge within myself and was capable of making intelligent decisions. This assurance was one of the Faith's greatest gifts to me. I checked any decision with the Bahá'í teachings, my own inner voice and the opinions of knowledgeable others, and I appreciated knowing that I was in charge of my own life and accountable to myself.

In those days, I was going to Feasts every nineteen days and participating in Bahá'í Community activities. When I use the term "Bahá'í Community" I don't mean that the Bahá'ís all live together "in community". I mean that we live in the same local area. There were Feasts, usually organised on the first day of each Bahá'í month. In the Bahá'í calendar there are 19 months of 19 days each with four intercalary days or five such days in leap years. The months are named after the some of the attributes of God like Grandeur, Sovereignty and Will. Even the names of the months are uplifting to me!

The Feasts were held in the homes of Bahá'ís, and that immediately gave a level of intimacy, a sense of family. There would be about 10–12 people at each Feast. The Chairperson of the Local Spiritual Assembly would welcome the guests and thank the people who were hosting the Feast. The hosts would have chosen prayers and readings from the Bahá'í writings, and given them to various people to read. When that was over, the chairperson would ask the secretary of the Assembly to report any news or plans. Then there would be a consultation with everyone free to offer their views, comments or suggestions. After the consultation there would be a closing prayer, and then the host would provide the guests with refreshments. That was the time to chat to friends and enjoy the company of my fellow Bahá'ís.

There was such love and fellowship in those gatherings that attending a Feast was very nourishing for me. I could go to the Feast feeling irritated or troubled or depressed, and I would come out feeling uplifted and happy. It was like an oasis in a storm. In many places where I have lived I have become very closely involved with the Bahá'ís who were living in the area, so meeting them regularly, sharing prayers and activities and plans has been a wonderful addition to my life. There are a lot of laughs, and it is fun too.

Of course, as with any family, there are also many challenges. Because the Bahá'ís are from different backgrounds, the cultural mix is exhilarating and challenging. The principle of the elimination of prejudice is lived beautifully, and there were people that I would never have met if I had remained in the society where prejudice was part of the social fabric.

Growing up in St Louis, I had never met people from other cultures or really any background that was different from St Louisans. Oh I tell a lie: there was an exchange student from Sweden at my secondary school for a year. In all my moving around in the early part of my life, I met other white Americans and some Canadians, but I had not met black people socially at all nor had I met people of other cultures. I considered that a great loss. I never did understand racial or cultural prejudice and to find friends from many cultures as I did in the Bahá'í community was just wonderful.

There are nine Holy Days in the Bahá'í Faith. Some of them are days of great joy and celebrating, others are days of commemorating the passing of the central figures of the Faith. Because we believe in all the "Divine Educators", like Jesus Christ, Moses, Abraham, Zoroaster, Muhammad, we could actually celebrate all the Holy Days of all the religions, but we would never get any work done. I had been used to celebrating Christmas, Good Friday and Easter. Now my life had become marked by the rhythm of the nine Bahá'í Holy Days scattered around the year.

One particularly interesting Holy Day is the passing of Bahá'u'lláh, which is commemorated in the early hours of the morning. I usually slept for a few hours before the meeting, and then I slept again after returning back home. The commemoration almost felt like an overnight flight between continents: a time that doesn't belong to the day before or the coming day, so a kind of time outside of time. It was magical, and I would leave the meeting around 5am when dawn is just coming, and the world is silent and clear.

As a teenager in search of a potential partner, I was able to use my new-found identity as a Bahá'í to gain some understanding of the people that I met and men in particular. When I met a new person, I would mention "Bahá'í" just to see what their response would be, and that would tell me quite a lot about them. If they didn't even wonder what "Bahá'í" meant, I would assume that they were not as interested in unusual spiritual or religious matters as I was. However, I had to be careful and not judge too quickly because some of my best friends had been people that I didn't even like on first meeting. If the new person asked what "Bahá'í" meant, then we could get into an interesting conversation about new ideas. I realise now that I used my Faith to challenge people and perhaps learn a little more about them.

I had stopped drinking alcohol, which was unusual in those days when university students usually drank beer on campus. My faith was so important to me, however, that it was a small inconvenience just to say "no thank you" when I was offered a drink. I have never regretted eliminating alcohol from my life at that early age; in fact I feel it has been an enormous strength and support for me. My father had wanted me to become knowledgeable about wine, but I didn't like it, so I guess he was disappointed in that. He was a man who drank with style, particular wines with particular foods. Even he gave up drinking later in life because of health. Later when I had a family, my life was so much easier without alcohol than I feel it might have been with it. When my children grew up, they made their own decisions in this respect.

I had never seen my dad drunk or unruly because of alcohol. I noticed that some people became a little more relaxed and pleasant after having had a drink and others became ugly and even violent. I was bewildered by such a huge range of responses. Some enjoy alcohol with a semblance of style. Others drink to get drunk so they can behave in ways that they would not normally allow themselves to, often at the expense of others. I had seen people who habitually drank moderately turn to drinking excessively when life became hard. Because I did not feel confident that I would have the strength to remain a moderate drinker if life became really painful, I was unwilling to take that risk.

We live in a world where we might hope to create unity within ourselves, within the family, the neighbourhood, the community, the city, the nation, and ultimately the world. I can't imagine how any of us can use alcohol as long as there is even one person who becomes violent or dangerous as a result of its use and does harm either to themselves or others.

As I explored my faith I became ever more committed to making my life meaningful and helpful to people in whatever way I could. I longed to serve humanity without perhaps knowing what I meant by that, but knowing that I wanted to contribute to a better world. At that time in my first effort to create a meaningful life I chose to think in terms of marriage rather than developing a career because I so much wanted to be a wife and mother. Being settled with my spiritual life enabled me to feel more secure in the thought of being a wife and raising children.

I had never wanted to live with a man without being married to him. I had the experience of living in close proximity to people in universities who had very different habits and values than I did. That was enough for me. I realised that I didn't want to live with someone so intimately unless we were married. I had particular needs. For instance I needed sound sleep, and I was easily disturbed. I was sure my husband would care enough for me to be considerate of my needs.

The people around me in universities didn't seem to care how much noise they made late at night. I found the noise problem so difficult in one university dormitory (where I actually had a single room) that I had to come up with some way to shut out the noise. I had a clock radio that had a timer, and it had a plug in the back for people who wanted to plug in a coffee pot, so it would come on early in the morning. It also had a night time function whereby the radio could be set to play for a half an hour before going to sleep. Well, I had a hair dryer that made sufficient noise to reduce the sound of people in the halls, so I used to plug the hair dryer into the clock radio and set it to run for half an hour when I was going to sleep and that helped me enormously.

I was also very particular about the food that I ate. I really liked good quality food. I used to sometimes make grilled cheese sandwiches when I didn't get to the dining hall for a meal, or wouldn't eat what they were serving. I made my sandwiches in my room by buttering bread, putting some good cheese in between the slices of bread, wrapping the sandwich in aluminium foil and then ironing the sandwich in its foil! I had other tricks as well. I had an electric frying pan and a coffee percolator, and there was a lot that I could do with both of those appliances, like cook vegetables or make stews. Sometimes I just went out for a meal.

I was particular about cleanliness and caring for my things. I met people who were not at all as particular as I was. Some people were especially messy and even dirty with respect to their clothes and their room. I was unimpressed. For all these reasons, I felt I would prefer to either live on my own or with a husband.

Bahá'u'lláh recommended marriage, and I believed that marriage was a good principle in terms of raising children and positively contributing to the world. It felt like part of a spiritual path to have someone to whom I was committed, whom I loved, with whom I could share my life so I wasn't so self-centred. I wanted to share my life in a structured way. To me marriage was a kind of fortress for protection, growth, and development of the couple as well as of the family and the community. I would rather have been married at least once, even if it failed, than never have been married at all. It simply remained for me to find the man, and I didn't expect that to be particularly easy because I had pretty set ideas about what was important to me.

I started to monitor my actions with my friends and family to be sure that I was being as truthful and considerate as I could be. Because of this I thought I had become a nicer person because I had become more concerned with others and my treatment of them, wanting it to be fair and just. I don't think I was mean, nasty or evil beforehand, but I know I was less selfish after becoming a Bahá'í. I believed all of that augured well for the possibility of marriage and children.

I decided to volunteer at the Bahá'í House of Worship in Wilmette in the summer of 1964. It was a magnificent building with a dome on Chicago's North Shore that looked like concrete lace. It attracted many tourists all year long. I found out that Philip O'Brien was co-ordinator there, so I wrote to him declaring my undying devotion to doing whatever I could to help as a guide for tourists and do my bit for the Faith. I said that I would even be willing to clean the dome of the House of Worship with a toothbrush if necessary. When I think about that now it was a little over the top, but I was so enthusiastic! He replied to me saying that he didn't think it would be necessary for me to scrub the dome with a toothbrush but that my efforts would be appreciated by people in over 250 countries, islands and territories of the world. That was OK by me.

When I went to Chicago to spend the summer guiding at the Bahá'í House of Worship, there was no fear or loneliness – none of the feelings that I had experienced just the previous year when I had gone to Chicago to work for the summer. On the contrary, I couldn't have been happier or more fulfilled. I was going to do something for which I was needed. I was going to work to help the Faith, and that felt like the most meaningful thing I could do.

When I first went to the House of Worship to work as a volunteer guide, it was Philip who welcomed me there. He was an actor, and he had wanted to do something special for the Faith after becoming a Bahá'í. He gave up his job in television in California and went to the House of Worship to supervise the volunteer guides, talk to groups and generally deal with the public in all its myriad forms. That was quite a task. I was very impressed with this man who would relinquish working in his chosen career to do something for the Faith that he loved.

I remember he said to me that he was terrified of speaking to groups. When he was acting he had a script and that was fine, but just to get up and talk to people about the Faith was really frightening for him. He did it, but it made him nervous every time. He would get physically sick to his stomach each time he had to give a talk on the Faith because he wanted his talk to be really good. He succeeded in that although he didn't realise it himself. He had a sharp and quick mind and could answer questions remarkably well. His talks were challenging, interesting, inspiring and funny. He always said that we should never try to tell everything about the Faith because that would only confuse people, so he made the whole concept simple and understandable. If he hadn't loved the Faith so much, he might have been less worried about presenting it well.

The House of Worship was open from 10am to 10pm in the summer seven days a week. Ideally there had to be five guides on duty all the time. Well, that was some job. Volunteers are not as reliable as paid people generally because they think that someone else will step in easily if they can't. People would phone up and say: "I was meant to guide today from 2pm to 6pm but I have a little cold, and I am going to stay at home." Philip would say: "You will feel a lot better when you look up at that dome and feel the energy here." And they would come!

With the best will in the world, however, there were still times when there were not enough people available. In the House of Worship there was an upstairs and a downstairs that had to be covered as well as a book shop and an auditorium where a 10-minute slide show about the Faith was put on when people wanted to see it. That makes four spots where people were needed. The fifth guide could float around to help out or give breaks. Hundreds of people would come to see the House of Worship at any given time. It is a tourist attraction, and whole tour buses would arrive there, sometimes several at a time and often without notice. The organisers of the tour buses often phoned first to let us know they were coming, but not always.

When guides didn't turn up we had to somehow cover that spot. We couldn't always find someone to do so. Once I arrived at the House of Worship to guide and Philip was standing outside so he could see the entrance to the upstairs auditorium as well as the downstairs area with books and displays. I asked him why and he replied: "I am the only one here, and I want to be available if anyone comes to see the building." The other guides had let him down. I really felt needed then. Just one other person made such a difference. One of us could cover the upstairs and one could manage the downstairs.

I had to find a place to live while I was working at the House of Worship for that summer of 1964. Luckily I was able to find a little apartment in the same building where I had lived after returning from California to Chicago. It was a slightly larger place in the basement with a bedroom, living room, kitchen and bathroom. I really felt like I was progressing to have an apartment with a separate bedroom rather than the one room place with the Murphy bed that came down from the wall. The building was a strange shape, a bit triangular, and this flat was in the bottom corner. I walked into the hallway and barely noticed the water pipes that lined the hall ceiling. The bathroom and kitchen were on the right, the bedroom on the left, and there was a living room straight ahead. There was a rather dull green carpet on the floors, and the walls were beige. Oddly the walls of the rooms were not exactly squared off because they slanted as part of the building's triangular shape. It had rather sparse, simple furnishing so I could have my record player as well as books and little things that were important to me. The windows looked out onto a tree-lined pathway slightly below street level. Even though it was an unusual apartment it was simple, and I thought it was great. After Philip and I got to know each other a little bit through working together, I invited him over for a meal. He walked in the front door, looked up at the exposed pipes under the hall ceiling and exclaimed that the apartment was gorgeous while raising his eyes to heaven! His beautiful blue eyes were so expressive that I could only laugh when he did that.

In those days I could fit everything that I owned in the trunk of my car, so moving around was pretty easy. It was a lucky thing too because I moved a lot during those years. I sometimes felt as if my car was my real my home.

During that summer I was in the process of transferring to Northwestern University. I felt that it had a great School of Journalism, and I wanted to go there. I had been in touch with the admissions department of the university, and I had arranged to have my transcripts sent from Lake Forest College and the University of Illinois. Everything was in order, and I heard from the Director of Admissions to say that all was well. The only thing left was to have a medical examination. I found that a rather strange requirement and I didn't remember ever before being required to have a medical exam for admission to a university, but this was Northwestern, a very prestigious university with an outstanding journalism department, so I was willing to submit to this strange requirement because I was very keen to be a student there.

I went along to the appointed doctor and was surprised to see that he didn't have a stethoscope or anything that indicated he was a medical doctor. He criticised me for changing majors and universities and then going to California in the previous September instead of continuing at the University of Illinois, even though I did go back to the university in February of that year. I thought those were very strange questions for a medical doctor to be asking me.

Then suddenly it occurred to me that this man might be a psychiatrist, and he was trying to see if I was mentally stable because I had not followed the usual route in terms of university work. I began to feel threatened by him. I said that I found that travel and experience were often better teachers than classes. I saw nothing wrong with changing my mind about what subject I wanted to study and finding a university that had a great department in that subject. Where in the past I might have been intimidated by such a man in authority to the extent that I would have been unable to answer him, I found the strength to do so when I recalled a phrase in one of my favourite prayers, *The Tablet of Ahmad*, which said:

Remember My days during thy days, and My distress and banishment in this remote prison. And be thou so steadfast in My love that thy heart shall not waver, even if the swords of thine enemies rain blows upon thee and all the heavens and the earth arise against thee.

Be thou as a flame of fire to My enemies and a river of life eternal to my loved ones, and be not of those who doubt. (Bahá'u'lláh, 1991a, p.211)

I kept calm and collected and finished the conversation with this man, was accepted at Northwestern University and was delighted that I had come to an understanding of what might have been happening during my "medical examination". I realised that my faith had given me a greater trust in myself, and a genuine feeling of self-confidence. This confidence supported me to take my intuition more seriously and to trust my sense of this doctor's agenda. I had a right to change my mind and value different ways of learning, even if those ways might not have been seen to be in the service of my academic achievements.

I got to know Philip as a good friend during that summer because we spent a lot of time together. I worked about six hours a day at the House of Worship. When we could take a break together, we would go out for a meal. He was very funny, and we had a lot of laughs and could talk and talk for hours about anything and everything and always have something else to say when next we had a chance to talk. There wasn't a subject that we didn't discuss. We seemed to have a lot in common. He was sophisticated, cultured and all the things that I found very attractive. He happened also to be very good looking. Because he was 16 years older than me, I was sure we would always be just good friends. I never thought for a moment that he would have been interested in me as a wife. For this reason I didn't allow myself to admit to my growing love for him and never really looked at the possibility that our friendship might have meant more. We got along really well, so I was delighted to be working for him even as a volunteer. If someone couldn't come to guide, then I would fill in for that person. It was lovely being in the House of Worship, so close to Lake Michigan. I could sit and read a lot of the time. That suited me fine because I have always been an avid reader.

People from all over the world came to the House of Worship as tourists, so I answered questions about the Faith all day long, and I learned a lot. I helped Philip in lots of ways, sometimes writing letters for him as a secretary. When I started my course at Northwestern University I was in Wilmette, very near to the House of Worship, so I continued to see him regularly even though I no longer worked as a volunteer guide. We spoke on the telephone several times a day, and I really enjoyed his stories.

I was so excited to be seeing an actor who had a lot of experience in life, in the arts, with great taste, who was such fun to be with. I never thought of our meetings as "dates" because I was aware of just being with someone whom I thoroughly enjoyed. I always held that feeling that we might not always be doing this, and that someday someone else would be accompanying him or me, and I wondered how I would deal with that. I felt rather frightened of losing him. As I look back now I see that clearly I was falling in love with him as he was with me even though we hadn't admitted that to each other. We went to the theatre or to concerts from time to time. We both loved that, and I saw how much he loved the theatre. I noticed in some plays that he would be on the edge of his seat as if wanting to be in the play himself. I introduced him to my friend who was one of the best talent agents in Chicago and he began to get work in the theatre. That made him very happy.

One day our growing love for each other finally came out in the open. Philip called me and said that a friend of ours was going to phone me because he had told her that we were getting married. He said that he had been at a party over the weekend and she had said to him: "Wouldn't it be nice if you had a spouse to go to these parties with?" He told her that he was getting married soon and he wouldn't tell her who it was, adding that he couldn't say anything until we got consent from our parents.

He tortured her by keeping it secret but phoning her to ask questions like: "Do you know where we can get a non-fattening wedding cake?" Finally her curiosity got the better of her, and she rang him to say that she had figured out who it was. She reckoned it was me because nobody knew whom either of us was seeing, and if we were seeing anyone, then we had to be seeing each other. He told her that she was right, but that he didn't want the word to get around yet. I remember it was a Monday, and we had gone out to lunch together. On the way to the restaurant, he had actually been singing: *"I want to get married"*. I had ignored it and never thought another thing about it.

I had just arrived home when Philip phoned me saying that our friend wanted to check with me to see if it was true that we were getting married and he told me the whole story. He asked if I would go along with it as if it were a game and tell her that it was me. I agreed because he had caught me off-guard. Ordinarily I wouldn't have said yes to such a charade. She phoned, and I confirmed that Philip and I were getting married, asking: "Do you think that he would lie about a thing like that?" After that conversation, I phoned him back immediately and said that I was furious because once that news got out, it would prevent me from any chances I might have with anyone else, and it was a lie because at that stage we hadn't agreed to marry. I didn't like lying. He said that he thought it would be a great idea for us to marry but he didn't think I could get consent from my father to marry a man who was so much older than I was.

Suddenly in that conversation I came to the realisation that this charade had been Philip's way of asking me to marry him! I then knew beyond a shadow of a doubt that Philip wanted to marry me and he was too unsure to ask me directly. It was not just a question of whether or not my father would agree to our marriage, but rather would I be interested in marrying someone who was 16 years older than me? I was more charmed than ever by him when I saw that Philip's way of proposing was actually quite a shy way of doing so, and I knew both that he loved me and that I loved him although we had not yet had the courage to speak those words.

I said I also thought it would be a good idea for us to marry, and I thought I could get consent from my father, so I would phone him now, but he had better get consent from his father too!

I telephoned my dad, who answered the phone by saying that he had had hepatitis and jaundice and was on a diet with no alcohol and no fat, and I ought to know what that would be like for him. He added that he knew I wouldn't phone unless I wanted something and asked what I wanted adding that it was midnight in Geneva, Switzerland where he lived, so I woke him up. That wasn't a great start to my important topic of conversation! I said that I was so sorry but that I had to ask him for consent to get married.

He asked whom did I want to marry, and I told him it was Philip. He said that he was afraid of that. He asked if Philip loved me, and I said yes, but I was lying because Philip hadn't yet told me that he did. Then he asked if Philip could support me, and I said yes and again I was lying because I didn't know if he could. My father asked what he made in terms of income, and I said I didn't know, so he said I should find out. Then my father agreed to give me his consent pending my finding out how much money Philip made. It was done!

I phoned Philip, and he had his father's consent too. His father was a little surprised that Philip needed his consent because Philip was then 37 years old, and he asked if Philip would consider marrying me in the local Catholic Parish Church in Troy, New York. Philip said that it would be fine with us, but he didn't think the priest would marry us as Bahá'ís. In those days, such things didn't actually happen, and his father knew it, so he didn't insist any further on that idea.

There followed endless letters back and forth to my father to assure him that everything was alright. He did eventually sign the letter of consent and came to love Philip after awhile. I didn't question it at the time, but looking back I realise that normally it would have been the man who asked the woman's father for consent to marry his daughter. That was the usual pattern when I was growing up, but quite frankly neither Philip nor I thought of the idea that he might phone my father. If I had been living with my parents, and I had been out on a date, I wouldn't have hesitated to wake my parents with excitement if the man I loved had asked me to marry him. When I think now of the conversation I had with my father, I realise how much worse it would have been if it had been Philip on the phone to him at midnight in Geneva. They had met already because Philip had driven me to Montreal from Chicago some months before when my father was there on business. I imagine that my father would have wondered if we had a romantic connection at that time. I would have protested that we were just friends, but I feel sure that my father could have seen through my protestations and recognised that I really did care for him. My father would also have thought of all the reasons why we shouldn't be involved with each other like that he was so much older than me and that he was an actor without a stable income and that I surely could do better. Philip on the other hand would have equally protested all of those issues and stood up to my father. They were both quite strong willed individuals, and I dread to think of the outcome if they had spoken on the telephone on that eventful night. At least my father would have softened his reaction to being awakened at that ungodly hour because it was his daughter.

After Philip and I had made the decision to marry each other and gotten consent from our fathers, we had no hesitation and said "I love you" many times to each other.

I was absolutely thrilled, and I really enjoyed such an unusual method of agreeing to getting married. Perhaps I had to be somewhat tricked into it, or I would have run a mile before committing myself to marrying any man. The way that it all happened might seem unromantic to some, but just because Philip didn't get down on bended knee to propose, it worked just fine, thank you very much. Philip and I got engaged a year to the day after my mother had died. That was a good omen, I thought. One evening after that, when we were having dinner at a restaurant that Philip frequented, he was telling the waitress, whom he knew, that we were getting married. She looked at me and said: "It is better to be an old man's darling than a young man's slave!" We all laughed, and I think I agree. Philip didn't want me to work. I was happy with that because the freedom of being at home gave me the much needed time and energy to research health and healing for myself and the family. Of course what I didn't realise was that I would have to work 24 hours a day at home. I had no idea. I had never before in my life worked as hard as I did when I had my family.

Now when I look back on my choice to marry a man who was 16 years older than me, I can see that there were some limitations to my choice. In principle I would rather have been married to someone who was nearer to my age, but in practice, Philip and I were extremely well suited and very much in love with each other. I usually found men of my own age rather dull, and therefore was more than willing to let go of any possibility of finding such a man in favour of marrying Philip. I grew up for the most part without siblings and in the company of older people. I usually got on well with people of my age, but I felt I learned more from older people, so I preferred to be with them. Sadly, because Philip was so much older than me, I was always likely to be left by his dying well before me. At 21, however, I didn't realistically think ahead to that. It was enough for me to think about my joy in marrying the man of my dreams without concerning myself too prematurely with who was going to die first even though I am now his widow.

We arranged to be married on the 23rd of May, a Bahá'í Holy Day and Philip's birthday, so I was his birthday present on a Holy Day! We had about three months to get the wedding organised. Because Philip knew so many people from working at the House of Worship, we invited a large number of people. Members of my family came from St Louis, although my father was unable to come from Switzerland. Members of Philip's family came from Troy, New York, and some of his friends from New York City came too. There were hundreds of people there. I bought a beautiful pale-pink, beaded wedding dress at Bonwit Teller in Chicago. I was delighted that Philip and I went shopping for the wedding dress together, overthrowing the old tradition that the groom should not see the bride before the wedding in her dress. Philip was my best friend, and he had wonderful taste, so who else did I have to go with me who could do such a good job as him?

I particularly remember trying on the dress, and it was so stunningly beautiful that I gasped. It was such a simple design, with little cap sleeves, a round neckline and full skirt to the floor. It was not white but the palest of pink, and it was beaded all over except for the sleeves and the waist and a panel at the bottom of the skirt. I know that if I had been a child and had seen a woman in it, I would have thought that she was a queen or a princess. It had to be ordered because they didn't keep those dresses in stock. We also decided to have a stole that wrapped around me with some of the beaded detail on it, and I got a pink hat in the style of a light turban to wear with it. We didn't want me to wear a veil. After all, he knew what I looked like! We had such fun together choosing that dress. It was enormously exciting. It is, without doubt, the most beautiful dress I have ever worn, and even after Philip had died, I put it on and felt great. It was tighter in the waist than it had been when I had first worn it, but I could still zip it up, and I felt just great in it again. I kept it all these years, and my daughter wore it when she got married. She looked absolutely beautiful in it, and I was delighted that she could wear it.

We had chosen readings from the Bahá'í writings and asked friends to read them. We were married in the downstairs auditorium at the House of Worship, and asked a friend to give a little introduction and explain to the audience something about the Bahá'í wedding, which was rather different in form to Christian weddings. There was no priest or minister to do the job. According to the Bahá'í law, all each of us had to do was to say: "We will all, verily, abide by the will of God." (Bahá'u'lláh, 1991a, p.104)

Even so, after the wedding was over, the people had read their pieces, and the House of Worship choir had sung, Philip's father turned to his wife and asked: "Do you think they are really married?" We were! We arranged the wedding on a Sunday, so everyone could go to the weekly worship service at 3 o'clock upstairs in the House of Worship after the wedding. The first thing that Philip and I did as a married couple was attend a service in the Bahá'í House of Worship, and that was really poignant for both of us.

The wedding reception was held later that day in a hall at Northwestern University. We were utterly exhausted by the time the reception began. After awhile, Philip just wanted us to leave and go to the nearby hotel where we were spending our first night together. I insisted that we had to cut the wedding cake, and as soon as we did, we got out of there to begin our life together. It was a lovely event, and I was so delighted to be married. I felt as if I had come home. We had a very special romantic night together in terms of intimacy, but we were also absolutely exhausted, so sleep came very quickly. I think my exhaustion overcame any nervousness I might have had for our first night together.

The next day we left Chicago and drove together to New England and New York, where Philip was longing to introduce me to friends and family because he was so proud of me. As much as I wanted to be with him and to meet these friends and family, I found it really hard to figure out who I was as Philip O'Brien's wife, Mrs Philip O'Brien. I was naturally shy in company in those days, and very likely to remain quiet much of the time. On our honeymoon I was even quieter because I had just changed my name, and my identity. I had not come to really understand who I was in this new role. I was like a tender new shoot just breaking its way through the earth, and I felt very vulnerable, longing to be the "perfect wife" who knew how to behave and what to say in any circumstances, and I felt far from that.

We moved to Glencoe, Illinois, north of the House of Worship after we were married and lived there just over a year in a little apartment above a pet-grooming parlour. I have a story that might amuse you. After a few nights in our apartment, I decided that our bed wasn't hard enough for my back, so I suggested that we get a board to put under the mattress to make it more firm. Philip wasn't interested, and I was suffering, so I decided to get it anyway. I arranged for it to be delivered to the pet-grooming parlour downstairs, and when Philip was out, I got it from the people in the parlour and I took it upstairs and put it under the mattress. Philip came home from the theatre that night and threw himself down on the bed as usual, but the bed didn't give in the same way it had before. He looked shocked, and then he looked at me in massive disapproval. He had such big expressive blue eyes. I was never in any doubt about how he was feeling.

He didn't do anything about it once it was there, and he discovered that the bed was much more comfortable with the firm support of the board under the mattress. This little cameo illustrates something of the dilemma with which I was faced. I was confused in my new identity and didn't know how free I was to be self-initiating and self-defining. I didn't know what I was meant to do as "wife". Was I meant to concede to his wishes even when he wasn't being supportive? Was I meant to get on and do it myself even though he might not approve? Where is the line between the compromise that is needed in marriage and continuing to be an independent person? There were lots of little moments like that. Anybody who has been married will recognise times of such dilemmas. I was only 21 years old, married to a man who was then 38 years old, and I was sometimes very confused about my role.

In the midst of all of this we had both been elected to the Spiritual Assembly of the Bahá'ís of Glencoe, and I was elected secretary. That was my first time being secretary of an assembly. Philip was very helpful in teaching me how to write minutes and keep records and deal with correspondence and that sort of thing. Here again he was the elder, wiser teacher, the authority, and I was grateful for that at the time. Indeed allowing him to have authority enabled me to feel protected. He continued work at the House of Worship for a while, but he was gradually getting back into acting again. Later that summer, after he had fulfilled his two-year contract he stopped working at the House of Worship. He then began to work as an actor in commercials and in the theatres in the Chicago area.

I found that it was difficult for me to adjust to being married in the beginning. I had had a pretty active life as a single person and suddenly I was at home more during that summer while Philip was often out working. We were having some building work done in the flat, so I had to be there for carpenters and various people to come and fix up the kitchen or put in a shower or something like that. It wasn't as interesting being the "housewife" as it had been being the student or working and meeting people. I found that summer rather lonely. I went back to the University in the autumn, but I got ill and missed too much work to continue, so I withdrew. I had to find out what it meant for me to be a wife, and I also wanted to have children. I felt that we needed to do so fairly quickly since Philip was so much older than I was. Those were my priorities alongside my service to the Faith.

One day I went to a party at the home of some Bahá'í friends. When I arrived at the door, I must have looked awfully troubled because the wife said to me: "If you make it through the first year, you will be all right!" I was so downhearted and having someone see what was wrong with me just took away my anxiety right away. Along with my delight in feeling that I belonged with Philip and to Philip, I was still struggling to find out where I was still free to be myself within the marriage. That is part of what is so intense about the marriage commitment.

After about six months, I had made the adjustment and felt really committed to the marriage and to being myself in the context of my marriage. I certainly continued to work on that feeling throughout the relationship. One day, there was a request from the National Spiritual Assembly of the Bahá'ís of the USA for two people to go to Ireland to serve the Faith there. Because of the name O'Brien, people were asking Philip if we were going, and he was saying no. Then one night, we began talking and saying that our dearest wish was to serve the Faith in whatever way we could best do it. We also wanted to raise our family somewhere other than America: particularly in Europe. Philip looked at me and said that he would go if he weren't married. I said: "What does being married have to do with it, and I want to go too." We both wanted to raise our children in a place that was more spiritual and less materialistic, and Ireland seemed to fit the bill perfectly, so we decided to go.

By that time I was pregnant with our firstborn, and I longed to live in a place where life was simpler. We stayed up all night after having decided to move to Ireland. We rang friends in California, Bob and Keith Quigley, Keith was Bob's wife. I thought it most unusual that a woman's name was 'Keith'. We told her we were going to pioneer in Ireland. "Pioneer" is a term used by

Baháʼís who go to another place to help with the work of the Faith. We were going to live our ordinary lives, work, raise a family, and just be available to be on a Spiritual Assembly or help in any way we could. We were so excited about our new adventure. My father, his wife and daughter lived in Geneva, so we would be closer to them. Philip's father and his wife loved the idea of visiting us in Dublin.

We had some rather interesting conversations with the Irish Consul in Chicago. He gave us a price list that must have been from the early 1900s! It said that a haircut cost the equivalent of about $1.00. We said that we wanted to have a little land with a house. He said: "Sure, just about every house comes with five acres!" Not true!! We did find out that actors, artists, authors and musicians didn't need work permits there, so that was an advantage, and Philip could look forward to working without any problems.

We had a dog and were considering getting another dog to keep him company. It was a miniature dachshund named "Irving Katz". We knew that there was a six-month quarantine situation for animals when we went to Ireland. The Consul looked at us and said: "Sure, they say six months, but when you get there…!" Then he winked several times as if he knew something. We were supposed to take from that statement and the wink that we wouldn't have to leave the dog for six months after all. So we bought another little miniature dachshund called "Zelda". If we had really believed that the dogs would have been kept away from us for six months, we would have given Irving away and not included Zelda at all because we didn't think it would be fair to any dog to leave him in a kennel for six months. We hated parting with our dogs for that amount of time, and it didn't do them much good, but we believed that little wink from the Irish Consul in Chicago. How foolish and gullible we were.

This was late May of 1966, and we were leaving in August, so we had less than three months to get ready. We wanted to take things that we thought would be important. One of those things was a king-size bed. They were just new then. We went to Marshall Fields in Chicago and looked at beds. I wanted a really hard bed for my back. After the salesman had shown me what he had in hard beds, I asked: "Is this definitely the hardest bed you have?" He replied, "Madam, the next hardest thing I could offer you is a coffee table". Philip and I both cracked up laughing at that one. We bought a cradle for the baby and a few toys. We also bought a refrigerator. We knew that we would have to have a transformer, but we liked American refrigerators. In Dublin, a friend thought it was very funny that before our furniture had arrived, we said that we were going out for meals and not eating at home because we didn't have a fridge. This was in Southern Ireland in the mid 1960s where fewer than 18% of the population had little fridges. They simply went to the shops daily to get fresh food, but we were not used to doing that!

Aside from the king-size bed and the American refrigerator, we had only a little furniture, books and personal items in our place to pack up and ship. We also bought loads of natural vitamins because we feared that there wouldn't be anything like that in Dublin. We were used to the idea of a health food store locally, and we didn't think we could expect that there.

When I was nineteen years old I was a university student planning a life including a career, and that was as much as I could imagine for my life and my future. Just two years later so much had changed - I had found a faith that inspired me enormously and I was married to the man of my dreams whom I met through that faith. Together we chose to go on an adventure that would change our future in ways we could not begin to foresee at that time and it was all in the space of less than three years. That was a lot of change in a short time, and the following three years were going to be characterised by still more change again.

On Reflection

We all make choices that may feel like big risks at times. Some of these choices shape our lives and change their course. It could be the choice of a partner or a career or a place to live or a pursuit of an interest or passion. All of those choices will have a big impact on the direction of our lives. When we make the choice, we may feel both excitement and fear, but something inside us urges us on and encourages us. If our choice is accepted by those close to us, they will also encourage us forward. If it is not accepted it may feel like a rebellion and it will probably feel like a necessary rebellion.

Look back over your life and at the times when you have taken decisions that have changed your life considerably and set you on a very different path than you had been on before. Look at how you felt while you were making those decisions and how you feel about the outcome of your choices. Ask yourself if you are content with the outcome, if you would still make the same choice given what you know about how your life has turned out so far as a result of those choices.

For those things that you have done that you have really appreciated and that have benefited you, see if you have been able to be grateful for having had the wisdom to take the risks that you did and for the learning that you have gained as a result of having taken them. All too often we just do not appreciate ourselves for the wisdom that we have that leads us forward. We seem to dwell often too much on our faults and shortcomings, and it is really important for us to acknowledge what we have done right and how we have made some good decisions in our lives. It doesn't matter if anyone else knows about it or agrees that we did something of value, but all we need to do is admit it to ourselves and appreciate ourselves when we deserve such credit.

CHAPTER 5
Pioneering Spirit

When it came to leaving America, we had 17 pieces of luggage and two dogs. We took the train to New York City where we stayed for a few days before departure. We saw Philip's father and Betty, his wife, and some old friends, and after some tearful good byes we boarded an ocean liner called the Nieuw Amsterdam. As the ship departed New York Harbour we left behind our old life in America and watched the Statue of Liberty fade in the distance. The ship was enormous. The food was great, and in the bathroom we could choose between ordinary baths and seawater baths. That was pretty impressive. We were exhausted from all our goodbyes to friends and relatives and all the organising and endless packing. I was pregnant, so I was more tired than usual anyway. We might have enjoyed more of the facilities on the ship, but we mostly just prayed and slept our way across.

After five days at sea, we docked in Cobh (pronounced 'Cove') on the 18th of August, 1966 and I cried with joy when I saw the beautiful green coast of Ireland for the first time. I was struck by the many different shades of green on the hills in front of me. Just as I was taking in the beauty of the land, an official came to take our dogs from us, and put them into quarantine. I hated to see them go, and I knew I would do what I could when I got to Dublin to get them released as soon as possible. Despite what that man had implied in the Irish Consulate in Chicago, our dogs remained kennelled for the full six months. Philip had to collect them from the kennels on the very day that our son, Scott, was born at the Coombe Hospital in Dublin. The baby was born, and the dogs were released on the 18th of February, 1967. Everything was happening at once. It was a Saturday and Philip rushed out to get the dogs, took them home, put them into the house, and then rushed over to the hospital to be with me at the time of the birth. It was hardly the welcome home for them that we would have wished, but it wasn't long before I was home with our new baby, and we were all together again.

On our arrival in Cobh, we had arranged to rent a car. It was so small, I don't know how we managed to get our suitcases into it, but we did. You know they drive on the wrong side of the road! Philip drove to Dublin because I didn't know how to drive a manual car. I was used to driving an automatic. We arrived in Dublin and looked for the Moira Hotel. We had a hard time because the streets changed name every few blocks, and that was most confusing, but we found it. We checked into our hotel, got to our room and went to bed, dog-less and exhausted, but we had arrived in Ireland where we were going to create our new home. We woke up in the morning, and I opened the curtains and saw, across the road, The Irish Health and Herbal Centre! I couldn't believe it. There was the health food store. My prayers had already been answered at least to some degree.

This was 1966, and our first task was to rent a house. That didn't take us long, and we soon found a lovely four-bedroom house near to the city centre of Dublin for only £500 a year! That seemed really good, too good to be true. That was less than £10 a week. We couldn't believe our luck. The house had a lovely back garden and front garden, living room, dining room, study, kitchen, a bathroom upstairs and a little toilet room downstairs and a garage. This rent remained the same for three years, if I remember correctly.

Then we had to contact the Bahá'ís in Dublin. There were nine in the city centre, so there was a Spiritual Assembly there. There was one Bahá'í who lived just outside of Dublin, and there was one who lived in Cork, and that was it. Fortunately for us, a wonderful man, O. Z. Whitehead, an American actor who was a Bahá'í, was there as well. Because Philip was an actor too, and we were all Americans, we had much in common. We became good friends and saw a lot of Zebby, as his friends knew him.

We had very much wanted to help with the local Spiritual Assembly in Dublin city, but our little house, so near to the heart of Dublin, was in County Dublin and not in the city centre, so we couldn't be part of the Dublin Assembly. The civil administrative boundaries are also the boundaries for Assembly areas, so we were living in what was County Dublin, not in the city. Philip and I thought that it was a good idea that we were not in the Assembly area at first because he was a very outspoken person. He might have offended people before we had become better acquainted with them. In our early days there, his American style of saying whatever he felt might really have been misunderstood and people might have found him offensive or hurtful.

We were welcomed to attend all the Baháʾí events in Dublin city centre but we were not able to vote in the annual election of members of the Spiritual Assembly because we were not resident in Dublin City. The Spiritual Assembly is responsible for organising regular Feasts every 19 days, for making sure that there are appropriate celebrations of Baháʾí Holy Days, for planning and carrying out any interesting events for the Baháʾís and their friends, and for any administrative tasks that are necessary.

We enjoyed attending Feasts every 19 days in Dublin at Zebby's flat, which was on Fitzwilliam Square, and we gradually got to know our new friends. Because there were no other Baháʾís in County Dublin at the time, there were no Baháʾí activities there either, so our little group joined the community of Dublin City for their activities. There was a Baháʾí Centre on Morehampton Road. The caretakers were an English couple who were both in the theatre. Feasts were often held there as well as other activities. Actually when I think of it, there were a lot of creative and theatrical people in the Baháʾí Community of Dublin at that time.

Another job I had to do was to find a doctor to deliver the baby that was due in early February of 1967. I went to a man who was Master of the Coombe Hospital at the time. I had a lot of questions, and Philip wanted to be with me at the time of the birth. The doctor was not very communicative. I was a little unsure about how to deal with that, but I accepted it as the style of doctoring at the time. Every time I would come home from seeing him, Philip would ask me if I made sure that he could be with me at the time of the delivery, and I would say that he wasn't terribly clear. Every time I saw him I would tell him that my husband wanted to be there for the delivery, and finally one day, he agreed to that. Then later, he said that my husband could be there if there were no other mothers delivering babies in the delivery room at the time. There were three delivery stations in the delivery room, so three mothers could be delivering their babies at one time. I found that a rather frightening thought and I wondered about the simple concept of privacy for such an intimate event in any parent's life. But I realised I would just have to wait until I was in labour to see what would happen. The final message from my obstetrician was that even if there were other women delivering babies in the three-station delivery room, he would deliver my baby in my room so my husband could be there. That was fine with me. I felt very reassured by that message.

And so we settled in. The Irish authorities were so shocked and grateful that anyone wanted to move into Ireland at a time when everyone seemed to be moving out, that they gave us permanent residence visas.

Our furniture and belongings arrived from the USA about three weeks after we had first docked in Cork. We then moved from the hotel into our rented house, and a few days later a customs official came out to check our things. We were especially worried because of the cartons of vitamin pills that we had in the shipment. It turned out to be no problem, however, and everything was passed.

It was wonderful living in Dublin then. We felt so safe knowing that we could walk anywhere in town at any hour of the day or night fearlessly because there was very little crime in the city. We could be in the countryside within minutes from our house, and the fields were varying and beautiful shades of green because of all the rain. The people were charming and very helpful. We were enchanted. When we first were there, we went to an Irish pantomime in the theatre and couldn't understand any of it because of the accents. They would have said that *we* had the accents, but…!

We had our first real home. I hadn't lived in a house since age seven, and I dearly loved that house. Someone once said to us that within a few years of living there we would know everybody in Ireland. We didn't understand what he meant when he said that to us, but soon it became clear, and it was true. You would always know someone who knew someone else. People were all connected.

Philip and I spent a lot of time getting the house in order. We weren't used to having just one or two electrical sockets per room, and it surprised us to find only two sockets in the living room. We preferred the atmosphere given by lamps rather than one lighting fixture in the middle of the ceiling, so we needed far more sockets in every room. We also needed extra shelves and various things done.

Terry, a builder who was recommended by a friend, came over nearly every night, so we were getting to know him quite well, and we considered him a friend. One evening, we had some of our friends over for a Holy Day

Celebration. I had prepared a selection of readings from the Bahá'í writings and asked different people to read them. We sat listening to the beautiful words of Bahá'u'lláh in the living room. There was a lovely atmosphere. After the readings, there was gentle conversation while I went to the kitchen to get the refreshments ready. In those days I really loved cooking, so I always made cakes and biscuits and various treats. Terry had been working in the garage. When I called to him and invited him to join us for refreshments, he came to me, and his face was white as if he had seen a ghost. He said that he couldn't eat with the other people, and he preferred to have his food in the garage. When he had first come to work with us he wouldn't have refreshments with us but asked to have them while he was working, and gradually we persuaded him to take a break and join us. We had gotten used to stopping for a cup of tea and cakes and chatting and laughing together. We had thought he was just shy with us in the beginning, but we felt that he had become very comfortable with us during the time that he was working in our home, so we felt he would be just as relaxed with our friends. Therefore it came as a complete shock when he told me that he felt unable to join us in the usual way because other people were there. We suddenly began to feel that Terry was not just being shy, but that he actually felt inferior to us and our friends in a way that we would never have wished. He felt himself to be lower and therefore needed to keep himself separate. We did not want anyone to feel that way, but we honoured his wishes on that occasion. In time he did feel comfortable with all of us.

We were going on pilgrimage in November 1966 to the Bahá'í World Centre in Haifa, Israel. I was just six months pregnant, so I could still travel by plane. We flew into Tel Aviv and stayed overnight there before going by cheroot (shared taxi) to Haifa, a drive of about 1½ hours. We stayed in the pilgrim house, which was located very near the Shrine of the Báb, the gold domed building halfway up Mount Carmel that overlooks the Bay of Haifa. There were ten Western pilgrims and nine Eastern pilgrims. The Eastern pilgrims stayed in another Bahá'í house down the road from the Shrine. These days many more people of all cultures and backgrounds go on pilgrimage at the same time, as many as 400 people or more at a time are on each pilgrimage. They are too numerous to be housed in the pilgrim house, so they stay in hotels.

I remember my first visit to the Shrine of the Báb. We were asked to remove our shoes, which we did. We stepped into a spacious room with white walls and beautiful Persian rugs covering the floor. Directly in front of us was an archway through which we saw a place lighted by many candelabras and decorated with fresh flowers above where the remains of the Báb were buried. The energy in that room was dynamic, charged, alive and vital. Someone read the Tablet of Visitation aloud, and we stayed quiet for that. Then we were invited to say prayers silently by ourselves.

I was reminded of the stories that I knew of the Báb's life and of His wisdom and the horrific persecution that He and His followers experienced. He was in prison, sentenced to death because of His ideas and beliefs, much like Jesus Christ. He was perceived as a threat by the local government and clergy, and they thought that if they killed him, they would stop the spread of his ideas. The Báb was martyred (killed) in a square in Tabríz, Iran, on the 9th of July 1850. It is quite a story. He was in His prison cell explaining His wishes and last instructions to His secretary and followers. He hadn't finished when a guard came to take Him to the square where He was to be shot by a regiment of three files of 250 men each – that is 750 shots to kill one man with His follower who chose to be martyred with Him! The Báb said this to the guard who came to take him out to the square for his execution:

> Not until I have said to him all those things that I wish to say can any earthly power silence Me. Though all the world be armed against Me, yet shall it be powerless to deter Me from fulfilling, to the last word, my intention. (Shoghi Effendi, 1956, p.52)

Nevertheless, He was ordered to go. A spike had been driven into a pillar from which two separate ropes were hung, one for each person. In whatever way these two men were suspended, the Báb's follower was able to rest his head on the chest of his master. Sam Khan was the head of the regiment and was particularly distressed at this job expressing his wish not to perform the execution of such a holy man. The Báb said to him: *"Follow your instructions, and if your intention be sincere, the Almighty is surely able to relieve you of your perplexity."* (Shoghi Effendi, 1956, p.52)

Sam Khan did just that; he ordered his regiment to shoot. After the smoke cleared, the remains of the Báb were nowhere to be seen and His follower remained alive and unscathed beside the wall on which they had been suspended. Only the suspending ropes were severed. The onlooking guards knew that a body shot with 750 rifles could not just disappear into the atmosphere. The crazed people searched everywhere and finally found the Báb, alive and unharmed, in his cell finishing what He had to say to his other followers. When He was finished, He then told the Guard that He was ready to go, and He was again taken out to the square where He and His follower were once again suspended for execution.

This time, Sam Khan and his regiment would have nothing to do with the execution, so a new regiment was called. This time, the bullets shattered the bodies of the two, the Báb and His follower, but didn't touch His face. The remains of the Báb were hidden and preserved safely despite much persecution of His followers until they were finally interred in the Shrine built for that purpose in Haifa many years later. This incredible story, which is historically documented, demonstrates the kind of power that I felt in the Shrine of the Báb.

We finished praying in the Shrine of the Báb, and then we were ushered into the next room, which was the Shrine of 'Abdu'l-Bahá. I walked into that room which was not unlike the one for the Báb, but the décor was a little different. There were green shutters on either side of the opening into the place where there were candelabras and flowers. The energy in this room was completely different. There was an immediate, palpable sense of joy and love. It was sheer bliss. There was a lightness and refreshment just walking into the room. The Tablet of Visitation for 'Abdu'l-Bahá was read, and then we were left to our own private prayer. We then went back to the pilgrim house quite astounded at the experience of the energy in the Shrine and the different feeling in each room.

This was 1966, and it was only three years since the first Universal House of Justice had been elected. We knew a number of people who were members of the House of Justice. We went out to dinner at the homes of several of them. When we weren't elsewhere for dinner, we were fed in the Pilgrim

House. When the time came, we moved on in our pilgrimage and spent two nights in Bahjí, the house where Bahá'u'lláh lived for the last years of his life.

The Shrine of Bahá'u'lláh is across the Bay of Haifa in 'Akká and is next to the mansion of Bahjí. My experience of visiting the Shrine of Bahá'u'lláh is different from that of visiting the other shrines. Walking towards the Shrine I felt as if I were going to meet my God. I felt a great sense of reverence and humility. The Shrine is laid out differently from the others. We first walked into a short hall, which lead to a rectangular indoor garden surrounded by pathways covered with Persian rugs. The room where Bahá'u'lláh's remains were buried was to the right, and there I saw candelabras and bouquets of flowers. The roof was high and there were windows near the top of it, so the plants in the garden could reach toward the sunlight.

I sat on the floor beside the garden, and as I sat there, I felt as if I could do my best work and be the best I could be. I felt completely supported and wisely guided, as if I had everything I could ever need to fulfil my life's purpose and do what I needed to do in this life.

When we went into the Mansion of Bahjí, where Bahá'u'lláh had lived and where we were to spend the next two nights, we were shown the doorway on which the original owner of the mansion had inscribed this message in Arabic:

> Greetings and salutations rest upon this Mansion which increaseth in splendour through the passage of time. Manifold wonders and marvels are found therein, and pens are baffled in attempting to describe them.

Our guide gave us the English translation of this message and the message seemed providential because Bahá'u'lláh lived there from 1879 until his passing in May of 1892. It was here that Bahá'u'lláh wrote many of His tablets and letters. It was here that He met with visitors. This was so very different from His time in the prison in 'Akká where He had been from August of 1868 to November of 1870. After that, He and His family were placed under house arrest in various houses in and around 'Akká until they moved into the mansion of Bahjí.

We were ushered up a flight of stairs into the main living area in Bahjí. All the bedrooms surrounded a central open space overlooking a balcony that went right round the house. Philip and I had one of those bedrooms. Our room was only a few steps away from the room where Bahá'u'lláh slept and received visitors during the last years of his life. The energy in the room of Bahá'u'lláh was very powerful. Because we were housed in a nearby room for two nights, we could go into the room of Bahá'u'lláh at any time for private prayer, meditation or reflection. I had never felt so close to God as I did in that lovely and simply furnished room that was maintained in exactly the same way as it had been during Bahá'u'lláh's life. I was particularly touched by Bahá'u'lláh's slippers that were carefully placed beside the mattress on the floor. There was something that felt so ordinary and human about seeing those slippers there. It almost felt like they were just waiting for Him to come into the room to get ready for bed again.

We had our meals in the pilgrim house, which was beside the shrine. During the day, we were able to walk around in the gardens, to go into the shrine for private prayer or visit friends. It was an amazing time to think that we could actually sleep in the same house where Bahá'u'lláh had lived. It is almost unbelievable now when I think back on it.

It was in this house where Bahá'u'lláh was visited by the English Orientalist, Edward Granville Browne from Cambridge University. He was one of the few Westerners to meet Bahá'u'lláh. He described their meeting in this way:

> The face of him on whom I gazed I can never forget, though I cannot describe it. Those piercing eyes seemed to read one's very soul; power and authority sat on that ample brow; while the deep lines on the forehead and face implied an age which the jet-black hair and beard flowing down in indistinguishable luxuriance almost to the waist seemed to belie. No need to ask in whose presence I stood as I bowed myself before One who is the object of a devotion and love which kings might envy and emperors sigh for in vain!
>
> A mild dignified voice bade me be seated, and then continued: "Praise be to God that thou hast attained!…Thou hast come to see a prisoner and an exile…We desire but the good of the world and the happiness of the nations; yet they deem us a stirrer-up of strife and sedition worthy of bondage and banishment…That all nations should become one in faith and all men as brothers; that the bonds of affection and unity between the sons of men should be strengthened; that diversity of religion should cease, and differences of race be annulled - what harm is there in this?…Yet so it shall be; these fruitless strifes, these ruinous wars shall pass away, and the 'Most Great Peace' shall come…Do not you in Europe need this also? Is not this that

which Christ foretold? Yet do we see your kings and rulers lavishing their treasures more freely on means for the destruction of the human race than on that which would conduce to the happiness of mankind.... These strifes and this bloodshed and discord must cease, and all men be as one kindred and one family.... Let not a man glory in this, that he loves his country; let him rather glory in this, that he loves his kind..." (Browne, 2004, pp.xxxix-xl)

From Bahjí, we were taken to visit other houses in which Bahá'u'lláh and His family had lived. We saw many rooms that had housed the Holy Family during those years. In some ways it felt almost too much. It was more than my tiny mind could take in, and I knew that it was a most meaningful experience, one that would stay with me for my whole life.

Philip and I were made especially welcome at the Bahá'í World Centre because I was pregnant. I felt really special because of the extra attention and care that I was given, and because people went out of their way to give us gifts for the baby. They were so warm and caring and generous. I prayed that the baby would be healthy and that I would be able to guide the tender little soul in its life.

The nine nights of our pilgrimage seemed to fly by, and we were soon back in Dublin getting prepared for the birth of the baby. I felt so blessed to have been able to go on pilgrimage while pregnant. I remember just after we arrived back home that I couldn't find a beautiful embroidered piece of cloth with a picture of 'Abdu'l-Bahá on it that was a gift for the baby. I was so upset that I prayed about it before going to sleep. In the night, I dreamed about where it was. I woke up in the morning and found it straight away.

And so we continued to settle into our new home in Ireland, "the Emerald Isle". We had an interesting experience with the telephone. We were used to the American system where you phone to get a telephone in your new home, and they ask what kind you want, what colour you want, what services you want and whether you want it installed tomorrow morning or afternoon. It was not so in Dublin. Philip contacted the Telephone Company, and they said we needed to fill in an application form. He did that, and they said they would take care of it. We waited and waited and waited. We finally became impatient. We contacted them again, and they said they would be dealing with it shortly. This went on a few times. Eventually after some weeks, Philip went down to the office and asked them what they were doing about our telephone. They said that they were dealing with it. He asked if we could have an appointment for them to come out to install it. He was told no because they didn't know when that might be. He said that if we had an appointment, then we would be sure to be in when they came. The man said: "Sure, if you're not there when we call, we can always come back!"

Well, there was not much that we could do except wait. And wait we did. We did actually have a telephone in the house, but it was dead and had been so since our arrival. We were not too worried about making phone calls to friends because, of course, we hadn't met many people at that time, but it would have been helpful to have had a telephone to get our lives in order. We went on with life "telephone-less", and one day, suddenly, I heard the telephone ring. I answered it, and a voice at the other end of the line said, "We are connecting your telephone now, and here is your number"! Philip and I looked at each other in massive disbelief wondering how a country could run like this! It had taken months. All they had to do was connect the line and phone us!

We had been particularly concerned about not having a phone as the time of my baby's birth drew closer, so we were hugely relieved when we had phone service. My child was due on the 10th of February. Because this was my first pregnancy I rather expected to go into labour on that day or near to it, so I was surprised when that day came and went and still no sign of the baby.

I saw my doctor for an appointment the following week and told him I was worried that the baby was so late. He suggested that I go into hospital on the 17th to have the baby induced if labour had not begun by then. I really didn't know what to expect. We had a minor complication in that our dogs, the ones that had been in quarantine for a full six months since our arrival in Ireland, were due to be released on the 18th. Philip delivered me to the hospital on the evening of the 17th. He stayed home that night, and first thing in the morning, he rushed out to the kennels to collect the dogs. He took them home and put them into the kitchen and then came to be with me at the hospital. It was not much of a welcome for our dogs, but we just had to deal with it.

Fortunately I had gone into labour naturally on the morning of the 18th, but I had no idea how long it would take or how tired I would get. At some point in the afternoon, Philip arranged for a birth trainer, whose classes I had attended in Dublin, to come to help me because I was so exhausted. She arrived, and I regained my strength and courage. She stayed with me well into the evening, encouraging me to breathe through each contraction and finally it was time for delivery so then I was wheeled into the delivery room.

Fortunately on that Saturday night when our son, Scott, was born, I was the only one in the delivery room so Philip was allowed to be there with me. We made history because Philip was the first husband to be present at his baby's birth since the hospital had opened in 1826. Also I think it was the only night ever when there had been only one woman delivering a baby in that delivery room, equipped as it was for three mothers. As soon as my son was born, I asked Philip: "Does he have two of everything?" Philip replied: "No, fortunately, there are certain things of which he has only one." I have no idea where I got such a question, but it was the first thing I could think to say after the long labour and joyful birth. Scott had been born around 10:45 in the evening, and I was so elated after he was born that I couldn't get to sleep right away.

I had been determined to breastfeed my baby, but when he was first born, he seemed to have a problem latching on to my breast. I was so inexperienced that I didn't know what to do, so on the night of his birth, a nurse came in to help me. She must have spent an hour and a half trying to get him to suck properly. She claimed that there was something wrong with his chin. She felt that if his chin was not shaped properly it would hamper his ability to latch onto my breast. I was just shattered by her persistence. It wasn't that I was ungrateful, but she actually wasn't helping me. Despite my lack of experience, I began to succeed with breastfeeding. I was surprised when nurses came in to see me because they had never seen a mother breastfeed her baby. In those days women were kept in hospital for a while, so I must have been there for a week before I was allowed home.

I found that I was breastfeeding Scott successfully from the moment I arrived home from the hospital. Then I came down with the flu. The doctor came to see me and said I should not go near the baby for 24 hours because I was ill. So Philip took over looking after and feeding the baby. After that period of having only the bottle baby Scott liked the bottle better, so I fed him with both for over five months, but I wasn't pleased about the situation. I had so longed to be a breastfeeding mother who successfully breastfed her baby. I had no idea that the whole procedure would be so complicated. I learned later that when a mother gets a cold or flu, she should continue to breastfeed her baby because her milk provides immunity to the baby who has already been exposed to the cold or flu virus by the time the mother shows any symptoms of the illness, and nobody could prevent that.

It was such a surprise to witness that our little house which had been home to Philip and me as a married couple, was now home to our family. We could hardly believe it. As tired as I was, nothing could stop me from being awestruck by the change that had occurred in our focus. Where before we were concerned about getting our home in order and managing day to day activities, enjoyable as they were, now we really had someone else to care for, to love, and to see growing and developing. We were so excited that when Scott was asleep we often just stopped what we were doing and went to look at him in his little cot just to watch him breathe.

It wasn't all rosy however, because I, like many first time mothers, hadn't had any idea what it would be like to have such a small being completely dependent upon me. I had rather thought that he would fit into our schedule. The truth was that we fit into his! Sometimes that was just fine, and I have to admit that sometimes I was mildly depressed because my life had changed so dramatically, and I found that I hardly had any time to think about what I needed or wanted to do without having to minister to the needs of a tiny being. I realised that I had a lot to learn about parenting a baby, but I was eager to learn. I was absolutely shocked by the relentless nature of caring for a newborn as well as by how tired I felt.

After a while I recovered from the exhaustion of labour and birth and from the flu and adjusted to a mother's schedule, and then we were all fine. Part of the adjustment was that as little Scott got older, even by three months, his system was more settled, feeding was easier, quicker, and he didn't suffer from colic or wind as he had done in the early weeks, which made caring for him easier than when he was first born.

Because we wanted several children, we didn't delay and I became pregnant again very quickly. I was thrilled! In the summer of 1968, only 17 months after my first child was born I was happily sitting on my bed in the Coombe Hospital about to deliver my second baby. This time, we were in the new Coombe Hospital, which was bright and airy, and this delivery was far quicker and easier than the first. Because I was so comfortable, I was knitting with Philip sitting beside me until it was time to go to the delivery room. Labour and delivery all occurred within the space of about four hours. This was a very different experience than the first one, and I was delighted to have a baby girl for my second child, giving me one of each – my two beautiful children. We named her Shannon, and she was just gorgeous. I was more comfortable about motherhood and caring for a baby this time, and I was especially pleased that she was a girl because I thought we would be able to share a lot and have a lot of fun together.

Before I had my second baby, Philip had read an article in *Time* magazine about a group in America called La Leche League. It was a group of breastfeeding mothers who had gotten together and written a book about breastfeeding. They realised that nurses and doctors knew little or nothing about breastfeeding, and they wanted to help. They organised themselves to help other mothers who wanted to breastfeed because so little was known about breastfeeding in our society. I got their book before Shannon was born and read it, and I was well equipped to manage breastfeeding this time. I was determined that this baby would not get a bottle at all. That worked, and I became the kind of breastfeeding mother that I had originally wanted to be. I became actively involved with helping other mothers in Ireland who wanted to breastfeed as part of the La Leche League in Ireland. Philip had to laugh because he would sometimes come home from working in the theatre to find between 10 and 15 mothers with nursing babies in our living room as we were finishing off a meeting. He would quietly sneak upstairs, go to bed and read!

Young mothers need to have support for breastfeeding. Having a young baby is such an emotional experience, and the mother can lose confidence so easily because she can feel so uncertain about whether or not she is doing the right thing. It is not only emotional support that is needed for breastfeeding mothers; it is also the knowledge of what to do when there are problems. I used to get depressed every time I heard of a baby who wasn't being breastfed.

Even in The Hidden Words, Bahá'u'lláh says:

O SON OF BOUNTY!
Out of the wastes of nothingness, with the clay of My command I made thee to appear, and have ordained for thy training every atom in existence and the essence of all created things. Thus, ere thou didst issue from thy mother's womb, I destined for thee two founts of gleaming milk, eyes to watch over thee, and hearts to love thee… (Bahá'u'lláh, 1975, pp.32-33)

That seemed to me to be a real endorsement of breastfeeding for infants from the Bahá'í teachings.

From the time of marriage I realised that my dearest wish was to have a family and to be the best wife and mother that I could be. I thought that nothing else was as important as that. I no longer gave any thought to other aims or desires in the way of a career, at least not while I was caring for young babies.

Philip had a career, and I felt that I was the one who supported him and the family so that he could be out working. That felt just right. I also had my faith and my need to improve my own health and to ensure that the family was healthy. That was more than enough to do. I couldn't have been happier then about my new life and my family. I loved cooking and looking after everyone. The days were filled with lots of work to do but it was work that I thoroughly enjoyed because it arose out of my love for these people in my life. Even when I got frustrated or overtired, I felt a kind of contentment in knowing that it was worth it because I loved them.

I really felt that I had made some key decisions in my life and that I had been right to do what I had done including becoming a Bahá'í, marrying Philip, moving to Ireland and having children. I felt as if I had made some bold choices, and I had begun the kind of life that I would have wanted to live, where I could live somehow undisturbed by judgements and opinions of people around me. I felt free of the past that had been very difficult for me and I had a sense that I was creating a life for me and my family that might not include the kind of hurt that I had experienced both in terms of illnesses and of loss of people close to me. I was determined to create an environment that was healthful in every way for my little and beloved family.

Philip and I got to know quite a few people as time went on and we made some friends. Our children going to school also opened my world, and I got to know mothers of other children and more people all the time. Philip was at the same time meeting people in the theatre and in his work and I was meeting people through my own projects, with La Leche League, and later on when I taught natural cooking. Soon, we felt like we knew everyone in Dublin. At least it was true that almost anyone we met knew someone else whom we knew.

Then, one day after living in Dublin for quite a while something happened that made us realise that there was a quality to these people that we didn't see at first. We had been like babes in the woods in our naiveté and innocence. Suddenly we realised that some of the Irish people had a habit of telling us what they thought we wanted to hear. We were used to the way Americans spoke to us. They are quite outspoken and straightforward on the whole. They will challenge you if you say something that doesn't quite seem right. The Irish would just agree and smile. Because the language was the same, we didn't know how these people expressed themselves when they weren't comfortable with a new idea we were discussing – we had assumed they would be as outspoken as we were – and yet we discovered that they would not tell us straight out, but would agree with us whether they really agreed or not.

We became very depressed because there were people whom we had felt were close friends, and we suddenly saw that they didn't mean what they said. As time went on, however, we adjusted and learned to read between the lines. That was when we got to know who was really trustworthy and who was not.

And so I was a Bahá'í making a home in a foreign land for myself and my family. In those early days the National Spiritual Assembly of the British Isles which included all of the UK & Eire had asked the Bahá'ís in Ireland not to discuss their faith with others as a mark of respect to the prevalent religion of the country at the time. I found that very hard. One of my greatest joys was to talk about the Bahá'í teachings with people who were interested and who asked. Nevertheless I had plenty to do with childbearing and raising my children. In many ways it was an idyllic life.

In 1969 we bought a house and decided to add on to it by building a whole new kitchen and enlarging some of the rooms. In some respects we were engaging builders to build another house onto the house we had purchased and it was quite a big task. We had been living in a lovely but small four bedroom house, but it was a rented home, and we wanted to be in a house that we owned. We expected to have more children, and we had a strong nesting instinct and a need to be even more settled and rooted in Dublin. We so loved our life there and continued to see living in Ireland as a wonderful place to raise our small family. All in all we felt that we had made a good choice, but we did feel that we were bursting the seams of our present house.

The builders had been working on the refurbishment for months, far longer than they originally promised. We soon began to realise that their smiling faces often led to empty promises. Finally, after what seemed like forever, they said we could move in to the house. At that time we ran into huge problems with the move. A few days before we were due to move, they smiled and said to us that they needed our washing machine and tumble drier so they could have them ready and installed for when we moved in with our two small children. We duly disconnected them and sent them over planning to do without them for a few days so they would be all working when we got to our new home.

It happened that Philip was producing a show called *Big Maggie* by John B Keane, which was touring in Ireland, and he had to go to Waterford where the show was playing at the time of our move. He arranged to be present for the day of moving, but then he had to go away for a few days. On the appointed day we arrived in our new home, expecting everything to be in order with only our own personal belongings to be put away. Well it didn't quite work out like that.

We moved in to the house and discovered that not only were the washing machine and tumble drier sitting in the hall, so were the bathtubs! We were horrified. As soon as our belongings were delivered to our new home, Philip left me and the children there and he went to Waterford for the next couple of days. We did have a friend staying with us, which was great because she could help me deal with the situation. What we didn't realise was that the builder was about to go bankrupt. We learned that the hard way soon after our move.

On our first night in the house, we were absolutely freezing because it was November and the coldest time of the year in Dublin. There had been no heat in the house since the other owners had lived in it. With all the building, many of walls had been taken down, and new walls had been built. We had managed to borrow an electric heater, which I put into our bedroom. On that first night and several subsequent nights, the children, the dog, the guest and I all slept together in the king-size bed just to get a little warmth. We could barely believe that we were in such a degree of disarray. It was like camping out in what we expected to be a well equipped home!

Philip was not amused when he arrived back home from Waterford, and he ranted and raged at the builder saying we were all going to stay in a hotel for the weekend at his expense, so we could warm up and have baths and get ourselves comfortable. Well the following week, the builder did manage to install the bathtubs, the washing machine and the tumble drier before announcing that he was going bankrupt. So we were left still with a lot of work that needed to be done and to top that off, we had to pay for own our hotel accommodation on that eventful weekend. Looking back I guess that last part was not such a huge sacrifice as it was so cold and uncomfortable in the house that it was well worth the expense to have hot water and general warmth.

Philip and I both reacted differently to the situation. Philip became glum and depressed and unhappy with the way the builder had lied to his face time and again and told him everything would be finished on this date and then that date and then another date. The whole process had been delayed and delayed, so we were moving in about four months later than we had expected. Once there, we saw that the jobs had not been done as we had expected at all.

Each time Philip would tell me how upset he was about it all, I would say we should just be grateful that we are here in our house, and yes things needed to be done, but they would be done. I was always thinking about how wonderful it was to be as far along as we were. He found it hard to see my viewpoint. I guess I found it hard to see his. Looking back, of course, both were valid, and he had been much more involved in the face to face experience of negotiating with the builder all the time and debating about each thing that had to be done in the house. Philip must have been severely disappointed with the builder who promised him all that he wanted but didn't deliver most of it. I was not involved with those negotiations and hadn't developed a relationship with a man whom I trusted to do what he said he would do like Philip had. It was easier for me because I was in the background looking after the children while Philip was dealing with it all.

I always said to Philip: "Let's remember our humble beginnings". I really felt that strongly. I just felt so lucky to have a home at all. I couldn't get worried about the irritating things that had to be completed because I knew they would be completed, and then we could forget about them.

It took us several months to find a new builder, and it took that new builder a further nine months to complete the work. During that time there was so much dust throughout the house that my beautiful little girl never wore a dress. I had to keep her covered up in overalls all the time. I didn't mind that for Scott because he was boyish and loved watching what the builders were doing and generally getting dirty. I just felt that a little girl who was as feminine as Shannon should be in a dress at age three at least some of the time. However, finally the house was finished, and we could relax.

It had been hard work and we were tired, but oh so grateful to be there and have a lovely home that suited us and the way we wanted to live. There was much that was exciting and full of promise for me and my family, but all was not entirely well, and I will tell you more about that in the next chapter.

There was further development of the Baháʼí community in those years. In 1971, some Baháʼí friends of ours who lived in Limerick met a lot of people who by some miracle suddenly were interested in becoming Baháʼís. If I remember correctly there were over a hundred people who became Baháʼís at that time. They didn't all stay, but a good many of them did. There were a number of young people in this group, not under-age people, but young. Parents became worried, wondering if their children had espoused a cult religion. That certainly wasn't the case, but it was a difficult time for many people.

I always thought that if I had children who were joining a Faith that advocated no drinking of alcohol nor taking of leisure drugs, I would be very happy with that because it would eliminate a lot of problems. Of course, I understood what being a Bahá'í meant, and for those who didn't, I could understand their fears. There were a few cult religions around at the time, and people were afraid that this was one of them.

In 1972 the first National Spiritual Assembly of the Bahá'ís of the Republic of Ireland was elected. That meant there were nine people elected to serve on the National Spiritual Assembly for the coming year. When this National Assembly had been elected the Bahá'í community in the Republic of Ireland had its own administration and therefore was no longer under the jurisdiction of the same Assembly as the UK. Philip was one of the nine elected to the very first Irish National Assembly. After its formation, the National Assembly created an exhibition that toured Ireland, appearing in hotels all around the country explaining the faith and telling people what it meant to be a Bahá'í. This was done to help to ease the worries of people whose relatives had become Bahá'í.

Today many more people are in communication with the Bahá'ís in Ireland through the National Spiritual Assembly there, and understanding of the Faith has grown dramatically. Bahá'ís are involved in all sorts of projects to promote respect of human rights, the equality of men and women, moral development, the prosperity of humankind and world citizenship. It is not just the Bahá'ís in Ireland who are involved in such projects; it is the Bahá'ís all over the world.

We lived in Dublin for twenty years, and we loved our life there. Philip worked in the theatre and the television. After three years we bought a house and moved in. Our new home was within the city limits of Dublin, so we were able to participate in the Spiritual Assembly of the Bahá'ís of Dublin. We often held Bahá'í Feasts, Holy Day celebrations, and other activities in our home. One of the things that we loved about the Irish was that they had a deep sense of spirituality. They were people with wonderful senses of humour, a touch of the Blarney stone, and when we got to know them, they were loyal and trustworthy friends.

On Reflection

We all go through changes moment by moment, hour by hour, day by day. We respond very differently to the changes that we choose than to those that are thrust upon us by circumstances or other people. When we choose the change, we have adjustments to make, but we feel empowered. When change is forced on us from an external source, we often feel disempowered and helpless.

One of the keys to coping with change is to recognise those things that we can change and those that we cannot change. I have often said, if we don't like what is going on in our lives, we may change the circumstances or if that is not possible, we may change our attitude towards those circumstances. We, as human beings, are equipped with the ability to change and to make choices about how we change. We can use our imagination and change our beliefs, habits and expectations, but to do so we need to know ourselves. Every decision is not a decision about what we must do, but a decision about who we are, and when we really know who we are, we are better able to make appropriate decisions.

Whatever is going on in our lives, it is how we look at it that matters. It is our relationship to our life that is important. Nothing in our world has any meaning except the meaning we give to it. We often tell ourselves little stories [beliefs, assumptions, or ideas] about how the universe is, and act as if our stories are true. The stories we tell ourselves determine how we will perceive the world around us. These stories form the meanings we put on things, and we then consider them to be fact.

Look back at your personal values that you uncovered in the last chapter and spend a little time wondering if you are living according to your own personal values as fully as you would like in areas of your life, such as:

Relationships, faith, spirituality

Health, body and sexuality

Finances, home and career

Imagine how you might feel if your values were more present in those different areas. In other words, how might you feel differently if you were really living your values?

In order to really gain something from this exercise, imagine an ideal image of yourself. This is an image of you living exactly as you would like to live including all your wisdom and values and sense of what is most important. Take some time to build a strong picture in your mind.

Then imagine yourself as you would like to be, as this ideal image, and take your list of values and take another sheet of paper and evaluate each of the above aspects of your life. For instance list first your important relationships and for each one ask yourself as your ideal image:

What am I doing in this relationship that feels right and good and according to my values?

What am I doing in this relationship that doesn't feel aligned with my values?

What might I do differently to bring my actions into line with my values so that I can be more true to myself in my relationship with this person?

Do that with each of your relationships. Look at your friendships, your relationship with your family, with your partner, with your work colleagues, and your spiritual friends.

Then do the same with the other categories, but always as your ideal image, so that you can evaluate the situation from the point of view of your most authentic self.

Remember, you don't need to do all these exercises in one sitting. You may do whatever feels necessary at any given time. During the course of this exercise, feel as if you are creating a relationship with your ideal, so that you can begin to gain a different perspective on your behaviour and how you feel about your behaviour in all these different areas of your life. As you get to know your ideal self better, you will be more easily able to live as you would wish to and to recognise areas in your life which cannot be changed right now and to accept that to be the case without losing sight of that future ideal, so as soon as the opportunity to change does arise, you are ready to grasp it and become the person you want to be.

Chapter 6
Flew Away

Tara was a beautiful baby girl who was born on the 23rd of May, 1971. My husband and I were enjoying our life in Dublin, and we already had two gorgeous children, a boy of three, and a girl of two. My pregnancies had been wonderful, and I had given birth naturally in the hospital, so I really felt happy about having another baby. The time was right, but this pregnancy was very different.

I remember that Tara was conceived in August of 1970 at a time when Philip and I were longing for another baby. Philip had said, and I had thought it was a joke, that he wanted a baby born on his birthday, which was 23rd of May! I wanted both to please him, and I wanted a baby, but I didn't care when it was born. I thought the idea of thinking one could orchestrate a baby's birth on any particular day was selfish and shallow at best, but I really wanted a baby. We had been hoping for a pregnancy for a while, but it hadn't yet happened. We were eager to conceive, and I was willing to plan a May baby, which meant the baby would need to be conceived in August, but beyond that, I couldn't guarantee that the baby would be born on Philip's birthday.

That August a dear friend of ours had drowned off the coast of Limerick. We were the only ones of his friends who had a telephone, so the police were due to contact us when his body rose from the sea. We cringed every time the phone rang thinking this call might be the police. It was during that sad and tense time that Tara was conceived. A few nights later on a very stormy night in Dublin, the police from Ballybunion in the West of Ireland phoned at about 10 pm to say that our friend's body had been recovered. Then we heard a strange thudding sound outside at the back of the house. The next morning we looked outside and saw that the storm was so bad it had caused the stone wall on one side of our garden to collapse. Philip had to go down the next day to identify the body, which was an unimaginable task.

For each of my previous pregnancies, I had known immediately after conception that I was pregnant. This time, I was absolutely sure, after Philip and I had made love, that I *wasn't* pregnant. I was completely shocked when I found out some six weeks later that I was in fact pregnant, and my first reaction was to say to myself "oh dear, there is something wrong here". Although this sounds very irrational, from then on and for no real concrete reason, I was anxious about the baby and felt something that I had never felt with previous pregnancies: an ominous feeling that there was something wrong with my baby. I carried that fear all through the pregnancy. Every morning when I woke, I was afraid. Even on busy days, when I had a quiet moment and turned my attention to my pregnancy, I became frightened.

I was upset; I wanted to be enthusiastically awaiting the baby's birth, not living with a constant feeling of disquiet. In my other pregnancies, I had experienced occasional fears for the baby, but this was very different. This was a real sense of foreboding. I certainly was not a person who was inclined to harbour hugely irrational fears. I had always been a very intuitive and perceptive person, and I could often figure out people and situations far faster than others could. After my children had been born, I noticed that my normal intuition had become sharper, and I really understood "mother's intuition" which made me even more trusting of my feelings about my new pregnancy.

My fears seemed so unreasonable to me that for a long time I felt I couldn't really talk about them to anyone. My other children had been perfectly healthy. There was no reason to believe that there would be anything wrong with this child, nor that there was any tragedy in the atmosphere, but I couldn't stop feeling my terrors. I absolutely adored my children, and I devoted my life to my family. I so much enjoyed taking care of Scott and Shannon. Children of two and three are so full of wonder and awe and eager to learn that they are just great to parent because of their joy and mischief and innocence. Of course they had their squabbles, and I sometimes found that upsetting, but it didn't stop me from enjoying their company and wanting to teach them drawing and painting and cooking and all kinds of things that interest and involve children of that tender age. Because I was so happy with my children, I thought it would be wonderful to have at least one or two more. I imagined a family of three or four children before I would stop.

I mentioned my sense of foreboding to Philip, but he dismissed it and was unable to understand my concern. Philip was busy working in the theatre, and whenever he was in a play, he gradually distanced himself from me in a way that I found very difficult. Also because he could not relate to my fears about this pregnancy, I found that I eventually had to talk to other friends about my feelings, rather than to him, because I just couldn't keep it to myself. Before that time, Philip and I had talked about everything with each other like best friends. I didn't know if he was preoccupied with his role in a play or if he just found it too painful to even consider the possibility that there might be something wrong with this baby. I was terrified for my baby, and I didn't know if I could cope with what was ahead. However, I still had to live my life, look after my husband and other two children and suffer this ongoing anxiety that sometimes felt a bit lighter or disappeared briefly, but was, by and large, always present.

I had dreams about our friend who had died just before the baby had been conceived. I remember one dream in which he came to me to say that everything would be all right, and I wondered what that meant. Of course everything would be all right, and that still didn't mean that the baby would live. I imagined that my dream was meant to console me and help me to be more trusting and optimistic, but I couldn't just relax into a sense of ease like the way I had with the other pregnancies.

A few weeks before the baby was due, I had a very unusual symptom. I was out driving with my children, and I saw stars or spots in front of my eyes. I felt frightened because I didn't feel safe driving with impaired vision like that. I got home and I phoned the doctor, who said to me that I should wait until my next regular appointment, which was scheduled a couple of weeks later. In the meantime I decided that I had better not drive around in case it should happen again.

At the time of my regular check up, I walked into the doctor's office and he looked at me as if he had seen a ghost. He immediately rushed me to a clinic and insisted that I have a blood test. We went back to his office, and without explaining anything to me, we simply awaited the results of the test. When they came, he told me that I was severely anaemic, and I would have to come into the hospital immediately for transfusions and large doses of iron. I was flabbergasted. I had never before experienced that in a pregnancy.

Why would I suddenly on this occasion have become so very anaemic when it had never happened before? I didn't know what to do to help myself. I was amazed that I had been functioning so well despite severe anaemia, running a household with a husband and two children, dogs and cats. I had been tired, but I didn't think I had been excessively tired, and I was sure that I was tired because I was heavily pregnant. I had been eating very healthy food, and I had felt far better than I imagined anyone who was suffering from severe anaemia would feel. None of this made sense to me except as a further sign that things were not right in this pregnancy. I was so worried, and I felt so helpless.

I went into the hospital for massive doses of iron and blood transfusions. I reacted to the excess iron and transfusions by getting a severe cold and cough after it. I was particularly annoyed because I didn't like the idea of taking another person's blood into my body. I had gone to great lengths to cook really healthy food, and I was sure that the blood donor would not have been as careful as I had been.

In my ordinary daily life, I would have preferred to use complementary therapies to help myself or my family, but I didn't know any natural remedies that might have brought my iron level back to normal in such a short time. This was a time when I had to follow medical advice. Even though there is no objection in the Bahá'í teachings to the giving or receiving of blood transfusions and I felt no spiritual conflict, but I still felt somehow contaminated by someone else's blood, nevertheless I knew I was helpless and had no other choice.

The doctor told me that if they didn't bring up my blood count before I went into labour, I would probably die during childbirth because I would not stop bleeding as my blood would not clot properly. That is scary enough to be grateful for the blood that I got, but it still didn't feel right to me. Much later I found out that seeing stars in front of your eyes is a symptom of severe anaemia. I wondered why the doctor had been so casual when I had phoned him about that some weeks before. As I look back I see clearly that my whole experience in this pregnancy was of being out of control.

Then it was time for the baby's birth, and the doctor chose to induce the baby by breaking the waters. Because Philip wanted to be present, and he was in a show playing in Cork, he could only arrange to be with me in Dublin on a Sunday, so the doctor agreed to induce the baby on that day. And guess what? That was Sunday 23rd of May, which was Philip's birthday! I couldn't believe after all that I had been through that the baby was actually going to be born on Philip's birthday, as he had wanted. That to me was a kind of miracle, and I briefly began to feel a little more at ease and even hopeful.

However it wasn't long before I was in a terrible mood because it was a dark rainy day, and being in labour, after my waters had been broken, with a serious cough was no joke. The pain of the contractions mixed with the pain of coughing didn't contribute to my mood. When I was feeling particularly low, a nurse offered me 50 milligrams of pethidine to help the pain saying that I had at least another two hours to go before it would be time to push. I accepted the pethidine, but I was angry at feeling the need to do so because I preferred natural birth. Taking that drug didn't make any difference to the intensity of the pain: it just made me feel drunk and disconnected, while the pain continued, so I still wasn't happy. Contrary to the nurse's authoritarian statement that I still had to endure at least two hours of contractions and coughs, all of which hurt, I was wheeled into the delivery room and told to push after just about half an hour. I didn't feel I could even push very well because I felt drugged. All in all the experience was horrible, especially in contrast with my last birth, when I delivered my baby girl just about four hours after the doctor broke the waters, and I still had a smile on my face because it had all gone so well.

When Tara was born, the doctor, who was Master of the Coombe Hospital in Dublin said, "She is a beautiful baby". I replied rather sarcastically, "You see so many of them, I'll bet they all look the same to you." He said, "No, she is really beautiful." He was right; she was really lovely. Babies are typically born with blue eyes, and her eyes were deep purple. She looked very like my firstborn son, Scott, which meant she looked like me. My other daughter looked more like my husband.

Philip and I were not sure what to name her, and secretly in my own mind, I had the feeling that I wanted to name her "Jane" like me, but I felt embarrassed and like I might be feeling selfish to want to do that, so I never told anybody. We discussed names, and we decided to name our new baby "Tara". It is a beautiful Irish name and seemed to suit our new baby very well. I never let her out of my sight. On the second night after she was born, I was dozing in bed, and her cot was beside me. I had a private room. I saw a nurse open the door and come towards the cot as if to take it to the night nursery, and I said, "What are you doing?" She said she was going to take the baby out so I could get some sleep. I said, "I am sleeping fine; that baby stays with me!" I was a breastfeeding mother, which was most unusual in those days, so I wanted to be available to feed her whenever she wanted feeding. I had a camera with me in the hospital, but somehow didn't feel inclined to take her picture.

I took Tara home about a week after she was born. Ordinarily I would have gone home after three days, but I had a fever for a couple of days in the hospital, and they wanted to keep an eye on me. I just wanted to go home. I was so distressed that the doctor insisted on my staying in the hospital that I wrote a note to my husband telling him to get me out of there. I don't know why I wrote to him because I could just as easily tell him when he came in to see me that morning, but I just needed to get my feelings onto paper, so I wrote. It made no difference however, and I was stuck in the hospital until my fever had abated.

Tara was fine and feeding well for about two weeks, and then she developed a most peculiar behaviour where she would cry and tighten up as if she were in tremendous pain, then relax and start hiccupping. This happened every once in a while. I took her to several doctors. They didn't see her occasional strange behaviour pattern when they examined her, so they told me she was fine. I knew she wasn't, so I was angry and frustrated about being dismissed as an over-protective mother.

Not being heard in that way was so horrible and frightening, and I didn't know how to get a doctor to take me seriously. One day I was in a doctor's waiting room. I had been to see the doctor with Tara, who seemed fine, and I was waiting after our consultation while he prepared some homeopathic remedies according to the way I described her symptoms. As I was sitting in the waiting room, Tara began to go into her kind of spasm, and I said to the receptionist that I needed to show my baby to the doctor exactly then. She said that she couldn't interrupt him, and by the time she began to take me seriously, the spasm was over, and I felt helpless and hopeless again.

Finally I was visiting a friend who had seven children of her own and whose husband was a doctor. She took one look at Tara and said, "She is a sick baby". Finally someone else saw what I was seeing. What my friend had noticed was that Tara was sleeping with her eyes still partially open. I was grateful but also terribly frightened. My friend suggested I take Tara to the clinic at Temple Street Children's Hospital the next morning to her friend, a paediatrician there. That night Tara didn't feed for about 14 hours. I tried spooning milk into her mouth, and in the morning when I lifted her arm, it just fell down limply; there was no strength in it. When the doctor saw her, he said that they would have to take her into the hospital. "This is a very sick baby", he said. I knew that was the truth. We went up to the ward, and I gave her to a nurse who took her into the room where she would be kept. Then I spoke to a doctor in the hall and said, "If Tara is going to die, I want to be with her". I felt I had to be clear about the possibility of her death. She said, "We don't like to talk about that". I said, "You have to talk about that. I was with her when she was born, and I want to be with her when she dies." To me the whole idea of a doctor who didn't like to talk about the potential for death in such a situation was unbelievable. I would have imagined that the doctor might have wanted to prepare me for possible loss, and yet I was the one who brought up the subject. I was astounded that I had to talk about the possible death of my beloved baby.

I find it hard now to describe the roller-coaster of emotions that I was experiencing at that time. It felt as if all this trouble with Tara was happening at a distance. Events had taken over and were happening so quickly that I felt numb and was going through the motions of what had to be done. At the same time I felt terrified and helpless, as if I were in the path of a tornado. Despite the forebodings of my pregnancy, I still longed for all those warnings to be wrong and clung to the hope that this nightmare might end happily. Philip was there with me, but I think that he was able to remain more hopeful at times than I did. We were on automatic pilot, like zombies being dragged through a very confusing and excruciatingly painful maze.

Tara had been admitted into the hospital on Friday. Philip was in a Neil Simon play, *Plaza Suite*, at the time, so he went out every evening to the theatre. On Saturday, he went to the hospital to see her on his way to the theatre in the evening. When he came home, he told me that they wanted me to send down milk, and she was looking good. I just said, "don't" as in don't get your hopes up. On Sunday, I prepared a bottle of milk, and we took it down. When I saw her, she seemed to be gasping for breath, and I asked a nurse what it meant. She said that the baby was pretty OK. I didn't think the baby looked "pretty OK" at all, but I was not a nurse and I reluctantly accepted what she said. We were exhausted and needed to go home, but it was really difficult to leave her there in the hospital. Philip and I drove home, and no sooner did we get home than a nurse from the hospital rang to say that Tara had taken a turn for the worse. We drove right back down.

I rushed into Tara's room and wanted to hold her, but she was all strapped up with tubes going into her, so all I could do was put my hand on her chest. Although there had been this ominous feeling all through the pregnancy, it was still a massive shock to realise that Tara had deteriorated so fast. I knew she had taken a turn for the worse, but I didn't really want to accept that she was actually dying. Then the doctor came and said to me that she could give Tara a shot of adrenaline to keep her going a little longer. Here was that doctor who didn't want to talk about my baby's death just a couple of days ago, and now she was telling me that a shot of adrenaline could keep my baby alive another 10 or 15 minutes. There was no more hope than that, another 10 or 15 minutes of life prolonged by a shot of adrenaline, and that was truly unbearable. It was all really more than I could take in. I was in shock and very numb, but I said, "no". She died, and I expected to be able to tell that she had died, but because there were tubes pumping medicines into her, I couldn't be sure that she was gone. The nurses assured me that she had died.

Philip and I drove back home, each of us feeling heartbroken, shattered and destroyed. We sat down at the dining room table. Shannon, our three year old daughter, asked, "How is Tara?" I said that she had died. She just burst into tears, and so did I. Then Scott, our son who was then four and a half just crawled up on the arm of my chair and put his arm around me like a little old man, and we all cried together.

We were at home in shock, when the telephone rang, and it was a nurse from the hospital phoning. Philip answered the phone, and she asked him to come down to the hospital with me because they had laid out Tara's body in the hospital chapel. The nurse said that she wanted me to see her in that way since the last time I had seen her she was in a hospital room with various tubes and equipment, and it was not a good last memory to have. Philip and I went back down to the hospital then, and we were ushered into the chapel where my beautiful baby's body was laid out. The nurse had put her into a lovely white dress, and her eyes were closed. I wept, and put my hand on her forehead. It was so cold. As I look back, I wish I had picked up her body and held it close to me one last time, but touching her forehead that was as cold as marble and then kissing her goodbye was as much as I could manage. I was just overwhelmed with grief. This is the kind of unbearable moment that I can never forget. I can still see Philip and me in that room with our beloved daughter's body.

Although I don't drink alcohol, my friends insisted that I have some Guinness for the shock and because it was considered nourishing for mothers who had just given birth, especially breastfeeding mothers. The night of Tara's death, I had one bottle of Guinness, and it tasted awful and gave me such a bad headache that I chose to just stay with my shock and distress. I know many people would have gone to the doctor and been given tranquillisers, but I needed to keep my wits about me as much as I could because of my husband and my other children.

The next day, Philip went to the hospital to collect Tara's body in a small coffin, and brought it back home to pick me up so we could to take it to a beautiful little graveyard in the Dublin mountains where we had bought a plot for it. We had planned to take Tara's body for burial privately just on our own because nobody else knew her. However a couple of friends who loved us dearly and wanted to be with us, appeared at the hospital when Philip was picking up Tara's remains. They were very special people to us, so we were glad to have them with us. We said some prayers at the graveside, and then the little coffin was lowered into the earth, and we had to say goodbye.

Sometime after the burial, we were given the results of the autopsy and found out that the cause of Tara's death was purulent meningitis, a most aggressive form of meningitis, and hydrocephalus. A nurse at the hospital explained to us that if she had lived, in a couple of weeks her beautiful head would have begun to expand, and we would have found it terrible to watch. We were grateful that Tara did not have to suffer for long with such a dreadful disease. I had heard of parents with babies who had been desperately ill for months, and then subsequently died despite all the loving devotion and care the parents had lavished upon the child. I felt that I wouldn't have had the physical and emotional stamina to keep up such a routine only to watch her die after a long time of our intense care. She would have been our only focus, and our other children would have suffered enormously too.

Life at home, after Tara's brief time with us, was a matter of trying to keep functioning, but that was extremely difficult. Because of our other two children, I had to keep going, and yet my heart was broken. As much as I tried to continue with life as usual, I was deeply grieving, questioning the meaning of this devastating experience, and longing to feel as I had done before the tragedy of Tara's death. My usual joy and enthusiasm seemed like an imaginary memory.

I received a letter a couple of weeks after Tara's death that really helped me. A friend of mine, who had also lost a baby just a month earlier, said that her father wrote to her after the passing of her daughter: he said, "there are some birds that soar very, very high in the sky. At times they would wing their way down over the ocean, touch the waters and fly up into the heavens again." He continued that a baby who dies early was such a soul, "and it was sufficient for her to live but a moment on this earth and go back to her creator." My friend added that "Tara" in Arabic means 'flew away.' This was a perspective on the brief nature of Tara's life that began to give me some kind of peace. Nonetheless it has taken an extremely long time for me to accept that some children are only here for a brief time and to try and make meaning of that.

Losing a child is one of the hardest things to find meaning for because it is so tragic. No parent should ever have to bury a child. It feels like it is against the natural order of things, and yet clearly people die at all ages in all circumstances. I was in touch with Nora Weeks of the Dr Edward Bach Centre in the UK. She wrote to me and said, "yes, indeed your little daughter just came to greet you and to say she will be waiting for you until you go to her. No need to answer this, but later on let me hear how you are."

We received a letter from the Universal House of Justice, the international governing body of the Bahá'ís throughout the world which said: "We offer you the thought that in spite of the apparent tragedy you have set a new soul –'immensely exalted above all infirmities of body or mind' – on its eternal journey, and through your prayers and the love of God you may be related to Tara throughout eternity."

These letters and many others helped me to feel loved and supported, but nothing could dull the pain of losing my beautiful baby girl. Sometimes it is hard for people on the outside to understand the need to make meaning for people involved in tragedy, but it is a necessary process because without meaning, tragedy is really unbearable.

I always knew that life was difficult and that I would have sacrifices to make in my life, but I couldn't think of anything more painful than the death of my baby girl. I walked around not knowing what to do with myself, how to hold the agony, how to understand something about why her and why me. I remember feeling that there must be something really wrong with me at a very deep level or this wouldn't have happened. I sometimes felt as if the death of my little one was some kind of divine chastisement for crimes I never realised I had committed. Even though I tried so hard to be a good person, it was hard not to wonder if such a painful experience was a fateful punishment.

When faced with the enormous power and ruthlessness of death, I stood watching, helpless, vulnerable, and like a frightened child. I was only too well aware of my powerlessness. At times I thought it was all my fault. My mind kept wondering if I had done this or hadn't done that, maybe my baby would have lived. When I tried to discuss my feelings of guilt with my husband, he couldn't understand them. He knew how difficult it would have been for her life to continue for a long time, as she became more and more ill. I knew that too, but it didn't stop my wondering and questioning and a whole host of feelings that Tara's death evoked in me. I also remember thinking for a time that if sex leads to death in this way, I would have preferred to avoid it.

However I knew that sex was joyful and usually didn't result in pain and death, so I wasn't prepared to give it up.

For many years I shut down my intuition because it was just too painful to have had such fears during my pregnancy and to see them come true. My foreboding had probably helped to prepare me for the loss, but I felt too vulnerable to go through that again.

To this day I don't know what my husband did to grieve Tara's loss. He had to be in the theatre each night to do the show because he was an "old school" type of actor who felt "the show must go on!" I saw him do his job when he had been deathly ill, and nothing would stop him unless it was his own death or something that actually prevented his being able to function. Maybe he felt he had to keep strong for us all, but I rarely saw him grieving. Perhaps he threw his pain into his work? Whatever he did to grieve the death of his daughter who was born on his birthday, this loss certainly drove a wedge between us. In the wake of that experience, I knew that I had to become more independent because I couldn't depend on Philip to be there with me as my closest friend and companion as he had been. As much as we loved each other, our ability to communicate seemed to have deteriorated because of this experience. I wondered if he blamed me for Tara's death, but he assured me that he didn't. I couldn't blame him for her death, but I was aware of a kind of deeper blame that I only fleetingly noticed towards him. Just because Philip was the man with whom I had fallen in love, married and chosen to have a family, he was instrumental in the chain of events that led me to the pain I was feeling at that time. I knew that if I had never known him, I might never have made such choices and therefore have avoided the searing pain of this loss because I would have remained on my own, single and childless. That is not a scenario that I would have really wanted, but I just wished that the pain would cease, and I couldn't imagine that it ever would. I didn't realise that the death had done considerable damage to our relationship, which we didn't have the skills or appropriate help to overcome at that time. In many cases the death of a child or a miscarriage can cause a marriage to end, and we didn't know that we needed help to deal with Tara's death. I couldn't identify what was wrong, but I knew that something was, and in those days I blamed myself.

I was not just suffering emotional pain, but I was also physically grieving. I was still producing milk for a baby who was no longer there, and it was heartbreaking. When I went to the obstetrician for my check-up at six weeks, he asked, "How is the baby?" I replied, "She is dead." He was shocked. I think part of me partially blamed him because I didn't think that he was as vigilant as he could have been. I felt that her susceptibility to such a virulent illness might have been made worse because of his negligence that prevented him from realising that my iron levels were becoming severely depleted. I felt that if he had checked my iron levels more regularly, this might not have happened. Not only that, but I later heard that there had been an outbreak of meningitis in the hospital around the time of Tara's birth. It may not have been the same kind of meningitis that she had, but nevertheless it was worrying. Rationally, I knew that nothing I could do or say or that he could do or say could bring Tara back. I could only attempt to accept that this was God's will, and she was in God's hands. I felt that if I were not meant to have her with me, I would rather have her be in God's tender care where she would be safe and nurtured.

I was somehow held together by my family, my little children who needed me and my faith. Gradually I threw myself into life with all of that, but the loss was always there. Losses of this nature never go away. It took me years to come to a real acceptance of her death. Gradually the pain faded, but it still recurs sometimes, usually when I am least expecting it. I miss her, miss knowing her, miss watching her grow up and become a beautiful woman in her own right. I feel that she is waiting for me in the next life, and that we will meet each other and become acquainted when I join her, but I really miss her here now.

In my grieving, I longed to be pregnant again, and the next pregnancy began about five months after Tara's death. About six weeks in, I started to bleed. A friend from Belgium was staying with us and was cooking for us. She insisted that I eat very healthy foods to give this new being the best possible chance for life. However one night, I simply had a miscarriage.

The doctor came to the door and rang the doorbell. When I opened the door to him, he asked me what I was doing answering the door because I should be in bed. I said that someone had to put the children to bed and deal with the household. There was nobody else at home. My Belgian friend had decided on this evening to take a walk and was gone for quite a long time leaving me alone with my two young children aged nearly four and two and a half. The doctor examined me, and said that I would be fine, and there was no need for any further procedures. I just needed to take it easy for a while to recover.

Although I believe in life after death where children continue to grow in love and safety, it took a long time before I began to emerge from the nearness of death. I was so full of grief at the time that I couldn't tell anyone about that pregnancy and that loss because I knew that if anyone looked at me with sympathy in their eyes again so soon I wouldn't be able to take it. I would have broken down in tears again. I always found that if something is painful to me, it somehow becomes more real and more painful when other people know about it. Thank goodness for my two other children, a boy and a girl, who gave me a reason to keep going because without them, I can imagine myself feeling truly lost and possibly just giving up.

On Reflection

No parent should have to witness the death of their child. It is an event that profoundly affects us because it is not according to the proper order of things. Parents are supposed to die before their children. When a child dies, it is an enormous loss. Parent/child bonds are arguably the most potent bonds that are possible to have in a life. As parents, we never expect such a loss because we know we are meant to die first.

What may be less obvious or less explored is the huge loss of potential and dreams of what our baby might have become. The death of an infant can be a most extreme experience of loss of future as well as loss of present and past. When an adult dies, we feel a huge loss of memories, of the past and of what we shared with them, and depending upon their age, there is more or less of a potential future ahead of them that we might have shared. When an infant dies, there is more of a sense of what was to come, and it is that ripping down of the future that feels so incredibly painful. One of the many reasons that we have children is to build a sense of the future and to make a contribution towards it. When that potential future of love and contact and growing with each other is gone, the emptiness is vast.

The question 'why' is so hard to answer in the experience of infant death. If the child were older, we might have better understood the reason for the death, like illness or accident. Even when there is a medical reason for an infant death, that still doesn't stop us demanding why? Why them? Why me? Why us? It seems so utterly unfair to allow a child a moment to glimpse this life and then to reclaim it.

One of the ways of coming to some kind of understanding of the death of a child is to look at the soul's journey and to wonder what was it about that child's soul that the journey into life and out of it had to be so brief. It is also important to look at what the life and death of the child meant in the family and to the family. Children who live through the death of a sibling or who are born after that death may experience grief and survivor guilt even though they may not call it that or be able to name it until much later in their lives, if indeed they ever can, but they will be affected by it. It is often very hard for children to understand that their baby brother or sister has died and what that means. It can be heartbreaking to see their pain. That is, of course, above and beyond the pain of the parent. It may be that losing a child helps us to understand our own pain and that of others more than we might have done otherwise. That may feel like small compensation for our loss, but we may be more compassionate and understanding as a result of it. Nevertheless, we never forget that child, and we are always aware of the empty space in our hearts and our lives. For those of us who believe in life after death, we may be consoled by feeling that the soul exists somewhere, but we still cannot pick up our child and hug her or touch her.

It may be important to us to wonder about our own lack of control and inability to change the outcome and save the child. Infant death is an event that brings us face to face with our helplessness, and that really hurts. Losses due to the death of loved ones are among the most difficult events we ever face in our lives, and we find it extremely hard to come to terms with them. The loss of an infant may bring up some of the most profound feelings of confusion, lack of meaning in life, and possibly even a crisis of faith.

Most people understand that the loss of an infant is very significant. Yet despite this there may be an unconscious expectation that recovering from the grief should be quicker than it may actually be. This can be especially the case with miscarriage. Friends and relatives can suggest that we should have moved on thinking that it is not as if someone really died! Comments such as, "You can have another baby", can be made in an effort to minimise the grief, but really they deny the depth of the pain. There is no doubt that people say that kind of thing to try to be helpful and look forward, but inevitably such comments end up being very hurtful however kindly they were meant. There is sadly often a feeling that a baby who has been miscarried can be easily replaced. But no matter how briefly we have had a child either in life or in the womb, we are inextricably bound to that child, and the loss is just as devastating as the loss of any loved one.

The death of an infant at a very young age or a miscarriage calls into question beliefs about when the soul joins the body and some very deep questions about the nature of life itself. This can be exceptionally painful for the parents who have been deeply involved in the pregnancy and are facing the loss as well as their own existential questions. That kind of attitude makes bereaved people stop talking about their loss even though they are still in a great deal of pain.

If there is any problem with conceiving after the loss, the inability to share grief with people who are close becomes almost unbearable. This causes some people to live in a kind of emotionally-closed limbo in which they have a deep feeling of failure. It can take many years before these feelings are understood, and the parents have made any meaning out of such an important loss in their lives, and there is no guarantee that the parents will ever really come to terms with the loss of their baby.

It is so important to personally honour the depth of the soul connection that a parent has with any child who has died even if that deep connection is not honoured by their culture and the people around them. It is sometimes the case that men and women grieve differently. Therefore, even though both parents are suffering, they may do so in very different ways leaving one or both feeling left out or misunderstood by the other. This often comes as a surprise and a big disappointment to any partner who expects their spouse to respond as they do. When each partner is in such pain, they have little or no energy left to be understanding of the other's different style of grieving, especially if that other doesn't seem to be showing distress in the same way.

A pregnant woman experiencing her baby growing inside her is touching a sense of eternity and already developing a spiritual connection with that child from its earliest beginnings. She feels deeply touched not just on the outside but deep within her physical body. Having experienced that relationship, a woman is never again the same. At a very physical level, she is participating in carrying forward an ever advancing civilisation, and that goes back to the beginning of human life and connects forever into the future. A woman's growing sense of spiritual love for this unborn child is so deep and huge that the devastation of feeling life slipping away causing the loss of that deep connection leaves an incredible sense of homesickness. If it is the woman's first real experience of such a connection, its loss is even more devastating because she might not even realise that she is grieving the loss of the powerful internal connection to the physical continuation of human life as well as the death of her baby. For the mother, the loss of a child is not just an emotional and spiritual pain; it is very much a physical pain as well.

When any child is born, there may be sadness at the loss of the interior connection that the woman has felt for nine months with her growing infant that she may not even be able to name. It may well be that loss which is at the root of some of the post natal depression that some women experience. There is very little said or written about the deep internal physical bond that a mother has with her unborn child partially and possibly because it is so profoundly meaningful and yet so deep, primal, unconscious and unfamiliar that she may never recognise exactly what it is.

Breastfeeding, as important, vital and bonding as it is cannot really equal having a life within her body. The relationship of a mother to the baby in her womb is as close as many people may come to a true spiritual connection. Even those people who have had a spiritual awakening may not find an experience of connection to equal that of feeling a new life growing within.

Having a life developing within our body takes us beyond our physical identification into that existential mystery of: 'my internal world is a universe, and there is a life growing within me.' That is something completely different from feeling 'I've got a body, and I feel attached to something or in relationship with something or someone'. Many women will admit that there may not be anything else that can match the profound spiritual experience of having a baby growing inside her body. In no other way is the spiritual brought into the physical world as it is during pregnancy.

A woman can really feel the energy field of her baby although she cannot see it, and she feels profoundly in tune and connected to the life force through that developing baby in her womb. Most women will say they can feel that tiny new being mixed in with their own being. The miracle of procreation is creativity at its height. It is clear that the father/child bond is just as deep and profound because both people have conceived this new life and therefore that sense of creative miracle is experienced by both mother and father at the birth of their baby. However, the physical nature of the mother/child bond, especially during pregnancy, cannot be disputed nor replicated in any other way.

It is this profound connection both personally to the new soul growing inside her body as well as to the passage of life and the development of humanity, i.e. to eternity, that makes many women love being pregnant, be willing and eager to have many pregnancies, feel deep sadness when the time comes to leave pregnancy behind, and find sex when it is simply for pleasure and bonding and not for the purpose of conception just that bit less interesting than when it was for the possibility of entering into the mystery of life through pregnancy. It is enormously painful to lose all of that. When a baby dies, there is so much taken away that it is no wonder that the mother may feel somehow betrayed by the physical world, and maybe even punished at some level for something that she may not even be able to imagine because the loss is so deep, the hurt so profound in every way. She may mistakenly feel that she wouldn't have had to suffer such enormous pain if she hadn't been somehow at fault. However, despite all that, women who lose babies often long to be pregnant again, and they look forward to having another baby.

Chapter 7
A New Beginning

I did have one more pregnancy before my childbearing years came to an end. I was so very grateful to have a fine healthy boy who was born in 1973, just over two years after Tara's brief life. I know that Philip and I did not try for a baby immediately after the miscarriage, but time was marching on. Philip was still 16 ½ years older than I was, and we still wanted another baby for its own sake. I was pregnant again in late September of 1972. I remember feeling very frightened about being pregnant again, but it wasn't the same kind of foreboding. My fear was natural after my previous experiences, but this time I knew intuitively that everything was going to be all right. I remember sometimes during that pregnancy I even wanted to eat the same kind of food that my mother used to feed me, in a longing to go back to that feeling of safety.

I had my last baby at home thanks to a local doctor who delivered him. After my previous experiences in the hospital, I decided I wanted this baby to be born at home. I phoned local doctors, but they all said that they were no longer doing home births. Then several days later I got a phone call from a doctor who lived just a few blocks away, and he said that he would do a home delivery for us because we lived so near to him. That doctor had to search through all the "O'Briens" in the phone book to find me because I hadn't left him my phone number when he had initially said no. That must have taken some time because there are quite a few "O'Briens" in Dublin!

It was a Friday when the doctor came to see me and wanted to induce the baby, who was several weeks late. I had experienced the previous two babies being induced by breaking the waters, so I said, "No thank you, I would rather wait. When the apple is ripe, it will drop." He replied, "I hope the baby is born alive!" I guess that remark was supposed to force me to change my mind, but I remained steady. The next day, Saturday, labour began naturally at about 10.30 in the morning with mild contractions. By late afternoon I knew that the birth was coming closer because the contractions were longer, more frequent and more intense. I phoned the midwife, whose name was Nurse Pain, and invited her over to join us for dinner, which I cooked. We all ate together, and then I went up to my bedroom. Philip washed the dishes before he joined me to be present for the birth and to help out. A friend came over to put the other two children to bed. Nurse Pain was there, and when she felt the time was right, she phoned to ask the doctor to join us.

I had done natural childbirth classes, so I knew how labour progressed. I was getting to the transition stage of labour, just before it is time to push, and I was practising the breathing I had learned for that stage of labour. The doctor looked at me, and he said, "You know, Jane, sometimes it helps to pray." I replied, "Yes, Doctor, sometimes it does, but now is not the time!" I was aware that during transition stage some women become very aggressive. Even the mildest mannered woman can have a complete change of character and shout and speak in a very unpleasant and unfamiliar way. I guess my response at the time was mild in comparison.

The baby was born quite quickly. After his birth, the midwife was preparing a syringe of ergometrine, which was normal procedure in hospitals to prevent haemorrhaging. I had spoken to the doctor beforehand and asked that he not give me that shot unless I haemorrhaged. I had read that ergometrine was a derivative of LSD, and I didn't want to have that in my body just after delivery unless it was really necessary. He said to the midwife, "No, we are not giving that." The doctor picked up the baby to examine him, and found that he was just fine. A few days after the birth, the doctor came to see me, and he said that I looked a little anaemic, although it would be no use to take a blood test because it wouldn't have been accurate just after I had given birth. However, he thought I should have six iron shots. I had four, but they affected the baby so badly that I said to the doctor I won't have any more. The baby cried for hours just a short time after I had each shot. I assumed that something had travelled through the milk from the shots. I later began to take iron tablets to assist whenever I became anaemic, and I closely monitored my blood count to catch any signs of anaemia before they became serious. I realised that I was inclined to become anaemic when I was pregnant or breastfeeding.

I was perfectly delighted to have a new baby boy, whom we named Brian and the whole family was overjoyed. Nothing could prevent my wondering about Tara, how she was, who she was, what it meant to be in a world that I could barely imagine. I remember one time when Brian was about five years old; he was in bed before going to sleep. He said to me, "I don't know why God let me live and Tara die because I am the littlest boy in my class, and my writing isn't very good." I was so touched that I knelt down beside him and hugged him. I explained to him that we were delighted to have him in our family whether or not he is little and his writing isn't very good, and that some children die early, but we can't really understand that. I also assured him that God wanted him to live and that Tara had to do other things in ways we couldn't imagine.

I was delighted to have three children in this life, two boys and a girl, and felt terribly lucky to have them. In the distance I was also aware of the two children in the next life that I would meet again one day, and yet they and that meeting seemed almost unreal and not possible.

It was at this time that I had to really think about whether or not I wanted any more children. I loved being pregnant, having babies, breastfeeding and looking after growing children, but as much as I loved that I had to acknowledge that I couldn't continue to do so forever, and one day I had to call a halt and say no. I also wanted to focus on the beautiful children that I already had without my attention to them being interrupted by another pregnancy and baby that would demand a lot of attention and take it away from them.

Each subsequent child meant another couple of years when my own life, my personal ambitions and my interests, had to be put on hold in favour of looking after the baby as well as the other growing children. As much as I loved doing that, I also had things that I wanted to do. Philip was not so affected by that choice as I was because he was free to go out and work and follow his career whether we had any more children or not. I was at home looking after the family. After much inner searching and thought I decided that I would have no more children. By that time I was in my 30s. I had had all my children between ages 23 and 29, and that felt right for me. Other people do it differently. Now many people are having children much later than they did when I was getting married and starting a family. I am glad that I had my children when I was young, and I am glad that I stopped when I did. It was a difficult decision to make, but I felt that the time had come.

On Reflection

Some of our most difficult decisions are the times when we actually say no to something that we love. When somebody else tells us no, or when circumstances cause difficulties, we are involved in the decision as a recipient, but we are not the cause.

For example, choosing to end a relationship is enormously difficult, and that is a decision involving someone else, but often we have to take ourselves in hand and say no to ourselves. That is still difficult for us even if it doesn't actually involve anyone else. In this section I would like you to look at the habitual attachments that you have had that have been difficult for you to end or change, for example: leaving a job, letting go of an addiction, changing any personal habits, ending a friendship, leaving a country, separating from a parent and leaving home.

Look at some of the hard decisions you have had to make, the ones that involve other people and the ones that are for you alone. Notice how you feel about yourself and the amount of strength that you had to gather to make such a decision. Sometimes we fail to admire ourselves sufficiently when we have made a difficult decision. It is by looking at these achievements that we often dismiss that we can really see our own strength. We deserve to value our inner strength, and not ignore it.

Sit quietly with a piece of paper and some coloured markers, and just dream about the times when you have said "no" in your life, what the results have been and how you now feel about having done that. Wonder about the level of courage that you had to muster to do so and give yourself real credit for doing so. Draw an image of how you see yourself as someone who can say "no" in difficult situations and spend some time with that image.

Then dream about the times when you might have said "no" but you didn't. Look at how your life has been affected by your lack of "no" and see how you feel about that now. Then imagine and draw an image of the part of you who sometimes doesn't say "no" even though you might wish to do so. Spend some time with that image.

Look at your ability now to say either "yes" or "no" in different circumstances and see how that ability serves you. Draw an image about your ability to make choices and be discriminating and then spend some time with that image and really take in the value of your capacity to discriminate as well as recognising that you might not always get it right. Ask yourself how you feel about that and if you are willing to accept that you are not perfect and do not necessarily make "the right" decisions all the time. Actually that is called being human.

CHAPTER 8
Growing and Glowing

Health has been a major concern for me my whole life. When I say health, I mean more than just physical health. I know that there are several aspects of human beings that need to be nourished: the body, the feelings, the mind and the soul or spirit. My first authority is Bahá'u'lláh, so I use His teachings as a guideline for everything else. While my young family was growing up, I was most focused on physical health through cooking for my family.

There are no dietary laws or restrictions in the Faith, but I followed the words of 'Abdu'l-Bahá who said:

> The food of the future will be fruit and grains. The time will come when meat will no longer be eaten. Medical science is only in its infancy, yet it has shown that our natural food is that which grows out of the ground. ('Abdu'l-Bahá, 1923, p.453) *This quote is attributed to 'Abdu'l-Bahá. The reference is quite old and may not be entirely accurate, but it does reflect something of the spirit of some of the writings.*

Before we were married Philip gave me a book called *Let's Eat Right to Keep Fit* by Adelle Davis (1954), and it inspired me to adopt a healthier diet. The book described taking extra vitamins and minerals and eating a high protein diet. I read that with enthusiasm because my health had been poor since I was severely ill as a child. Since then I had experienced continuous bladder problems, lack of energy, little stamina, and I usually got every cold and virus that was going.

I wanted to find ways of healing myself from within. I knew that my health would probably deteriorate as I got older, so it was important that I take responsibility and start finding ways to improve it while I was young. My approach to health is very personal and not to everybody's taste, but it helped me a great deal, so I share it here. I was on a mission of discovery and I was willing to experiment.

Growing and Glowing

The last doctor I had visited in Chicago, shortly before getting married, had suggested that I see a brain surgeon. He said to me that he could operate and perhaps re-educate the cells of my brain to take over the functions of my bladder. The operation might stop the urgency and frequency of wanting to pee and prevent the frequent infections that I experienced. He said, however, that I might become paralysed on one side of my body, so I said, "thanks, but no thanks!" It was then that I decided I had better see what I could do myself, so I was on the trail of health and healing. Also because of Philip's age, I wanted to feed the family in a way that would keep us all healthy.

I started by using wholewheat flour rather than white flour and honey instead of white sugar in my cooking and meal planning. Then I gave up eating beef, because a woman who taught childbirth classes in Dublin said that there had been studies in France that showed that women who ate beef were more likely to get toxaemia. My mother had had toxaemia before I was born, and I had been born by Caesarean early because of her illness to save both our lives. Hearing what this woman had to say I decided that we would give up beef. That was a bit of a shock to me and my family because we had been raised on beef, and we felt that we should have it or else we would die! Happily I discovered that I was able to get minced lamb for casseroles and burgers, so that was OK and we found that we didn't miss beef as much as we thought we would. The butchers in Dublin were most accommodating and willing to provide us with whatever cut or type of meat we wanted. In the end, given my mother's experience and wanting what was best for my own pregnancies, I was glad to give up beef. After my first pregnancy was over and the baby was born, I couldn't even look at minced lamb again, and I never went back to eating beef.

I loved experimenting with cooking for the family because it made life more interesting. I used to think about what people ate in the early days of America or in Biblical times, and the food seemed to be based on staple grains plus vegetables and fruit, chicken and red meat when available. The foods of the past seemed quite simple compared to modern tastes, and I wondered if we could simplify our diet.

Of course, I was cooking for five people with varying tastes, and while they usually enjoyed what I cooked, there were things that one or the other didn't eat or like. I was searching for a set of principles by which I could decide what foods to use in our diets.

I was ready to discard my old and inappropriate theories of how the body works and what foods are necessary for good health, and to enter unknown territory.

I devoured everything I could find on the subject. With each new book, I would try new ways of cooking and eating. My exploration of food and diet was challenging and interesting. In Ireland at the time it was common to cook the same meal on specific days of the week and a large portion of the population had fish on Friday. The other days might be similarly organised, so Monday would be stew day, Tuesday might be shepherd's pie and so on. And it was not just having the same food in the sense of basing the meal around meat or fish, but it was actually often the same recipe week in week out. I didn't work that way at all.

Philip never knew what we might be getting for a meal. He was continually surprised. He used to joke that everything looked like a cooked army uniform because I used wholewheat flour instead of white flour and brown rice instead of white rice. He sometimes came to the table clucking like a chicken because he knew we would be eating sunflower seeds and nuts. That was his way of gently teasing me.

I did cook some wonderful meals though, and he remembered them well. He thought I was really a good cook. It was fun and exciting to me to translate favourite recipes into more healthy recipes even if it meant that bread and cakes didn't look as white as they normally would. I remember growing up with the understanding that the best way to a man's heart was through his stomach, so it was important to me to be a good cook and to have Philip enjoy my meals. This was not a wholly altruistic consideration for me it must be said because I loved good food, and I wanted to have great meals myself too.

One of the very earth-mother type of things I did was to grind wheat into flour, and make bread from that. In the beginning it was a really hard job because I had a simple hand-cranked grain mill, something like a meat grinder. Grinding grain is a much harder job than grinding meat because grain is harder. I threw my back out doing it in the beginning until I was shown how to stand while using the grain mill in a way that protected my back. One day I discovered electric grain mills. That seemed like a little miracle to me. I suggested to Philip that it would be a good idea to get an electric grain mill, but he wasn't too keen (possibly because he wasn't the one cranking the handle on my old manual one and throwing his back out doing it).

I had been raised with the idea that a wife manipulates her husband until he wants what she wants and he thinks it is his idea. I gave up that way of being later on, but in the early days it was the way I worked. Basically I didn't want to be manipulative, but I wanted us to consult on every decision and to want the same things for a better quality of life. Sadly, in this instance, Philip wasn't really getting the point about my need for the electric grain mill. Then one day, and this wasn't my plan, it just happened quite innocently, I asked Philip to grind the flour. He had had no idea how hard it was to actually grind wheat grain into flour and was quite surprised when he did it. He came triumphantly from the grain mill with his little container of flour having stopped after grinding enough flour for one loaf of bread. I usually baked three at a time. He then said that he thought we should get an electric grain mill! We did.

This whole experience of seeking health through diet was exciting and frightening at the same time. When I became pregnant with our second child, I gave up eating meat entirely. That took some guts to do because I had been raised with the idea that if we didn't have meat and therefore get enough protein, we would die. I feared for my children and for all of us. However, I said prayers every day for guidance, and despite my fear, I felt that I had to take the risks associated with giving up meat because I knew that the rewards might be far greater than the chance that I was taking. So I studied and read everything I could get my hands on in the way of information about how to feed us without meat.

There were two sisters in Wicklow who made delicious natural yoghurt in various flavours. We bought so much of it that they delivered it to us. I think we probably bought more of it than the shops. In the 1970s yoghurt wasn't as popular as it is now, and few people knew anything about the good bacteria in it. We ate yoghurt. I cooked loads of fresh vegetables and served fresh fruit. I made delicious cakes and biscuits from my freshly ground wholewheat flour and I was quite proud of that. I baked my own bread. I got up early in the morning and made fresh oatcakes for breakfast.

My health improved and Philip and the children's health really were good. For many years Philip had frequently suffered from bursitis in his shoulder, which is an inflammation caused by a sports injury or an underlying rheumatic condition. It is exceptionally painful, but he never had it again after he had been eating my food for a while. I noticed, however, that while our health was good and mine had improved, we were still getting colds and flu and coughs more than I wanted us to. The children never had an upset stomach, but we were getting sick too much. I didn't like it. I still didn't have much energy, and I didn't like that either. I kept reading, and I looked at other people who also got sick pretty regularly. I looked at animals and birds and didn't see them sniffling or getting fevers. I wondered what to do. I prayed, and then I read about macrobiotics. The word itself sounds like an illness or a scientific subject. It was a system of life based on the complementary opposites of yin and yang. George Ohsawa had written about it, and there was interesting evidence to support it. It actually seemed quite scientific. There are no particular dietary recommendations in the Bahá'í teachings, so I could only research what I could find elsewhere.

Embracing a macrobiotic diet meant giving up honey and dairy foods. According to Ohsawa, cow's milk is really food for calves and we lose the enzyme for digesting milk when we are about two years old. I took this on board, although I did love dairy foods and puddings and such things. Cheese was a favourite. I also loved sweetening things with honey rather than sugar and felt terribly righteous in doing so. It was more expensive, but I didn't use all that much. When I first read about macrobiotics, it seemed too extreme for me, so I dismissed it for a while. I was really enjoying our food, but still, we weren't up to the health standard that I imagined, and I hated to see the children coughing and sniffling and being sick from time to time.

I used Bach flower remedies that were very helpful in dealing with problems, but still it wasn't enough. I read about Dr Bach and loved his story. He saw disease (literally dis-ease, or being ill-at-ease) as a problem of lack of alignment between the soul and the personality. He was n extremely sensitive doctor who discovered the flower remedies by his own response to the flower as he walked the countryside in England. Apparently when he handled the flower, he would experience the condition that the essence of the flower would heal. I found the remedies especially helpful with children because they are non-toxic, easy to understand and can be used by anyone. That is the way he designed them. He wanted them to be available to all people. Later I qualified as a counsellor in the Bach Remedies, so I could help others with them, and I still use them today as and when I need them.

Despite all these changes, I had to look more critically at our progress. I still had bladder frequency and frequent colds and coughs. The children also got colds and coughs. Therefore I wasn't convinced that what I was doing was working as fully as I wanted it to do. There was great improvement, but I still needed more energy. Who doesn't need more energy with children and a home to run?

I didn't know what else to do to improve our health. Then one day I just decided, in consultation with Philip, that we would attempt a macrobiotic diet and see how we got on. We both agreed that if it worked, we would be glad that we did it. So, for about a year and a half, we struggled with it. We began cooking with a lot of brown rice. I made miso soup frequently. We would go for a couple of weeks without dairy foods and honey. I would sweeten things now with raisins, sultanas, dates or apricots. We were getting better, and I couldn't deny it, but it was really hard to create interesting meals without the good old dairy foods. I really missed them and honey as well. I guess they are addictive. I began using beans, seaweed and having more fish too. When I was really bored and couldn't think of something exciting to cook for a macrobiotic meal, I would turn to good old smoked salmon and have it with rice and vegetables. Somehow that kind of meal satisfied us and helped me to get back on track and to experiment with recipes again.

I had read the few books that were available about macrobiotics, and I had written to people in various parts of the world asking questions about things that I didn't understand, so my name was getting out and about. It was really hard to maintain my dedication and enthusiasm, when the rest of the world seemed to be eating completely differently. One day, however, I got a phone call from a woman who was in Dublin and had gotten my name from the macrobiotic centre in Boston to which I had written a few times. I was in heaven to have someone who knew more about this kind of cooking nearby. She came out to the house and stayed with us for a few days. During that time, she cooked for us. The food was great. I spent my time washing pots. She used more pots for her cooking than I ever had, and the food was just delicious. She had cooked in the Macrobiotic Centre in Brookline under the direction of Michio Kushi who was the leading person teaching macrobiotics in America at the time.

She thought it would be a good idea for me to go to Boston for a while to learn macrobiotic cooking because I had not experienced it, and that would help. I was pregnant with Tara, and it sounded like a really good idea. Philip and I consulted. We both agreed that if it were going to make a big difference in the health of the family over time, we would be well advised to make the sacrifice now. And so I was off to Boston in a few weeks time with my two children who were then three and two, and I was about three months pregnant with Tara. It was quite an undertaking with two such young children and I had a push chair for twins. In those days such push chairs were really heavy. I was lucky, however, because wherever I went people were very helpful to me. Of course nobody knew I was pregnant as well because I wasn't showing then.

We got to the macrobiotic house in Boston where we would be staying. It was one of those lovely large colonial houses with more rooms than I was used to seeing in homes in Dublin. There were no carpets on the wooden floors, so I was aware of every little noise that my children made and feared we might be disturbing someone. The house was on a beautiful tree lined street amidst other houses of similar design. I imagined that most of the other houses had been one-family homes at one time, but I didn't know if they remained so. This one seemed to be filled to the brim with macrobiotic adult students all in residence.

We had food cooked by expert macrobiotic cooks. I watched the cooking and kept notes of recipes. I noticed the biggest change in my daughter, Shannon. It wasn't, at that time, such a good change under the circumstances. As she adjusted to the standard macrobiotic diet and was not having the food to which she was accustomed, she became irritable in a way that she had never been before. That was a shock, and it was difficult because there were other people living in the house. My son, Scott, didn't seem to be so affected by it, or maybe he was more difficult anyway as a child, so I didn't notice a change. Shannon was usually so easygoing and delightful that to see her becoming more demanding and irritable was a surprise. I was relieved when after a few days she settled down as much as any children do when in strange circumstances living in close proximity with other unfamiliar adults and no other children. We stayed in the house for a couple of weeks, and I was able to absorb quite a bit of experience in cooking without honey and dairy foods.

I found it really hard to be in a strange place with two young children, so I decided that I would ask a friend of mine, Nancy, who lived with her family in New York if we could visit her there. She was someone I had known from when Philip and I were first married. She was another Bahá'í who was interested in healthy living and had been using health foods for years. We used to have great fun in Glencoe, near Chicago, just after I was married because we both loved cooking with good food. I was a new wife who loved cooking and Nancy was a great cook. She had more practice because she already had three children and had been married longer than me. As a mother who stayed at home, she had the opportunity to experiment with food. I wanted to be 'the perfect wife' so Nancy and I experimented a lot with cooking and finding new ways to make healthy food delicious.

She had written to me some months before I went to Boston asking if I had any suggestions because her three children had been coughing every night for six weeks, and she wasn't getting any sleep and was having a really hard time. I wrote back and suggested that she try macrobiotics. I was very careful to say that she should change their diet gradually. Her children were older than mine, and they would have been more attached to other ways of eating. I told her that there was no need to try the extreme form of macrobiotics, which was for curing serious illnesses by making them eat only brown rice for 10 days. That was the way in which macrobiotics had been mentioned in some books at the time, but I felt that approach would be too extreme, and the children would react against it. I said that there were great ways of cooking macrobiotically, and she would be able to learn it quickly as she was living in New York where she could go to cooking classes easily.

Some months later Nancy wrote to say that she had started them on the brown rice diet and within a day or two all the coughing had stopped. They didn't want to try the diet, so she asked them what it would take to make it worth their while. They said a trip to Florida for their next vacation. She agreed, and they stuck to the diet. She was really desperate because she had been unable to sleep due to their coughing for so long. It worked, and she was finally able to sleep again. That was a huge relief for her.

It seemed like a great idea to phone Nancy and ask if we could spend some time in her home with her because she had children, and I thought it would be easier for me and my children to be with her and her family. She was so pleased to hear from me and to know that we could spend some time together that she came to pick us up at the house and we went to her home near New York City. When we got there, she said that she served dinner late, like 8.30pm or so. I was surprised, but she said it was so her children would be so hungry they would eat anything! Nancy had learned much more about macrobiotic cooking than I had. She was a great cook anyway. Her food was just beautiful and somehow my children settled down better at her house than they had in Boston. We spent about a week there, and we really had fun trying different recipes and the children enjoyed playing!

Then it was back to Dublin for us. I had had all the adventure I could handle under the circumstances and I guess the old nesting instinct had kicked in and was playing on my mind. I had gotten a great boost of information and experience of the cooking, so I was encouraged to return home and get down to doing my own cooking.

And so it began. I got home and I was far better able to create meals that were good and satisfying. During the months of my pregnancy I found myself having a lot of fun in the kitchen, using seaweeds and miso for soup and other dishes. I no longer had to revert to dairy foods and honey, although I still relied on smoked salmon from time to time when I just couldn't think of something interesting to fix for a family meal. I made sweet desserts with fruit, raisins and sultanas. I made delicious breads, cakes and savoury foods from all sorts of things – vegetables, beans, chick peas, rice, millet, buckwheat, and there was so much variety that I could hardly believe it. People imagine that when you give up meat, there is no variety. I could take leftovers from one meal and turn them into something completely different for the next meal. I made a lot with pie crusts including delicious seaweed pasties that were deep fried. One of my favourite foods was tempura – deep-fried vegetables or fish in batter. It is available in Japanese restaurants. We all loved it. I also made what I called an apple pie pizza which was like an apple pie mixture made with lemon peel, vanilla, sultanas and arrowroot for thickening on a wholewheat pizza dough or an ordinary wholewheat pie dough. That was a real delight.

I was on a roll and life was an adventure. I found myself able to do more work in a day than I had ever dreamed possible. I was feeling good and healthy and active and full of energy. My health had improved dramatically. I had been used to getting cystitis very frequently, and since changing to a macrobiotic diet I never got it. I didn't have as much trouble with my bladder in other ways as well. None of us got colds and flu with the same frequency as we had previously. The children didn't feel the cold. I remember one very cold winter's day in January when the sun was shining in a nearly cloudless sky. That was very unusual in the winter in Dublin. It was such a lovely day that my two children got dressed in their swimming suits, took large towels and went out into the front garden to sunbathe! I don't remember how long they stayed there, but it was a cold day. I remember that the teachers in school were always commenting about the fact that they were never cold.

Another example of how the diet helped to improve our health was once Philip had a problem with a kind of dizziness and pain down his left arm. He thought he was having a stroke. This happened a few times, and he went to the doctor who investigated and discovered that he had a little bit of arthritis pinching a nerve at the back of his neck. He came home and went on the brown rice diet – that is he ate nothing but brown rice for ten days and drank bancha tea or cereal coffee. The arthritis disappeared, and so did the problem.

One interesting effect of dietary change is that I didn't experience body odour any longer. When I had eaten meat and the usual fare that I was fed growing up I had body odour just like everyone else did, but with a macrobiotic diet it seemed to disappear.

When I was in hospital at the time of Tara's birth, I was getting food from home, so I didn't disrupt my eating habits. However, because I had become so severely anaemic, I was given blood transfusions, and the morning after having had the transfusions, I had body odour. This was the first time I had noticed body odour on myself for ages, probably since having stopped eating meat, and I was sure it was because I had just taken in quite a lot of a "meat and sugar eater's" blood! I didn't even have deodorant in the hospital because I had forgotten what it was like to consider body odour in my life!

I might have wondered if the macrobiotic diet had made me anaemic, but I knew other macrobiotic women who went through pregnancies without getting anaemic. I had been far stronger in my pregnancy than ever before despite developing anaemia, so I was sure that my bout with anaemia was not as a result of the macrobiotic diet, but it was something that was particular to me.

At the time of Tara's death, I found that it was only by throwing myself into my life, continuing to take care of my family, and learning more about health and healing that I stayed sane because it gave me a sense of purpose. Looking back on it, I believe that it was because I had these supportive structures in my life, Faith, prayer, healthy eating practices, and a desire to learn more about health that I had something to hold onto when so much had been lost. It is wonderful to live well when times are good with important values and priorities and to take care of ourselves physically and spiritually. When crisis hits, it is more needed than ever to have those kinds of structures in place.

Despite the enormous loss that I carried with me all the time, life was busy, demanding and rewarding. I enjoyed being helpful to people, learning about the effects of food on various illnesses and knowing something about what I was doing with regard to feeding my family. My children were far healthier than I had been as a child, and that stood for something. I was also far healthier than I had been as a child or an adult. That was great, and I thoroughly enjoyed the adventure of going to my doctor for diagnosis and then going home and resolving whatever health issues we had with food, diet, or Bach remedies and homeopathic treatments.

We had some fun times with the doctor. I remember saying to him one time that I didn't know why he gave me waiting room space because I would see him for his diagnosis, but I wouldn't take drugs or give them to my family. Because I got anaemic easily when I was pregnant or breastfeeding, I used to have to get my blood checked regularly. Once I went into the waiting room and the doctor said: "What you need, Jane, is a good steak!" He smiled, and so did I. He wanted to see what I would say to that. I said: "Oh, you have no other patients who are anaemic, is that true?" He replied that he did have a number of other patients who suffered from anaemia. I said: "Well, they are all meat eaters, so having a good steak isn't the answer, is it!" We both laughed.

One of the most difficult things for a mother is the inevitable childhood illnesses that run through families, so all one's children get ill within a short time of each other. This happened to us with measles – in those days, it was considered natural for children to have measles, and there was no vaccine. Some authorities even agreed that measles was an important developmental illness that children should have. All three of my children came down with measles at the same time. Two of them had a very straightforward experience of the disease. Scott, however had a little problem. The doctor came over to examine him one Friday. I observed that Scott was sick, had a fever and the spots had come out. The doctor looked at his ears and warned me about an ear infection that could lead to deafness. He wanted to give Scott antibiotics. I objected to the use of antibiotics unless absolutely necessary. I understood that once the spots had come out, the illness was on its way out. So I asked the doctor to give me 24 hours. I asked if he could come back the next day to see how Scott was. He agreed. I got the feeling that the next day was his day off, and he was making an exception because of my desire to avoid drugs.

As soon as the doctor left the house, I dove into my books of remedies to find the appropriate homeopathic remedies and gave them to Scott. I also knew that cabbage leaves are good for bringing down fever, so I put some cabbage leaves under his head as he was lying on the sofa in the kitchen to be with us all. Philip came in, looked at his sick son lying there and exclaimed: "He looks like a salad!"

I was actually quite frightened because I certainly didn't want my son to go deaf. According to my understanding of macrobiotic theories, measles is a discharge of unnecessary elements that are in the body from birth, and it is normal and natural for children to have the measles. Therefore I wanted to be sure that my children had the measles in the healthiest way. The next day the doctor came back and checked his ears, and he said: "they aren't any better, but they aren't any worse either. They weren't that bad in the first place." When I heard him say that I wondered why he had not been quite so clear in the first place, but I did feel very relieved. Scott's hearing was perfect after that illness, so he was unaffected by it. He even went on to become a singer and a sound engineer, thus testifying to the clarity of his hearing.

My understanding is that drugs can stop the progress of a disease, and I believe that it is important for the disease to run its course and come out. In the case of a fever for a child, I had read that the fever was actually the healing process, and unless a fever was dangerously high, it would be better in the long run for the fever to be allowed to run its course. I would certainly use medicines in many circumstances, but I did object to their overuse especially if the illness were part of the body's own healing mechanism. The difficulty was in knowing the difference between circumstances that required drugs and those that didn't. Therefore it is up to anyone's best judgement in consultation with an understanding doctor to decide how and when to use drugs.

The use of medicines and vaccines is a very controversial area. There will be many who will disagree with my approach. It is important for me to live according to my own philosophy and values, and this is an example of how I attempted to do that with my children. I know that sometimes drug use is absolutely vital and life saving. For me, this was a time of researching when it was useful and when it might have been counterproductive.

According to macrobiotics and to some other theories of illness, disease is an attempt by the body to discharge foreign, harmful and unnecessary things. Disease can be seen as a healing crisis or a discharge from which we can learn. It is not always a discharge of actual physical elements, but frequently it is a response to emotional conflict. How many times have we gotten a sore throat or cold because of something that we have not been able to say openly and clearly? Do we get ill when we wish to avoid something in life that we prefer not to do and are unwilling or unable to say no to it? Illness, according to Dr Bach, is an opportunity of the personality and soul to realign themselves. How many of us would not need to get a cold or the flu, if we knew we could phone in work occasionally just to say: "I am staying home today because I need a day for me!"

You may think that all this focus on food and what we put into our bodies created a situation whereby it was impossible to go anywhere – to a restaurant or away for a holiday. Not so, and I will tell you what I did. One weekend, Philip and I and the children – we had only two at the time – went to a hotel in the country. I took my rice, a pressure cooker, a two burner electric cooker, and I just handed the rice to the chef and asked him to include it with vegetables and fish for my meals. It was rather fun when I cooked a pressure cooker full of rice in our bedroom, however, because as soon as I turned on the little electric cooker for the first time, all the electricity in the hotel went off. Philip ran out to check to see if it was our little cooker that had caused the electricity in the whole hotel to fail, but it wasn't. When the electricity was restored I just completed cooking my staple food quite happily. Much of the time I would simply eat fish and vegetables in a restaurant or when away on holiday. Philip and the children would eat what they fancied from the menu. The children were sometimes rather fussy about food in hotels anyway, so it wasn't so easy to find something that they enjoyed.

I used to send the children to school with rather unusual lunches, and I was concerned about my children getting food from other children. One child was quite happy about the lunches, and another was very embarrassed by them. I could always tell when they had other people's food that included sugar. My son would have to go to the loo many times when he came home from school. My daughter would lose her balance and fall. Within a couple of hours, they would moan and groan and become irritable, and we called it "sugar tears". When people eat sugar, it gives them a real boost to a very high point of blood sugar in a false sort of way. They feel good initially, but when that boost wears off, they feel more down and depressed more than they would have done if they had not had the boost. Whenever the children had sugar, there would be this reaction, and it was especially noticeable because they didn't have sugar normally at home, so their systems were very sensitive to it.

I was aware of the bad effects of sugar on people's health, so much so that I didn't provide sugar in its white form at all for the family. It is very difficult in this modern life to keep children on healthy diets when they are exposed to so much refined and processed food. In a way it does require them to have to deal with having a foot in two worlds. That is a good thing because it teaches them to be themselves and not to just fit in, enables them to see alternatives, and learn how to make choices. It is difficult and a challenge but worth it for their overall health and fewer sleepless nights for parents. I guess my own health problems really forced me to question and to take risks that I might never have done otherwise.

One day, when some of our friends were away, Philip took their children to the zoo for the day. When they returned, I had cooked a dinner of lentil soup, fish, chips, brown rice, vegetables, and I don't remember what there was for dessert – maybe apple pie pizza or something like that. I always left potato skins on chips because I liked the flavour, and there was more nutrition available in the skins. It was what I thought was a good, relatively normal, dinner. Not for these children, however. When Philip was driving them home, one of them said: "Philip, the food in your house is desperate." Philip took them to a fast food restaurant on the way home! I thought it was very funny.

Occasionally Philip took the two older children away for a weekend especially when I had a new baby just to give me a break. They had white bread and packet soup for dinner in the hotel. My children smiled at the waitress commenting on how delicious the food was and exclaiming: "If only Mommy could cook like that!" All Philip could think about was how much work, energy and love I put into my home-made cooking. He had to keep himself from laughing when the children spoke like that to the waitress. I loved hearing the story of it because it just shows how innocent children are. However, when I had put so much time and effort into cooking our meals, trying to make them tasty and interesting, I have to admit that my feelings were hurt a bit as well. It was not easy for me to try to meet the taste demands of the children and to look after their bodies at the same time. I started my focus on diet when they were so young that they knew nothing else and hadn't accustomed themselves to other food, which they would have missed if I had made the change later. Nevertheless they were sometimes easily seduced by the world of sweets, fast food and easy to prepare meals. We can all be seduced by that at times.

After I had developed my understanding of macrobiotics and felt confident and well able to cook a good variety of dishes, I spent many hours giving cooking classes to people in Ireland. The classes were usually held in my home, but I also held them at a local adult education centre and at a friend's home in Tralee. The best part of it all for everyone was that we would eat the food at the end of the class. Because I was teaching a kind of cooking with which people had no experience, I demonstrated how I cooked the food while explaining my reasoning. The students did not actually do the cooking. I usually prepared the elements of a small meal in the classes, and I had anywhere from 10 to 18 people in a class.

I really enjoyed sharing what I had learned with the class. I would always get nervous beforehand, hoping that I had all the ingredients I would need and that I could answer any questions. There was a great sense of pleasure for everyone when it came to tasting time and people actually enjoyed the tastes. I made pates, chilli without beef, delicious French onion soup without beef stock, and a wide variety of pastry dishes, both sweet and savoury. As I have mentioned before, I had invented my famous "apple pie pizza" which was simply wonderful made with sultanas, lemon peel, eating apples, vanilla and cinnamon. I thought they were amazing and tasty dishes. I had gotten so used to my diet, however, that I always wondered if I found these foods delicious only because I had changed my habits. So I was never sure if people who were not used to this kind of food would like what I had prepared. When they loved the food, as they usually did, I was delighted. They kept coming back to the cooking classes, so I guess that was a good sign.

Because doing the cooking classes was very important to me, I forced myself to establish boundaries, to practice saying no, to handle challenge, to be challenging and to prioritise. I was learning to value myself enough to say no to things that I didn't want to do. I was a loving, caring person, who dearly wanted to please my family and friends, so I went out of my way, often neglecting my own interests, to please or help others. Therefore I needed help to begin to recognise that it was right for me to make choices that might not be what others would have wanted. My cooking classes were so important to me that they gave me a good reason to begin to stand up for myself.

At that time I needed a reason to say no, whereas now I usually find it easy to say no if I don't want to do something or feel something is not right for me, and I find that people still care for me when I say no. This was a hard and surprising lesson for me because I found it really difficult to say no to anyone, family or friends.

I grew and developed as a person despite the difficulties that I experienced doing something a little bit unusual in a very traditional community. My cooking classes were at times inspiring and at other times challenging. I remember a difficult participant in one cooking class. Every time I would speak about some effect of food on health like the benefits of brown rice over white rice, for instance, she would laugh and challenge what I said. Eventually I looked at her and said, "I didn't force you to come to this class, and I realise that you don't like what you are hearing. However, if you kept quiet and listened, you might actually learn something. You don't have to use anything that I say after you leave here, and you don't have to stay, but since you are here, you might as well finish the class." She stayed quietly and came back to the next class as well. This is another example of how I was learning about not just being a dutiful woman, wife, and mother. I was also experimenting with becoming more of a working woman, even though it was in my own home.

For a little while we had a house guest who came home from work, handed me his trousers that he wanted me to wash in time for his next day at work. This was about 7 pm, and the class started at 7.30. I said to him firmly that I had a cooking class starting shortly, and I was not here to wash his trousers. This was a friend of a friend, not somebody we knew well. I was shocked that anyone would have the nerve to suggest such a thing to me. I might have been helpful at another time, but not on cooking class night! Later, I called this guest "The Most Great Last Straw". After him I put an end to inviting guests to stay in our home unless they were close friends or family.

A discovery that revolutionised our diet was that of soya foods – tofu and soya milk. I had always loved puddings and milk products even though I didn't like to drink cow's milk. I went to two soya food conferences in the USA in the early 1980s. I wrote my first book called *The Magic of Tofu* in 1982 and it was published by Thorsons Publishers in the UK in 1983. At the same time as I was very active in organising a large conference for Baháʼís from all over the world in Dublin. I was exceptionally busy at that time, and one thing that I had to do to create the book on tofu was to test out recipes on my family, so every night, there would be something with tofu or soya milk in it for dinner. I doubt that any of us have used tofu that much since that time. I do still use soya milk quite regularly. Soya milk and indeed other non-dairy kinds of milk, like rice milk or oat milk, have provided me with milk for all sorts of uses without the excess mucous formation that some people with lactose intolerance experience from cow's milk.

I was, over the years, becoming better and better known in Dublin for my views on diet, and I was occasionally on the radio. At first I was terribly nervous about being on the radio, but later on I became quite comfortable. I was always pleased to see people improving their lives and health by making simple dietary changes. I was especially pleased that macrobiotic eating was not expensive, so it was available for anyone.

When Scott was 18 and living in London, he phoned me one day to tell me how grateful he was that I had taught him how to eat for health because he was "soooo sick now", and knew what to eat to get better! He then sent me a postcard of a skeleton, which says, "Miss your cooking"! Although it was challenging for the children when they were young to be eating so differently from those around us, later on as adults they were relieved to know the difference between when and how to look after themselves with their diets and when not to worry about it. I only learned much later on that when Scott was a teenager he would sometimes cook bacon rashers in my kitchen when I was out. I never knew it. I don't know how he covered up the very distinctive smell, but I congratulate him for having managed it. I did know when he and his sister smoked as teenagers. They were not able to hide that from me, but I surely never noticed the smell of bacon!

On another occasion, while I was pregnant with Tara, Philip had been to Cork to give a talk on the Bahá'í Faith and a young woman heard him, got talking to him afterwards about food, and she determined that she would visit me to learn about macrobiotic cooking. She was a devout Catholic, and I respected that, so I never mentioned anything to her about the Bahá'í faith. She came out to the house frequently, and we cooked together and ate together too. She was in the theatre, as was Philip, so they had a great deal in common. We lost touch for a while, but one day after Tara died when my children and I were at a Bahá'í Summer School being held in Dun Laoghaire my friend came to the school to give me her condolences and sympathy on the death of the baby. She stayed and met some of the other people who were there, investigated the claims of Bahá'u'lláh and decided to become a Bahá'í. She is still one of my dearest friends, and she thanks Tara for the gift of the Bahá'í faith.

Eventually I felt that I had done about all that I could do at that time with regard to improving my diet and finding natural medicines. There were great improvements in my health and my children were healthier than I had ever been as a child, and yet I knew there was more to learn. I looked at other people with families who ate macrobiotically and the women didn't suffer from bladder frequency as I did, nor did they get anaemic regularly as I did. I still regarded myself as something of an invalid because every day I was reminded that my bladder was not working properly as I always had frequency and urgency. The fact that I no longer got cystitis, as I had so often in the past, was testimony to the effectiveness of dietary change, but I still had not found the whole solution.

In trying to figure out what was wrong and what to do about it, I would imagine that maybe the high fever I had from the encephalitis had caused my bladder to become somehow pocketed, and I would have to empty the little pockets more frequently than if the bladder were still whole. I don't think that there is such a thing, but it was my mind trying to find some explanation, believing that if I knew what the problem was, I could then look for solutions. I just kept visualising myself as strong and healthy, and wondered what to do next.

It wasn't just because of the bladder problems and anaemia that I felt sickly. When we first moved into our second house in Dublin in 1969, I was unable to get up enough energy to wash the kitchen floor. That shocked me and made me feel weak and helpless. By the mid 70s through dietary change I had strengthened to the point where washing the kitchen floor was just one of many things I might do in any day. Nevertheless experiencing severe illness at such an early age had really left its mark on me. At that time I had been so fragile, and I had been treated as sickly by my whole family, so I got into the habit of feeling as if I were more frail than other people around me. That frailty made me fear that my life might be short, and that I mustn't therefore take it for granted.

That is part of what really drove me to heal myself because I didn't want to waste my life through having no energy and allowing my health to deteriorate as I got older. I had experienced my body collapse into illness frequently enough that I wasn't sure that I could trust it. I dreaded the possibility of being a burden to my husband or my children. I think this fear had partially come from having experienced too much illness and been around too much death to really trust that I would live a long life.

I also think that having children had increased my fear of my own mortality both because it put me in touch with life and death through miscarriage and losing a baby, but also because I was aware of being a very important part of my children's life. My death would have a huge impact on them, and I would have hated to be absent from their lives. I had a deep (almost irrational) emotional impulse to be proactive in staying well. I am sure that many people would not respond to illness in this way, but my drive to be healthier seemed to be an important part of my development and thus I was strongly committed to searching further for answers to my health problems.

It wasn't just aspects of my physical health that were not up to a level that I wanted, but I knew there was something else that I couldn't identify; something that was wrong. I can only describe it as a kind of inability to feel all my feelings. I would notice Philip getting angry and saying what he felt, and then getting over his anger. I noticed that I seemed not to get angry. It may seem like a small thing, and it is one thing to be able to control anger, but it is quite another not to feel it at all. I also couldn't understand why I would sometimes hide behind Philip and let him do most of the talking when we were with friends. All in all I just knew that there was a lot more about me that I didn't understand, so I was eager to continue my search for the knowledge that would help me. I realised that as I improved my health, I also helped my family and others to improve because I could share what I had discovered. Thus it wasn't just healing through food and complementary therapies that I sought but healing through self-discovery. I spent quite a while wondering what to study next.

On Reflection

As an adult and a mother I became responsible for the health of my own and my children's bodies. As I grew and developed I realised that nutrition was only a small part of the picture, and that as much as I was on a path to knowledge, I was also on a path to personal discovery. I'd like to use that lesson here, by inviting you to reflect on your own relationship with your health and how you nourish your body.

In what way do we take responsibility for the health of our adult bodies? This is a question that encompasses food, exercise, spirituality, attitudes, beliefs, feelings, and how we heal ourselves when we are ill. Food is certainly a very big part of how we nourish or don't nourish our bodies but it is not the whole picture.

If we start to uncover the underlying meanings and experiences that are caught up with food, we see that food plays an enormous part in our lives. We can use it as a reward or punishment. We can become addicted to some foods and really abuse our bodies with it. Food can replace sex and intimacy. We can get into such rituals and habits about food that it can become like a faith: *I must have this food or create that ritual with food to celebrate or commemorate this particular thing.* Think of the family sitting down to their favourite meal to celebrate a loved one coming home, or the binge eater punishing themselves by gorging on "trigger foods" until they are physically sick. These are both positive and negative rituals that give away our emotional relationship with food.

We are usually completely unconscious of this emotional attachment because somehow we tell ourselves that food is just food. We eat, and we have always eaten, and that is all there is to it. Food is our constant companion for as long as we live. Living with food can become so habitual that it is like living with a person so long that we just take them for granted and ignore them. Food is our most constant partner from birth to death, so in some ways it is our most intimate relationship. It is not until we go on a diet, or a fast, or until we get ill that we may begin to question our food habits and what kinds of foods are best suited to our particular body, lifestyle and situation.

The kind of food we are used to eating depends partially on culture and environment, and the habits of our families. Added to that we are bombarded with directions and rules about what and how we should eat. Blanket instructions for everyone do not necessarily solve our own particular food problems.

Ask yourself, what foods do I know I can eat comfortably that make me feel good? What foods do I know make me feel uncomfortable physically when I have eaten them? What food makes me feel bloated, windy, tired, erratic, sleepy, or sluggish? What foods would I like to find out more about to decide if they are good for me? How much do I eat foods that contribute to my wellbeing? How much do I eat foods that make me uncomfortable? Why do I eat foods that don't work for me?

Even if you know a lot about the current food theories and what is considered good or bad, your body is very individual and actually may not agree with you. It is important to treat any instructions you might receive with a question rather than blind obedience to an apparent authority. We need to develop our own sense about what we eat. Different stages in our lives may also require adjustments and different foods to keep us functioning well.

At times most of us eat compulsively and thoughtlessly. Next time you eat something that you know doesn't agree with you, ask yourself why do you do so? Is that a punishment for a particular act or self hate? Do you eat that because you just like the taste of it, and you don't care what it does to you?

Do you sometimes eat something that you know makes you feel bad because you need an excuse just to go to bed and take time out? In our culture, most people are only allowed to slow down and take time out when they are sick. We have such a strong work ethic that we often have to make ourselves sick just to have a break.

Think about what you do when you are not well. Do you rush to the doctor immediately for anything and everything? Do you simplify your food and attempt to work with your disease? Do you know how to adjust your diet, so that you can co-operate with your illness by eating simply? Do you ever wonder what your illness is trying to tell you or what it is protecting you from?

As we grow and develop often our needs change, and we need to be alert to those changes. When we are very active, we may need different types and amounts of food than when we have a more sedentary lifestyle. If we are working to become more sensitive and caring, we might eat differently than if we want to be more daring and courageous. Food affects our moods as well as our physical health.

It is helpful and interesting to keep abreast of changing views on dietary health and to be aware of your body's changing needs. Finding the right diet is not a quick fix or a situation where once you do some research, experiment with different ways of eating, settle on a method that works for you, and the job is done for life. It is about continuing to be aware of your body's needs because they are dynamic and constantly changing. Don't be put off by this seeming complexity however because what is important is to realise that we can make significant improvements in our health by adjusting our diet even in small steps.

Chapter 9
More Things in Heaven and Earth

My focus in life was changing. Up until this time I had been involved with raising my children and researching food and nutrition. I had more answers to find because I still had some physical symptoms and there were some emotional issues that I didn't understand. It was not just the ever-present physical symptoms in my body that drove me to search for more ways to improve my health. I liked some of the rather different choices I had made such as my decision to become a Bahá'í and my choice to explore how changing mine and my family's diet positively affected our health.

It wasn't much of a stretch for me to think that there must be other ideas in the world that could improve our lives in all sorts of ways. I didn't want to sit back on the sidelines, I wanted to learn, to grow and make changes. I was a rebel with a cause. I enjoyed my search, the challenges that I met, and I was eager to explore whatever was there that piqued my interest. I felt that I had a radar that was able to pick up signals from things that would be of benefit.

In the summer of 1979, the family went to visit my father and my sisters in California. Because of a recommendation from our dear friend Zebby Whitehead, I went with the children to see a woman called Dr Viola Petit Neal. She ran the Biometric Research Foundation. She had a system whereby she would measure what she called the brain radiation and the emotional co-efficient. The brain radiation was about a person's intelligence and showed what kind of work would best suit or most fulfil the person. She said that it often happens that there are people of high intelligence who should be offering their gifts and talents in some way to the world, but because their emotional co-efficient is not at the appropriate level for their intelligence, they simply are unable to be successful in the world. It is a shame because much wonderful work is lost to the world in this way. She gave us exercises to bring our emotional level into balance with our intelligence, and I did these exercises daily with the children for seven months.

The exercises involved looking at geometric shapes in particular ways. She said that in the Ancient Greek universities, before students even applied for entrance, they would spend about a year coming into the halls of learning and concentrate on geometric shapes that were drawn on the walls. This was a fascinating concept to me but I never heard anything like it from anywhere else although in some way I felt it made sense, and I don't know why I felt that way.

She said that people of the time thought that doing that kind of meditation made a person more intelligent. Actually what it did, she explained, was to balance their emotional level with their intelligence level and then the people were able to be more productive.

Having done these exercises in the early 1980s I realised that my own intelligence had improved between taking an IQ test in secondary school and passing the test for Mensa in the late 1980s.

These days we talk about emotional intelligence and spiritual intelligence. We understand now that somebody can have a high IQ, but if they are emotionally illiterate, unable to communicate and relate with other people, they are going to be very inhibited in terms of how they interact with the world. Equally someone who is emotionally intelligent but has not developed their ability to think cannot be so effective in their lives.

If intelligence and emotional understanding are not supported by spiritual values as well as appreciation for and care of the body, people have a less than ideal way of being in the world. Part of the task of living effectively is to learn to understand our bodies, feelings, mind and soul, so they all work together helping each other rather than getting in each other's way and causing difficulties.

Zebby was so keen that I see this woman and do what she said that I felt it was important, and I also felt it made a significant change in the children and me. It was a subtle change, and perhaps not so easy to describe. In some ways I think it opened the doors to all the new things that I did afterwards.

Then the eighties came upon us. Time was moving on, the children were growing up. I was feeling disturbed. Life had changed, and I wasn't getting along so well with Philip. That had been the case for a while, but it was more difficult at this time. With hindsight I feel sure that the loss of Tara in 1971 and my miscarriage in early 1972 would have had a profound effect on my marriage. Those events alone could easily have broken up a marriage right after they occurred. I have since read that the death of a child often precipitates a marriage break up, so I guess it is rather surprising that Philip and I stayed married for a long time after that.

It seemed as if my world was somehow falling apart. I had always said that I didn't mind having a hard time, but I would like to have some idea about how long I might have a hard time for. I had some friends who were very interested in astrology, and I began to see that astrology could be very helpful psychologically and that it might also give guidelines about how long events in life might take. For instance, particular planets that had an impact on my life at any given time could help me to understand what I was experiencing in my life. I didn't expect to be told exactly what would happen but just to get a kind of map of the planetary configurations that were around and what they might mean.

I realised that it was important to maintain my own ability to differentiate between what was right for me and what was not. I wasn't naïvely expecting somebody else to solve the dilemmas in my life. There is a lot of scepticism in the West about such things as astrology and mediumship. Some people, depending on their beliefs, may prefer not to consider such things. These are philosophical and spiritual questions that I really delved into and questioned critically, partially because of some of the public scepticism that is out in the world, because I wanted to be clear about the Bahá'í guidance on the subject and partly because I was sceptical myself.

I feel it is a sign of health to question things that are mysterious before putting yourself into the hands of other people, particularly if you have had a difficult time in life because it could create a crisis of Faith. One may find it difficult to confront experiences that throw our world into question. Some people prefer not to do that, and others are happy to explore differences of opinion and beliefs. I was experiencing difficult times, and while I was sure that there is real intelligence in life, I felt as if I was being thrown onto my own devices to either sink or swim.

As I explored these esoteric arts I also sought guidance from friends and family, but I was looking for guidance from an intelligent system that could give me objective information in my search for understanding and meaning.

I was curious about whether astrology worked or not, and I was willing to try it out in my own life.

I attended classes in astrology in Dublin. I realised, however, that whatever I might learn, I wouldn't be in any position to read for myself, so I asked if there was someone who might do a reading on a tape and post it to me. I was directed to a woman who lived in London.

I wrote to the woman, and sent her my date, time, and place of birth. She duly replied returning a tape with her reading. Her name was Pam, and she has become a lifelong friend. She used astrology in a psychological way to do just what I needed. I think of astrology as a kind of weather map, but it is the weather of our emotional or psychological landscape and our growth patterns. It could help me to understand whether there were storms or wind or rain expected, and how long these weather patterns might last, so that I would have a clearer idea of what I might expect in my life for awhile.

I was suffering a lot because of the difficulties in my relationship with Philip, and Pam was helping me to understand at a psychological level what was happening, and how the movement of the planets were signposts for the coming changes. She said that I was experiencing a transit of the Planet Uranus to my Sun. Uranus is a planet that rules lightning and electricity, and I could expect surprises in the same way that lightning strikes in rather unpredictable ways. She said things will suddenly appear that have not been there before and for which there is no warning. I could argue that she was warning me of this possibility, but still she could not identify exactly what might emerge. She said that the main purpose of Uranus is to remove from my life anything that is not working and to leave me with what is truly right for me. Well, that is exactly what happened.

I found the study of astrology to be very interesting in the way that it can help people to understand themselves and what is going on especially when the circumstances of life become difficult. Pam's astrological guidance helped me to better understand my emotions and navigate through the more turbulent times.

I went to Devon to study Huber astrology for two summers. It is the basis of the astrology that Pam practised. I found that Pam made more sense of the guidelines offered by the movement of the planets than most other astrologers. Very often I would write to her after having attended a class or discussion in astrology and I would say that I didn't think it was the same subject they were talking about. She brought astrology to life and drove it into my understanding by explaining the mythology and mystery of the planets, which made it feel magical to me.

I was very grateful that I was able to afford to have regular astrological readings done by Pam because she was especially good, but readings were expensive. I always wanted whatever I found of help in life to be easily available to everyone. Today there are some excellent astrologers available through newspapers and the Internet. I am most familiar with Jonathan Cainer who is one such astrologer. He, like Pam, uses astrology to help people to understand what is going on for them internally in a psychological sense. He is poetic in the way he writes his daily predictions. Pam is also poetic - she once said to me that the planet Pluto carries the energy of a single blade of grass breaking through the earth. I loved the imagery of that statement.

Pam went to Yale Divinity School, and became an ordained Episcopal Priest. Long before any thought of becoming a priest, Pam struggled mightily with her growing Christian Faith and her practice of astrology. Historically it seems that there has been quite a lot of conflict between Christianity and the practice of astrology. Although I was brought up Christian, I don't remember being aware of this conflict. In May 1983 Pam outlined her concerns in a letter to her local vicar. I loved the clarity of that letter, so with her permission I enclose the following excerpt:

> ...this dilemma is terribly important to me both morally and spiritually.
>
> The question stands: Does astrology work at the hands of the Devil? Is it fundamentally evil? I know it works; the question is under whose auspices?
>
> I find it puzzling that a body of knowledge which is purportedly evil should have brought me to a Christian renewal. It seems further odd that a system which cherishes God's perfect intelligence and acknowledges the existence of His divine plan should be intrinsically negative. Astrology mirrors God's will, His love and divine purpose. The understanding of astrology (i.e. God's plan) is faulty only in as much as humans are imperfect -ungodly, incapable of fully apprehending God's will. Astrology offers tiny glimpses of that scheme He has made for us - but only isolated ones often out of context. The astrologer is only all too conscious of his/her limitations vis-à-vis prediction and forecast.

Modern astrology, unlike its ancient practice, focuses on moral development. Individuals are shown aspects of character which help/hinder growth. Astrologers work closely with psychologists now in developing personality inventories as well as plotting periods of stress/and or comparative peace for individuals who suffer emotionally/mentally. Student astrologers are taught that the stars do not condemn us to one act or another. They merely offer us reminders of our inherent weakness and need for discipline. No serious astrologer pretends that he/she has a direct line to "fate". To the contrary, most astrologers beg the issue of prediction, forecasting altogether by simply not doing it. They simply stick to character analysis.

Occasionally I will make quite precise predictions but only when I have questioned my own motivation, the impact it will have on the individual and when guided by an inner voice which does not contradict common sense and human caring. Forecasting is not my sole interest. What is important to me is to lead others to a tolerance of self, which allows them the possibility of becoming servants of the Kingdom. While astrology, as practised, appears to reinforce egocentric views of the world, I've found that when individuals have come to know themselves through this method (as opposed to pure psychological therapy), they are able to step outside their immediate worries because they know there is purpose in their suffering, that each difficulty brings challenge and opportunity for developing character and that someone known as God has and will guide them appropriately. For the heathen or agnostic this is a beginning. What concerns me is that I too might be thought heathen.

How astrology works has perplexed millions. The scientific materialists among astrologers (not exactly religion's favourites either) insist that astrology works by some causal relationship between the planets and human behaviour. They cite the Moon's effects on tides, female menstrual cycles, and criminal behaviour as evidence that the planets probably have a similar albeit unquantified as yet impact. My own experience is that astrology is a mystery--one that has on occasion thrilled me with its inner balance. Jung's belief that it worked by the synchronistic effect is closer to my understanding, although it too leaves certain questions wide open? Who developed synchronicity?

Biblical references to astrology abound mostly in the Old Testament. Many are contradictory. What does stand out is God's insistence that He does have a Plan and that He doesn't like others playing with it. (Isaiah 44-48) Yet, the New Testament opens quite clearly with a revised interpretation of the "astrologer". Three Wise Men from the East are led to Christ by the Star of the East. (Matthew 2: 1-12) It would seem that if God was truly contemptuous of the Magi, He would not have warned them in a dream not to go back to Herod.

Although I don't presume to equate myself with those who followed the Star in the East to Bethlehem, I share their journey by proxy in travelling via the stars to find Him.

In a more recent communication with Pam in September 2001, she asked that I add the following piece on her behalf:

> Were I writing that letter today it would come from a vastly different level of sophistication insofar as I now ponder astrology from the standpoint of lawyer-priest. Certainly I hear Matthew 2:1-12 (The journey of the Magi-astrologers) in a new way. For me the Gospel now represents God's gracious patience and ingenuity in reaching out to all people wherever they are, in whatever language available. Birthing a relationship with/to God is the point of the Magi's encounter with Jesus. God sees people far off on foreign lands yet draws them near. The language by which God seized me first was plainly through the stars.
>
> Eighteen years later, I'm still dazzled by astrology's gift to human understanding, but am very clear of its spiritual inadequacy before the face of God. Eighteen years downstream, God no longer speaks to me through exclusively masculine language.

I have included Pam's words because they in some way reflect my concerns about contacting astrologers. I consulted these people because I didn't know where else to go and I needed help with feelings and events in my life that I didn't understand. I wanted some positive way of dealing with them.

After I had known Pam and benefited from her astrological understanding for some years, she suggested that I see a medium. I had no idea what to expect, but I trusted Pam and was happy to follow her recommendation. Pam had originally learned astrology in New York working for a major publisher and had read many books on the subject. When she came to London, she learned a lot about mediums by preparing birth charts for over 200 of them. Although I didn't really understand the phenomenon, I did visit two mediums at different times, whom she had recommended. She knew very reliable people. I found that the mediums I visited at Pam's suggestion were able to give me a kind of help that no one else was able to do. They were able to get down to the principles underlying events, so that I could look at them in a more detached way and understand the learning that was there for me.

My first visit to a medium was to see a man called Owen Potts. I was nervous because this was a new experience for me, but as soon as I met Mr Potts his manner put me at my ease. Although he had never met me before, he was able to tell me very accurate things about my life that he couldn't possibly have known. He was also able to reassure me in many ways. He seemed to be able to understand me and to offer answers to some of my questions. There wasn't anything outrageous or unusual about my session with him; he just spoke to me quite simply. I don't now remember what he told me, but I do remember seeing him from time to time when I was visiting London, and each time I felt helped by his clarity and insight.

Later, when Pam felt that I had progressed, she suggested that I see a trance medium. She explained that there are physical mediums who can link into the physical aspects of a client's life, like what was happening with their job, relationships, daily life and such, and there are trance mediums who deal with what is going on underneath all of that. Mediums who work in this way go into a trance and allow a spirit to use their body to speak to the client.

Pam thought I was ready for a real cosmic leap at that time. I went to the trance medium she suggested, the wonderful Ivy Northage at the College of Psychic Studies in London[1].

When I first went to see Ivy Northage I was completely stunned because she gave me such a clear outline of exactly what was happening in my life. It was in December 1985, just two days after my birthday. I had travelled to London to look at houses, since I was planning on moving to London the following summer.

At the time Philip had been working in London for a while. He had begun by working at the National Theatre in *Jean Seberg*, and then he was in-

---

1   The College was founded in 1884 by a group of highly respected scholars and scientists to investigate psychic and mediumistic phenomena that were the subject of contentious debate at that time. Since then the College has grown to incorporate the broader area of human consciousness and spiritual development while continuing to focus on the development and understanding of mediumship, psychic ability, and healing, and the scientific knowledge that supports them. The College trains and prepares professional psychics, mediums and healers in a safe and thorough way.

vited very shortly after that to work in the NT production of *Guys and Dolls*, taking the part of Lieutenant Brannigan.

I was left on my own in Dublin for about two years. Although I was exceptionally busy because I had full responsibility for the children and the household, I also had time on my own to think. I realised that Philip and I had been growing apart, especially since he was absent from our lives for such long periods of time. When we did get together, which was not often, we were finding it more and more difficult to communicate with each other. I felt a degree of tension and defensiveness between us whenever we were together for any length of time. I felt more and more that there was something wrong between us, and I didn't know what to do. I had been feeling this way for many years and didn't know how to improve it. Any chance at reconciliation became more remote when he was living away for so long.

As a result I finally decided to ask him for a divorce. It wasn't entirely that I wanted a divorce, but I didn't know what else to do to resolve the situation. At the time, I couldn't initiate the procedure for divorce in Ireland because there was no legal divorce available there. The only way we could get one was to take it through the British legal system. Philip did not start proceedings, and I was unable to start them, so it seemed as if I had to move to London to resolve the matter. I was never clear about why he wouldn't start them especially because he did so very shortly after I moved to London.

It wasn't just about getting a divorce. I wanted to move to London for many reasons. I wanted to train as a psychosynthesis counsellor. I was passionate about Psychosynthesis, its wisdom and its effectiveness. I knew how much it had helped me and I wanted to be able to use it to help others. I imagined that everyone would want to grow, develop, learn about themselves and change long standing habits that no longer served them just as I had. There was no counselling training in Dublin at the time, but there was in London. Although Scott, my eldest son, had already moved to London, and Shannon, my daughter, was planning to go there when she finished secondary school in about six months, I also wanted my youngest son Brian to be closer to his father. I could imagine that Brian and I would be left rattling around in a big house with two dogs and two cats, while the rest of the family was in London. I felt as if I were being left behind and I didn't like that idea much. I hoped that if I were closer to Philip we might be able to resolve the issues between us. I really felt the need to develop a profession for myself because I feared that I would not be able to support myself when the time came unless I did.

I consider it a privilege to have continued to see Ivy Northage once a year for 12 years. I also attended her course in spiritual realisation. As she explained to me at the beginning, she was a trance medium, which meant that she would close her eyes and go into a trance, which is a very relaxed state of mind. When she was in trance, she was taken over by the spirit, Chan, and she would speak to me with a different accent and use of language. The philosophy that Chan espoused fitted in beautifully with my beliefs, helped me to trust in life and God, and to be more open to new opportunities than I might otherwise have been.

Ivy, or rather, Chan, told me that I was embarking on a new cycle. She said that I had developed myself to a degree that I had used up what I had to gain from past circumstances and was therefore moving on to a new life. She assured me that this unsettling time, which was fraught with fear and doubt for me, was just as it was meant to be in terms of life, growth and development. She said:

> Now the important thing, Dear one, is to understand on a conscious level what exactly is taking place, which, as I've tried to explain, is a movement through life of the degree or point of development in a very wide and general sense. This embraces your personal, your spiritual, your mental [development], and of course everything physical in the way of activity, you see. It is not in any way confined to one aspect or another. It embraces the whole, so your first realisation then is to come positively to the conclusion that all this apparent unrest, inconclusion, apparent doubts and contradictions are merely the furniture or the décor of the room in which you happen to be. They are not happening to you as a person. That is the first thing you've got to be quite positive about.

She went on to say:

> Having decided therefore that you are, so to speak, subsidiary to these varying degrees of unrest and so on, you now look to that which is most relevant to your need at this particular point. It is awfully important when these things are happening to us to know that they come a step at a time, so that everything pertaining to that next half an hour, that next hour, that next

evening, that next day, as it were, will take its own course, moment by moment, hour by hour, day by day. So, you are not now looking over the fence at 'well now if I do this, what about that, and what about that'. You say 'this is here to be done', and you get on with it because it could be a finalising of one thing, which will terminate that, or it could be an introduction of that which would again bring you nearer to the new level.

She gave me these two guidelines for when I was experiencing difficult times:

a) It is important not to take difficult times personally.

b) It is vital to stick with what is right in front of me rather than what is two steps away, or five days away, because I won't really know fundamentally what could be coming.

Ivy was encouraging me to trust life and to manage the challenges in small step by step portions. This was an invaluable teaching to enable me to deal with enormous change. By making sure that I did what had to be done at the time, without trying to guess the outcome, I saved myself many other difficulties. I learned always to do what had to be done to the best of my ability.

She said that my divorce was just one of these circumstances that were coming to an end. She said that my work was changing, but I wasn't leaving behind my previous training. It was that my work was entering a much more "scientific, spiritual, therapeutic area". I recognised that description as one that fitted perfectly my plan to become a psychosynthesis counsellor. I didn't think that it could have been said in a better way, and I took that as an endorsement of my plan.

She spoke to me about the nature of relationship, and how I needed to treat relationship similarly to the way I needed to treat any circumstances, just deal with the here and now, without looking for an assurance for the future. She said:

One's emotions are extremely unpredictable. The tendency is [for people to say to themselves] 'I have suffered so much from that, I am not going to make the same mistake. This time I am going to be sure before I commit myself, do you see, I want to know if this is really going to continue. I want to know if this is really serious, and so on.' All of which, Dear one, forgive me, is non-existent in this step by step thing, do you see. So again with your relationship, Dear one, you are not going to ask if it is permanent or if it is going to last… You are going to say 'am I enjoying it at this moment? If I am, I am going to make the most of it. I don't care what happens tomorrow or the next day, I am enjoying this now.

Her words resonated deeply with me and I felt that if I found myself involved in a relationship again at a later time, I would manage it differently. This was a very wise directive, one that is much easier to hear than to do, but with time and practice, I became much better at living it.

When I looked back at my meeting with Ivy, I noticed that there were two aspects to what she had said. On the one hand she focused on some of the detail of what was going on in my life and helped me to put it into perspective. On the other hand she was a teacher of spiritual development who showed me how I could get more out of life.

In our sessions, Ivy occasionally mentioned one of my relatives who had passed over. When each session was over, and Ivy was coming back from the trance state as if she had just been in a deep meditation, she always had something special to say. Once she mentioned a man who wanted to give me a white chrysanthemum. This was a dear friend of the family who had recently died, and who loved those flowers. I was delighted.

I noticed that each time I went for a reading, Chan was able to speak to me about the particular details of my life at the time and to explain and clarify any areas where I might have been uncertain, enabling me to move forward more surely. I was always surprised by how much Chan really knew about what was happening at the time for me, as well as whatever thoughts and feelings I had that were causing me concern. I could not imagine that such knowledge could come from anything other than the spirit world. No human being other than a close family member could have been so accurate. I regarded Ivy Northage as one of the all too rare "wise teachers of life". She had her own wisdom, which Chan enhanced. In those days I knew of no other way to find such helpful and wise counsel, and I would still today seek out a good medium for wise guidance.

Although I know that mediums are becoming more accepted in mainstream society, there is still a lot of scepticism about them. Of course, I have no doubt that some are better than others, and some suit particular people but not other people. All I can say is that my personal experience of them has been very positive. I haven't felt misled or manipulated in any way by any medium I have consulted. They have simply given me the confidence and support to act on what I felt was right for me to do at the time. I consider myself fortunate to be able to have had annual sessions with Ivy Northage, whose trance work was legendary.

From a Bahá'í point of view, we are urged to investigate the truth for ourselves. In writing this book and in mentioning these things which are quite private to me, I was concerned that people might be very judgmental about my interest in astrology and mediumship. Therefore I wrote to the Universal House of Justice, the international governing body of the Bahá'í Faith, asking for guidance particularly on the subject of writing a book that told a good deal about my life as a Bahá'í and about my consultations with astrologers, mediums and the like. Here is an excerpt from the response that I received:

> The House of Justice warmly appreciates your having written to ask for advice on this matter, and was touched by your sincere motive to share your experience as a way of being of service to others. You mention that many different people and belief structures have been a source of consolation, healing and guidance to you over the years, including therapists, and healers, in addition to your drawing on the writings of Bahá'u'lláh. You also make reference to astrologers and mediums. The Guardian did, indeed, reply to many queries by individuals regarding the relationship between these latter genres of belief and the Faith, and made it clear that the Bahá'í Faith should always remain clear from any such practices. We share with you the following excerpt '…it is absolutely essential that the Teachings should not be confused with the obscure ideas related to numerology and astrology and the like. Individuals interested in them are free to believe in and credit such ideas, and to make any inferences and deductions they desire from them, but under no circumstances are they expected to identify them with the principles and Teachings of the Cause. We must at this stage preserve the purity and sanctity of the Bahá'í Teachings….' In light of such guidance from Shoghi Effendi, the House of Justice asks that you make a clear distinction between Bahá'í belief and any form of occultism that you may wish to credit…. The House

of Justice wishes you all the best for the publication of your book and thanks you for your thoughtful consideration of this matter. (Universal House of Justice, 2001)

In light of this guidance, the reader of my story should understand that my interest in astrology and mediumship is purely a personal one and not connected with my Bahá'í belief or practice. The Bahá'í teachings discourage paying too much attention to such ideas and practices, but do not prohibit individuals from exploring them as I have done. That discouragement served to give me a sense of discernment in my investigation of these phenomena and to find people who were well qualified and respected in their work. Because my experiences with these practices have had such positive effects on my life, I share them with you here without asking you to believe in them.

I find these words from the Universal House of Justice such a comfort. On the one hand they reassure me of my individual freedom to use my own heart, mind and soul to pursue truth and self knowledge to the best of my ability in my own way while on the other they simply ask me to be clear about the distinction between what I learn from astrology and mediumship and what I understand of the principles and teachings of the Faith. I would strive always to do that in any case.

In the summer of 1981 I was planning a trip to California to see my ageing father. I didn't get to see him often, and so I wanted to go with the children to pay him a visit. Shortly before leaving, I discovered an article about Rolfing in a free magazine that I picked up in a health food store.

What I read about this system of body improvement seemed to make a lot of sense. Rolfing is a method of deep tissue massage that re-establishes proper balance in the body. The theory of Rolfing states that when we are born and are still very young, we use our body in the correct way. When we first learn to walk, we usually do so in a perfectly upright manner. They say, however, that as we age, as we copy the habits of our elders and our peers, as we experience trauma, accidents and illnesses the body's proper alignment gets thrown out of balance and we no longer hold ourselves in a straight manner. This lack of alignment in the body affects the flow of energy and the functioning of organs. In my case, when I started treatment I had a pear-shaped figure with my hips bigger than my shoulders. After Rolfing, my hips and shoulders were in proper balance and proportional to each other. I looked more balanced, my clothes hung better on me and my posture was much better.

Since I was going to be in California, I arranged to have my first ten sessions of Rolfing with a woman who lived in Santa Barbara, over a period of about four or five weeks. Usually it was one session a week for ten weeks, but because there was nobody doing it in Dublin at the time and I was in California for only a short time, I had to do it faster. I loved those Rolfing sessions, and I felt better. They didn't take care of my health problems, that is to say those things didn't improve just because of the Rolfing, but they started a whole new phase in my life. One of the important hypotheses of Rolfing is that buried memories are stored in body cells and that when we work on the body deeply, such as in a Rolfing session, these memories can be released. Sometimes people remember buried trauma during these sessions, but for me it triggered memories that began to emerge about six weeks later.

I returned to Dublin from California in early August with my younger sister. She stayed with us for a while, and then she and I went to London for a few days of theatre-going and generally amusing ourselves while Philip stayed at home looking after the children. During that time I found an ad in a theatre magazine which said something like: *the microchip method of weight control*, which I read with interest and made an appointment to go to the place. It was a hypnotherapist's clinic on the Fulham Road, which no longer exists now. I was particularly interested because my weight was always going up and down, and I explored any avenue I could to stabilise it. I was not afraid of hypnotherapy. Not long before that I had done one or two Silva Mind Control courses, in which they said that a hypnotherapist could help people with difficulties in life, and assured us that we were always in control of our minds. Some people believed that a hypnotherapist would be able to control their minds, but I was sure that no hypnotherapist would force me to say or do anything that I didn't want to say or do.

I spent a little while talking to the people who ran the hypnotherapist's clinic and determined that when I returned to London in September I would attend the clinic and do some real work on what I felt was my weight problem. I remember that I rarely visited London from Dublin, but somehow in that September I was due to travel to London twice. I don't now remember why. I said goodbye to my sister after our few days in London, and she got a plane back to California. I flew back to Dublin, and was there until my next trip to London that happened in early September 1981.

When I visited London I usually stayed in the Tara Hotel in Kensington. My life in Dublin was so active with our menagerie of children, dogs and cats, that I never had much time to myself at home. So it was quite a luxury to arrive in London and to find myself able to do what I wanted to do when I wanted to do it. I really enjoyed the time I spent in that glorious city.

Within a day of arriving in London on this trip, I went to the hypnotherapist's clinic, and the therapist dangled a pendulum in front of my eyes and asked me to relax and did all the things that hypnotherapists do. I was a willing subject, so I did relax. Because my presenting issue was a desire to lose weight, one of the first questions he asked me was this: "Was there anyone close to you or in your family who was overweight?" As I replied yes, suddenly memories began to emerge, memories of me being sexually abused by a trusted close family friend. I was shocked, horrified, astounded and all kinds of words like that which can only give a glimpse of my deep feelings that these memories stirred up within me. I certainly couldn't talk about this to anyone else. I thought my mind was playing tricks on me. I left the clinic after about an hour of experiencing these memories and went to the hotel. I was meeting a friend of mine to go to the theatre that night.

Usually when I attended the theatre, I would have to go to the loo before the show started, at the interval and at the end. This time I didn't have to go to the loo at all the whole time I was at the theatre. That means I went five hours without having to go. This was completely unheard of! I had another session with the hypnotherapist during that trip, and more memories emerged.

Later in the month I was back in London and saw the hypnotherapist again, and again memories of abuse came up. I was in complete turmoil inside. Part of me believed these memories and knew that they explained so much about my life, my illnesses and my insecurities. The rest of me wanted so much for them not to be true. When I was at home with my family I couldn't stop thinking about those horrible memories, but I didn't have the courage to talk about it at the time. I planned to return to London a few months later, in January of 1982, when I was going to have a week of intensive hypnotherapy.

My abuser had been dead for a long time, so I couldn't take any direct action against him. I couldn't talk with my family because I couldn't talk about it at all. I was too raw, too much in pain at the confusion. I felt so guilty and worthless. I felt like I didn't deserve to have been married, or to have been a Bahá'í. I thought I was dirty, evil, rotten to the core, and fatally flawed. There was neither understanding nor forgiveness coming from my mind or heart. It was all too shocking for me. I felt as if the floor had dissolved under me, and I was falling into an abyss.

My earliest memory of being abused was at age three, and I have memories of abuse up to age 14. I remember saying to the hypnotherapist at one stage that I could understand how a child of three, five or seven might not have remembered, but I couldn't understand how a child of 14 wouldn't remember being abused. He explained to me that it only takes a few events of a frightening and shocking nature to make a young child bury those and any subsequent memories of such events.

Strangely, I found that I didn't have to go to the toilet for long periods of time when these memories were coming back to me. It made me think that my urinary frequency had not only been an after-effect of having had encephalitis, but that there was also a psychological aspect to this condition. I was both astounded and relieved because I could see a new direction to travel in order to work on regaining my health.

For three years after those revelatory sessions in London I wrestled with my thoughts and feelings and tried to pretend that none of this was true, but in the end I could no longer deny it. I did more work with the hypnotist during that time, and gradually I came to an understanding of why I had buried the painful memories. If an experience is traumatic enough, the mind protects itself from the impact of the trauma by burying the memories somewhere very deep. Those memories may not re-surface at all, but sometimes and in some circumstances they do return.

I sympathised so deeply with that little child in me. I had never before been so acutely aware of my inner child, but when these memories emerged they were of me as a child. As an adult I already knew that my life had been difficult when I was younger. My parents were divorced at a time when such a thing was a rare event, which seemed shameful, and I knew that my mother felt she had failed. My mother was sick and dying when I was a teenager. Now I was seeing yet another difficulty, and I marvelled at the strength and endurance of me as a young child who could survive it all. I was left with a sense of awe at the power of the mind and even a feeling of fear in the face of its power. I had to remember that the power of the mind is there as a protection, which enabled me to remain whole, sane and intact. In order to maintain sanity, sometimes we must forget, repress or deny the things we cannot comprehend.

When the time came for my intensive week-long session with the hypnotherapist, my body reacted very strongly. In the week prior to my departure for London, I got a kidney infection and fever of 104 degrees. I had told my family that I was going to London to do a course in self-hypnosis, which was a reasonable lie and was as much as I could admit at the time. Because the "secret" of being abused is such a secret to the child, the adult who is remembering the events is really frightened of revealing it to anyone. Somehow all that original fear is present at some level in the body, so I wasn't surprised when my body responded by getting ill. My body had frequently gotten ill in my life, and I was used to it. I did my best to take it easy while I had the fever, and I kept talking to my body saying things like: "You had better get over this because we are going to London to see the hypnotherapist on Monday no matter what condition we are in." I said: "You trust this person; you talk with him and you tell him what has happened, and you are safe." "There is no point in being sick. It won't stop us from going. You might as well get better." I repeated like a mantra: "Every day in every way we are getting better, better and better."

We were hosting a Bahá'í wedding in my home on the Friday before my trip, and while I asked friends to help out so that I didn't have to do much, I still wanted to appear and take part in some way. I woke up on Friday morning and the fever had disappeared. I was weak, and I had lost about 10lbs. (What weight problem!) The wedding was beautiful, and I was able to be present, but I didn't have much strength.

The next day, Saturday, I woke up in the morning again with no fever but this time with no voice. I laughed, silently, and I said to my body: "Oh, that is very funny, you think that if you don't have a voice that we won't be able to talk to the hypnotherapist about all these things." I suggested that if we couldn't talk, we were going to write it, so we might as well get better before Monday.

I took it as easy as I could over the weekend, and I packed on Sunday. First thing on Monday morning I was on the plane, and as soon as I arrived in London I checked into the hotel, left my bag there, and went straight to the hypnotherapist. I was coughing and sputtering and feeling pretty weak, but I was there, and I could talk.

During that time many memories emerged and my feeling of shock and horror continued. There were changes, and I wasn't going to the loo as often. I was emotionally exhausted and still quite shattered by it all. I felt alone, isolated, frightened, angry, enraged, deeply saddened to name just a few of the many feelings that I experienced during those few, intense days.

When I was back in Dublin, I really felt that I needed to see someone who was nearby, and I didn't know anything about counselling at the time, so I contacted the hypnotherapists there. I could tell just by speaking to them on the telephone that I couldn't trust them like I could the one in London. My mind wasn't going to open up and share its dark hidden secrets with just anyone. It had already in its own way chosen the hypnotherapist in London, so I stayed with that.

In April I was off to London again for three days. This time I didn't have to go to the loo for periods of eight hours, and that even continued for a while when I was at home. Then I chose to tell Philip. He was very understanding about it, but he asked a lot of questions. He was a curious and bright person who wanted to know. Ordinarily I would have been fine with that, but when he asked questions about this particular experience, I began to feel more and more nervous. I felt I had to go to the loo because of the nervousness, so I got frightened, thinking that real progress would be stopped. I had to say to him that I couldn't discuss it any more.

When you have been sick for a long time, and suddenly there is an indication that significant improvement is there, it is so discouraging when that improvement disappears. I know that was hard for him, and indeed I didn't remain in that blissful state of having to go to the loo only every eight hours, but it was an indication that my body was a good barometer regarding the validity of the memories that were coming up. I was in a very vulnerable state, and my emotions were all over the place at this time.

I went once more to the hypnotherapist in London, where more memories emerged, and then I felt that I had done as much as I could do with him so there was no need to continue the work. I felt that any further work on these issues would have to be local to me in Dublin. I was exceptionally busy at home at that time, so I felt that I had to postpone any further hypnotherapy work for a while. I was heavily involved in organising an important Baha'i conference that was to take place in Dublin, I was writing a book, and raising my young family. All in all, I was rushed off my feet and it was all I could do just to focus on the tasks in front of me, so I put everything else in my life on hold for a while.

On Reflection

Sometimes our most difficult task is to do something contrary to what those around us believe, and yet it may be very important to do nevertheless. Often we may decide to do something because we have been inspired to do so, and it may be in conflict with what our loved ones and society believes or thinks. Often they take our decision personally and feel offended by it, when really all we are attempting to do is to follow our own inspiration. Our motivation is not to hurt our loved ones or to go against our society, but our inspiration to take the next step feels important to us. These kinds of issues arise often when we fall in love and choose a partner, or when we choose a career or even just change our beliefs about particular things. Look back over some of your experiences and see how difficult it has been for you to make the choices you have in the face of the judgment of those around you.

We often slip into believing that our personal evaluation is the truth and that somehow comforts us and helps to give us a kind of security in an uncertain world. This apparent comfort may be shattered quite shockingly when we meet something in our life that is not according to the way we believe life is. If we are happy enough to live with uncertainty, diversity and insecurity, then we can be far more flexible in the way we meet the world around us.

If you believe that your viewpoint is the truth then it will be extremely difficult, nearly impossible, to hear another viewpoint that is at variance with your own. If instead you hold a belief in diversity then you will welcome hearing another viewpoint that is different from your own.

Let's conduct a little test like a kind of experiment – ask yourself, how did you respond to the contents of this chapter? Look at how you felt about the various subjects. Did you dislike any of them? Did you choose not to read any of the sections? Notice your reactions, and ask yourself if your reactions reflect your own values or the values of loved ones or colleagues and people around you, or your cultural or religious background. These questions may be very difficult for you to answer, and you don't have to answer any of them, but you might find them helpful even just to consider.

Are you happy with your response to what you have read, or would you like to have responded differently? If differently, in what way would you choose to respond? Ask yourself how you generally tolerate difference. What have you done in your life that has been different or at odds with people or the society around you?

CHAPTER 10
Growing Up

I submitted the final draft of my book to Thorsons Publishers at the end of May, 1982. The Bahá'í Conference came and went in June of the same year. It took a lot of work for an entire year to prepare for the Bahá'í Conference, and I had neglected other work at home for which I had to make good.

During that time, I also spent a good five months writing my book, and it took me another six months or so to feel as if I had put my life at home back in order.

My book was released in May of 1983, but I had little to do with it because I was living in Dublin, and it was published in England. There were a few reviews, and then it sold at its own pace. Admittedly, in 1983 a book on tofu was not going to be a best seller!

I turned 40 that year, and I had always understood that life begins at 40. Philip was away working at the Royal National Theatre in London, but my children were there to wish me happy birthday. My youngest son, Brian, had tried his hand at making me a birthday cake. I was enormously touched by all the loving care that I received, and yet Philip was not there.

My relationship with Philip had been deteriorating for a while. I was getting better, stronger, feeling a sense of freedom and power that I hadn't felt for a long time, but even as I grew as a person, it was becoming more and more difficult to communicate with my husband, leaving me with a feeling of tension when we were together that was palpable and not very pleasant.

In our early days in Dublin we had been much more in love and united. In many ways it was just the two of us because we had no family there, and only a few friends. We thoroughly enjoyed each other's company and really didn't want much else except to be together. Then gradually Philip got more and more work in the theatre and eventually in movies, and I seemed to have more and more babies! I think the atmosphere of being in a Catholic country where large families were common was contagious. It seemed as if all Philip and I would have to do was pass on the stairs, and I would be pregnant again. I was pleased with my fecundity really because we certainly wanted to have children and because of Philip's age we didn't want to delay. While I was 23 when our first son was born, Philip was nearly 40, and time was always marching on.

As the years went by and I was more involved with the children, getting out more, meeting other people and Philip was more involved with his work, we seemed to have less time for each other. Because he was away so much, I realised that I needed to develop a life of my own, so I was simply not as available to him as I had once been when he was around. Already I was noticing a level of closing down in me, and I found myself wondering if there was something wrong in our marriage.

One year Philip was away for five months in total, and I was feeling bereft, especially because the children were so young. I remember wondering what I was going to do, and feeling as if I wouldn't have had the strength to take a stand and confront him, and even if I did, what was I going to confront him about? He had to work, and I had to look after the family. I somehow couldn't identify a problem. Some of it seemed as if it was about our communication, but we couldn't even begin to communicate if Philip wasn't there.

It was also about living separate lives and the drifting apart that comes with that. At the start of our marriage and for a long time we did have an ability to communicate. As we saw less and less of each other, we became strangers. Looking back I find it interesting that I didn't feel that our gradual alienation from each other was significant enough to take a stand about his long absences. I somehow felt wrong or that I shouldn't feel that way. I reckoned that because I had chosen to be married to an actor, he was allowed to be away, and I was supposed to look after the family, and that was how it was, whether I liked it or not. I felt I was living a variation on the theme of "You made your bed, now lie in it!"

One possible solution to the long separations might have been for all of us to move to London because that was where Philip would have been most likely to find work. But then I realised that no matter where we lived, Philip could be asked to be on location somewhere else. I remember when he went on the maiden voyage of the new QEII as part of an advertising campaign. We could hardly have lived on board ship!

It was very sad, this drifting apart. When the tension built, I became delighted when he was away, but then I started to ask, is this a marriage? It felt more like a long-term liaison with occasional home visits. I do think that for people married to show-business spouses, no matter how much they may love each other in the beginning, if they don't make sure to spend enough time together they can lose that connection.

When Philip was away I was sustained by an idea of our union, a memory of him that kept me going, but I was not having a daily, ongoing experience of his presence. We were not bonding every day over shared experiences, mealtimes with the family, shared tasks, sharing the same problems, making love to each other, and spending time with mutual friends. Those are all bonding things, and the less and less we did it, the more and more I felt the loss and lack of it. I started to feel we were not the right partners for each other, when really the issue was that we were simply not seeing enough of each other.

I was starving for attention. I didn't look outside my marriage for an affair, but I certainly became involved in creating my own interesting events and finding a network of friends. Thus in Philip's absence I was forced to get on with my own life. We had established a marriage and a family, and then he disappeared for a lot of the time. Because of that, I had to become very independent in order to survive psychologically, physically and practically.

Ironically, rather than being pleased that I was managing so well in his absence, I fear that my capability might have made him feel insignificant. I found it almost impossible to be strongly independent and capable, managing everything on my own while he was away and then to become somehow more submissive when he came home, which seemed to be how I felt I needed to be in order to be in relationship with him. I don't think that was actually the case, but it felt as if my boss was coming back to tell me how to manage things when he returned. That didn't feel at all comfortable. I was so sure that he would be proud of me and my ability to manage, and yet it didn't feel as if he was when he returned home and found things a little different than when he had left.

There wasn't much that was different. I might have rearranged the furniture and become involved in the odd course that interested me, but I guess he may have felt threatened by all of it. But I just couldn't sit at home all the time waiting for him. Our family couldn't be put away like dolls when playtime was over to sit silently and patiently until next time.

What was I to do? Our relationship was crumbling, and yet we continued. In 1977 we had bought a mobile home on the coast of Ireland in a little village called Kilmuckridge. I spent much of the summer there with the children, and Philip joined us when he could.

It was virtually impossible to plan any kind of holidays all together as a family because Philip never knew when he would work, and the children had fixed school holidays. We really enjoyed the mobile home, however, and that served us well for a few years. It was just glorious to have nothing to do but watch the children, make meals and go to the beach.

At that time, which was long after Irving Katz had died, we had two standard poodles and they would be there with us, which was great fun in a tiny mobile home! There was no telephone, no post, and no interruption. I loved it. Also it was a rather up-market mobile home with a shower, toilet, and a nice kitchen including a refrigerator, so I wasn't roughing it!

It felt as if Philip and I had reached a kind of plateau, and I held a new hope for our marriage. Still there was a kind of loneliness that I also felt. I had friends who would complain to me about their husbands, and that raised more confusion for me about my own circumstances and what was realistic or fair to expect. I concluded that I enjoyed having a certain amount of freedom and times when I could make decisions on my own. Yet still I had a niggling feeling that I wasn't sure about our marriage.

Then two things happened that changed everything. Since I was young I had had an investment in America that I thought was tiny. It was one of the few investments that I had left having used the others to buy property and to support the family while Philip was away. Then in late 1979 I was notified that this tiny investment which was in forest land, was being taken over by a big paper company, and I was about to receive something in the region of a million dollars more or less from it.

I was amazed, stunned, as was Philip, but he said he wanted nothing to do with it. I thought that was a really odd response, and I couldn't understand why he was angry. When I heard what he said, I felt almost guilty about my news. I recoiled into myself and almost wished I had never had such news nor received any money.

I had already been feeling uncomfortable about the state of our marriage. In the beginning I felt that whatever we had was our joint property, but by that time I was not at all sure of my trust in him.

At the time I didn't really understand what Philip meant, but in hindsight, I can see that he might have feared that my imminent wealth would tip the scales of our relationship and give him a feeling of insignificance and if ever there were a man who would not be considered insignificant by anyone, it was one Philip O'Brien, but perhaps he neither knew that nor felt that at the time.

He seemed to be deeply resentful of my ability to manage in his long absences and that was only made worse by the news that I was receiving more money. I had always had a small income and had periodically in the past received some distribution of money but not nearly that amount. I took that as normal, but sometimes I felt that Philip resented the fact that I had some money. It was only once at a very stressful time that Philip in any way indicated that he was resentful, but I was shocked when I began to understand that it might be very difficult for him to have a wife with money. I never thought of it as a problem until then and now that 'problem' was growing bigger.

I arranged with my father to join him in California for a short time to invest the money while Philip stayed home to look after the children. I was delighted to have that injection of funds, but I was scared that I would get too used to having a lot of money. I felt absolutely sure that it would not last, and I would need to provide myself with a means to make a living for when the money did run out.

And that brings me on to the second thing that happened. Well Philip was out of work for about three years. So suddenly we were at home together all the time, or so it seemed. I guess it was either feast or famine in our relationship, but that really didn't work for us. Philip kept himself busy and set about converting our house on the outskirts of Dublin into flats, so we could sell them individually. That occupied him some of the time, but he often complained about the lack of work available. He would watch the news on television and see the unemployment figures and worry. He noticed how few jobs were available. I said to him, "Look you only need one job: that's all". But I don't think that helped to assuage his insecurity.

We got on each other's nerves during that time, so much so that we would even argue about picking up the children from school. It wasn't that we didn't want to do it; it was that we both wanted to do it just to get out of the house for a time. It was a relief to have a break from the tension.

I kept teaching my cooking classes and working on the Bahá'í conference, but he was so afraid of missing auditions that he didn't work on the conference until the last couple of weeks. I found his tendency to put life on hold while he waited for work hard to understand. I thought it would be better to just get on with life. It was as if he sat in a waiting room rather than living his life because he was always thinking, well he might get that call.

I remember once, during this time, when Philip said to me, "You know we will be together through all the worlds of God, in this life and in the next!" I thought to myself: "oh help" and I said, "Look let's just get through today!" It is funny when I look back on it, but not so funny when we were living it.

Philip and I shared a lot in common, our Faith, the children, the theatre, movies, books. We both loved to read. He would read very fast, and often he would read in bed at night with the light on. That was fine if I had gotten to sleep when he started, but it was not so fine when he did it before I went to sleep. I would lie awake, but I wouldn't say to him that he was keeping me awake, and he wouldn't ask if the light was disturbing me. One day I just got up out of the bed, and said, "I feel like a battery hen!" I went into one of the children's rooms, and I slept in the extra bed there for a month. That had an impact, and from then on he would check with me first if he wanted to read in bed.

But as much as we shared the same interests, there were many areas in which we had different rhythms. For instance, I was better in the morning than at night. I could get work done in the morning, my mind was clear, and I was effective. By the time night time came, I was tired and just wanted to get to bed so I could get up early, about 6 am. That gave me an hour of quiet before I had to get breakfast ready and wake the children up and take them to school. That hour was my own special time when I could read prayers or some inspirational writings and then just dream and muse and be able to have my own thoughts without interruption. It felt like a magic time just for me.

Philip, on the other hand, would work until late, come home from the theatre and not be able to go to sleep right away. I had gotten into the habit of taking a cup of coffee up to Philip each morning when I got back from taking the children to school, and I knew I was angry with him when I stopped doing that after many years.

When he was tired, he would talk and talk and talk. When I was tired, I just wanted to be quiet, and if I couldn't go to sleep, just to rest in my own thoughts. He would start a conversation and keep at it, and I could hardly respond because he would just keep talking at me. I found that irritating, and felt that he was ignoring my needs, because he didn't acknowledge how tired I was.

When we had an argument, usually about something very small, like why I hadn't put something away, or endless things like that, we would stop talking for a while, not days, perhaps hours. Then I would suddenly see the funny side of it, and think to myself, "How could we be arguing about such a little thing? It is hardly worth the angst and tension that is in the air and the cold shoulder treatment." Then I would start to have fun, begin laughing and joking with the children, and gradually he would come around and do or say something silly to get our attention and join in the fun.

All in all, I closed down more and more to him, and yet I would communicate in an animated way with friends on the telephone and in person. I remember once when I said that I wanted to go to visit my father because I hadn't seen him for a long time. Philip responded by telling me I was crazy. He never approved of my having much of a relationship with my father because in some ways Philip blamed him for not being around for me when I was a child due to my parent's divorce. I on the other hand couldn't hold onto that anger for my father because I recognised that insofar as he could be, he was good to me. I didn't like being told that I was crazy at thinking I wanted to see my father, so I didn't appreciate that response.

Then in September 1983, Philip got an audition for a musical called *Jean Seberg* at the National Theatre in London. He went over for the audition, then came back home. He was recalled and had to go over again a couple of days later, and they kept him there. He came home at the weekend to get some clothes, and that was it. He was gone.

By that time the children were 16, 15 and 10. Scott was involved with friends, and he was more interested in spending time with them, watching television, taking time out to go for a walk and having a smoke that I wasn't supposed to know about. He and his friends would spend most weekends in our home. He had a band in which he played the guitar and sang and they would practice in his room. My office was directly under his room, and you can imagine what it was like with the drum and other instruments going immediately above my head, but I was pleased that they were there and enjoying themselves in a safe place.

Shannon, our daughter, was very sociable and she worked every Saturday in town at a clothes shop to make money for a holiday, and I really admired her determination to be self-sufficient. She had loads of friends and was active and out a lot of the time.

Brian was just 10 and often at home with his brother and friends or with me. He would sometimes have friends come over, but at his age he had to rely on me or their parents to fetch his friends or take him to their homes. Nevertheless we had an active and busy household.

And so it began, our new life with Philip away working in London. Philip and I would speak on the phone or write to each other occasionally, but by and large there was a sense of freedom that I felt in just being at home in Dublin with the children. I wasn't longing to do anything in particular except to begin to understand myself a bit better, and to look after my children. I loved my children and enjoyed my time with them, but I was now seeking more understanding, more fulfilment in different ways than I had done before. I was embarking on a new path that would change my life for the better and would eventually provide me with a profession that I loved, although I didn't have any idea when I began that I would become a professional.

On Reflection

We often hurt ourselves and each other by being unable to communicate, to listen, and to honour the other. We sometimes have expectations that are not appropriate. We often don't know how to take responsibility for ourselves or to let go of the other person when that might be necessary.

Relationship is a very important part of life, and we need to be mindful of our relationship to ourselves as well as our relationship to others. In these days, it is far more acceptable to get help when we have relationship problems than it once was. There is help readily available, and it is to our credit to seek it out in order to strengthen our relationships. It is never easy to ask for help, but we have no training in how to be in relationship, either with ourselves or with anyone else. Consider your important relationships, and ask yourself if you need help to make the best of them. Be brutally honest with yourself, and then if you do need help, find ways of getting the help you need.

Some suggestions about help for your relationship might be couples counselling or individual counselling. Even one partner examining herself or himself can do much to heal a relationship if both partners are not ready or available to seek counselling together. There are many books that can throw light on relationship difficulties and how to address them. There are courses that couples can take to help communication. If you seek help and continue to look for what works for you, you are more than likely to find the help you need. In seeking a counsellor, be sure to choose someone with whom you feel comfortable and whose counselling style you appreciate.

Look at your important, significant relationships and note down the things that are working and the things that might not be. Notice if you are secretive about the things that are not working for you. Also wonder if you are getting appropriate support, for example, from friends and family: is their advice in your best interest, or do you find it unhelpful at this time? Notice if you have any negative emotions about admitting that this part of your life might need more support? Perhaps you are feeling a little ashamed or embarrassed. In recognising and acknowledging these feelings, if they are there for you, you are taking a huge step towards being true to yourself. Feel proud of yourself for taking that first step and ask yourself: are you willing to seek more neutral, objective and professional help?

CHAPTER 11
Psycho What?

I was longing to understand the workings of the mind because my experience had shown me how powerful it was. I had devoted myself to exploring the role of food in health and had found a great improvement in my own health. Now, I saw that the role of the mind might be equal to or more powerful than that of food and nutrition. That was such an exciting thought to me. I had uncovered the issue of my childhood trauma when I was under hypnosis, and I knew that there was more work to be done on that issue. However, I also knew that there was a lot more to my interest in the workings of the mind than that.

I read a most beautiful book by Piero Ferrucci (1982) called *What We May Be, The visions and practice of Psychosynthesis*. While I was reading it, I felt as if I had come home. It made so much sense. I could see that this book seemed to grasp the complexity of the human being, and to explain that our seemingly disparate drives, needs, and desires might be harmonised and able to work together in a healthy and productive way.

These are just a few of the aspects of ourselves that we need to embrace and manage:
- our body
- our needs: biological, physiological, security, belonging, love, self-esteem, knowledge, meaning, aesthetic appreciation, realisation of our potential, service
- the senses
- feelings
- impulses
- desires
- imagination

- our thoughts
- our belief systems
- trusting our intuition
- our will
- our Self or Soul
- our personality, which is the vehicle of the Self.

Although we are born with all these aspects within us, we are not given any kind of instruction manual to help us navigate through the various ways in which they interact and work with each other, either positively or negatively. I was deeply saddened by my lack of understanding of how I worked. I wished I had learned more about how I could manage my needs and drives and all the things on that list when I was at school. So I was thrilled to see that there was such an understanding and even more importantly that there was hope of harmonising what sometimes seemed like warring elements within me. Psychosynthesis seemed to be the next phase for me: I knew it could lead me and maybe others to better health in every way.

Psychosynthesis is described as a "transpersonal psychology". It sees each person as a spiritual being who is having issues with human problems and doesn't focus on just the problem. It holds two views: 1) Each person is a "Self" or a soul who is a unique individual with a purpose in life, a huge capacity for love, intelligence and creativity; and 2) Each person is also a human personality with an interesting blend of physical, emotional and mental capacities. People usually seek the help of psychosynthesis counselling or courses because of the pain they experience in life. It is through a growing relationship with the Self and its purpose in life that the individual is able to find the motivation to change, to grow and to find resolution and meaning in the painful experiences they have undergone.

Because of its interest in the Self or soul, I wondered how psychosynthesis and religion might relate to each other. Dr Roberto Assagioli, the founder of psychosynthesis, said:

> Psychosynthesis does not attempt in any way to appropriate to itself the fields of religion and of philosophy. It is a scientific conception, and as such it is neutral towards the various religious forms…Psychosynthesis does not aim

nor attempt to give a metaphysical nor a theological explanation of the great Mystery – it leads to the door, but stops there. (Assagioli M.D., 2000, p.5)

Psychosynthesis is not identified with any particular religion or spiritual approach. I was really happy with that because I didn't want to follow a dogma, nor align myself to a particular philosophy in order to be involved with psychosynthesis. I saw psychosynthesis as a science of the soul and the personality, and as such, it fit in very well with my religious beliefs. One of the Bahá'í principles is that science and religion go hand in hand. I felt that by understanding psychosynthesis I would find a way to live my Faith more truly because I would be able to better understand myself as a person, to change destructive habits, and to lead a more fulfilling and effective life.

Assagioli was a student of Freud, so he was rooted in analytic thought, but like Jung, he suggested that we are more than just our drives and our pathology. We all have potential as well. Although he doesn't philosophise about that or make a religion out of it, nonetheless it is something that resonated with me.

I applied to do a Foundation Year in Psychosynthesis at Eckhart House, the local psychosynthesis organisation in Dublin, in the summer of 1983. Miceal O'Regan, a Dominican priest who was a man with a great breadth of vision and Catholic understanding, was the director of Eckhart House, and he taught courses there. I did a preliminary course for a week in the summer first, and then I began the year's course, which usually took place on one weekend a month. There were explanations of theory as well as exercises to give us an experience of the theory. Thus I learned not just by listening to lectures, but by participating in group interaction, meditation, visualisation, reflection, writing and drawing.

Meditation is a profound system to help us relax deeply and to enable us to become aware of thoughts and feelings that are deeper than our normal waking consciousness. The subconscious mind speaks to us in images, not in sentences and paragraphs. We are most familiar with subconscious messages or activity in our dreams. Meditation leads us into a state that is similar to the nearly sleeping or dreaming state, where we are more available to impressions from the subconscious. When we develop a relationship with these images we can come to understand ourselves at a deeper level than if we were just talking about things. The meditative state provides a place in which to explore our feelings, experiences, beliefs and to communicate with a deeper presence inside that I can only describe as my soul or an experience of me that is more neutral and less involved with the minutiae of day to day living.

As I became more comfortable with meditation, my counsellor was able to guide me into a meditative state and help me by introducing the use of imagery. Working with images bypassed my conscious mind and my sceptical, critical nature, which only too easily said, "Oh no, this cannot be right, it is ridiculous." It is our subconscious mind that holds our programmes, deep emotions, memories and experiences, and it determines our life. Regardless of what we may think or believe about ourselves consciously, often the subconscious mind tells a very different story. By working with an image of any dilemma I was experiencing, I opened the door to a lot of repressed material that, once aired, no longer blocked my energy.

One of the things that I appreciated about psychosynthesis and with psychosynthesis-trained counsellors and psychotherapists is their real understanding of the contra-indications to meditation. I have seen books and met other practitioners who have no understanding of the fact that meditation can be extremely dangerous for anyone who has had any psychiatric problems or history. Meditation, as wonderful as it is, is not suitable for everyone. I cringe when I see any unguarded recommendations that everyone should meditate. Meditation can have disastrous effects for someone who has had a psychotic episode or has ever heard voices, even if any of these things have happened a long time ago. When Miceal spoke of meditation in the context of the course, he warned us that meditation is not just about good images: there can be images that are very frightening. We can work with them, but the meditative state is not one to be played with nor entered into lightly.

One of the subjects in our course was that of the body, feelings and mind. I really enjoyed focusing on each one in turn and coming to understand their functions individually. I am always surprised now when I ask someone, "What are you feeling about that?" and they respond to me, "Well I think…" A feeling is not a thought and vice versa, but they are often confused. One of the difficulties that people experience is that they are often unable to express feelings in a healthy way. Some feelings are perfectly acceptable like love and joy, enthusiasm and optimism, but other feelings like anger, rage, grief, sadness and despair are often denied because we think of them as being unacceptable. Actually we have our feelings for good reasons, and they need to be acknowledged and expressed. I find that much of the difficulty that people experience within themselves and in relationships is because of unexpressed feelings. I know that I thought of myself as someone who didn't really get angry. I found out in the course of therapy and psychosynthesis courses that I did get angry, and it was fine and healthy to do so. I also learned how to feel my anger and express it in appropriate ways that were harmless to myself and others.

I had weekly sessions with a psychosynthesis counsellor, and she frequently used imagery with me to help me deal with my feelings and their effects on me. One of the exercises that I remember most during my time with my counsellor was that I had to do a meditation on my body before every session. I imagined an image of my body, and then I drew that image. The first image I got was of a heavy black lead weight, and the second one was one of a vase of dead black roses. I saw quite clearly that I didn't have a very positive feeling about my body! Over the three years that I spent with this counsellor, I gradually came to get vibrant and alive images of my body as a beautiful creation, which of course it is.

I'll give you another example of working with images. One day I went to my counsellor with a seriously painful back. I had arrived after having just been to a chiropractor who had managed only to make my condition worse, and I was having trouble walking. I sat down opposite my counsellor. She invited me into a meditation and led me into a more relaxed state. Then she invited me to picture my back. I saw in my imagination a very dark brick wall. It was tall and thick and black and was preventing me from moving. This is how our conversation went:

Counsellor: Describe how your back is feeling, and what your experience is of this very painful back.

Jane: I "spoke" in my mind to this wall telling it how difficult it was for me to walk and what pain I was feeling.

Counsellor:	Would you be willing to ask the wall what it wants from you?
Jane:	It wanted to keep me hidden.
Counsellor:	Would you be willing to ask the wall what it really needs from you?
Jane:	It really needs love from me.
Counsellor:	Now I invite you to become the wall briefly. Just take on the role of the wall, so you can speak to Jane sitting in the chair.

As soon as I did that, I was suddenly in the midst of a terribly frightening memory of being abused. I experienced the fear and pain, the feeling that I was surely going to die because I didn't understand what was happening to me. I just cried and cried in front of the counsellor. It was as if a dam had broken, and I felt as if I would never stop crying, but gradually I did stop. It was as if that pain in my back was giving me a way into a memory that was in some way controlling me and blocking my progress. The feelings that had been present at the time of the memory were too much for a small child to process, so they just got buried in my body. After I had experienced the feelings and released that memory, my counsellor gently brought me back to the present day and time. She dealt with any questions I had. After that session, I went off home and my back got better very quickly. Each time we worked in that way with imagery, I realised something profound about my life or I triggered the release of a memory and feelings associated with it, and then I would notice an improvement in the way I was feeling or in the way my body behaved and I gradually started to heal my physical infirmities.

I began to have an enormous amount of respect for the faculties with which I was born: my body is constantly working for me, taking care of my life in the world. It actually works for me 24 hours a day. It never goes on holiday or asks for a day off. It deserves my genuine care and attention.

My feelings include my emotions as well as my physical senses: vision, hearing, touch, smell, and taste. All emotions are useful signals to us when we acknowledge them. They are just different kinds of signals than the ones that we receive from our senses. They give us information about what goes on within us as well as what goes on around us. It is easy to accept what I consider to be positive feelings. It is often difficult, however, for me to accept hostile or negative feelings like anger, aggression, rejection, inadequacy, failure and despair. Pain looked at and held, heals, but pain pushed away is very destructive. When I have been able to allow myself to feel very difficult emotions without trying to deny them or to push them away, I have found that they eventually lighten, and they bring me to some new realisation.

My mind is a wonderful thing, which helps me to move through the world. It can be extremely effective and positive. Equally it can be extremely destructive and negative. When it links up with my feelings, then its capacity to be positive or negative is simply increased. It can be enormously creative, and it can cause me to act on my perceptions and the impulses that come from both my intuition and my instincts. When my mind is sharp and clear, I can be most effective in my life. Thus my awareness of how I am in any given situation comes through my body and my feelings but it is named and identified by my mind. Without my mind, I couldn't identify or act on any of the signals that are given to me by my feelings and my senses.

Even the term "mind" is not as simple as it may sound because we have our concrete mind, which deals with practical, concrete reality as we know it, and the intuitive mind, which works much more creatively with images and impulses. We can get an idea with our intuitive mind, but it takes our concrete mind to bring it into reality.

What is really of interest to me is that we grow up with certain ideas and belief systems that were part of our families. When we become adults, we may have very different ideas and belief systems to our parents, but unless we become aware of our original constructs that we grew up with and sublimated and that are no longer working, we are in conflict. These constructs, formed from our earliest childhood right up to maturity are a natural and essential part of life and serve an important function in enabling us to blend with our family. It is only when these constructs differ from our current beliefs that they cause conflict. We are often unaware of these inner conflicts and the simple act of becoming aware of those differences helps us to integrate them and to find peace.

Therefore, we don't have to have experienced extreme difficulties in childhood to benefit from the teaching that psychosynthesis provides. For instance it is sometimes the case that our parents want us to pursue a particular career or life path, and although we may choose to fulfil our own heart's desire and take a different path, we may find that we don't become as successful as we think we should. Some of our lack of success may be due to guilt over going against our parents wishes, and when we realise that we still hold that guilt deeply within us and can begin to heal it, we may then become successful in our chosen career.

Then I was introduced to the idea of sub-personalities, which came as an enormous relief to me. As part of understanding this concept, we did an exercise with one other person on the course. That person asked me, "Who are you?" not once, not twice but repeatedly for several minutes. Each time I responded with a different aspect of myself: I am a wife. I am a mother. I am a friend. I am a cook. I am a housekeeper. I am a Bahá'í. I am a student. They went on and on. Each of those identifications was a sub-personality. In just a few minutes, I had identified 50 people that "I am" and I hadn't completed the list. After I finished the exercise and looked at the list of the different people that I am, I was rather astounded. I was also delighted because I immediately thought, well, if there is something not working in one or two of those areas, then there are many others about which I feel content. So my problem area is not all of me.

I was interested to know that some of the more important Sub-personalities, like "mother", are actually made up of our experiences of our own mothers, other mothers, mothers that we liked, mothers that we didn't like. So in my role of mother, I was responding to both good and bad experiences I had had throughout my life. In some ways I would be mothering like my mother. In other ways I would be mothering in rebellion to what my mother did. It was all very complex, but it meant that I could begin to think about how I behaved as mother and change my behaviour if I would rather do something differently. The same applied to "wife" and any other sub-personalities of mine. As well as these more externally-recognised sub-personalities I also had more internal, pervasive sub-personalities like the one who continually criticises me, or the inner child, who feels frightened, hurt, abandoned, and lost and whom I really needed to get to know, care for and protect. In my private moments at home, I often felt that my tears were her tears that she had been unable to express all those years ago. I realised also there are many sub-personalities that we can never know.

All of these ideas were very new to me. I was someone who read a lot and yet I had never come across psychosynthesis and its vision. I was very excited about what I was learning. In my time at home between my weekends at school, I began to realise how important it was that I was spending time learning more about myself. My growing understanding of myself was leading to a greater sense of inner strength. That inner strength came from a growing freedom from old, destructive habits and fears that had dictated my life and robbed me of my free will. This freedom came from the slow and painful experience of examining my behaviour with my counsellor and resolving any behaviours that were rooted in the past, like the example of my painful back.

There are people who wonder why anyone would spend time going over such painful issues. I can certainly confirm that doing so is worth all the effort because I was finding a real sense of my own free will and a renewed ability to make choices. I was no longer operating on automatic pilot, reacting to events just as I had always done, and was learning how to take some distance and choose my responses. I felt that my own self discovery, painful though it was, seemed to be giving me a degree of psychological freedom that I had never before known but that I could really enjoy.

And so the life of my inner world, which included my feelings, thoughts and belief systems was going through an enormous change that would improve my health and my effectiveness immeasurably. Already I noticed that my bladder was responding far more normally than it had for years. My recurring back problems stopped recurring. My endless bouts of colds and flu lessened dramatically. My experiences of inappropriate guilt and shame decreased, and I began to feel a new sense of my own value and worth that was more substantial than I had previously felt. Before I began the course and the weekly therapy, I would feel enormously guilty about the slightest mistake. My feelings of guilt had been far beyond what was reasonable given the small nature of the mistake or failure, but I was beginning to understand that and gain perspective. All that was needed was an apology and a correction where possible. I was learning to feel my anger and express it in ways that were appropriate but not harmful. All of these things were happening, and it was a very difficult but very rewarding journey.

Philip was working away in London in a show at the National Theatre called, *Jean Seberg*, and he came home at Christmas time. We wanted to work on the problems in our marriage, and we sought help from some friends. However Philip had been offered another acting job at the National Theatre, and it was to play a role in *Guys and Dolls*. The drawback was that if he accepted that role, it would mean he would be away from Dublin for at least a year. During his Christmas break, he made the decision to take the part, and he soon left. Then it was real. Then I was on my own with my children, managing our household as well as being landlady for our other house that we had let out as flats.

I had originally thought that he would be gone for a few months while working in London. I never dreamed that he would be away for well over a year or more. I didn't know what might happen after that. At times over a period of a couple of years when we were arguing, Philip had threatened to divorce me but he never did anything about it. Therefore I had to wonder if he was choosing to put himself in London for such a long time as his way of saying goodbye to me. We were not communicating well enough to discuss it, and I was afraid to ask what he meant by that for fear of his answer. I had mixed feelings about his going to London. On the one hand, there was a great deal of tension between us when we were together, and I didn't miss that. On the other hand, this was my marriage, and he was the father of my children, and I just felt abandoned.

Although my husband was gone and I felt lonely, I was not entirely on my own at all. I had some dear friends who helped in whatever way they could, even to the point of saying to me, and meaning it, that I could contact them any time if I had any problems. A wonderful woman helped in our home, and I will always be grateful because she was a true friend to me, supporting me, keeping the place in order, helping with the children and anything that became necessary in a busy household. My two older children stayed awake later than I did usually, so there was someone who would let the dogs out into the garden last thing at night before bed. It was very comforting to have older children who could take some responsibility around the house. They looked after their younger brother, each one taking care of him for one day a month when I had a psychosynthesis weekend. I was at the stage of gradually letting go, giving them a little more freedom bit by bit. There is a very delicate balance to this task, and parents certainly do not always get it right, but it is a kind of half and half mark, and I am sure I made errors, but I wanted to support them where possible and let them take the lead where possible.

As much as I enjoyed being at home and looking after the family, I also really looked forward to the next psychosynthesis weekend. At one of the weekends, Miceal spoke about the art of "disidentification", as he called it. He said it is the "art of remembering that at any time, I am more than any of my experiences". When I heard that, I began to see that when I got caught in any negative feeling or thought I would know that there were other options available in that moment. That negative thought is not my only feeling or thought. I knew it would pass because that was not all of who I am, so I needn't be consumed by it. Thus I could have some perspective even when I was in some intense emotion. That was extremely helpful. As a result of that principle, I gradually was able to find within myself that neutral point that I called "the Observer". With that neutral "Observer", I would experience thoughts or feelings and at the same time be able to step back and observe myself thinking those thoughts or feeling those feelings.

Using this tool I could decide if I wanted to continue those thoughts or feelings in the same way or a different way. I especially noticed this principle when I was obsessing about something that I should say or do in response to a disagreement, and I would be thinking "you should say this or that to the person". That thought could circulate in my mind rather relentlessly. Then if I didn't want to continue the repetition of the same idea, I learned to say to myself, "All right, I have heard what you have said. Thank you for your input, and we are doing things differently now." I began to understand that if I hadn't said what I wanted to say at the time, then I can just forget about it. Alternatively I can, if I still wish, bring up the issue later and say to the person, "You know I was thinking about our argument, and I came to think this or that".

In some ways these years were the most painful in my life. In other ways they were the most exciting and joyful because I was actually becoming stronger. It took a lot of work and a long time but I was getting better in terms of my physical health and in my ability to feel my feelings, to observe my behaviour and to express myself clearly. Psychosynthesis counselling was working. Towards the end of the foundation year we were asked to do an exercise. We were asked to look at where we have been, where we are now, where we are going and what we need to get there and then to write a "Once upon a time story" about the journey of our lives. I want to share mine, so you can see how profound it was for me:

My Story – June 1984

Once upon a time, I was engulfed in a big ball of fire; and every time I turned to be near the warmth, I was burned; and the flames seared my body so that it was raw and tender and painful and weeping; and I crawled with my badly deformed and bruised body through this ball; and as the top layer of skin began to close over and heal, I would once again look for warmth and comfort; and once again, the flames would burn too hot, and once again, the wounds would burst open and fester and bleed and weep. I longed for release. I cried for someone to hear me, for someone to answer, for peace, for joy, for comfort, for rightness, for being; and yet I found only the same sequence of events again and again and again. I longed for death as release. I could see no other place where I could go, no direction in which I could turn.

So, I built walls around myself thinking, "maybe, if nobody knows I am here, maybe I won't feel the pain of too much loving, maybe, I won't feel the pain of desire, of need, maybe, I can dispense with needs and desires"; so the walls grew, and they became stronger and thicker; and I knew how to move through the flames with speed, carrying my sturdy walls, and I learned the rules, what was right and what was wrong; and I tried and tried and studied and learned, and still, my body was damaged, and I was alone and hurting and still crying out for help, for someone to love me and care for me; but nobody could find me, and one who thought he loved me, loved the walls because they gave him the distance that he needed, so he didn't have to look at his own self.

The longing, the niggling sense that much was missing, the searching everywhere for a clue, a key! The fire was hot and full of power, and I took on the power to maintain my walls and negotiate this life, and I learned well, and did what I was supposed to do. I played the game by the rules; and still

I was lost to myself and to others, abandoned and alone, in spite of the fact that most people wouldn't have seen that.

I searched through God and religion from which I took, in addition to a real sense of security, more rules, more guilt, more sense of non-acceptance of myself, of my rotten inner core, of my badness, inherent in me. I tried to be good. I was kind and generous and caring, but I still felt bad. I couldn't see my anger, my pain – I couldn't look.

Then suddenly somebody loved me and saw through the walls and loved me for who I am and began to help me take down the walls little by little, one chip at a time, and I began to trust, little by little. I had thought that I was honest, but how could it be honest to build walls and hide who I am? I had thought that I was caring, but I was simply terrified of losing a friend, a loved one, terrified of separation, abandonment.

With the help of my friend, I dragged my weary and blistered body to the wilderness and in that deep and private place, I began to look at where I was and who I was. The air was cool and clear and crisp; so I could take out the little parts of myself one by one and examine them and see how they fit or if they fit or if I wanted to change them; and then came the job of sorting, of removing, of replacing, of organising, of deciding what to keep and what to dispense with. Some of the things that I removed, I did so with much pain, and some fell away easily; and it was a huge job and required much attention, but my body was feeling cooler, and healing was taking place; and in order to feel the cool breeze against my pain-ridden body, I kept chipping away at the walls, and the pieces fell away, and the breeze came in to me and healed me.

Then, with more help from my friend, I found that I could walk; and my foot was unsteady, my step, hesitant; but I moved forward out of the wilderness and toward the mountain. It was a long and arduous journey, but somehow I grew in strength as I walked along, and somehow I kept going. I couldn't turn back, and then my friend noticed that I wasn't rotten; and he bade me look at that, and I did; and I resounded with shock and surprise; and then he showed me that I was beautiful and kind and caring, and that I could feel and did feel anger, jealousy, hurt, pain, fear; and with all that, that I could love and feel and care and help and be; and then he bade me endure separation and rejection, and I did, and I was growing in strength and in being; and my body was becoming more whole and beautiful; and when I travelled up the mountain, and the way grew steeper, and I lost my foothold on the loose rocks, still I progressed and knew how far I had come and how near I was to the top of the mountain; and I was being, and I was dropping my rules, and I could feel acceptance and love and well-being; and I had survived, and I had improved, and my body was becoming more and more beautiful. And I know that when I walk through the snow at the top of the mountain and see the sun and the bright clear sky and receive my bouquet of red roses, I will have arrived at my own womanhood, my sense of being of well-being, of being loved for who I am, not for the walls around me.

The most frightening part of it all was learning to allow my sense of openness and trust to let what happens happen. I can flow like a river, float like a leaf in the breeze and live with the magic, mystery and strength of my trust in life. As I trust more and more, open up more and more, I am learning to love, play and have fun. Also, it was terrifying to look at myself, but if I am loved, and I know that, I can do so more easily. I know my strength, power, fun, magic, joy and peace. I can love even with pain, hurt, anger, despair and rejection. These qualities are mine, and I can continue my life trusting in my qualities.

I am reaching my being, finding who I am. The journey is long, and I am weary, and I am coming to the end of it, and I am grateful; and I will, when I reach the end, know who I am and be able to show myself to others.

I am seeing the perfection in it, the need to confront the issues, the need to examine, and so it goes on, and I am healing.

AND THEY ALL LIVED HAPPILY EVER AFTER

THE END

I still look back at that story and see how poignant and relevant it is to me and this personal journey of self-discovery.

For the first year of regular counselling, I spoke only with my counsellor about my abuse. I was unable to speak about it in the group during the psychosynthesis weekends. I could hardly speak in the group at all. I felt so timid and nervous at the idea of speaking. When I did manage it, my heart beat hard and loudly beforehand, and afterwards I felt exhausted.

After the first year, there was a summer school in England run by the Institute of Psychosynthesis in London where I attended a course in Gestalt and Psychosynthesis. The facilitator was excellent. Gestalt is a very down-to-earth psychological system that marries well with the soul approach of psychosynthesis. There was a session with the group on a Friday night. Several people were expressing powerful feelings, and suddenly I began to speak. I told my story about how I had only recently remembered that I had been sexually abused as a child. I told them about the pain and the agony I had felt when I was remembering it. I was shaking all over and deeply crying. I kept forgetting to breathe, as we do when we are afraid of something. The facilitator stood behind me with her hands on my shoulders saying, "Keep breathing, in and out, in and out". It was like an almighty torrent of energy that poured from my lips as I, for the first time in a group, shared something that was so painful to my heart. I was feeling hot and cold and when I was finished, I was completely exhausted. However, I had done it; I had shared my pain with other people whom I trusted in the group.

After it was over the facilitator told me what courage it had taken for me to do that. She said that when I went back to my room that night maybe someone should go with me and sleep in the room with me because I might not want to be alone. Somebody did walk back with me and was willing to sleep in the room with me, but I said I would be alright. The facilitator said that if, when you are in bed tonight, the shaking in your body should start again, let it happen. Don't worry about it and don't try to stop it. She said that my body had to release all that pain. She said that I had to be careful because I had just opened my heart in a way that I had never done so before. She said when you go home, you will have to take care of yourself. If you are cold, make sure that you put a sweater on, if you are lonely or wanting company, phone a friend and ask them to come over just to be with you. She said that if I took care of myself now, I would soon be able to open myself up emotionally in a way that I had never before been able to do. She repeated that it was extremely important to take care of myself now and for the foreseeable future because I would be extremely vulnerable after this experience. The facilitator told me that memories that came up in hypnosis have to come up in daily life so that the feelings connected to them can be released. She said that would be the next stage and it was difficult and very painful, but the only real healing would come when that had happened. I had already experienced a good deal of that with my counsellor.

I went back home and I did take care of myself, and I was improving. I could feel my life getting better. It was still early days, and there was still much to do. With all the pain, there was the joy of a kind of psychological freedom that came from getting to know myself better. I felt very vulnerable, but I was really learning to be my own observer. When I was hurt or disappointed, and when I would feel vulnerable or dependent or weak, I would also be observing my behaviour, so that I wasn't so completely engulfed in every experience. This was a gradual development. It certainly didn't stop me from feeling any emotions very deeply, but it did enable me to recognise behaviours that I wanted to change. I would then go to my counsellor and say that I had had an experience of getting my feelings deeply hurt by what someone had said. I had then withdrawn from that person for a period of time, but I would rather have responded differently. We would look at what happened, and we might do some work with imagery around my feelings and the experience. That work would lead to another memory where I might have been hurt before, but wasn't able to express the feeling, and that would free up more energy and enable me to have a choice about my behaviour later on, somewhere down the road when another such incident would occur.

The release of memories would cause a realisation, what we call an "Aha!" experience. That would help me to see the pattern and how it was that I would always respond in a particular way to a particular type of situation. The process of changing that habit took some vigilance and discipline and careful observation of what I was doing. I did change, however, and I went through the necessary steps to do so.

For anyone who has never experienced counselling or psychotherapy, I can say that it is a wonderful system. I was able to speak with my therapist about whatever was on my mind, whether it was issues with my marriage, my children, my childhood, my physical health, my longings and dreams and desires, and whatever else. I could count on gaining some insight and seeing some aspects to my concerns that hadn't occurred to me before. Sometimes those insights would come from me, just by airing my thoughts and feelings. Other times, my therapist would guide me to an understanding. Often I would be wondering what it was in me that was causing people to respond to me as they did. For instance, if I was feeling worthless, then people around me might be more inclined to treat me badly. My feeling of worthlessness might not have been one that I acknowledged in myself. Once I realised that I felt that way, I could then decide whether or not I was truly worthless. I could also experience the sadness about feeling that way about myself because such a feeling just doesn't do justice to me.

Having a therapist present when I speak these thoughts is important and the therapist is a witness; they hear me when I speak. If I can speak my heart and my pain, my confusion and vulnerability, my anger and despair to one person who really hears what I am saying, that in itself is very healing. That is why it is so important for people to be able to speak candidly to their loved ones. Just saying something, no matter how foolish or "negative" or painful, gets it out into the air and frees the person of it, so he or she can consider it more clearly. A good therapist is worth their weight in gold to me. I don't go to therapy any longer because of some huge issues that I have, but I go to therapy to have a kind of consistent time and space when I can be myself and look over whatever may be on my mind about which I want a better understanding. It is like having a best friend who has the skills to help me to bring about the kinds of changes I want or to just be with me in whatever way I am without judgement and without an agenda.

And suddenly the year was over. It was summer holiday time, and the children were home from school. At times they went away to visit their father in London. They went separately because he was, by that time, living in a flat not far from the National Theatre, and there wasn't room for more than one child at a time. I was looking after myself as I had been advised. I was still in a quandary about the state of my marriage, still wondering what to do, if anything, but thinking that there was something wrong. Philip had come home for a little while to get some furniture for his flat, and he had nearly cleared out our living room, so I began to think about what I wanted to do to replace the furniture. I went to London during the sales and found a sofa that would work for a reasonable price. It was sent over to us in Dublin, and there was more to do as I looked around the house. I had applied and been accepted to do a degree course at Trinity College, Dublin in Single Honours Psychology. I was still concerned about having a profession, and I knew that there was no training in psychosynthesis counselling on offer at Eckhart House at the time. I was continuing with weekly therapy to work on my issues. I saw that with each realisation, there would emerge another layer of understanding to be absorbed in the slow step by step process that seemed to take such a long time, but in some way ensured my continuing sanity. I knew that if the process of recovery from my abuse had been too quick, I might not have managed to stay afloat and take care of all that needed care around me. Even though I may not have been perfect in discharging my duties, I was certainly adequate. I looked forward to the coming year and the new things that I would be learning.

On Reflection

In our world we seem to value thinking and mind above all else. We are not encouraged to listen to our bodies, to look after them well and to really value them. Many of us hate aspects of them and do as much as we can to change this dreadful vehicle that carries us through life. While there are great movements towards improvement, we often go to the gym to whip our bodies into shape or go on diets or have cosmetic surgery, and why is all that? We are so unsatisfied with our bodies.

Our bodies are very finely tuned advanced pieces of equipment that deserve our best attention. They give us loads of information about our inner world, how we are feeling, how we are responding to whatever circumstances we meet. They also tell us a good deal about people around us. If we have an instinctive response to someone that makes us feel uncomfortable, where do we feel that discomfort? We feel it in our bodies, but we do feel it. Our bodies are very sensitive and wise, but if we fail to listen to them or attempt to understand what their message might be we are not using a powerful resource within us.

Remember that your body works for you 24 hours a day every day. It never asks for a holiday or even a day off. Look at how you feel about your body. What do you like about your body? What do you dislike about your body? In what ways do you struggle with it? How would you like to change the way you feel about it? Are you able to interpret your body's signals, for instance, if you feel unwell, are you able to identify a cause that might have contributed to that dis ease?

Equally our emotions are often a dirty word. When we feel unacceptable emotions, and many of us are so programmed not to even feel them that we don't, but when one tiny unacceptable emotion sneaks through our defences, we bury it, feel inadequate for feeling it at all and pretend that we are 'fine'. When people want to control us, they accuse us of being overly emotional.

I'll let you into a secret: Our feelings are all there for a reason. Anger and rage, compassion and love all have their uses and can be expressed in a healthy way that takes care of us but does not harm others. Even jealousy and greed can help us to identify where we might need to put our attention. If we are jealous, we may be noticing that somebody else has a quality that we need to develop in ourselves. If we feel greed, it may be that we are not attending to looking after our material needs well enough. Our feelings give us information about what is going on within us and around us, so it is valuable to notice our feelings. Even the most negative feelings when we are feeling helpless and inadequate can be a portal to a new insight if we are able just to allow ourselves to feel those feelings until they move into something else. Our feelings are changeable like the weather, and we can be pretty sure that whatever we are feeling at a particular moment can move on to being another feeling if we simply allow ourselves to feel our feelings.

Fear is a feeling that most of us attempt to deny. If we are performers, and we experience stage fright or audition nerves, we attempt to cover those feelings up and hide them even from ourselves. The more we cover them up, the more they inhibit us and make us unable to perform at our best. If, however, we consider our fear to be coming from a little frightened child within us, we can help the situation enormously. We can speak as a parent and say to that frightened child, "It is all right. I know you are frightened, but I am here with you, and we are going to do this together." If we communicate with the frightened part of ourselves in that way, we find that the little child actually loves to go out and perform. Once it is reassured, it no longer prevents us from doing our best work. It may sound ridiculous or simplistic to imagine our fear coming from the frightened child within us, but it is worth an experiment to see if it helps.

Now put your attention into you feelings. What feelings do you appreciate and enjoy? What feelings do you dislike and wish to avoid? What feelings do you deny and skip over? What feelings do you really fear? What would your life be like if you were able to admit to and feel all the variety of feelings of which you are capable?

In the West, in our schools and universities the mind is king. We work hard to improve our minds, to learn and to be able to evaluate and discriminate. What doesn't get mentioned however is our belief systems, and I am not talking about religious beliefs here. Our positive beliefs might be very constructive, but most of us have some very powerful negative, destructive belief systems, especially about ourselves, to say nothing of learned prejudices about particular others. These are the underlying programmed responses or inner voices that cause us to sabotage ourselves when things are going well or to feel bad about ourselves or others.

Mind is a very powerful thing, and it responds to what it has been taught from early childhood: things that we may not even remember. Inner belief systems that have come from parents or teachers or close family friends when we were growing up may not be appropriate for who we are today. We may be completely unaware of some of these beliefs that cloud our thinking and responses. That is why it is useful to question what our deeply held beliefs are about ourselves, others and about life.

What do you believe about yourself? Do these beliefs do you justice? Do you have particular groups of people that you dislike? How strong are these dislikes? How valid are they? What is their source? Also what do you believe about life, and the meaning and purpose of your life? Would you like to change any of your beliefs? Consider these areas carefully and ask yourself if you are satisfied with your beliefs or in what ways you might like to change them, if you could.

One of the things that we often wonder about is who we are. There are so many levels of that. We can wonder about the roles we play, and there are many of them, such things as mother/father, daughter/son, friend, person, woman, man, cook, driver, etc. There are also the questions about the meaning of our existence and the purpose of our lives. Ask yourself the question, "Who are you?" Alternatively, you might ask a friend to repeat the question to you many times, and you could do the same with your friend. In either case ask that question over and over for a few minutes until you come up with a list of answers, so you can see how many roles you play. Look at your responses and ask yourself if you feel comfortable with each of them. If you don't feel comfortable with any of them, ask yourself in what way you would like them to be different, and how you might begin to change your behaviour in those areas.

These are questions to allow yourself to daydream about, so you can really feel your way into your responses and not simply treat them in a kind of mechanical matter of fact way.

Father in Alaska, early 1940s, a few years before I was born

Mother in the 1940s

Father in the 1940s

Mother and Father on their wedding day

Baby Jane

About four years old

In Canada at my stepmother's farm

My high school graduation

Later in university

My soon to be husband, Philip

The Bahá'í House of Worship North of Chicago where we were married

Wedding photos by Buck Rodgers

During our wedding ceremony

A new begining

Leaving the wedding

On our way to the wedding reception

Life as a new mother

with my first standard poodle

Photo by Mary Healey

Philip when he was older

CHAPTER 12
Transformation

Now I was getting serious about wanting to be able to work, and I felt that a degree course would give me a professional path alongside the vocational training in self-development that I was doing. I thoroughly enjoyed walking through the Trinity College campus from one class to another. My schedule was not overwhelming: rather it gave me interesting insights into university life, and the way in which psychology is taught at university level. Those were the days when the walkman had just been marketed, and I carried my walkman tuned in to songs by Emma Kirkby or music by Bach or Handel while walking between classes. It was a glorious feeling. There was something magnificent about that kind of music in such a setting. I felt as if I could have been on a film set taking part in a movie about some very important historical moment.

I enjoyed the courses in psychophysiology and the history of psychology. I wasn't so keen on the course in statistics, and was far more interested in deeper human experience. Thus when I attended the weekends in Eckhart House and participated in a course called "The Way of Transformation" taught by Miceal O'Regan and the staff, I felt more grounded in the reality of what psychology meant to me. This course was based on a book called *The Way of Transformation, Daily Life as Spiritual Exercise* by Karlfried Graf Dürckheim (1980), which clearly outlined the process and progression of transformation in the context of our connection with the Divine, the God within, or our inner Self. The year served to continue and deepen my healing and provide me with further support during the process along with my regular weekly therapy.

My university work forced me to focus my conscious mind, which is the rational, critical, decision-making part of me, on the demanding study of academic psychology. Because my conscious mind was so well occupied with its study, it was no longer able to hold its iron grip on my subconscious mind, which is the less accessible storehouse of memories and repressed emotions. It seemed as if I had used my conscious mind to suppress a lot of my painful feelings as the more I gave my conscious mind something to do in the way of academic study, the less it behaved like a policeman controlling my subconscious mind. I found my studies challenging and absorbing during the first year of my course in psychology, and I wanted very much to do well. So with my thinking brain so tied up with academic study, my subconscious mind could have the necessary freedom to process the flood of repressed emotions that emerged in my personal therapy.

The conscious mind is very diligent and in repressing all of those emotions it was practising what it perceived to be its job. Mainly its job is to maintain the *status quo*, to keep things as they are and not to rock the boat with change or improving life. This hardworking little trooper gets used to its familiar patterns and can aggressively try to stop any possible changes. It has to be constantly reminded that it is all right, and it will survive, that it is safe and protected. So with so much now coming to the surface and demanding attention and processing, every new realisation that came to me in each therapy session could have been perceived by my conscious mind as a threat. Fortunately it was so busy trying to succeed in my university course that it could hardly bother with anything else. It almost wouldn't notice the changes that were occurring, at least for long enough for my subconscious mind to embark on change and get a little used to it.

While I was involved with working towards my psychology degree, I was also studying at the weekends in the course on Transformation. These sessions were emotionally very nurturing and supportive. We would spend a good deal of Saturday doing various body exercises, experimenting with gesture. Miceal told us that just as particular states of mind cause us to adopt various stances or gestures, we can also change our states of mind by choosing to adopt particular gestures. So, if I am depressed, and I walk around with my shoulders slumped over and my eyes glued to the ground in front of me, I might actually lift my depression just by standing up straight and lifting my eyes to look straight ahead. That is an oversimplification, but it illustrates the importance of gesture. One of the things that I often do in my work with clients is ask them to adopt a particular gesture to express what they are feeling, and that helps them to come into relationship with the intensity of their feeling, so they can experience it and it can be released.

Then on the Sundays we would focus on a particular quality, like power or vulnerability and explore that. After the weekend, and before the next one, I would notice that I would have experiences in daily life that would show me different aspects of the quality on which we had focused. This illustrates that when we pay attention to something, it grows. For instance we focussed on power one Sunday, and I noticed during the following month all kinds of experiences of power. In some instances I found myself able to assert myself appropriately at times when I might not have done so previously. In other instances, I became aware of my powerlessness in a particular situation, like with respect to the fact that Philip was away working in London, and no matter what I might think or feel or need, there was nothing I could do to change that then.

In many respects I was accomplishing more than I had in a long time in terms of my life. I enjoyed learning, growing and changing. I loved being with my children and found our busy life at home very fulfilling, and yet still I was asking myself questions about my marriage. Personally I was transforming my inner world through therapy and the course on the Way of Transformation. Educationally I had embarked on a degree course in psychology that could be a stepping stone to working in the world, particularly after my children had truly left home, and perhaps sooner than that because I felt they would have been old enough to deal with a working mother. And yet within my marriage it had never been necessary for me to work. I felt very insecure just not knowing what might happen with my marriage, with the fact that the children were growing up and would soon be leaving home. There seemed to be a lot of change around, and I had no idea where I might find myself in the future.

I was in awe of the power of the mind, and I saw that some of my health problems were not just physical, but there was a strong psychological component, and that I could actually make a change in that. This concept and experience felt nothing short of miraculous to me, and I was thrilled at all the new things I was learning to assist this process of psychological transformation. I found even just the idea of transformation somehow magical, mysterious and absolutely thrilling. I thought of transforming base metal into gold, something that the old alchemists claimed to do. That was miraculous, but far more miraculous was the fact that we could change our health and destructive habit patterns by changing our deep inner psychological belief systems and releasing painful emotions. That I could take my basic flawed self and work to release its highest potential: that I could perform a sort of personal alchemy and find my inner gold, what could be more miraculous than that?

I thought that transformation came from the grace of God, and was a gift. I was thrilled not just because of the changes in my physical and emotional health that I could see progressing, but also because my deepest desire was to fulfil my soul's purpose in my life. I found it hard to tell the difference between what I wanted in terms of my personality and what I wanted at a deeper level that was a response to what I saw as the voice of my soul. Whenever I had a choice to make, especially important choices like what to do about any career direction or about anything to do with my children or marriage, I longed to make a decision that was right according to what was best for me and for all of us. Therefore I always questioned my motives. Was I making this choice out of some aspect of selfish desire, or was I choosing because of a directive from my soul or higher self? This was a real struggle for me because I wanted to act with integrity and from the highest possible motive. As I learned more about sub-personalities, the little reactive parts of myself, and other aspects of my body, feelings and mind, I felt I was becoming clearer, more honest with myself, and better able to hear that still, small voice of my soul. I determined to live a rich and meaningful life and to complete my life's purpose. Then I knew I would be able to leave this life with no regrets.

My thoughts and feelings and wonderings rolled on, and I was intensely occupied with my degree, my weekend classes and my regular weekly therapy, which enabled me to continue to come into relationship with a very frightened and vulnerable part of me who had been abused as a child. I was also very busy with looking after the family and managing the household.

The idea of transformation continued to enthuse me, and the force or energy of transformation seemed to be operating throughout my life. I was thrilled just by what the word 'transformation' conjured up for me. It put me in touch with that wonderful poem from childhood, *The Night before Christmas* by Clement Clarke Moore. I include that poem because it is just lovely, and illustrates to me a magical story of transformation including joy, wonder and the forces of nature. My childhood experience of Santa Claus was probably one of the first times I became aware that I could play a part in making changes in my life. I could want something, ask for it, behave in a way that would show my parents that I should receive what I wanted, and then simply wait and hope that my actions and preparations would yield the results I desired. Whatever I received from good old Santa Claus seemed like a real transformation from my old life as it had been to a new life with more of what I wanted. For children, the experience is made very magical and appealing to encourage them to want to earn Santa's generosity, so they can get what *they* want, and conversely, so their parents can get what they want by encouraging good behaviour. But more than that, it is about learning to work towards a change.

> 'Twas the night before Christmas, when all through the house
> Not a creature was stirring, not even a mouse.
> The stockings were hung by the chimney with care,
> In hopes that St Nicholas soon would be there.
>
> The children were nestled all snug in their beds,
> While visions of sugar-plums danced in their heads.
> And Mama in her 'kerchief, and I in my cap,
> Had just settled our brains for a long winter's nap.
>
> When out on the lawn there arose such a clatter,
> I sprang from the bed to see what was the matter.
> Away to the window I flew like a flash,
> Tore open the shutters and threw up the sash.
>
> The moon on the breast of the new-fallen snow
> Gave the lustre of mid-day to objects below.
> When, what to my wondering eyes should appear,
> But a miniature sleigh, and eight tiny reindeer.
>
> With a little old driver, so lively and quick,
> I knew in a moment it must be St Nick.
> More rapid than eagles his coursers they came,
> And he whistled, and shouted, and called them by name!

Transformation

"Now Dasher! Now, Dancer! Now, Prancer and Vixen!
On, Comet! On, Cupid! On, Donner and Blitzen!
To the top of the porch! To the top of the wall!
Now dash away! Dash away! Dash away all!"

As dry leaves that before the wild hurricane fly,
When they meet with an obstacle, mount to the sky.
So up to the house-top the coursers they flew,
With the sleigh full of toys, and St Nicholas too.

And then, in a twinkling, I heard on the roof
The prancing and pawing of each little hoof.
As I drew in my head, and was turning around,
Down the chimney St Nicholas came with a bound.

He was dressed all in fur, from his head to his foot,
And his clothes were all tarnished with ashes and soot.
A bundle of toys he had flung on his back,
And he looked like a peddler, just opening his pack.

His eyes-how they twinkled! His dimples how merry!
His cheeks were like roses, his nose like a cherry!
His droll little mouth was drawn up like a bow,
And the beard of his chin was as white as the snow.

The stump of a pipe he held tight in his teeth,
And the smoke it encircled his head like a wreath.
He had a broad face and a little round belly,
That shook when he laughed, like a bowlful of jelly!

He was chubby and plump, a right jolly old elf,
And I laughed when I saw him, in spite of myself!
A wink of his eye and a twist of his head,
Soon gave me to know I had nothing to dread.

He spoke not a word, but went straight to his work,
And filled all the stockings, then turned with a jerk.

> And laying his finger aside of his nose,
> And giving a nod, up the chimney he rose!
>
> He sprang to his sleigh, to his team gave a whistle,
> And away they all flew like the down of a thistle.
> But I heard him exclaim, 'ere he drove out of sight,
> "Happy Christmas to all, and to all a good-night!"
>
> Clement Clarke Moore (1823)

As adults we seek transformation because we want change, whether it is in our health, our work, our relationships, our living arrangements or our financial position. When we look for a change in that way, we make preparations, we take action, like children being good for the year, then we "hang up our stockings" and wait to see what our actions have evoked. The results may be different from what we expect either positively or negatively or both.

The mystery of transformation seemed to be with me much of the time. What thrilled me the most was that I could participate in the force of transformation, like the force of nature, and make changes in my life and in myself for the better. Here are some of the thoughts, feelings and ideas that "like visions of sugarplums" danced in my head: Transformation is a gift. It normally comes with a feeling of grace around it because it is not something that we can will into being. We can create the circumstances that might enable it to happen, but then the result is based on a kind of "X" factor that is beyond our control.

We seek many kinds of transformation even of our physical being through diets and particular make up, dress styles, and even cosmetic surgery, but these seem somewhat less dramatic than the psychological transformation that we can go through when dealing with serious life challenges. Transformation is a force of nature that is always present. There are so many forces of transformation in nature like the sun, wind, water, and fire each carving and sculpting the living world. Within the soil, the energy of a single blade of grass breaking through the earth is both forceful and magical and a beautiful example of transformation. Even as night follows day is a transformation. The difference between a beautiful scene in the daytime and at night is simply remarkable. Even as night-time comes, at first the sky is all dark until suddenly we begin to see the first stars begin to shine until eventually the night sky is filled with starlight. It is magical.

We experience transformation in every moment, even when we are not aware of it, as we pass through the stages of our lives, through external events, and when we choose to make changes in our lives. Initially transformation chooses us, until we learn to take responsibility for our actions, for the way in which we create our world. Are we victims to chance and circumstance? When we walk out of our door, are we innocent bystanders? Are we creators? Is it possible that as I am, so I create my world? Is it that the old Hermetic axiom is true, and as above, so below? Could it be that I play a large part in creating my own reality in the sense that energy follows thought?

Poignantly, transformation most frequently occurs when life does not behave as we expect it to, or doesn't match up to what we have learned life should be or do. This is when the Mystery of Life, that which is outside of our control, can break through our controlled reality. Miceal O'Regan coined a phrase to describe such times. He called them "disclosure moments", which are moments when we have a profound realisation about our understanding of life, our relationship to ourselves, to others and more particularly to the force of life itself. These are moments when we may have some choices but mostly we are aware of the power of the mystery of life.

Here are some of the conditions under which disclosure moments can occur:

CONTINGENCY is a word that means dependent upon something else. I may see my life as contingent which means that it is dependent on some other force greater than myself, so I am not in control, as I would like to be. That is a positive experience when life is good, and I feel that it is great to be alive and I am grateful to that greater force, which I feel has rewarded me.

It can be a negative experience when I am having a difficult time; things are not going the way I want them to go, so I feel punished. Therefore a disclosure moment would be to realise that I have been living strategically, hoping that good actions would lead to good results and expecting that bad actions would be punished.

Actually through these experiences I suddenly understand that I can't control life, and my life is not about being rewarded or punished, but about living authentically and with integrity. In other words, good living is its own reward whatever the consequences.

DIALOGUE or COMMUNION is about being in relationship with another person. When I am in a loving relationship with another person, I may have a sense of the mysteriousness of life. I am excited and feel privileged to have met my loved one. This can be extremely positive when it is an open, inclusive relationship that is working well.

When things aren't going well in the relationship, I can feel a bit persecuted by the mystery. This can mean my fear of losing the relationship or being hurt can lead to feelings of jealousy or possessiveness. If I become jealous, and yet I want to hold on to the relationship, I may be pushed towards a new way of being, as if a mysterious force is urging me to relinquish my jealousy or my possessiveness in order to keep the relationship. This is a case of developing the ability to let go of the reins even though that might lead to loss. Doing so might also preserve the relationship, while jealous behaviour might be more likely to ensure its end.

Through dialogue I can learn to transform my behaviour and thereby preserve my relationship. I can learn that I can manage my jealousy and possessiveness. I can learn that if I let go of something that is dear to me, it may come back of its own will and then be truly mine as long as I treat it with respect and trust and not with jealous possessiveness.

COLLAPSE of ORDER in our personal lives can be a very painful as well as a very creative moment when the *status quo* is disrupted. That allows a new, unexpected experience. It may be connected to intense emotions over what is lost that help us to get in touch with a deeper, more soulful, more poetic experience of ourselves. We tend to have quite a negative association with collapse of order, which makes us work very hard to maintain orderly structures.

When our structures get kicked down anyway, when a loved one dies, when we lose our livelihood or worse, those can be very deeply creative moments. We may either settle for total destruction and give up, or we may learn to sit contentedly amid the ruins. I loved that image of learning to sit contentedly amidst the ruins.

Once we can do that, we can also get up and move on in a new way, but first we must sit there, which means accepting what has happened. *It is the attitude with which we engage with the changes in our circumstances that determines our response to them.* Often that ability to sit contentedly with enormous change does not come easily and only comes after we have expressed as much as we need to our feelings about how sorry we are that this all happened and how difficult it has been.

Further we can find great relief in letting go of the things that have taken a lot of energy to maintain. It can be huge release, whether it is something that is visited upon us or a change of our own making. It is why people choose to walk away from houses, sell belongings, and move to new countries. It is a way of unburdening ourselves of the things that we no longer wish to nourish, nurture, sustain and maintain. It is an act of simplifying our lives.

When the usual order of my life has collapsed and I have fully expressed my painful feelings, *when I have sat with the chaos and been still*, I learn that a new order can be created that may work even better for me.

DISENCHANTMENT is a feeling that occurs when we are let down by our expectations about what is good or spiritual and what is to be expected from what is good or spiritual. An example of that might be the myth of Santa Claus. We may have been taught to believe in Santa Claus as a beneficent and generous figure who gives us things we want if we are good. In a way Santa is like a good God or father figure. When later we discover that the Santa Claus story is just a story that our family acts out, we experience a sense of disenchantment with life and what we thought was good and spiritual.

We may be deeply disappointed that this story, which has been with us all through life, was simply a lie. We wonder if we can trust those around us who told us about Santa Claus in the first place. Thus we develop a level of distrust or suspicion of those people whom we had previously trusted. We may attempt to hide that feeling by cloaking it in the knowledge that we are somehow privileged now because we are old enough to know that Santa Claus is not real.

Later again I may discover that the myth of Santa Claus is saying something about being cared for by life, and therefore I have transformed my initial belief and ensuing disappointment by giving that experience meaning that satisfies me after all. This double switch is a disclosure of the nurturing lies we have created as a family and as a culture as glue that holds us all together.

Thus I am initiated into a greater myth of humanity, and I find a deeper layer of meaning beneath my adolescent disenchantment and I become an adult.

REMORSE is a feeling that can lead us to changing our behaviour and making amends for wrongs we have done. When we feel genuine remorse we are really sorry for something that we have done. That feeling can make us determined not to do something like it again and enable us to apologise or take action to correct the mistake.

I have noticed that saying "I'm sorry" can be excruciatingly difficult for some people, and yet it is a simple phrase to say. I don't know why we seem so preoccupied with acting perfect, but it is such a relief when I learn that it is all right to be human, and it doesn't take much to learn to say those two little words and mean it and make amends. The ability to do so makes life much easier and more pleasant because I am not always monitoring and second guessing my behaviour, so I can be more spontaneous and have more fun. I can take risks knowing that the occasional mistake will be forgiven.

INADEQUACY and FEAR are sometimes connected. I am struck by the lengths that we will go to, to make sure that we don't feel inadequacy or fear, and if we feel those horrible feelings, we hide them from everyone including ourselves. This again is unfortunate because if we are able to sustain them and care for ourselves while we are experiencing them, we are able to live more truly and to know that we can soothe ourselves and grow from all our feelings even the frightening ones.

These are feelings that I have tried to pretend were not there. In recent years, however, I have allowed myself to stay with these feelings. I notice especially in the middle of the night I may wake up with these feelings, and when I just stay with them, allowing them to be present for as long as it takes, they may become a portal for a new insight to come through. I noticed it particularly with respect to writing my MA dissertation that I would feel frightened that I couldn't do it. This was my last chance to get a degree, and it would have a huge impact on my ability to work and earn some money, so it meant a lot to me.

I would just lie awake and let my fearful and inadequate feelings swim around within me. Then suddenly I would realise something; a new thought would come through that would revolutionise my thinking and enable me to see that there was indeed something that I could do. Then I would feel fine and know that I really did have something to offer. That new feeling and realisation would enable me to go back to sleep and later to act on my new idea.

DESPAIR is an excellent opportunity for transformation. It can be a journey into that place where we don't know the answers. This can be the most painful and at the same time the most creative place within our Self. We are often talked out of despair by well meaning friends and relatives, when actually living in our despair may be the turning point for us.

Despair, like other feelings, needs to be felt and expressed at least to ourselves, so we do not deny that we are feeling it. Despair is an existential state, which also includes a sense of meaninglessness and helplessness. It is deeper than disenchantment. It is a feeling of hopelessness or uselessness. It is like a journey into the void or the emptiness within us when we feel as if we have been drained of everything and have nothing more to offer. It can really feel like the end of the line; a time when we wish we were dead and feel there is no purpose in our life. When despair gives way, and we no longer feel it, we feel released or cleansed like the earth after a spring rain and we can start anew.

I know when I am in my deepest despair, I feel as if I am holding on to life by a thin thread, and I am at the bottom of that thin thread hanging, like the Sword of Damocles. I also know that if I go any further down, I will lose myself, and when I realise I am in that spot, I say to myself, OK, you have to come out of this. You cannot continue this any more. I begin to choose to come back to functioning slowly, and I acknowledge that even though I feel so desperate life is still worth the effort. Then when I have lived through my despair and come out again I feel refreshed and ready to live again in a hopeful way. Sometimes, however, when I have just carried despair in the background, without actually feeling it, I have felt myself burdened, exhausted and sometimes rather sick.

We experience transformation in relationships to ourselves and to others, in our body, our sexuality, our material and financial life, emotions, and in our mind when we change our deeply held belief systems. We see it in nature, music, art, literature, work and institutions, in short everywhere in the world around us. How could we not be interested in something that so involves us?

I see prayer, meditation, sex, counselling, psychotherapy, and genuine self-examination as agents for transformation. They are catalytic forces that change us and the energy around and through us. There are many other agents for transformation, some of which are within our control and some of which are decidedly outside our control and dependent on the forces of life and nature. Such things as trauma, death of loved ones, and near death experiences all play their parts in our individual transformation. At one time, I thought that everyone should have a near death experience because I was aware of how precious I felt my life was after mine. It made me determined to make my life count and to do what was meaningful to me. Over time I became aware that there are other events that cause people to really savour life, and a near death experience might not be the way for everyone.

There is much that we can do to assist our own growth by bringing ourselves to account each day, monitoring our thoughts, feelings and actions to determine their quality and decide which ones we are happy with and which ones we would like to change.

The year between September of 1984 and September 1985, which was the start of my degree course and the Way of Transformation weekend sessions, became very transformative for me. During the course of that year I considered issues surrounding my marriage and what might be done about it and finally reached some life-changing conclusions. With the best will in the world, which I believe both Philip and I had, I realised that we couldn't really work on our marriage when we weren't even in the same city.

On Reflection

The times when life does not go as we expect it to, or believe it should, cause disclosure moments (a phrase coined by Miceal O'Regan) and transformation. These experiences have an enormous impact on us. Often we are left reeling with confusion, sitting amid chaos, feeling a huge range of emotions including grief and rage. Sometimes we attempt to bargain with God. We return to that childlike state where we ask God as if He were Santa Claus: "if I behave myself, will You change this outcome (that I hate)"? When our world and our expectations are shattered, and we are left helpless in its wake, it takes

Transformation

time to come into relationship with how we are and who we are in our new circumstances.

One of the ways to help ourselves is by expressing the negative emotions and continuing to do so until we feel spent. Expressing our disappointment, anger and hatred about an uncalled for change is a little like panning for gold in the old Gold Rush Days. We keep expressing those feelings that seem to be erupting from us until we don't feel the need to do so as much or as strongly. Gradually our reaction to the event heals over and leaves a scar, so yes, we will get a memory of the old feelings whenever something evokes the memory of our experience, but it won't be nearly so raw and painful as in the beginning, and we will have gained something in the process. We will have gained a better understanding of ourselves by learning from the experience.

There are also times during terribly distressing experiences when we feel at one with God and the universe, and as if we really understand what has happened entirely, and we feel completely cared for and held by life. Those are usually not feelings that we need help to overcome because we usually enjoy them and feel good. It is the other kind of feelings that come only too readily where we feel tiny, victimised by God and the universe and filled with pain and rage that we need to overcome.

Look back over your life and notice the true turning points in your life. Ask yourself, how much you have learned and grown from each experience. See if there is any unfinished business about any of those experiences and by that I mean look deep inside yourself and see if there are any lingering angry, embittered, or unhappy emotions that you feel towards those experiences. If there are, think about how you could release them. Wonder about getting help so that you can express and release those feelings and reach a place where the experience is less emotionally charged for you when you recall it. When you can recall the experience and feel neutral about it, then you will know that you have done all that you can to resolve the issues and to heal yourself.

You may also wonder what kind of help to seek if you feel the need. I would suggest that you find a therapist with whom you feel very comfortable and have regular weekly therapy sessions for as long as it may take. Because trauma and difficult events affect our physical body, it would also be very helpful to make sure that you have some body work in the way of such things as cranial osteopathy, shiatsu, work with a McTimoney chiropractor, rolfing or acupuncture, just to name a few. Also learning to practice yoga or t'ai chi or qigong can be extremely healing.

Healing yourself is a magical gift because it also contributes to everyone else around you. It is like dropping a pebble into a pond: the ripples go out to others each time you heal yourself, and then they come back to you with more strength and wisdom.

If you need to have an idea of a few ways to come into relationship with your emotions you might try simply noticing how you feel several times a day and writing the feeling down. Then you will become more aware of the various feelings that are coursing through you on a daily basis. You might also write a letter to or from the angry part of you or the hurt and disappointed part of you or any other part of you that is experiencing uncomfortable feelings. The letter isn't for sending to anybody, but it is just so you can express your feelings freely. After you have completed the letter or letters, you might keep it for a while, and when you feel that you no longer have any need of it, you could destroy it.

Another very helpful way of looking after yourself is to write a very honest and forthright journal in which you say anything you feel like saying about anyone. Writing a journal, a kind of evening review, is not about the events that occurred in your life, it is more about how you felt about the events that occurred and how you might have responded differently to a particular situation than you have done in the past, if you did. Any journal must be kept in a way that it is not available for anyone else to read ever because you need to be able to really express your feelings in it. After all what you feel at any moment in time is not the whole story nor is it the way you might feel at another time. Just expressing your feeling is a very healing process.

Chapter 13
The Good Doctor

While doing the course in the Way of Transformation, I heard about a five-day course to be given by Dr Elisabeth Kübler-Ross in Northern Ireland, and it sounded so interesting that I agreed to participate. Thus I attended her Life, Death and Transition Workshop in 1985. I feel very privileged to have been able to spend that time with her. She was a remarkable woman, and I learned a great deal from being in her presence.

In case you have not heard of her, Dr Elisabeth Kübler-Ross was a Swiss doctor and psychiatrist who had spent years working with dying patients, people who have had near death experiences and people with serious illnesses. She had written many books on death and dying, and they have helped people to come to a better understanding of the fact that we are souls with bodies in this life, that our soul will continue into other realms beyond this one. She also helped people to express emotions that were powerful enough to paralyse the person. Once these deep-seated and long stored painful emotions were released, the person was free and emotionally available in a way that they never had been before. At one time I didn't even know what that meant, but looking back I can see that the release of such painful emotions helps us to be better able to feel our feelings again and to trust them and be warm and open hearted without the need for unnecessary protective barriers that keep us apart from others. Of course we remain able to protect ourselves emotionally but we feel freer to choose when to use barriers and when we can be open and trusting. That is very different from having those barriers always in place.

At the workshop, there were 93 people, some of whom were cancer patients, many of whom had lost children or other close relatives, all of whom were in pain for one reason or another. Dr Kübler-Ross, who always asked to be called Elisabeth, would invite someone to the front of the room to sit on a mattress. Gradually one person's issue would trigger that of another person who would ask to go to the mattress in the front of the room and deal with his or her own issues. If it was grief that they needed to express, she would give them a small cushion, so they could talk with their departed loved one and express what they felt had gone unsaid. I believe that doing so enabled them to feel a sense of completion and fulfilment so that they were not carrying the burden of things left unsaid any longer.

If they needed to express rage or anger, she would give them a piece of auto-radiator hose and a telephone book and encourage them to hit the book and speak what they were feeling. People would start tapping the telephone book and speaking in an angry tone of voice to the person at whom they were angry. Gradually, they would be taken over by their anger, so they would really attack the telephone book with the auto-radiator hose as in a fit of rage while continuing to shout their anger at the person. This was an extremely powerful technique because through it people were able to externalise their anger in a physical way and release from the body pent up feelings of anger that had been affecting them in their lives in a variety of ways. For example before venting their anger on the telephone book, people described feeling bitter and angry as well as cynical and unhappy, and often depressed. They found that after releasing that anger, they felt more relaxed and at ease with themselves.

Elisabeth knew that if we were able to release blocked emotions, our lives would regain the sparkle they once had, and we could experience the joy of life again. Although I was not able to express anger or grief in front of the group, I did manage to get up and speak. I got up in front of the group and said that I felt I had something to offer to people in the world, and I didn't know what it was, but I wanted to offer it to help people. That took enormous courage for me because I was not comfortable speaking in front of large groups, and yet I felt compelled to express what I was feeling. In some ways that felt like an enormous turning point for me.

During the workshop, aside from appreciating the use of the auto-radiator hose and the telephone book, I also learned that it was important to recognise and acknowledge that I am angry. That was something I rarely did before then because I didn't think it was all right to be angry.

After the workshop once I recognised that I felt angry at someone or something, I occasionally used a piece of auto-radiator hose to beat up and destroy a telephone book. That was especially effective for expressing the rage connected with my childhood abuse. Such things as beating up cushions or screaming in a place which is fairly soundproofed can be very helpful. Doing that allows the anger to be expressed physically, so it is out of the body and the being. Then we can be more loving human beings to those around us. I remember countless times when I have gotten really angry about something that may not really be that important. By expressing the anger physically in some way that is safe, I can still maintain loving relationships.

Elisabeth had said that if you are angry for longer than 10 seconds - the time it takes to say "no, thank you" - you are dealing with old unfinished business from the past. That means there are old memories of events that caused anger stored within you, and that anger was not expressed at the time, so it is still working within you. The anger doesn't just go away especially if it hasn't been OK for you to be angry within your family. When we get into the habit of repressing anger, it stays burning inside. It is locked away, but it is still burning.

For instance, when a child spills a glass of juice, and the mother gets furious, that is a sign that the mother is really angry about something else from the past. We all spill drinks sometimes. It isn't the end of the world. These are over reactions to small incidents that probably point to the storehouse of anger that hasn't been experienced or expressed.

Anger is not the only emotion that needs expression. The same is true of grief. If we don't grieve, we hold that grief in our cells, and it does affect our lives. The point is that if we repress the difficult feelings, we often repress the good feelings along with them. We can't be selective. Once we have started muting our emotional world, we tend to mute all experience, so we don't feel the good feelings or the difficult feelings. Eventually we find ourselves living in a kind of limbo that may feel safe sometimes, but doesn't allow us to truly experience life in all its glorious Technicolor.

Although I wasn't able to express grief and rage in that workshop, the experience of being there with people who did express those feelings made me realise that these emotions were present inside of me more intensely than I thought. So when I went back home, I was able to express the grief and rage in the relative safety of one to one work with my counsellor.

At our next counselling session we explored some role-play. My counsellor encouraged me to find some key phrases that helped me to access and express my pent up rage at my abuser. She asked if I was willing to let her use some of those key phrases and speak them in the room to role play what my abuser might have said to me. She did so, and for the first time in my life I was free to shout my rage at my abuser and beat up a telephone book.

After it was over and I was quite exhausted, she said that it was my rage that actually protected my sense of self worth, and if I hadn't held that rage as I did, I might not have managed to retain my sanity throughout all the years of abuse. Rather than being evil, my rage was what protected me. That was a shocking but very welcome realisation because it helped me to understand that my feelings of rage, which I would have considered wrong or bad, were actually what saved me, and that was a profound change of viewpoint for me.

After that time, I became easier with being angry, knowing how to express my anger and not hide it from myself as I had done in the past. I remember all my life that I had never actually gotten angry, and usually didn't recognise when I was angry. Sometimes Philip would detect something in my voice, and he would ask if I were all right. I would insist that I was because I was hiding my anger from myself, although, of course my anger would leak out as anger always does. Anger denied and hidden from our view comes out in a way like a snake hissing, when we make little snide remarks or say a few words to put someone down without actually having the presence of mind to address the anger at the appropriate event or behaviour that caused the anger in the first place.

Now much of the time I am able to feel and express my anger, and as a consequence I send out less confused signals. We have all experienced people who appear nice to us while we sense that they are irritated, angry or frustrated. Because their feelings are hidden, it is hard to feel secure or safe around that person because we have a feeling that there is something going on that they are not expressing.

I have noticed that I am also able to express my feelings in a safe way on my own at first, so that I don't hurt loved ones by acting on my anger before I have had a chance to weigh my options about it. That doesn't mean that I never let anyone else know I am angry. Once I discharge the anger physically or just recognise that I feel it and allow myself to feel it, then I can address the person who caused it and say quite calmly: when you did this, I felt angry, and I would prefer that you might have done that. But sometimes I also just plain get angry anyway.

One of the most important reasons that Elisabeth has done this work with anger is that unfinished business is a big issue for dying patients. As we near death, any unfinished business interrupts our love, and our capacity to be intimate. We don't want to be nearing death feeling that we have shut down to life, and it is our unfinished business that causes us to shut down to life. I feel very strongly that I would rather deal with any unfinished business I have long before I face death because by doing so, I will be better able to live freely, openly and lovingly for as long as I can in this life. I don't want to live a drab, colourless life. I want to feel and experience the colours and textures of that rich patchwork that is my life.

I found these five days with Elisabeth to be extremely important for me. I was really impressed by her, by her values, by her ability to work with dying patients and people with extremely complex and difficult emotional blockages. I read many of her books and watched videos of her. I admired her qualities, her capacity to deal with taboo issues. Up until then, the subject of death was rather taboo. People found it extremely difficult to talk about. She insisted that dying people want to be able to talk about dying and not have friends and relatives visiting them acting as if nothing is happening.

This period of time helped me to evolve my own basic value system, so that I could more securely know where I stood on the important issues of life and death. I had already established my value system up to and including marriage and family, but now I was being challenged by the fact that my children were growing up and by my need to find a meaningful profession, and I was considering what that profession might be. I felt I wanted to train as a psychosynthesis counsellor, and I also felt that I wanted to work with dying patients because Elisabeth had been such a wonderful example. That possibility seemed a long way away, and I didn't know if I would manage any of it.

On Reflection

What feels important to you from this chapter? Consider how comfortable you are about your feelings and what kind of unfinished business you might have in your life? What feelings do you avoid? Anger is not the only unexpressed or taboo feeling. We all have feelings that we wish were not there. Very often it is vulnerability and helplessness. For some it may be grief and sadness. Each of our feelings is part of being human and living in this life. Each helps us and gives us information about what is going on within us and around us. It is up to us to learn how to manage our feelings in a way that is safe for us and for those close to us but also gives us the right to our experiences. Feelings are neither right nor wrong. They just are. The more we enable ourselves to feel our feelings the richer our lives become and the more in touch we are with our inner world. Much of the unfinished business we have from the past is about feelings that we were unable to express at the time and that still live within us. Think over your life and consider what you have in the way of unexpressed feelings and if you are willing to find a safe way to allow them into your awareness and express them at least to yourself. Becoming more emotionally literate can help you to feel more comfortable with yourself in your life.

Also consider death. How do you feel about your own dying? What is your level of fear about dying? Can you think about it, wonder about it, have any relationship with the fact that you will die one day? Can you imagine what the world will be like when you are no longer in it? Do you have a will? Do you want to be sure that your possessions are given in a way that you choose to others?

How do you feel about the deaths of people close to you? Have you ever been with someone when they were dying? It can be a wonderful experience and/or a very painful experience. What has it been for you if you have accompanied someone in their last minutes on earth?

Do you believe that you cannot die? Do you believe that you are Spirit here and now? Do you believe that your Spirit has led you in the direction that your life has taken? Have you really understood and appreciated your right to be here on earth living your life and having experiences and have you felt value of your existence?

There are many more questions that may come out of this chapter for you. In many ways death is the most important event in our lives and coming into relationship with it can enable us to live more fully and choose more wisely how to use the time that we have.

Chapter 14
Breaking Through

Still the issue that troubled me most was that of my marriage. While life seemed to be improving in so many ways, there was still tension and discomfort in my relationship with Philip. I needed to go back to the beginning and to see if I could uncover some of the underlying reasons for disharmony.

The tone of the marriage had been set to a certain degree when we began our friendship in a work relationship, which gave Philip the authority because he was in charge at work. Also because of his age, and the difference between our ages, I think that he grew up in a generation where the man was the authority in the family. I had a similar expectation at the time of our marriage and for many years after that. Although I was able to challenge Philip at times, I soon became accustomed to a kind of power struggle that seemed to permeate our relationship to varying degrees.

There was an ongoing struggle between my deferring to him and thereby pleasing him and taking my own initiative, owning my authority and risking displeasing him in the process. This felt like walking a tightrope, I never knew how much of my own initiative would be accepted, and yet I had a need to act on my ideas. I seemed to have no jurisdiction in any area in the family. I had been raised to make sure that a husband thought he made all the decisions, whether or not that was true. That system worked for me for quite a long time, and I duly deferred to him to make final decisions. We consulted on things, but I accepted him as the final authority. Then I began to find that game rather tiresome, and I knew that I was more than capable of making many decisions myself. So I began doing just that.

This caused a strain in our relationship probably because Philip didn't expect it, but life was so demanding with three children and a household to run that we rarely had time to discuss anything meaningfully enough to both come to a joint decision about it. It was far more efficient for me to decide whether or not a child had permission to visit a friend on a particular day when I was the person who would take the child in the car and pick him or her up because Philip would be working. I could see sometimes that Philip felt unfairly left out, but the speed with which decisions had to be made caused it to be impossible to be sure we were both informed and on board with those kinds of things. Equally if we needed a new piece of kitchen equipment, I was sure that was my realm because I did the cooking and bought the food. It seemed clear to me that we had to rule over different areas of household life unless of course we were dealing with a major decision like where a child should go to school or when we might need to buy a car.

Much later on, I chose to be rebellious enough to leave him, come into my own authority, and negotiate life on my own for a time. I asked for the divorce to break the pattern of Philip being in authority. I felt like a teenager in a kind of rebellion, so I may have been responding to my mid-life crisis. Philip insisted on applying for the divorce and was willing to give it to me because he didn't want to be married to someone who didn't want to be married to him. Although I felt compelled to choose to divorce Philip, it was extremely difficult for me to do so. Because my parents were divorced, I grew up determined that my marriage would be forever. I was committed to doing whatever was necessary to make our marriage work. It was impossible to do that, however, when Philip and I were not even in the same city.

I had married him when I was just 21 years old, and in my late 30s and early 40s I began to believe that I had been really very young, inexperienced and perhaps not guided well enough to make such a weighty decision as marriage at the time. I had been alone at university before our marriage. My mother had died the previous year, and my father was thousands of miles away. Philip was so attractive and attentive to me when we were courting. Now many years into our marriage I had to question whether or not I loved Philip or if I really felt that he loved me.

Philip had become very authoritative and critical, and as a result I sometimes felt, when we were together, that he really didn't love me. He maintained his power in our relationship by putting me down. This was a rather immature way to maintain power, and it was certainly hurtful to me. Ultimately, his biggest power play was to move away to work in London and to think that I would still be there, should he decide to come back. I then felt that I was really being left out of the whole equation but expected to continue in the way I had done when we lived together. As my mother used to say, "He picked the wrong one!" I was not prepared to act happy families and be left alone, so I left him.

I feel that if we had been able to consult to find a mutual solution to our difficulties, and if he had really appreciated how very good I was at keeping everything going at home when he was away, I think we might have had a very different outcome. Philip just announced to me that he was going to be working wherever he was called to work, and I was left to pick up the pieces and to keep the household and the children going on my own. That would have been fine if he had really supported me from afar and shown appreciation for what I was doing to keep the family system running, but he didn't do that.

I am aware that because of Philip's age, he may have felt a greater urgency, a kind of soul's need, to fulfil his potential through his work as much as he could, but I was still young, energetic and attractive, and I simply felt abandoned by my husband. It was a really deep conflict for me and a very difficult decision, but ultimately I felt that I couldn't just sit and wait for something when I felt that there was a whole life out there for me if I just got up and claimed it. I really wanted to have a right to a life of my own expression with my husband on board, but that didn't seem to be happening at that time.

I had particularly noticed the change in our relationship after Tara died. Tara's death initiated a time when I began to come in to my own power and started to have a life of my own, teaching cooking classes and developing my capacities. I am sure that Philip felt threatened at the time because I don't believe he had expected me to do that. On the one hand, he was pleased with my activities, and proud of me, and on the other, he often wondered why I wasn't happy just being at home and being a wife and mother. In contrast I felt that I needed to be more active and involved in life aside from the traditional role of wife and mother.

I could have been a very happy wife and mother if I could also have had some life of my own. That didn't seem to be too much to ask. And so I just realised that while deep down I believed that we really did love each other, I couldn't participate any longer in a power struggle that was partly maintained by our own belief systems, which didn't seem right to me, and partly maintained by the steady flow of criticism. I needed to explore beyond that, and shake myself out of an archaic belief system that didn't feel to me to honour the real expression of love between a husband and wife that can come when each is an equal and interdependent part of the couple. I couldn't do that with him, so I chose to absent myself for a time while I gained a better understanding of my part in such a destructive duo.

I needed to find something of myself, to choose something for myself, to develop a profession and some kind of work or career, which had been completely neglected in favour of having a family. I rather blamed Philip for my lack of a career because when we were first married, I was attending university. There came a point where I was making a choice not to complete my degree, and he did not encourage me to continue, but rather enabled me to quit the university. He didn't seem willing to allow me to improve myself and develop a profession of my own. I know that this was not really his fault but I feel that if he had encouraged me to finish my degree I might have done so to please him. As it was I felt that it was right for me to discontinue my education. I rather wished he could have seen a reason for me to complete what I had started.

All through our marriage something in me felt strongly that I had to find a means of working to support myself despite having a comfortable life at the time. I felt too helpless without anything on which I could depend in the case of losing the financial security of my marriage. Because I had inherited money early in my life, we had been able to buy three houses in Dublin, leaving us with a security that few people have in the beginning. Still I didn't feel that I could depend on that to last. I guess I could have been considered at the time to have been neurotic because everything seemed fine, but some intuitive impulse kept me on track to find a career for myself.

Philip was a fine actor, and being married to an actor can be a difficult thing. You see, I couldn't depend upon his response to me because some days he would be one way and some days he would be another. It wasn't so much that he was moody, but rather he was sometimes in the character that he was playing in the theatre and sometimes he was more himself. Also he was a Gemini, and people of that sign can be notorious for behaving like different personalities. Therefore I found it difficult to know how to be around such a mercurial personality. I felt that I couldn't depend on him.

Perhaps one of the other strains on our marriage was having three young children. We both wanted all of our children and loved them deeply. Although I didn't delay, having had five pregnancies in six and a half years, I feel that it may have been harder for Philip to deal with teenage children, especially three of them, than it was for me because of our respective ages. I cannot ask him that now, so it is just a feeling I have had. I know that he adored our children and was a good father to them, but I just think that it became harder as he got older. Indeed it was often hard for me too, but I did have youth on my side. The death of baby Tara, followed by a miscarriage, certainly changed our relationship. I came to understand much later that many marriages fail after the death of a child. In some ways I think it is quite remarkable that Philip and I maintained our relationship at all after those experiences.

I understand that relationships go through phases, cycles, growth, deaths of ways of being, and emergence of new ways of being. That doesn't mean that there isn't love, but sometimes we are affected in ways that we don't really understand at the time. I recognised that something else needed to happen, and in many ways, I didn't know what that was. I had felt for many years that there was something wrong in our relationship. There wasn't much available in the way of relationship therapy in those days. I felt I had to take some time away just to come to understand something about myself and him and our relationship. Clearly I did want to resolve whatever was going on between us that didn't feel right, and when I resolved a lot of my own personal issues, I was able to communicate more clearly.

One of the things that Philip complained about was that I had changed. I found it hard to believe that he might have dreamed I would have grown through all the experiences in my life and not have changed. I dread to think what I might have been like if I had remained the same as I had been at 21. He never really explained to me in what way he thought I had changed, but I rather imagine that it was that I had become more assertive and firm in my determination to say what I felt. Although I hope and choose to believe that is not what he really wanted, I do wonder at times if perhaps he had wanted the awestruck, rather naive 21 year-old with whom he had fallen in love, who was a great audience for him.

When I was young and thought he was the greatest man on God's Earth, I listened attentively to everything he said with my doe eyes focused on him.

Who wouldn't want that? However, to have a woman with her own mind who doesn't necessarily think he is the best thing since sliced bread, but who loves him in a realistic way and speaks her mind is probably not what he had expected or really wanted. When I was younger and adored him and told him he was funny, intelligent, laughed at all his jokes and stories, he did fall in love with exactly that. All of this made me wonder if I had done something wrong in terms of my determination to grow and develop, and yet I felt compelled to do what I could to heal myself.

Many people might have assumed that the reasons for our divorce were largely due to the changes that had come about by my doing personal therapy work on my inner world. I know that inner work can cause huge changes in people's lives, but it certainly doesn't always cause the end of marriages and other stable patterns of life for people who undergo therapy. I knew that the difficulties in our marriage had begun long before I began therapy.

Someone said to me that I could regard divorce not as a breakdown, but as a breakthrough. I think that is more to the point. Neither of us was involved with anyone else, so there was no case of infidelity. Looking back, I see that there was tremendous advantage to our separation and divorce despite its difficulties because I became very clear about much that had compelled me to seek divorce.

Having chosen divorce, I also realised that as my two older children were completing secondary school they would soon choose to move to London to develop their lives and careers. I pictured myself rattling around in a big house with one child, two dogs and two cats, and I didn't like that picture at all. In fact, I didn't think I could stand it. Also I felt as if I had done all that I could in Dublin. I had been one of the key organisers of the Bahá'í conference in 1982, a major international event at the Royal Dublin Society. I had also participated in the organisation of a concert at the National Concert Hall with Emma Kirkby and Tony Rooley as well as a weekend of master classes for young singers in Dublin. I kind of wondered where I could go after that in that country. Even when I thought of other possibilities, there seemed to be plenty of reasons why I couldn't do them. So it felt as if doors were closing to me in Dublin. It felt as if it was time to move on.

Rather than complete my degree course in psychology at that stage, I realised that one of the main things I wanted to do was train as a psychosynthesis counsellor. There was no counsellor training in Dublin: I would have to be in London to complete the training. I was so impressed with the effectiveness of psychosynthesis in working with people and helping me to understand and resolve many things that had puzzled me all my life that I wanted to help others in a similar way. I felt that becoming a counsellor was my best hope for a future career. After all, I was over 40 and not likely to build any other kind of a career starting so late. How many people truly see mothering children and household management as an entry into a successful career?

I thought further that I wanted the children to have more access to their father, including my youngest child, who was destined to remain with me at least for the time being. I really wanted to work out the differences and resolve the problems in our marriage. However I wasn't in any state to do that for quite a long time because it did take a very long time for me to work through even some of the issues around my childhood. It wasn't actually until after Philip and I divorced that I was able to fully explore and work through my abusive childhood.

In consideration of all my thoughts and feelings and options, I determined that I had best not continue with my degree course in the academic year 1985-1986. I chose to continue my personal weekly therapy and make plans to move to London, where I could train as a counsellor and be near to my two older children. Scott was already living in London and had begun working as a sound engineer. Shannon was finishing secondary school and planning to move to London. Brian could continue in school there, and he would be able to spend more time with his father, his brother and sister. I was deeply saddened leaving Dublin and my home, and yet I felt so strongly that I had to make that leap of faith then. I knew if I didn't do so that I would be destined to remain in a relatively empty house with very little else to do that was really important to me.

Thus in August of 1986, I left Dublin. I had loved living in Dublin for those 20 years. I had made great friends, and life had been good in so many ways. As much as I wished it weren't so, I knew I had to move on, and still I found it really hard. In many ways, however, I have always been a big city girl. I grew up in some of America's biggest cities, St Louis, New York, Chicago, and Los Angeles. I liked the anonymity of big city life. It was not that I was doing anything wrong, but I didn't like being noticed and recognised wherever I went. I also liked the choices that were available in big cities. I enjoyed the culture and the variety of people, things, approaches to life and educational opportunities.

One of my greatest joys is the fact that Philip and I married again just about five months before he passed away, so I was able to realise my dream of resolving our difficulties. You may think it was too late because he died so soon afterwards, and I assure you it was not. This is a relationship that will endure into the next life.

Eventually over the 11 years that we were divorced, I realised that I did love Philip, and I grew to understand truly that he loved me. That was a real turning point for me, and it enabled me to know that I wanted to marry him again. We had talked about getting married again, but it hadn't happened. Unfortunately, when we finally managed it, in August of 1998, when I was 54 years old, and he was 71, we had only a few months together before he died. Those were wonderful months when we were able to make each other as happy as two people can be when one is dying. I thank God that we did marry again because I would have been devastated if he had died and we had not managed that. I will never forget how his eyes lit up every time I entered the room when he was in the hospice; how he really appreciated the strong and expressive woman that I had become; and how the last thing he said to me just before he died was that he wanted me to have a crown of jewels! What a testimony that is to the process that we had both undergone through the divorce and remarriage. We came into relationship then as individuals who were deeply committed and in love and knowing that our separation was coming soon. I will say more about that later.

On Reflection

The decision to end a marriage or partnership must be one of the most difficult decisions in life. Indeed there are many excruciatingly difficult decisions that we are called upon to make. When there are children involved and a long period of shared memories of fun and joy and pleasure as well as working through difficulties together, it becomes even harder to make the break. Contemplating making such a decision requires all the help that anyone can get as well as enough time to be able to evaluate the situation fairly.

There are certain things that we can spend our time doing in life, and the importance of a marriage or partnership is one of life's experiences that deserves a great deal of thought and attention. Nobody is perfect and no situation is perfect. Partnership difficulties arise mostly when there is a breakdown in communication: when one partner has lost trust, has not been heard, or feels betrayed. It takes time and work to repair the wounds that we give to each other, and in the long run, it may be worth putting in that time and work when something is of value.

There are very serious reasons to break up a partnership or end a marriage sometimes, for example when there is some form of abuse or neglect. However when there is no such case and the difficulties could be resolved with some work, we may find that our marriage partner who has been with us the longest is the one who deserves our attention most. When we get older, we often find that the people who mean the most to us are those whom we have known for a long time. Those are the people who know us through many different experiences. They carry our history and we might be better served to work on what we have rather than thinking there might be someone else out there who is better.

Often what happens is that two people break up, and in a short time, they may find themselves with a partnership that has the same or worse issues. The key to solving that problem is to do some inner work on yourself, and to get to know yourself better before you embark on another partnership. No matter how attractive you may be, there still may not be anyone out there who is as 'good' as your current partner.

Loving relationships are really the stuff of life, and the more we can encourage and support them, the better we all are.

CHAPTER 15

Look Out London, Here We Come!

Once I had made the decision to move to London, I thought that life would be fairly simple. I kept visualising myself living in London and working on my counselling training. It took more than that, however. I began to think about where I wanted to live, and what kind of a place I needed. I thought I needed a house that would be big enough for the family. Certainly Brian would be with me, and I wanted to have room for the two older children and Philip if things worked out between us. It seemed like a tall order in all directions, but I felt able to do it. I managed to take a day in London in December to look at houses just to get a flavour of what might be available, but it was so difficult to decide how to go about it. I came home wondering what to do because there were so many different areas. Then I decided that I had better think about selling our home in Dublin first and worry about housing in London later. I also decided that it would be better to focus on one area in London, and I chose Ealing because it was convenient both to the city centre and to Heathrow. I saw myself wanting to travel and to be able to get to the West End easily. Ealing had a lot of trees, and they were important to me. From another country, with only limited time to find my new home, I felt that by choosing one area I could make my house search more manageable.

Our house in Dublin was lovely, in a sought after part of the city, with four bedrooms, two bathrooms, a living room, television room/dining room, office and a huge kitchen. I even had a cooker with eight burners because I loved cooking and often made some complicated dishes. We had a garden of about a third of an acre, and it backed onto a green area filled with gorgeous old trees. I was sure it would sell easily. How wrong I was! We had an estate agent who said that I ought to have bread baking when she showed the house, so the smell of freshly baked bread would entice prospective buyers. I remember how many times I baked bread whether or not we needed it as a family just to tempt the buyers. It was a lot of work, and I wondered what prospective buyers felt. Not only did I have to really make sure the house was exceptionally clean and tidy, but I had to have bread baking as well! I had no idea that I would have to go to such lengths to tempt people to buy my home.

I was filled with resentment every time a prospective buyer would come into MY HOUSE even though I did want to sell it and move on. I did realise that it was only bricks and mortar but it was so reminiscent of the history of my family. It was really hard for me to let go. This estate agent even made me move furniture around because she felt that the way I had my home organised would not suit the Irish palate, which also infuriated me. My house was stunning and amazing. How could anybody not want it? There was so much of us stamped on it but at the same time it really was an outstanding property. It took a while, but we finally had a buyer. Once their offer was in place, I set about to find a new home in London.

On the night before I was due to spend a week in London to find a house, I discovered a lump in my breast. I was terrified. I nearly didn't take the trip but I knew that if I faltered for a minute, I would never manage my move to London, and I felt I had to move on. Clearly my children were not going to remain in Ireland after they completed secondary education. I also deeply felt that Philip had no intention of returning to Dublin any time in the near future if ever, and I refused to be left there on my own with a big house and one child and a couple of dogs and cats. I had to simply swallow my fear. I couldn't afford to lose my nerve then. I longed for Philip to be by my side working with me, but that simply was not happening. I realised I could deal with the lump on my return and I couldn't even think about it at that time. I forced my mind to turn off its conversation about the lump in my breast. I made the trip, found a wonderful house in Acton and I agreed to buy it.

I came back home and went to various natural health practitioners to try to do something about this lump. I was not satisfied with the results of their work, even though it was always my first response to health problems to check what might be available naturally. I remember on the way to the last natural health practitioner I saw, my car made a very strange thumping noise that I couldn't identify. I was really worried about it as I got near to my destination, so I stopped in a petrol station, handed the man the keys to the car, and said, please check this out. He drove the car and he suggested that I drive the car home and take it to my usual garage where they knew the car. He thought it would be fine. I then went to see the practitioner, and I found him rather strange. I felt uncomfortable with him, and I determined then and there to go to a surgeon because I knew that the only way to really know the contents of the lump would be to have it removed and biopsied. The Baháʼí Writings encourage consulting a wise physician on matters of health, and I usually did so alongside my complementary health approaches, but I feel that on this occasion my fear of what might be the case caused me to delay contacting a doctor. My car never made that noise again, on the way home or after that. I wondered what was going on, but I do know that sometimes when I am in turmoil, my physical world also reflects my turmoil. It was still a strange experience.

I remember the whole thing with such clarity, even now. I saw the surgeon, who said to me that I would have to come into the hospital in late morning, be put under anaesthetic, and the operation to remove the lump would take about 25 minutes. I would be unconscious for another 20 minutes after that, and I could go home later in the afternoon. The whole procedure sounded quite manageable, even though I was very loath to put myself back in the hands of a medical solution, after so many years of resolving health issues with natural remedies. But I weighted up my options and I reasoned that this was clearly a necessary surgical intervention because there would be no other way to be completely sure about what I was facing. Without a biopsy there would be no way to know for sure if the lump was a tumour. My fears needed to be assuaged with facts. I could hardly make an international house move while still wondering whether I had breast cancer or some benign intruder that could be removed easily.

I went to have the operation. I had agreed with the surgeon that this was simply an operation to remove the lump and biopsy it. I made it clear to him that if he thought any other surgery was necessary he was not authorised to do that without waking me and discussing it with me. I put those instructions onto the consent form before I signed it ensuring that nobody could do any additional procedure without my consent. That was extremely important to me because I wanted to be sure that I didn't wake up with one breast removed without having participated in the decision. Making those additions to the consent form gave me some feeling of control over what was about to happen to my body. After the operation, which I had just six weeks before the moving date, I was told that the lump was a benign fibro adenoma, which is most prevalent in teenage girls. I thought that was rather curious, but I was immensely grateful.

When I look back on this time I can recall the details easily, and yet I feel somewhat detached from my emotions. At another time, I might have been more aware of my feelings about this experience, and yet at the time all this was happening I was not. Aside from sheer terror, which was assuaged by the results of the operation, I had no time when I was moving house so soon to feel much else. Now when I think about this experience I hold no left over anger or fear that I need to express. I feel as if the moment has passed because the outcome was positive and so much else has happened in my life.

Philip came over just before the move in June to take whatever was his and that left me with the bulk of the household to sort and pack for the ferry ride to England. I had organised a moving company, and I thought we were on our way. I bought a new car to take out of the country. Then on the day when the vans were being loaded, the sale on the house we were leaving fell through. I was gutted, and I had to contact Barclays in London, who had agreed to give me a bridging loan. I went to a friend's home and phoned my stockbroker in California, asked him to speak to the people at Barclays to tell them I was good for the money. All of this was going on as my furniture was being packed up. Eventually on that very day, Barclays agreed to give me the bridging loan even though the house sale had fallen through. They realised that the house would be sold, and I am very grateful to them for trusting that enough to give me the money.

We were travelling out the next day, taking the boat from Dublin to Holyhead, and I was in shock at what had transpired. I didn't have much good to say about our erstwhile buyer. I was so exhausted and stressed that I went to have an Alexander Technique session just to ease the stress in my body. It worked and I slept pretty well that night, and we left the next day. Brian, Kay, a close family friend, and one tiny dog were coming with me along with some rather important possessions, jewellery and a few things that I didn't want the moving company to handle. I also had my mini-office that I needed for day to day chores to do with banking and house sale and purchases.

Because I knew I wouldn't get to London in time to collect the keys to the house, I asked Scott to do so, which he did. We arrived in Holyhead about 5pm, sorted out the car, and were on the road. I had no idea how long it might take to get to London, and to this day I don't know if I was driving terribly slowly, but it seemed to take ages. I did stop and rest by the side of the road for about half an hour at one point. I was so tired that I just focused on the car or truck in front of me on the motorway and followed what it did. It was getting later and later, and I was long past flagging. I was so tired that I began to think only of bed. About 1am in the morning we reached the area of Newport Pagnell, and for the first time in ages I saw a sign, which showed that the area had not just refreshments, but a roadside motel. There was a picture of a bed on the sign. I was so relieved that I would have jumped into the bed on the sign, if I could have done so.

We slept in beds, and the next morning proceeded to our new home in Acton. Scott was there waiting for us. He had been there all night. He had gone into one of the rooms, and because there was something wrong with the door catch, the door had closed and locked behind him, so he had slept on the carpet. He had been expecting us to arrive at any moment, so he wouldn't leave despite it being so late at night. I was so disappointed that I had no way of contacting him to let him know that we were not going to get there until morning, but there was nothing I could do. The next morning, after waking up to find that we hadn't yet arrived, he realised that he could get out by climbing down the drainpipe. It was such a relief to find him there when we arrived. He helped us unload and get a little organised. I apologised profusely because I had originally expected to arrive the night before.

Soon enough the vans pulled up with our belongings, and we began to sort ourselves out. We were there. We had arrived and were in our new home. I couldn't believe it! After all that, we had finally landed. Philip came out to the house to help us get settled. He was already well settled in our flat in South-east London, and we were able to talk with each other comfortably, but we were still planning on getting divorced. I invited him to come live with us in the new house because I still really wanted to work things out between us, but he wasn't interested in moving in with us.

I remember the first time I went to Acton Town Tube Station to take the tube. I was astounded to notice that I had gotten onto the tube platform without first having had to take a plane and come through Heathrow Airport to get to it, as I had to do when I lived in Dublin. I found that very exciting.

Brian and Shannon were living with me. Shannon was there only briefly because she was going to France for a year to participate in an educational experience there. Scott was living with Philip, and by then he was working as a sound engineer, so he had a schedule that was variable. I did notice, however, that almost every time Brian and I went to the supermarket and stocked our food cupboards, Scott would arrive at the door ready for dinner. It was remarkable. He seemed to have a radar that told him when we would have some nice food available.

Once we had a routine, we retrieved our two standard poodles and two cats from a friend who had taken them for a while during the course of the move. We felt safer with our animals in the house.

Gradually we got settled, and there was something thrilling about living in a Georgian house, which was in some ways typically English, and in other ways equipped with just what we needed at the time. We had to have some work done on the house, and that occupied us for quite a while. My psychosynthesis course began, and I was still enthralled by the magic of the new understanding about myself and human behaviour that I was gaining. I began regular therapy, and I was still uncovering issues to do with my childhood and the abuse I had suffered. I had no idea at the time just how much of my life had been affected by that experience.

I was able to make some changes in my obsessive behaviour. I realised that sometimes I would do or say something that would worry me, and I would keep turning the sequence of events over in my head: *he said, she said etc.* Then I found that if I simply said to myself, "All right, I have heard what you said" as if I were speaking to a small part of myself who was obsessing, "and now we are doing things differently". That seemed to end my obsessing, so I could relax and get on with life.

In the summer of 1987, Philip applied for our divorce, which only cost us £50 because we agreed on everything. On the day that he applied for it, a tree in my front garden fell down. I was impressed by the synchronicity of that small event. The final divorce decree came through on the 12th of November, which is the birthday of Bahá'u'lláh, a Bahá'í Holy Day. I felt somehow confirmed in my decision for divorce, even though I didn't like feeling that I had to make that decision. After all, we had been married on a Bahá'í Holy Day, so it seemed fitting that we would be divorced on a Bahá'í Holy Day as well.

I became very involved with Ealing Bahá'í Community and was elected Secretary of the Spiritual Assembly of the Bahá'ís of Ealing. That rather surprised me because I had never let anyone know that I could type or that I had any secretarial skills. I regularly attended Bahá'í Feasts and Holy Days as well as fortnightly Assembly meetings. Being involved in the Bahá'í Community gave me a sense of community and a group of people within which I began to find close friends.

I completed my course in psychosynthesis counselling in 1988 and was then qualified to see clients. I did let people know that I was qualified, but I didn't have marketing skills, and although I saw some clients, I had no concept of the fact that building a private counselling practice can take a very long time. I loved my work, and it was effective. There was something extremely rewarding about making a difference in a person's life, and I could see that happening with my clients.

Gradually I could see that money was becoming a problem, and I felt that I was paying more than I could really afford in mortgage payments. I became so frightened that I went to bed at night and would feel my whole body go stiff with fear, so I decided that we had better move house and find a way to reduce our mortgage payments.

In the summer of 1988 I sold our home in Acton at a significant profit and bought a new home not far from Brian's school, a home that he had seen advertised in an estate agent's. By then Brian was fifteen years old, and while he wouldn't have had much time left in school, we really loved the house. So we downshifted from our six bedroom Georgian house, which had been intended to accommodate the whole family, if necessary, to a three bedroom cottage in Chiswick. We had a smaller mortgage, and we were able to fix up a few things in the house because of the profit that had come from the sale of the first house.

I kept the house in its original cottage style. There was already an oatmeal coloured carpet in the downstairs, open-plan living/dining area. I put in William Morris "Strawberry Thief" curtains which had a lovely pattern on a deep Prussian blue background. This house really felt like our home. I had a beautiful Yamaha upright piano, which fit very nicely in the downstairs area, along with a sofa, chairs, a big dining room table, an oak desk and an over mantle mirror. The house was charming and very welcoming as soon as

I came in the door. I still felt optimistic then because I could see myself developing a counselling practice and managing very well. I had sold my home at a high point in the property market in 1988, and still I had enough capital to manage on the smaller mortgage payment until I found more work that would support us. That was the plan. Then in 1989 mortgage rates went up and tripled my mortgage payment.

Thus began a time when money was a huge problem for me, well rather, lack of money was a huge problem for me. In late 1991 when my money-worries had brought me to my lowest ebb Philip left to live in California for a time. Even though we had already divorced, we were still in daily contact, and I still somewhere deep within me imagined that he would rescue me. When he left I felt an enormous sense of loss, of the only person who might have offered to help me if things got really desperate. I will share more of that experience later when I talk about money.

Brian and I lived in our new home in Chiswick from July of 1988 to June of 1996. Within a few weeks of moving in to Chiswick, Shannon first went to live with a group of friends elsewhere in London and later got her own flat near to Philip's flat. Scott got married in 1988 and provided me with my first grandchild. I was a 44-year-old grandmother, and that felt just great. I was with my daughter-in-law when the baby was born, as was her mother. It was a wonderful experience. Scott, who had intended to be with her, was away working and couldn't leave. The baby was born a couple of weeks before they had expected, so he was disappointed not to have been able to be present.

I was able to continue to see Ivy Northage, the medium, once a year and to get her very wise recommendations about the progress of my life. It was amazing how on some occasions she would discuss the principles underlying what was going on in my life. On other occasions, she would give me extremely practical advice, which would almost immediately open the door to the next step that I needed to take. I was privileged to see her once a year for 12 years and to attend one of her self-realisation courses before she retired from working. She was an amazing character. She seemed like a gentle older woman whom we might see anywhere in London and not realise the effect she could have on a person's life. However, when she went into trance and her communicator, Chan, came through her face changed, her voice and mannerisms changed, and the wisdom that would come from her certainly helped me to manage my life and create a life that I wanted to live without which guidance I dread to think what I might have done. I longed to see her more often than once a year because I felt so nourished and helped by whatever I learned from that short meeting we had. That meeting was vitally important to me because it would set me clearly on a path that I understood and I felt as if I had been guided or advised by some divine mentor who really understood the intricacies of my personal life. She saw only a few people each week which is why I couldn't see her more than once a year, but that was enough to give me the encouragement that I needed. I was in awe of her talent and her ability to give me what I needed to shape my life.

Early in May 1991 I had a rather unusual experience. One day I was at home visiting with a friend of mine who was also a counsellor trained in psychosynthesis. We only met occasionally because he lived some distance away. On this occasion we spoke of Tara, and he said to me that he felt that I hadn't actually accepted her death. When he said that, I felt a strong movement of energy in my body. I said to him that I thought I had accepted it, but when I felt my body's response to what he said, I was thinking that maybe I hadn't. I asked if he could suggest anything that I might do. He suggested that I create some kind of ritual of my own to accept her death.

I thought about it, and I decided that I would see a medium on the anniversary of her death, which was coming up in the next month. A few weeks after that conversation, I was in a session with a therapist whom I saw a few times, and suddenly I felt a tremendous pain about three inches above my heart. It was excruciating. I felt it go down my left arm, and it felt as if someone was shoving a needle under the nail of my middle finger. The pain in my chest was the worst. I lay down on the floor, but I had to keep moving, so I lay down, and then I got up and walked around and then I lay down again and repeated that behaviour while this pain lasted. I had no idea what it was, and I tell you about it because it has bearing on what was discovered shortly afterwards by a medium at the College of Psychic Studies in London. The whole experience lasted about an hour and a half. Physically the pain seemed to be happening too high up in my chest for a heart attack. I felt as if I were being run over by a huge lorry for that time, and then the pain stopped, and I never felt it again. I had my heart checked some years later, and there was no sign of my ever having a heart attack.

After that experience I went again to the cranial osteopath whom I had been seeing regularly because the energy in my spine and the cranio-sacral rhythm was blocked. She was trying to bring the energy down to the base of my spine. I had been seeing her every week or two for months for that purpose. I saw her again after having had this experience of the pain, and she said that the energy was now flowing down my spine normally. It seemed as if the pain had released some block to the flow of energy down my spine.

The anniversary of Tara came on the 20th of June, which, if it falls on a Sunday, is Father's Day. It wasn't on a Sunday on that occasion. I went to see Keith Casburn, the medium and healer who had been recommended to me at the College of Psychic Studies, and I asked him three questions. I have already mentioned what he said earlier about my teenage ill health. I wanted to know something about Tara and told him how I felt I hadn't fully accepted her death. He did tell me that she was my teacher, and that was certainly true. I had learned so much from my grief over her death. We talked about that for a while. Then he said something to me that I had never considered. He said that I had become frozen in the moment in time when my baby, Tara, had died and he suggested that I see a healer or therapist to work through any remaining grief that I was still feeling about her death. He said that this kind of being almost paralysed in a moment could cause actual physical pain and a sense of being stuck in the flow of life. I said that I was sure it was true because I had experienced the pain of it about six weeks before, and I told him about my episode with the pain in my chest when with my therapist.

I asked what he meant by being stuck. He said it is as if you have been travelling in a car along a road, and the car has skidded and turned 90 degrees and now there is a wall in front of it and a wall behind it, and it can't move. He also said it was like being in an Oxbow lake. It was like going over the same territory all the time and not really being able to get into the stream of life. I said that was exactly the way I felt.

In my next therapy session I sat in the chair, and my therapist invited me to see Tara and to express all the grief that I could about her death. I was crying profoundly, and she encouraged me to continue that as long as it took. This was some 19 years after Tara had died, and I wouldn't have expected those feelings still to be there because I thought I had grieved for her, but I guess not. Anyway, suddenly in my imagination, I saw her as a young woman standing by a tree, and she was beautiful and grown up. My image of Tara was at that time changed from that of the baby who died to the beautiful young woman, my daughter, who is living in the next world. I was amazed and delighted. My therapist had said to me in the beginning that when all the tears had been spent, there would be room for joy and laughter. It was hard to believe, but once I had fully expressed the feelings, and the transition had occurred, I felt such unbounded joy.

After that was over I had to recover. It was as if I had had surgery, and I was really disoriented emotionally. Gradually I realised that I had become frozen in the moment of Tara's death, so she remained always my baby who died. The shift from the baby who died to my daughter in the spirit world was enormous. I felt that I could imagine her as a young woman in spirit, and that was absolutely wonderful. In one way she would always be my baby who died, but I could also have a relationship with her soul in a very different way after this experience, and that felt like a huge healing of my pain over her death.

It took me a few months after that to come back to normal and really feel the flow of my life again. In October, I felt the need of more work. I was interested because a few healers whom I had recently gotten to know kept telling me that *I* was a healer. I thought healing was a wonderful thing and yet I couldn't imagine myself as a healer. However, the idea of being a healer did seem like a ray of hope as an opportunity to do some more work. Another healer was recommended to me, so in November of 1991, I went to see the new healer for my first appointment in the Midlands, and she ushered me into her room. I sat down and said to her that I didn't know exactly why I was there, but I thought I was becoming a healer. She looked me right in the eyes and said that I was a healer, and I had been a healer all my life. She continued to say that there were two ways of coming into healing. If you choose healing, she said, then you have trouble with the power of it. However, if healing chooses you, and this is your case, you have trouble accepting the responsibility of it. Well, I was overwhelmed, and yet I knew I was in the right place because she seemed to know what I needed to discover in myself. I began seeing her regularly then for quite a while.

This might be a good point to say that, as you can see, a large part of my life has revolved around self-development of some kind. That has been a very central and meaningful part of my life. However, many people wish to do some work on themselves for shorter periods of time. Their desire to find help through therapy or healing is usually precipitated by a crisis, and they can do some very important work, which then puts them back into their lives again in a new and more effective way. It is not necessarily common for people to spend so much of their lives seeking further development. It is just as legitimate to embark on a short or medium term phase of work as it is to do what I have done. I am partly sharing my journey as a way of illustrating the many different ways that you can work on yourself and how effective these ways can be no matter how unusual or unconventional they may seem. I don't want to give the impression that once you start working on yourself, you never stop, and you get caught up in a sort of driven odyssey, always seeking answers to questions. In my case, one approach seemed to lead naturally to another, and even so, I wasn't spending all my time exploring unconventional avenues of help. I did have quite a full life in other ways, as I have also mentioned.

In terms of my personal life, it was the end of November of 1991 when Philip was leaving to go back to California to live indefinitely. I had a buyer for my home, which I thought would avoid any further problems with money, but the mortgage company refused the sale because the price was too low, they claimed. It was a time when house prices had gone down, and the value of people's homes was very low. As a result, I was trapped in my lovely home. I could neither sell it, fix it up to rent it, nor leave it. As much as I was happy to be there in my home, I felt the only way to solve my problem was to find work. Although I had developed a lot of skills, I was now 47 years old, and my work life hadn't taken me into the mainstream. At my age it was really difficult, if not impossible, to translate my skills into something an employer could make use of and find a way to join the workforce to earn a regular salary. So I continued to network, and to seek out work wherever I could. Pursuing healing and developing my own skills as a healer seemed like something that was helping me personally, but might also be another good string to my bow in terms of services that I could offer people.

I trained in healing through the National Federation of Spiritual Healers in 1992. From 1992 to 1993 I worked as a volunteer counsellor and healer on the Supportive Care Team which was a two year project in the cancer department of Hammersmith Hospital under Professor Karol Sikora and his colleagues. In England the value of spiritual healing, counselling, meditation and other complementary therapies in uplifting the life force of patients who are chronically ill with cancer has been recognised and has also been included in the supportive treatment provided by several centres. These therapies also have an important part to play in preventative medicine. In the UK there has long been cooperation between some doctors with some healers and complementary therapists. I found working at the hospital very rewarding. I was using my counselling and healing skills with cancer patients. I began by going to the radiotherapy waiting room and talking to patients waiting to have their radiotherapy. This was at a time when the new cancer centre was being built, so the facilities were basic and minimal. There was a lovely lady who offered cups of tea to the patients, and I was there once a week. I would just sit there and let people share their feelings with me. If someone wanted to speak to me privately, we could find some empty room somewhere, and that was not always easy or even possible, so we just made do with a small space anywhere. At one stage my supervisor considered hiring a counsellor to work one or two days a week. She interviewed a woman who required a room with a view all carpeted and curtained. I had to laugh because at that time, there was no room available that could have been made into a therapy room. She was never hired. I am sure now that there is a new cancer centre and all those niceties are there, but this was in a transition period. I was reminded of Dr Elisabeth Kübler Ross who would work with patients under any kind of circumstances, and I was pleased to feel that I was there to look after the patients without the need for formal room arrangements.

I also worked privately with a number of dying patients, and I was able to help them make the transition. It was so rewarding, and I felt like a midwife for the soul. There is something so precious about sharing some of the last few hours that a person has on Earth. I saw my first dying patient for an hour a day for nine days, and I felt as if I had spent a lifetime with her. During that time, she went from being an angry young woman full of rage to a peaceful person who was ready to accept her death and to help her family to adjust to it. I always had a little personal remembrance of the patients who died after I had worked with them. I had my own little time of grieving after their deaths.

One Friday evening, I was at home and a nurse from a ward in the hospital phoned to say that a patient whom I had seen in the radiotherapy department was there and asking to see me. I went there and sat with her for the evening. She was in pain. Her arm was very swollen. I gently stroked her arm and read prayers with her. She was saying that she didn't know what she did wrong to have such an awful illness. All she ever did was do her best to raise her children. She was from Jamaica, and she was very concerned about her children. I think that she had three or four children, and they were in their teens or older. I really appreciated being asked to spend time with her. I felt I was in my own small way making a little difference in someone's life, and that is the greatest feeling there is in life. The nurses were too busy to sit with her, and for whatever reason, she had no family with her at that time. I never heard any more about her, whether she lived or died fairly soon, but I just felt privileged to have been able to give her a little comfort for that Friday evening. I thought to myself I would rather be doing that than just about anything else because I felt valued and needed. How lovely it is to be able to help someone at that stage.

One young woman who was dying of cancer, came to see me once a week for about six or eight sessions, and each time we would talk about her dying and its effect on her husband and her mother. Then one day I was able to tell her that I had had a little memorial at home the previous weekend for my daughter, Tara. I had invited some close friends over, bought a lovely cake and some food. We had sat in the garden, said prayers, and celebrated her life and death. She was delighted with that story. She said to me that if she knew her mother would do that for her, she would feel fine about going. I never saw her again, and I heard that she died within a week after that meeting. I do know that very often a dying patient is waiting to hear some particular thing, to get some question answered before they feel free to go. Sometimes it is simply permission to go from their nearest and dearest relatives or to know that their children will be all right.

There was a woman who came to the hospital for treatment and was severely ill with a large tumour in her stomach. They thought she had only about 6 weeks to live. Her husband had died of cancer a few years before. She had a teenage son. I saw her, and together we talked about what she might do to help herself. I suggested that she didn't put a lot of pressure on herself and she enjoy the time she had left. She decided to see a healer near where she lived. She did so regularly, and the tumour shrank considerably. I don't remember if she had an operation, but in any case, she was able to live an extra year she had as a result of the healing. That gave her the time and energy to move back to her country of birth and find a place near her brother where her son could live, so he would be near family. Then she could go peacefully.

My work was not exclusively with dying patients. I also worked with cancer patients who went on to live full and interesting lives. Outside of the hospital I worked with singers and actors who were having difficulty with voice problems, audition and performance nerves. Because they have no other tools or instruments except themselves in their work, any underlying problems that emerge often show themselves directly in their working lives. It was so rewarding to watch their improvements in all those areas through our weekly sessions. I also worked with people who had issues like relationship or work problems, physical illness, bereavement, abusive childhoods and other negative life experiences.

I worked occasionally for Broadcasting Support Services on telephone help lines that were made available after television programmes with emotionally charged content, like those about abuse or rape or trauma of one kind or another. There were usually about 12 of us seated at telephones taking calls. People would phone up, many of whom had never discussed their experiences with anyone, but who had been hurt years before in a way similar to that portrayed on the television programme. I felt so privileged that they would feel comfortable to share their experience with me, an empathetic voice on the other end of the phone. Sadly Broadcasting Support Services stopped running their telephone help lines from London after a few years, so I was no longer asked to do that work.

My work with broadcasting support services led me to some very early morning work for GMTV. There were usually about six counsellors answering the phones. We would listen empathetically to the caller and make a note of the issue that the caller had reported. Later on, we would choose from amongst the callers the two or three, with a couple of back ups in case the calls didn't take much time, who could be called and with whom the television Counsellor would speak. I had to get up at about 4am and leave the house by about 5.30am to get to GMTV from Ealing in time for my work. I am not usually particularly good at that time of the day! In the fine weather, I would go to Embankment and walk over the bridge to the South Bank Television

Centre. It was glorious to see the sun coming up over the River Thames and just to be part of life at that hour. In the dark winter mornings, I would go to Waterloo station and walk from there. That was scary and uncomfortable because it was cold and dark. I was so relieved to reach the television centre, go to have a cup of tea and chat to colleagues before we began. That made the uncomfortable journey worth it. I would be finished by about 9am, and then go back home and feel jet lagged all day long because of the early start. I did this work only once or twice a week, with a rare exception of three times a week. I was sure that if I had that schedule every day, I probably wouldn't have felt jet lagged as a result of the unusually early start. Then later GMTV changed their telephone people and no longer required qualified counsellors to answer the phones, so I was out of a job there.

One time, an American insurance company that was going to set up a counselling department approached me, and I was going to be heading up the counsellors. I was taken out to lunch, and told that a contract would be following. I was so relieved because I felt my struggle was over. However, I never heard from them again, and learned later that they had decided not to put in the counselling department at that time, but to start with just medical issues. I was devastated about the loss of that dream. It was my fantasy that not only would I be able to work regularly and ensure a steady and reasonable income but I would be working in the counselling field and I was sure that this was an answer to my prayers. Because my life had been so improved by therapy, I still had my enthusiastic zeal about the work and was eager to share it with as many others as I could. In those days counselling was not as well established as it is today, and I longed to participate in helping to make it mainstream.

At the same time, I felt that I had completed a great deal with respect to my own healing, and there was still hope. My experience of healing had enabled me to re-establish a balance in my being that had probably not ever before been there. I was certainly getting stronger, and at the same time I was counselling and using healing with others. It was a great time in those respects, and my progress and development was very encouraging. I could say that I was far healthier than I had been as a young child, and my emotional life was more authentic than ever before. At the same time my lack of money was increasingly demanding, and caused me enormous concern.

I was facing the repossession of my home because my savings had been exhausted, and the high mortgage rates had taken their toll in every way. Part of my desire to search for healing in its various forms was that I felt if I could find and identify the faulty belief system within myself that was preventing me from being successful: I could find the solutions that I so hoped would be there. However, I will say more about that whole process in a forthcoming chapter.

On Reflection

How are you experiencing reading this book so far? What thoughts and feelings does my story evoke in you? How does your own life relate to mine and in what way do you see yourself as similar or different to me?

Now it is time to pause in the proceedings, and I would suggest that you take stock of where you are now, relax a bit and enjoy the moment. It is time to turn inward in a kind of meditative state. We can't get answers if we are always rushing around. We can only get answers by becoming quiet and listening to the deep inner voice which is the voice of our soul. There are so many superficial voices that we hear during our hectic daily lives that it takes some inward focus to create a life that we feel is worth living. Remember as Socrates said, "The unexamined life is not worth living."

Daydream a bit; feel as if you are sitting on a pier, dangling your feet into the water of a lazy river in the height of summer. The sun is beating down just enough. It is not uncomfortable, but it is pleasantly warm, and you are just enjoying the feeling of the water lapping at your feet, and the passage of the river. You notice a few boats, and a few people, and you have friends around but not nearby. This is a time for you to just do nothing and enjoy that. It is one of the lazy days of summer. Imagine and enjoy.

Chapter 16
Sex!

When I started writing this book, I thought I would not include a chapter on sex. The subject felt too threatening for me to do so, but as I come more into relationship with my life, I see that I really cannot ignore this issue. I am no expert on sex, but I have had some important questions that I think might be of interest.

As with most people, I am sure, sex has been an important part of my life. Even as a teenager, I remember buying at least one book on sex, although there were not many available at the time. However, when my hormones were racing through my body, and I used to get really excited seeing Elvis Presley on television, I knew that sex was interesting to me.

Prior to that time, when I was about 10 or 11, I was going over to visit a friend in her house, which I did frequently. Mary was my best friend at the time. When I arrived, I was ushered into a bathroom, and I found myself among several girls lying on the floor poring over an open book. It turned out that this book was one of Mary's sister's schoolbooks on health, and the page that was open described the sexual act and explained a woman's menstrual periods. I was left stunned. I couldn't believe it. The whole thing sounded impossible, wrong, ugly and well, how could the area from which we pee play such a major role in making love? And childbirth? Before I went home in my shock, my friends swore me to secrecy, with the warning that I needed to keep quiet because they said this was the time when mothers were meant to be explaining the facts of life to their daughters. My expectation was therefore that my mother would probably be explaining it all to me very soon. Well I couldn't really see that happening, but I agreed to wait and remain silent.

I waited, and I waited, and I waited. The weeks went by: only about three of them, but at that age a day seems like an eternity. Finally I could wait no longer, and I asked my mother, "How are babies born?" She was not really ready for that question. Her first response was, "I thought you knew". I said that I didn't, and she, bless her, continued with a pretty reliable explanation. She explained that when people are in love and married, a man puts his penis into a woman's vagina and then sperm come out and fertilise the woman's egg and nine months later a beautiful bouncing baby is born! Well that was all very well, and I had learned something about that, but I was rather annoyed that my mother had not initiated the conversation, so I had to put her on the spot just a little more, and said, "I don't understand; would you draw me a picture?" Well bless her, she even did that, and then I was satisfied that my mother had done her duty and explained the facts of life to me.

I don't know if the subject was ever raised again. My mother and I were living in my grandmother's apartment then, and I didn't really see much point in starting any further conversations about sex with her. She wasn't married, and my grandmother was a widow, so I guessed there was no sexual activity in that household anyway. Because I was still rather disgusted by the whole idea, I had no problem knowing that I didn't have to think about this until I was married anyway, so why worry now!

So by the time I started secondary school at age 11, nearly 12, I knew for sure that Santa Clause didn't exist and was a myth and I knew something about the facts of life. Beyond that I didn't care. I wasn't particularly interested in boys anyway, so it wasn't an issue. Having eliminated the Santa Claus belief and learned a bit about the facts of life, I felt I had made as much progress towards being an adult as I needed at that time. I didn't feel at all in need of having an interest in boys as well.

Of course at that age I hadn't realised what would happen when I hit puberty and my hormones kicked in. I first noticed that I would be interested in film stars and Elvis Presley, people who were far enough removed from me that I didn't have to think about ever being in the same room with them, and so I just noticed that I fancied them, and that I thought they were intensely handsome. Those thoughts and feelings entertained me for awhile.

It wasn't just Elvis Presley and attractive actors that appealed to me. I remember when I first lived in Chicago, Franklyn MacCormack, WGN radio personality, used to start broadcasting at midnight. I would be driving home from somewhere, and then I would hear his deep baritone voice reciting:

> How do I love thee? Let me count the ways.
> I love thee to the depth and breadth and height
> My soul can reach, when feeling out of sight
> For the ends of Being and ideal Grace.
> I love thee to the level of everyday's
> Most quiet need, by sun and candle-light.
> I love thee freely, as men strive for Right;
> I love thee purely, as they turn from Praise.
> I love thee with a passion put to use
> In my old griefs, and with my childhood's faith.
> I love thee with a love I seemed to lose
> With my lost saints, --- I love thee with the breath,
> Smiles, tears, of all my life! --- and, if God choose,
> I shall but love thee better after death.
>
> (Browning, 1954, p.57)

That would set my day and my week and my year. Franklyn MacCormack, whom I had never even seen, would read that poem, with which he started each broadcast, so beautifully that my heart would melt inside me. As I think about it now, that may have been part of the reason that I fell so in love with Philip O'Brien because he had such a wonderful speaking and singing voice.

Despite my daydreaming about romance I was still very inexperienced with respect to actual boys. I was shy and didn't really know how to act in the presence of a boy. Later, when I was about 15 or so, I did have a boyfriend for awhile, but in those days sex wasn't a big part of the experience, only kissing and cuddling. When I returned to school after having nearly died from encephalitis and was becoming quite attractive, I had a slightly older boyfriend for a time, and that was serious enough that he asked me to marry him when I was about 17, and he was about 23. He wanted to make love to me, but I declined in favour of waiting until I was married, and I knew I wasn't going to marry him. When he proposed to me I had only just begun life in a university, and I felt I was too young and had too much to do in my life before I settled down, so I said no. We broke up soon afterwards and that was a very sad occasion for both of us because I did love him. At only 17, I felt that I was hardly experienced enough to choose a husband for myself. Even though I did so at 21, those few years made a big difference to me.

Another thing I experienced in secondary school was that I went through times when I had a "crush" on an older girl. That meant that I really thought an older girl was attractive, and I liked the way she dressed and acted, so I wanted to copy her. I do remember wondering if that feeling meant that I was lesbian, but I don't think I really understood what that meant. I was too ashamed to talk to anyone about my feeling, so I left it alone and noticed that overall I was far more attracted to men than to women. I think that the fact that there was even an expression "crush on a member of the same sex" meant that there was something normal about my feeling, but because it felt sexual, it also felt wrong to me. Nevertheless much later when I learned about human development, I realised that it is a normal part of human development to admire and be attracted to people of the same sex as an adolescent.

While I seem to have digested the idea that sex was appropriate in marriage from growing up in St Louis with my mother, my father had a very different viewpoint. Although I didn't see him much because by that time he lived in Switzerland with his wife and young daughter, I did visit him in the summertime, and we discussed sex within marriage and outside of marriage. He let me know that he believed in fidelity in marriage, but he felt that it was a good idea to explore a relationship sexually before marriage to know if you and your partner were compatible. I respected his viewpoint and saw it as one which came from the fact that he had travelled and was more worldly and really had had more varied experiences in life than many people whom I met. I thought his opinion was wise because I felt it was validated by genuine experience. I was grateful that we did have quite an open relationship and could talk about anything and everything.

I knew that I wanted to get married and have children one day, but I felt I wasn't quite ready for that then. I was more inclined to listen to my father's opinion about life because I was aware of his level of integrity, which was extremely high, and of his serious way of thinking about life. He was someone whom I trusted far more than any of my mother's relatives and friends in St Louis except for one or two, with whom I didn't discuss aspects of sexuality. As my sister said about my father, "You could take his word to the bank." That was the truth. If he said something, he did it. If he were not going to do it, he would never act as if he were. I idolised him in ways, probably more so because I had not lived with him for much of my life growing up. Whenever I went to visit him and his family, my first question of him was, "Are you happy?" I worried about him and really valued him. I loved him as my father, and I liked him as a person and had tremendous respect for him. Thus I valued his opinions. We always had interesting discussions. He would always give me his opinion, without insisting that I agree with him, saying "This is my belief and experience, but you are in the situation, and you have to make up your own mind." He gave me a viewpoint of life that was international and accepting of different types of people. Through him I grew to appreciate people of many cultures and nationalities. I also grew to know that there was a life outside the one to which I had been exposed in St Louis that felt more vibrant and dynamic, interesting and fulfilling.

Because of my reading and interest in sex and my body and my cycles, I thought I understood when I ovulated and felt that I would know when it was safe to make love with a man and when it wasn't. I felt capable of making choices about my sexuality in an adult fashion because I felt that I understood my body. Looking back now, I feel I was sadly not nearly as smart as I felt at the time, but then that seems to often be the case with people of university age. Therefore in university I had a few relationships of sorts. I certainly enjoyed sex, and I felt that after my conversation with my father it was normal to experience it then even though I wasn't married. Also the moral climate was changing because birth control was becoming more readily available, and the book, *Sex and the Single Girl*, by Helen Gurley Brown had come out, so it seemed as if suddenly women were free of the fear of pregnancy if they had sexual experiences outside of marriage and it was becoming more socially acceptable to do so.

It was a time for what we thought was women's liberation. I guess for any woman to think that she could have sex with or make love to any man she chose and not worry about being left holding the baby did seem like a real liberation. I would now question that notion because I hardly think that it liberates women or men to be sexual without any real commitment or depth of a relationship, even if the fear of pregnancy is removed from the equation. I think that being sexual without commitment can open an enormous range of responses, some of which we would rather remained closed. There seemed to be no concern for sexually transmitted diseases, and I knew little or nothing about the age old ones like syphilis and gonorrhoea, except that they seemed to be of a time and place that was far from me. I guess the only real concern for me and many women like me was the possibility of getting pregnant.

Then in the summer of my 19th year I became a Bahá'í. I was over the moon about that. I read books about the Faith and attended many events, meeting a large number of Bahá'ís. It wasn't, however, until I had been a Bahá'í for about three months that I realised that the Faith, like most world religions, urges its followers to have sex within marriage only and not elsewhere. I was stunned and shocked because I felt an overwhelming love for humanity, and an overall excitement about what I had found in the Faith. I guess I was caught up in the 60s revolution of "Make love, not war!" I couldn't imagine that after having begun to feel a sexual freedom that had never before been available to women throughout history that I now had to make a 180 degree turn and re commit to a belief in sex only within marriage. I guess I was glad to have had the sexual experiences I already had, but it felt like now was the time to look for another way to express my sexuality, so I thought OK, that is a signal that I ought to get married. I enjoyed sex, and I didn't want to live my life without it. If my faith advised confining it to marriage, then I was prepared to do just that. As I reflect on the apparent ease with which I made that 180 degree turn, I feel that actually the idea of confining sex within marriage was my own ideal and though it didn't fit in so much with the emerging sexual freedom of the 60s, it fit in with my deeper beliefs that perhaps I hadn't really accepted until then.

On that subject, I remember a conversation between two Bahá'í women one evening. One said that she had only ever been intimate with her husband and paraded that fact as a virtue. The other one, noticing her tone of self righteousness replied something like, "Well then it wasn't difficult for you to follow the Bahá'í law! For me it was really hard because I was used to having a different fellow every night!" I thought that little exchange was quite funny.

Anyway, I was soon married to Philip and after the first year of marriage, we decided we wanted to have children. I had taken the Pill during the first year of our marriage, and that seemed like an appropriate use of this new birth control. During that year, I decided that I no longer wanted to use any form of drugs to interfere with my normal body cycles, and I really wanted to have a baby. I would wake up in the morning, dreaming of rocking a little baby in my arms.

I felt that not only did I have the appropriate arena in which to enjoy sex, but I also had the advantage of being sexual for the purpose of starting a family. I thought that it couldn't get much better than that! I was young and I got pregnant very easily. There was nothing as thrilling to me as making love with the man I loved for the purpose of conceiving a child with whom we could share our love. That was the purpose of my life and my love at that time. I was so happy. I was so attuned to my body and my life that I knew immediately when I got pregnant, and that fact was simply confirmed in a few weeks time by my body.

It wasn't long before I had my first baby, followed by my second baby, the loss of the third and the fourth babies, and finally my fifth baby. I had, through my experience of my babies, come face to face with the intensely positive result of sex, with my growing children who lived and gave us immense pleasure. However, I also felt the excruciatingly painful result of that same energy, with the loss of two babies, one by death at four weeks of age and one by early miscarriage.

That was just in my own little family, with my husband, in our marriage, where there was love and support. Yet I was also aware of even more horrific experiences of sex that many people suffer. Indeed I had suffered from sexual abuse as a child, even though I was unaware of it at the time. That was probably just as well because I imagine that I might never have had children if I had remembered my abuse and perhaps never have married either.

I surprised myself with my childbearing history. I was a young woman from a Protestant background who always thought I would have two children, a boy and a girl, and suddenly I was a woman with five pregnancies behind her and three children. I guess that living in the Catholic part of Ireland where women were encouraged to have as many children as God (or perhaps their husbands!) gave them, had a profound effect on how my little family developed. How grateful I am that I had all those pregnancies and have had the experience of more than just two children even if today I have only two living children. When we all meet in the next world, it will be a big family gathering, I would imagine!

Just as an aside, there is quite a funny story from our early days in Ireland. Philip and I had brought a king-size bed from Chicago to Dublin. These beds were quite novel in America, and I don't think they existed in Ireland at the time at all. Philip and I decided that we wanted to buy an eiderdown quilt for our bed, so we took measurements, and Philip went down to a lovely linen shop in central Dublin that advertised eiderdown quilts made to measure. When he presented our measurements, the sales person was quite surprised at the large size of our measurements and thought we must have made a mistake. He gave Philip two pieces of string, each representing one of our measurements and asked him to go home to check that we had measured correctly. Philip brought these pieces of string back home, and we looked at them. Then we decided that another couple of inches in width would be appropriate. The bed was six feet wide by six feet, six inches, long. Anyway, Philip went back to the shop and explained to the man that he was right and actually we would like the eiderdown slightly bigger than we had thought! The man was astounded and replied with, "What kind of an animal are you married to anyway!" Well I wasn't an animal, but we had a big bed. We thought it was all very funny.

I arrived at the beginning of my 30s, having already had my last child. Because I could not imagine having any more children, I felt it was a time to reassess the purpose of my sexuality. I felt that I had done enough for the next generation, and I knew it was time for me to make a decision about whether or not to have more children. I found it really hard to explore the possibility of being closed to further pregnancies. I had loved the whole experience of being pregnant, breastfeeding and nurturing a new little soul in my arms. I knew that Philip had also loved our experience of child bearing. But as hard as it was since I felt that he would have enjoyed more children, I knew that the time had come to say no, and I did just that.

I grieved for the loss of my childbearing years. It actually took me quite a long time to come to a final decision. I noticed that I would think of the reasons why it would be great to have at least one more baby so that I could raise four children or even one more after that, so I could have five children. I thought of how lovely it would be for my youngest to have a sibling with whom to relate. That felt like something similar to the closeness that my two older children had with each other. Then I thought about how the older two are close in age and by the time I began to wrestle with this issue I knew there would be quite a large age gap between my youngest and whoever might come next, so they couldn't really be experiencing similar things or play meaningfully together. I knew that if Tara had lived and I had Brian soon after her, then I would indeed have two groups of two children. In some ways I had wanted four children. I also noticed how much energy I spent looking after my children and I felt that I might not have so much energy for another infant. All in all it must have taken me a good year to make a final decision that I wouldn't have any more children and I grieved a good deal for the loss of that possibility.

Of course, hot on the heels of that decision came my questions about sex and what it meant to me, my husband, and my family. I have to say that although now there was the issue of birth control to manage when we had sex, having three young children was a big step in that direction. It was really difficult for me to feel relaxed and available sexually to my husband because I worried that my children would wake up and need our attention. I liked my privacy when I was sexual, and often privacy just didn't exist. We also had a lot of guests staying in our home, and that did not encourage marital intimacy either. To make matters worse Philip was often out at the theatre at night and got home after I was asleep, so all those things contributed to abstinence more often than we might have wanted.

Also, we had such busy, active lives that we were often very tired. I needed a reasonable amount of sleep, and I faded at night. Philip was more of a night person than I was. He would come home from the theatre and be wide awake, but I would be so tired after my day looking after children and the household that I would be sound asleep. Then he would do the laundry to settle down after his performance. That was great. It was as if there were elves doing some of the necessary housework as I would come down in the morning to find all the clothes had been washed as if by magic. As much as we had established our routine, it didn't provide for us the intimacy that we would have enjoyed, so in my spare moments, and when I was doing work around the house, I wondered about sex.

I had rather forgotten that people were sexual with each other for fun, pleasure, communicating and relating and not just for the purpose of procreation. For me, like for many women who have spent a significant period pregnant and raising children, sex had become very much associated with pregnancy. When the time of being pregnant is finished, there is a period of having to reassess sex once again, and explore being sexual without planning a pregnancy. I had even begun to wonder if our Creator had really intended sex just for procreation as was the case with some domestic animals like our dogs and cats. Our dogs, for instance, would play with each other quite a lot, but they would only engage in sexual activity when a female was in heat, and that was to create more animals. Our female cats would go into heat within what seemed like minutes after having given birth to a litter of kittens. That was more than anyone could bear, I thought!

I began to look for reading material that might help to answer my questions. I did wonder why there was this wonderful thing that two people could do with each other that was so nourishing and self affirming, and yet there was this caution attached to it: Enjoy, but not too much because you might end up with yet another pregnancy! I knew that all birth control methods were flawed. I certainly didn't want to take the Pill because I didn't like to manipulate my hormones in ways that might cause me trouble then or later. I didn't like or trust condoms nor did I want to use a diaphragm which seemed entirely too troublesome and rather old fashioned. Therefore the only sure birth control was abstinence. That hardly seemed fair.

Ireland in the 1970s and 80s was not renowned for having a large selection of books on sex. I looked in the local bookshop and found one book on sex that was entirely enclosed in a cellophane wrapper, on which there was a sign indicating that the book was only for married couples. I couldn't quite believe it. Surely anyone might want to know something about sex. So I communicated with some English and American bookstores and got lists of books on sex, from which I mail-ordered ones that appealed to me.

One of the most beautiful books that I found was *The Tao of Love and Sex* by Jolan Chang (1991). It was beautifully written and explored the wisdom of men conserving their sexual energy by pleasing their women without ejaculation except rarely. That seemed to provide a possible answer to the birth control issue, but not entirely because I knew that such a method was not foolproof either. Nevertheless it did seem to honour women in a way that much use of sex does not. I shared this book with my husband, Philip, who said it could have been written in fifteen pages, a response which somehow didn't encourage me, but also didn't surprise me because to follow the suggestions in the book would mean to change our whole way of looking at sex. I did continue to read a number of interesting books on the subject, which helped my quest but didn't provide the answers I sought. I wondered about the range of sexual experiences in my life and in the world from those that are beautiful and spiritual to those that are depraved and extremely damaging.

The Bahá'í Writings teach that sex should be confined to marriage, in concert with the teachings of many Faiths, and the use of birth control is currently a question generally left to individual decision in the light of Bahá'í principles, so I looked for natural methods of birth control. Although I was still confused about the role of sex in a relationship outside of procreation, I recognised that if I was going to explore this any further, I was going to have to find a method of birth control that suited me. I tried the "honey cap" but I wasn't that happy with it. I spoke with a close friend, who was Catholic, and who praised the benefits of making love without the meeting of penis and vagina, but that didn't really solve my conundrum. I learned about the temperature method of tracking times of ovulation, but all in all, I was just as puzzled as ever.

I had heard that there was an herb in South America that would prevent pregnancy for a long period of time, if taken by a woman. The native people would not reveal the secret of this herb because they didn't want pharmaceutical companies to sell it and make a fortune. It was simply a natural part of the environment and free to anyone. Again, while interesting and hopeful, this didn't resolve anything for me. I had my fertile times calculated by some computer service, but I couldn't really rely on that. I was in my early 30s, and it may well have been that as I got older I wouldn't have become pregnant as easily anyway, but that was no guarantee.

I held my confusion, and I explored these various methods of birth control with my husband, and we seemed to be enjoying sex for all those wonderful qualities that it gave us to do with communication, closeness, togetherness. Gradually I began to discover that I could enjoy sex without pregnancy as its purpose. I was also still grieving for the loss of that desire to be pregnant because I had so loved the experience of pregnancy, childbirth, breastfeeding and nurturing a new little soul to participate in life on Earth. However, I began to really understand, appreciate and live the reality that sex between partners is a wonderful way to enhance a loving relationship and build joy and trust.

As I reflect now on my experience, I remember also that I had gotten pregnant so easily in my 20s. Once I had truly decided to have no more children, I was really afraid of getting pregnant. My growing understanding of my body's cycles and finding that there were methods of birth control that I could use, even though perhaps not ideal, made me relax more into just the pleasure of intimacy and I finally let go of my fear of another pregnancy.

Then came the jarring discovery that I had been sexually abused as a child, and that really pulled the rug out from under me in terms of my sexuality. I became vulnerable and rather frightened and really didn't want to be sexual for quite awhile. I was deeply saddened by the impact that the discovery had on my ability to be intimate, but I also knew that such a response was inevitable. In a way the timing of my withdrawal from sex was not too bad because it was not long after that Philip went away to work in London, so I had time to myself to begin the long healing process.

And, of course, since I was no longer having sex there were no issues about birth control. My celibacy ushered in a period of reflection, healing and emotional growth that marked the end of my time in Dublin.

After I had moved to London and divorced Philip, I gradually began to feel that I still needed to come to terms with my sexuality, especially since I had worked through so much of my memories of my abuse, so I began my quest again. This time, however, I seemed to be able to find more resources.

As I continued my study, I wondered how it was that I had at one time felt that men knew all the answers about sex and I, as a woman, just needed to find my knight in shining armour who would lead me to all truth about my own sexuality. As I learned more about my sexuality, I was pleased to be taking responsibility for what was mine, especially because my body had been usurped at a very early age by an adult in authority without any consideration of my wishes or needs.

I began to believe that the reason I had assumed that men knew all about sex was that they knew much more about how they worked sexually because their sexual organs are so visible and available. Women on the other hand have sexual organs that are much more tucked away in what seem like secret places. So just because men understand their own sexuality more clearly and easily than do women, they don't necessarily understand their woman's sexuality. If she doesn't know how she works, it is likely that he won't either especially if they are unable to communicate their likes and dislikes to each other.

I did a short workshop based on Native American teachings organised by an American organisation called the Deer Tribe Metis Medicine Society. There I learned about a "full body orgasm" based on breathing that I could do myself to energise my body, and that set me free. I realised that I could manage my body, and that I could get to know how I worked sexually without relying on a man unless I chose to do so.

Through my reading, I also learned that there were other kinds of orgasms from full sexual intercourse to those caused by the stimulation of the clitoris, the only organ in a woman's body that exists purely for her pleasure. I could add to that the firebreath or full body orgasm generated by breathing. I learned about a woman's G-Spot and the Venus Butterfly technique. There are books about all of this. And so I realised that there were choices, and I could decide on how I was going to use my body and with whom, if with anyone.

I always found it puzzling that there was so little in the way of education about sex, when anything else that might be of interest to us often required vigorous training. Yet, here we are growing up in the West where sex is used to sell cars and refrigerators. Life seems to demand that we absorb and integrate on our own the enormous range of experiences from rape, sexual abuse, possessiveness and jealousy to the most glorious of sexual experience leading to unity between partners, experiences of oneness, and the creation of another soul. We have little encouragement to explore and come to understand what our sexuality is, and it is one of the most important forces in our world because it is the life force.

Many people in the West have grown up in families without any meaningful discussion of sex nor any forum where they can explore their thoughts and feelings about sex. I had heard that according to some Native American teachings, young people, when they became teenagers, were put with an older member of the opposite sex to learn about sexuality. That seemed somehow reasonable to me, but I was not part of that loop. I am astounded that we are so ill prepared to really understand our sexuality in what is meant to be an advanced society.

I also found some spiritual books that indicated that sex was basically, a spiritual experience, which opened doors in people's being that led to much higher forms of life and higher states of consciousness than might have been suggested by the usual concept of sex. I am reminded of the French slang for climax, la petite mort, which means "little death" and refers to the sense of spiritual release that is associated with climax and expenditure of the life force. I found out that in past ages, sex happened in the temples because it was considered sacred, and that people trained to be good at sex. The Native American teaching, according to what I learned from the Dear Tribe Metis Medicine Society workshop, was that sex was the catalyst force.

I also had to wonder about the moral laws of religion about sex within marriage only. Despite my decision to experiment with sex before I married, I began to see that I might have been wrong about that. Yet my choice after becoming a Bahá'í to save myself until marriage was also flawed, since no matter what I might have believed, I had been sexually abused, so I had begun my life in a way that was not healthy. I couldn't have made a genuine decision to be chaste before marriage because I was not chaste from a very early age, unbeknownst to myself. That seemed unfair. I know that the abuse was not my fault and I was a victim, but that didn't stop me feeling somehow tainted and spoiled by that experience, and as if no matter what I might have done later, I could not erase that original flaw nor make myself pure as the driven snow when I knew that I felt contaminated. I felt deeply disappointed that I had suffered such treatment that had affected me in so many ways and that couldn't be subsequently erased. I no longer blame anyone for this and see that life presents us with challenges of all kinds, and still it is sad.

When I had been sexually active in university in my twenties, my only fear had been pregnancy. However, now I had become aware of so many more sexually transmitted diseases I began to see wisdom in waiting until marriage. I had to admit that introducing sex into a relationship changes the nature of the relationship. Not only does it increase the risk of some life threatening diseases, but it activates forces over which we may have little of no control. The sexual force is a primal force, and for some people that is fine, but for others it can result in intense jealousy and possessiveness that could lead to murder. It is my belief now that we don't know what we might be unleashing as we open our sexual channels with another person, and the result may be extremely ugly.

Not only could we unleash forces that we don't want to have to grapple to control, but we make ourselves exceptionally vulnerable. I now believe that in an ideal world marriage or a genuinely committed relationship ought to be the most sane arena for the exercise of sexual activity, but I am aware of the huge amount of domestic violence that goes on in which marriage or committed relationship is not a bit safe. Nevertheless I surprise myself with feeling that I would ideally choose to be sexual within a marriage becuase I deeply understand some very serious results of inappropriate sexual activity. Marriage or commitment certainly does not solve everything, but it may provide a level of containment and safety for sexual activity if there is mutual respect and caring.

I also believe that there is a lesson of entitlement, and although we think we can do everything and anything that we want to do as adults, there are things that we may not be entitled to do. You know when we are children we have to learn how to cross streets. We have to laboriously be taught to look left, look right, and look left again and right again before we are able to safely cross the street if no car is coming. Until we are sure of that procedure, we are not allowed and are therefore not entitled to cross the street on our own. I think that this concept of entitlement applies in so many areas, and it strikes me that sex is one of those areas that is most important. I feel that if we took the time to really get to know someone before we opened ourselves to them and became sexual with them, we might be wiser. It is easy to imagine that becoming sexual very early in a relationship could happen before we knew that we could trust our sexual partner, so perhaps being sexual could be something to be earned after we tested out other aspects of a relationship.

I wonder if we realise how and in what way our current behaviour and apparent sexual freedom is affecting our lives and our world? I know that we all have a lot to learn, and I think that there must be very good reasons for the regulation and control of the sexual impulse. Just as our parents controlled our entitlement to certain privileges as we grew up, so too, perhaps, religion, at a different level, provides a type of parental concern that may limit the extent of our entitlement to sexual expression. This potential limitation may protect us from acting in a way that may bring us harm or emptiness. I don't believe that establishing boundaries and limits is wrong, although it can feel uncomfortable. I see it serving a purpose that in some ways we have lost now in our culture. We have become very consumerist, kind of like a fast food culture in terms of our sexuality; we want instant gratification and no longer see pleasure in anticipation.

There is also the issue of respect and reverence. These two words, like vigilance and discipline, are rather out of favour in our world today, and yet they are extremely important. Our bodies are sacred vehicles for the soul, and as such, they need to be respected and revered. How many of us grow up with any sense of reverence anymore? Sometimes we feel reverence in a forest or by the sea when we are surrounded by the intense beauty and thrill of nature. It is discipline and genuine vigilance that leads to freedom. I think of the discipline and vigilance of a trained ballet dancer. I also think of the discipline and vigilance that is required to change unconscious habit patterns and choose to behave differently from the way we have behaved in the past. That is all about work, but work that leads in a positive direction. Do we not need to apply respect, reverence, vigilance and discipline to our sexual lives? Are we not healthier and better off when we include those qualities in our lives? Is society not healthier and more ordered when we can access those qualities and make use of them?

Our need to contain our sexual urges is only part of the story. It is the life force that drives us to learn to walk as young children. If you have ever watched a child who is on the threshold of walking, it is an amazing journey. The child perseveres and continues despite frustration and disappointment to build the necessary strength in its legs to finally be able to stand, first in a wobbly way, and then more securely, and to put one foot in front of another and walk. Nobody can teach a child to walk; she has to simply keep trying. That is just a simple example of the power of the life force.

We seem to have taken this desire to experience the life force to extremes that are no longer in our best interests. After having struggled for years towards our right to express ourselves in whatever way we choose, we are now finding that we just cannot do it all and survive. In our hedonistic desire to experience stronger hits of the life force, we have turned to drugs, drinks, music, and found ever more sophisticated ways of getting off our heads. The 60s began a time of apparent liberation that was supposed to give us the personal freedom that would ensure our happiness, and yet we are still surrounded by a fair amount of misery and suffering, so has it really worked?

The issue of hedonistic freedom is about releasing powerful forces inside ourselves over which we have no control and for which we have had no training. There is no wise mentor, as in the case of Carlos Castaneda and Don Juan, who could give us the guidance and show us the limitations that are necessary for us to be safe as we try ever more elaborate means of increasing our sensation.

I remember my father told me how his father taught him to shoot a gun. In Montana in the West of the United States of America where my father, his sister and brother were living with their mother and father, it was standard practice to be able to use a gun. My father must have been about 10 or 11 when his father began his lessons. My grandfather would give my father one bullet, tell him to walk a mile, shoot it and come back to get the next bullet. That is how my father learned to use a gun that later enabled him to hunt bear in the northern woods of Canada and to provide for his family in Alaska. Not only was he a fine marksman, but he had enormous respect for the power of the gun. His father had taught him to respect the power that he held in his hand with a gun, and he didn't misuse that power.

It is not just in our personal lives that we have gone beyond what is wise in terms of experiencing life, but it is in our consideration of the planet and our fellow human beings. Since developing a major consumer mentality in which we had to have more and more of anything we wanted and could get, we are now learning that we cannot continue to do that. We have nearly used up fossil fuel reserves and in the process have upset the balance of nature and caused immense suffering to people, wildlife and the planet through climate change. It has come to the stage where we have finally realised that we can't just keep throwing everything away. We have to think about recycling, our resources are finite and so we cannot just have it all our own way.

In the toddler stage, we go about gaining personal freedom, but now we are really reaping the consequences of our own carelessness and entering a more responsible age where we are accountable. Thus we need to think about the consequences of our actions with respect to our bodies, our psyches, our families, our communities, and our earth and beyond. Where we thought we had a right to all the personal freedom we could find, and that would make us free, we now find that we are not ever free because there are always consequences to our actions. Perhaps our real freedom comes in knowing that.

Not only must we live with consequences of our own actions, but we must learn to live with the consequences that come from others' actions or "acts of God", by which I mean fate that is beyond our control. I have found the need to come to terms with surrendering to that higher authority within myself or in terms of life or some sort of spiritual force because I have so often had to relate to events and their consequences, which haven't even been initiated by me. Where is the freedom in that? Even in asking that question, I feel there is a freedom in knowing our limitations, knowing that there is a power beyond ourselves, and knowing that we need to respect that power and come into relationship with it.

My struggle has largely been to surrender to that higher authority, which I call God. I always longed to do just that. I prayed for guidance and help whilst recognising my powerlessness and my helplessness. That was all fine, while my life was manageable and relatively pleasant or even mildly difficult. However, when life overwhelmed me, as it did, and pushed me way beyond what I thought my limits were, I found myself being extremely angry. I even felt abandoned and punished at times by God. I felt as if I had been run over by a cosmic bulldozer. Then, very gradually I have seemed to come into a kind of co-creative partnership with that life force. That sense of working with the life force is born out of respect and knowing that I am not so much in control as I would like to be. I have found it extremely difficult to begin to attempt to learn to be with limitation in a wise and creative way.

In the next chapters, I will be looking at issues of suicide and death, examples of the cessation of the life force. These experiences have been my advanced training ground in terms of limitation, loss, pain, respect and reverence. In summer 1996, my beautiful home in Chiswick was repossessed, and that was the launch of a period of time when I could barely come up for air because the demands on me were so intense. There was no pause. In late September 1997, our eldest son committed suicide at age 30. In the wake of that tragedy, my then ex-husband and I remarried each other in August 1998, as we had been planning to do anyway. He died of cancer in January 1999. Just four months later, my father, then in his 91st year, died in May 1999.

This intense time was exceedingly difficult for me to live through, and I imagine that it might be also difficult to read about, so I would suggest that you take it slowly, a little at a time.

On Reflection

Sex is such a difficult subject to discuss in a caring and constructive way. Just mention the word 'sex' and you can get as many different reactions as you might get to seeing someone come towards you completely naked. There is a lot of secrecy around our attitude about sex, whether it is because we feel inadequate and not good enough at it or we feel a secret triumph in our sexual capacity. We are often competitive, and there is often a lot of unconscious comparison between our own sexuality and what we imagine is everybody else's. We assume everyone else is doing it enough, satisfied by it, comfortable with it, and yet we may assume that we just don't measure up. Even if we cover up our insecurities by a kind of confidant attitude, most of us have, at best, a vulnerable relationship with our sexuality. Our relationship with our sexuality is one of the most important internal relationships we can have because it forms a basis of where we feel our place is in society, along with our earning capacity, the kind of mate we have, the children we have, the home we live in. It is one of the ways in which we rate our status. Therefore our identity and self esteem is very dependent upon it. So much of how we judge ourselves depends on how we compare our sexual experience or performance with what we see in the media, which tells us what we should be doing, how often and how intensely we should be having sex, what we should be feeling, how many orgasms we should have, and how to be fantastic lovers. We are told we need to be liberated, experienced, confident, and competent, so there is constant pressure for people to be sexual. How often do we feel ashamed because we are not having sex much or, if we are, what if it hurts, or if it is unpleasant in some way or another? What if we don't enjoy the way we are having it with our partner? Where do we go for help when it is often so difficult to discuss, and there would appear to be very few 'experts' who can help us through the difficult times. We need to feel desirable, attractive and able to satisfy our partner sexually at all costs. However, whatever we feel at any given time about our experience of sex, we can be pretty sure that our feelings will change as we go through different stages in our sexual lives.

Growing up, some of us were able to discuss sex in our families, but I would think very few. Parents find it very hard to talk about sex with their children. If we feel a taboo against even talking about it with the people we know best, what do we feel about either doing it or not doing it? How refreshing it would be if we as parents felt comfortable discussing sex with our children. How nurturing it would be if we were able to reassure our children about the importance of sex, to enable them to respect their sexual impulses and to use them wisely, to protect themselves adequately in today's world, to make knowledgeable decisions about contraception and safety, when and with whom and under what conditions to be sexual with another person, and a host of other things that come up in our daily lives that relate to sex. How can we, as parents, encourage our children to keep open the dialogue about sex with us, so that they can get advice as and when they need it? How many children would even discuss sex with their parents? How many children ever think with any ease or comfort of their parents as sexual beings?

Our attitude towards sex involves beliefs and morality and a host of things that go far beyond the physical experience of sex. We have feelings about sex and those with whom we may be sexually involved. We have beliefs about the rightness or wrongness of sex in different situations. If we feel that it is 'wrong' to be contemplating or actually having sex with someone, we feel an enormous burden of guilt which colours our experience. Even with the degree of sexual freedom that is now available, people still hold beliefs and attitudes that may control their behaviour to such a degree that they can feel enormous guilt if they go against their own self imposed rules. Animals don't think about it or feel about it. They just do it when the time is right and the females are in heat. That seems very simple. Human beings are not so simple especially with regard to sex.

For people in long term relationships, it can be very difficult to maintain an ongoing sexual relationship. How excited do we get with someone we face in the bed every morning before they have even combed their hair or brushed their teeth! Partners usually have different sexual needs. One wants intimacy more frequently than the other. One wants intimacy in different ways or under different circumstances than the other. If we are not currently having sex with our partners, we need to wonder why.

We may feel that we only want earth moving sex, and that unless we are feeling really turned on, emotionally charged and ready to have mind numbing sex, we oughtn't to have it at all. How can we have that kind of sex with young children in the next room, or even neighbours who might hear us, or guests in our home? How do we enjoy a deep sexual relationship with our partners if we are not comfortable even discussing the subject?

If we don't feel sexually interested in our partners, we often feel enormously ashamed about that, particularly because we are sure that there is something wrong with us and everybody else is having great sex at home. What if, and dare I suggest it, we no longer fancy our partners? If we have been living with someone for a long time, had children with them, we may be a bit bored or feel that we know them too well, and they are just not that interesting or stimulating anymore. We may feel that sex is only right if we are feeling very romantic and very attracted to our partners.

Very sadly at times like this if we feel we have lost interest in our partners we may begin to think that we have the 'wrong' partner and that the 'right' partner is out there somewhere, so we begin to look elsewhere. We don't realise that as our relationship continues over time, love feels and looks different than it did in the beginning. Equally we may not realise how much we can grow and develop through regular sex with the same person over a long period of time.

What about when a woman is pregnant, and her belly changes from being slim and firm to being huge and floppy? When she gets bigger, she very often doesn't feel a bit sexy. I remember a lovely story I heard once. There was a man who was a lorry driver, and he would whistle at every pregnant woman that he saw. He said that he remembered how his wife felt that she wasn't sexy when she was pregnant, and he wanted to help other pregnant women remember that they were sexy during the pregnancy as well.

What about just becoming parents? Men and women in the West often seem to have a feeling that a mother can't/shouldn't be sexy. This is sometimes referred to as a 'Madonna/whore' issue. We have connected the idea of the Virgin Mary and motherhood, and something tells us that being sexually alive after becoming a mother is not right. Very often it is after children are born that problems develop in a couple's sexual relationship. Unfortunately in this kind of situation we often feel that we are alone and nobody else is like that. Some couples actually stop having a sex entirely after their children are born. That is really sad because a couple's sexual relationship is the glue that holds them and the whole family together.

We expect to have some sort of magical chemistry between us and our partners forever no matter how long we are together. Nobody has talked straight to us about the fact that most people have problems at one time or another with their sex lives. The truth of the matter is that we just need to have sex, often whether or not we feel like it. We need to put it into out diaries and schedules each week. If we are not physical with each other, we will not be bonding regularly, and our bodies won't be providing us with the glorious bonding chemicals that are released within us when our bodies make love together. It doesn't matter if we are enjoying it that much. It is something that we need to do if we want the glue in our relationship. We may be surprised that, as we do it more regularly, we find that we enjoy it more and more and we become more interested and adventuresome about it. There are numbers of books about bringing sex back into a long term relationship, once it has gone, and continuing it through the years.

One of my favourite books on the matter of long term relationships is *Sex, Love and the Dangers of Intimacy*. In the context of living with each other over a long time it says:

> When we have run around in bonding patterns, been parents and children to each other, pushed and pulled till we were exhausted, looked with horror and surprise and courage in the mirrors, yelled at each other and learned something about compassion through sharing our grief, after we have searched and found our gender identity, acknowledged our relationship as a third entity, raised children and spirit children and accepted death…a transformed life dawns…Then we continue to live our everyday, ordinary lives…We are now available to enjoy living with each other. And this is where the lust and passion comes in…Living with lust and passion is an attitude to life and not a style; it is not exclusively about sex, but it includes it…Sex is the celebration of intimacy - but it is also the place where many of our emotional and relational problems come out…Mature couples can actually have the best sex of their lives, if they understand the possibilities open to them. (Duffell & Løvendal, 2002, pp.219-223)

Because sex is so enormously beneficial for us it is a shame if long married couples lose that aspect of their relationship because they then may miss an opportunity to improve the quality of their relationship and their physical health as well. There is a surge of wonderful hormones that are released in vigorous sex that can help regulate blood pressure, reduce stress, strengthen the immune system, reduce the risk of heart attacks and prostate cancer, and relieve pain. Sex can be better than some really good workouts at the gym. It can also be a lot of fun and can help to smooth over some of the misunderstandings that grow between couples in long relationships. Those are just a few of the benefits of regular sex. (Doheny, 2010)

If you are willing and courageous enough to look at your experience of sex, to talk it over with someone you trust, and to commit to finding ways to include it in your life for your and your family's health, you will reap the benefits over time. Just begin to explore it and enter into the wonderful adventure of enjoying a good long term sexual relationship.

CHAPTER 17
Darkest Night

My next experience of death, and the most traumatic, was the death of my eldest son, Scott, which happened on the 27th of September 1997 when he was 30 years old. It was a Saturday, the first day of my course in Anatomy and Physiology. That class began at 10am and finished at 4pm. I remember sitting in the class and just after 3pm I suddenly felt a sense of tremendous joy in a way that I don't remember ever feeling before. I thought that it was because I had survived the repossession of my house just a few months earlier, had moved and settled and had begun my studies again. I love learning, and I hadn't taken a course for a while. We later realised that Scott must have died sometime shortly after 3pm.

I arrived home after the class and was rushing because I had to get ready to take readings and food to the Bahá'í Feast of Will that was being held nearby. A Bahá'í Feast is an event which happens every 19 days on the first day of each Bahá'í month as a devotional service and community gathering in the worldwide Bahá'í community. Alfred, a Bahá'í friend in our community, came to my house because he and I were hosting the Feast along with another friend. I didn't have a car, so he was picking me up.

As I got ready, the doorbell rang, and it was two policemen. They frightened me, and I attempted to dismiss my fear by thinking that the dogs must have been barking too much and a neighbour had complained. I felt that I certainly didn't have much time to deal with whatever it was then, and I didn't ask them in. When I think about it now as I write this, I wonder if I had some sense of the message they were bringing because I so much wanted them not to be there and to just have it be a simple matter of dogs barking so they could tell me and just go away. Most of all I wanted them not to be there at all. If I could have run away and hidden, that was what I would have wanted to do.

One of them asked me if they could come in. "Yes, OK", I said showing them into the hall. Then one of them asked if they could sit down. I am not usually inhospitable, but I wanted to get this over with. I showed them into the living area, and they sat on the sofa. Alfred went out into the garden and left me with the two policemen, not wanting to intrude on something which I guess he felt might be none of his business.

Then after a few minor preliminaries that I have forgotten, they asked if I was Scott's mother, and I said yes. I thought that maybe there has been an accident or something. Then one of them said, "Scott is dead." I screamed twice in shock "Nooooooooooooooooo, Nooooooooooooooooooo!" I ran out to tell Alfred and the man next door who was in the garden speaking with him. I came back in and asked these policemen what had happened. My mind was racing, not knowing what to do next. The policemen didn't know how it had happened just that he was dead. They said that they would take me to the hospital where the body was. Alfred said he would go to the Feast and tell the people there and also offered to drive me anywhere if I needed a lift. I told Alfred to take the food and the readings and go to the Feast and I left with the policemen.

I got into the police van and was driven to the nearby hospital. One of the policemen said he thought I was great because I had heard that Scott was dead and screamed "No" and thus expressed my shock. I couldn't respond to that. At the hospital I was told that Scott had dressed himself up in his best clothes and had hung himself. I was devastated. Looking back, I feel sure that the police took me to the hospital right away in case I might have done anything dangerous to myself or others after having received such news or just collapsed in my shock.

After waiting in the hospital a little while and expecting the body to come there, I was told that the body was being taken to another hospital. I phoned Alfred to ask if he could pick me up and take me there. He and Mali, another Bahá'í friend and host for the Feast, came to get me, and we went back home first. We had to be at the hospital to see the body at 10pm, and there was some time before that, so I wanted to go home to try to reach Philip, who was then in California. I couldn't reach him, and while I was at home, the Chairman of the Bahá'í Assembly and his wife came over. He asked me, "Why you?" and I replied "I don't know". They knew how hard my life had been for quite a while because of the repossession of my house which came after a long period of difficulties. They were really concerned with how I could possibly cope with another emotional burden such as this knowing that I had very few resources to support me.

Alfred drove Mali and me to the hospital, and we all saw Scott's body. It was definitely he, and he looked traumatised, as one would expect. It was a horrible and shocking experience for me to see him because I had given birth to him. He felt in some ways inexorably connected to me physically as my son. Now that physical connection was severed. His face was red, and his eyes were open. I tried to close his eyes, but they wouldn't stay closed. My heart felt as if it leapt out of my breast, and I wanted to jump in to him somehow, find him and ask what we could do or how we could help. But I didn't know where to jump or how. I stayed for a while, said a prayer, and then I left because I could do no more. I was feeling shock, nothingness, disbelief, and a kind of revulsion that I imagine can only come from having to see something that I never in my wildest dreams would have wanted to see.

There is a horror attached to any form of murder but especially, in my view, a wilful murder of oneself. The revulsion is not just about my feelings of seeing a murdered body that is so closely connected to me, but it is about the horror and the taboo of getting so close to something that is so shocking, at every level. In the days between then and the time when his body was laid out for viewing, I experienced being completely disconnected and yet needing to function for myself, the family, to help organise his funeral.

We went back home and found my other son, Brian, there when we arrived. He asked what had happened. Some friends had left a message on the answer machine expressing their sorrow at the news without saying what the news was, so he knew that something serious had happened.

I hadn't been able to reach him to tell him the news as he was working at a theatre in the centre of London that night. I had asked the police if they could pick him up and drive him to the hospital, but they said it was too far for them to go. I knew that I couldn't phone Brian to tell him of his brother's death and expect him to come home alone on the tube, so I decided to wait until he got home to tell him. I looked at him and asked him to sit down, and then I told him. In his shock, he thought about what we had to do. We decided that we had to drive to southeast London to where my daughter, Shannon, lived because it wasn't something that we wanted to tell her on the telephone.

Darkest Night

Mali, Alfred, Brian and I drove to her flat and on arrival, we phoned from a nearby call box to prepare her for what was coming. I went into the flat and asked her to sit down. She refused to sit saying she just wanted to know what had happened, so I told her standing in the hall. She didn't express her feelings at the time, but instead thought immediately of her father. I had thought of phoning the Californian police to ask that they find and tell him, but I really thought it better to tell him myself even though I would have to do it over the telephone. I would have preferred to tell him face to face. Since that was impossible, we had to content ourselves with the phone and so I prepared myself for that conversation, but we still couldn't reach him.

Alfred drove us all back home. He dropped Mali off at her house first, and then he drove Brian, Shannon and me home. We all needed to be together as a family at that time. We started making phone calls. Finally around 3am we reached Philip. He had been to the beach, and when I told him, he said that he had been feeling sick all day, and that a TV show called *Goodbye My Love* in which he had appeared had been shown on television in California that night. He said that he would make arrangements to come back as soon as possible. We spoke with a few others whom we could reach at the time, my father and my two sisters in California.

We went to sleep around 5am. I was still in shock. I was absolutely freezing, and I didn't think that my body could ever get warm again. I woke up two hours later and the first thing I remembered when I woke up was "Scott is dead." I kept thinking how there was no negotiation. This was one of the experiences in life where there is total helplessness.

It felt like a very violent experience of our smallness, our limitations. I couldn't say anything to Scott, and the first thing I wanted to do after I heard the news was to ask "why? What can we do? How can we help?" At the same time I knew profoundly that we were completely helpless and could do nothing. This kind of experience is one of feeling as if everything has been completely smashed up, leaving us in a degree of helplessness that I would have never thought possible. Then when we are in that condition, we can only realise that there is absolutely nothing that can be done to remedy something that is so incredibly painful.

We spent the next day informing people in London, Dublin, America, Haifa, Israel, all over. People came to see us and spend time with us. The next morning a friend phoned me to say that she had dreamed of her mother, who had passed away a while ago, the previous night. In the dream her mother was smiling, which was most unusual because her mother never smiled in her dreams. This time, she was smiling, and she was saying "Scott is so happy." After hearing my friend say that to me, it somehow eased my heart, and it felt like a communication from him to reassure me.

That night when I went to bed, the thought on my mind was not "Scott is dead": it was "Scott, I love you". That was a huge relief to me. It was as if I was suddenly able to access my feelings, and that they were not so rigid, so tight. This shift from "Scott is dead" to "Scott, I love you" felt like a step towards a kind of communication with the next world, a kind of reaching to what is now, and at the same time there was still this enormous, huge, tearing, ripping thing that had occurred.

The initial shock had seemed to paralyse me and to freeze me in time. There was a very tiny thawing I felt when I included my love for him as if I were somehow connecting with him in the next realm where he had suddenly catapulted himself. At the same time I was holding the mess, the pain, trauma, tearing and suffering that he had dumped on those of us whom he left behind. I was holding huge extremes of feelings.

It took us the next week to organise the funeral, music, prayers, readings, and that was really hard to do. Philip had come back from California, and he and I with our remaining two children and a close family friend sat for hours together working on the running order of the funeral. We were all in such pain that there was tremendous tension between us, yet still we got the job done, and the funeral was great. It was a celebration of his life.

Before the funeral Scott's body had been laid out in the coffin for viewing, and I felt relieved by the tremendous sense of peace and joy present in the room. Also, Scott looked wonderful. He was a handsome man, and while nobody would have said he was angelic in life, he certainly looked angelic in death. There was a strong presence, and I felt his energy while sitting with his body, as it was laid out in that very quiet and somehow rather artificial atmosphere with the room fresheners to help make sure that there was no odour arising from the body.

There must have been about 150 people at his funeral. People came from all over the world. He was only 30 years old, and yet he had obviously made an impact. People came from Ireland, America, and Italy just to name a few of the countries that were represented. The funeral took place in a chapel at a graveyard. Philip gave a eulogy, as did Scott's wife. Shannon and I both read prayers. Brian sang one of Scott's songs. We ended the funeral with an Irish piece of music played on the uilleann (say "illen") pipes, which was haunting and gorgeous.

Then we all went to the graveside and threw irises into the grave on top of the coffin. One of the members of Scott's band played the didgeridoo at the graveside. Some of us threw in the first handfuls of dirt to begin the actual burial of the coffin in the earth, and then the band members began to bury it. It was all very moving.

I remember immediately after Scott's death, I felt extremely vulnerable physically. I was coming home on the tube one Sunday, probably a week after the funeral and feeling so fragile physically that if I had died then, it wouldn't have surprised me. I guess I nearly wanted that to happen, so I could see Scott again. Strangely, while in that tube, I noticed a strong fragrance of a wonderful Native American tobacco that Scott loved. It was unmistakable. I looked around to see if there was anyone in the carriage that might have had something with that smell. Nobody looked like a Native American to me, or even vaguely unusual enough to have such a fragrance and I could only conclude that it was something for me from Scott.

I completed my course in anatomy and physiology and that somehow kept me sane. It was just about the only thing that I could do. It was something regular, despite being only once a week and it was fun. Otherwise I really didn't function well at all. Life was like walking through treacle. Just hauling myself out of bed to start another day became a major effort. I couldn't see much point in it. Although there were others for whom I cared and things that were important to me; they just didn't seem so important in the face of my son's death.

Then I went to see my father and my sisters in California. I came back home, and that is when the grieving really began. I cried and cried and cried. I didn't care where I was, on a bus, or a tube or walking down the street or sitting with friends. If I felt like crying, I did so. That went on for some time, and I had help from friends and counsellors. Sometimes even now it still hits me, the pain of it. For many months I would dream of him looking fresh and happy and alive, and he would communicate clearly with me. These dreams reassured me that he is well in whatever reality he now inhabits that I cannot see.

I looked back over time. I remembered hearing the words, "It's a boy" from 30 years before and how delighted his father and I were at his birth. That delight was now overshadowed by the words, "Scott is dead." How could I hold those two opposite feelings, experiences? The two phrases kept repeating in my brain: "It's a boy, Scott is dead, it's a boy; Scott is dead, it's a boy, Scott is dead."

About six months before his death, in April of 1997, Scott had experienced a time of being hypo-manic and was in the psychiatric ward of Ealing Hospital. At that time he had been diagnosed as bi-polar, or what used to be called manic-depressive. I knew he had experimented with drugs in the past, and his hypo-manic phase came about just after he had found a new source of cannabis, a drug that many people consider "harmless". At the time I read an article about how, on the contrary to this view of it as being a "soft" drug, some forms of cannabis cause psychotic episodes. The evidence was right there in front of me. Scott had spent the previous year without taking any form of recreational drugs, and suddenly he was smoking cannabis, and was catapulted into a hypo-manic experience. That doesn't sound harmless to me.

In that April of 1997, Scott was experiencing an intensity that I had never seen before. I remembered how it took me two whole days to admit to myself that I had a son with a mental illness and to figure out a way to get him to the hospital to be assessed. It wasn't easy, and I had to make endless phone calls to people, doctor's surgeries and others in the mental health sector in our locality. Most people wouldn't listen to me when I attempted to talk about my son's behaviour.

Scott wasn't sleeping, and he was smoking cigarettes constantly. He was staying with me and Brian at the time because he thought his wife was trying to control him, and he wouldn't go home. She was just trying to manage him and his energy. He was spending money like water, and his energy was very high. I had never before been around such energy. It was frightening. I hid in my room while making my phone calls and trying to figure out what was happening to him and what to do about it.

He criticised me and complained when I wanted to empty his ashtray by saying, "Don't disturb me, don't you know I am getting messages?" He felt all-powerful, as if he could do anything, and he was planning a musical tour around the world. He even spoke to someone in the Arts Council who said she thought he could get at least £25,000 for his plans.

Finally he said to me that he was Jesus Christ, to which I replied, "No you are not because you are not as loving as He was!" He said, "I knew you would react like that!" At times he told me that I wasn't supporting him, and I wasn't helping him. Sadly, I couldn't any longer "kiss it and make it better," like I could have done when he scraped his knee as a child. It was still very hard to hear that he felt I wasn't helping him. I thought that was the illness speaking. Interestingly there is a fine line between psychosis and genius, and often it was difficult to distinguish between the two. He would tell me his plans and I would begin to believe him and think that his ideas sounded good and exciting and interesting, then his wife would caution me to remember that his grandiose plans were not grounded and therefore would not be realised, certainly not in his condition as it was.

After what felt like days on the telephone I finally reached a man who worked in a mental health unit, and he was one of the first people to really listen to me because I said to him that Scott had a knife in his jacket pocket that looked dangerous. I added that I was afraid because I didn't know what he might do with it. The man told me I had to take the knife out of his pocket and put it away somewhere safe. I felt so dishonest doing that, and it was a really hard thing to do, but I did it. The man arranged for Scott to be assessed, after which he was taken in to the psychiatric ward. He spent only about four weeks there, and he was allowed out on weekends. Then he was released and seemed to be really well during that summer.

I had been included in a case conference at the hospital. That is quite a formal meeting with all the doctors, care staff, consultants and anyone involved in his case attempting to determine what was going on and to plan a course of action. I wondered, looking at Scott in this meeting, when he said that he wouldn't promise never to smoke cannabis or take drugs again, what I might expect in terms of his life in the future. I was wary and didn't think it looked very promising because I felt strongly that it was his excursions into the use of recreational drugs that had caused his hypo-manic state. I dreaded more of the same or worse. I looked at Scott and wondered to myself where else could he go after having been in the psychiatric ward of a hospital? He did seem to be enjoying the experience and loved going to art classes and participating in the life of his fellow patients. I couldn't imagine what other experiences might take his fancy? He seemed to have tried everything.

I knew how much he had wanted to be a rock star, how creative he was, how brilliant his musical compositions were. I was saddened because he seemed to attribute his creativity to drugs, and I knew he was wonderfully creative in himself and had always been so. I thought of his presence on stage, singing, acting, even just in the room. When he came into a room, you noticed him. He wasn't someone who just disappeared into the background. He intimidated people just by his presence. He had a warmth and a tenderness, as well as an ability to make penetrating statements that could be quite shattering to some people because they touched something of their truth.

From birth onwards, what was especially interesting about him was that he always would figure out something very, very quickly, whatever it might be: a toy, a concept, and then move on to the next thing, and the next thing, and the next thing. At one stage, I suggested that he go to see Keith Casburn, who is a sensitive and a medium, and Keith said to me later that all Scott wants is spiritual happiness; all he wants is spiritual development. I could see that in him. That was his hunger. It was this longing that I imagine fuelled his decision to move on to the next world and go home.

Still I couldn't help thinking that the choice to end one's life is not ours to take but is somehow woven into the fabric of our life and occurs by the will of some force other than ourselves. It feels at one and the same time like extreme arrogance or hubris, a spiritual longing, a response to the call of the soul, and also the effect of a disturbed mind. What strange bedfellows are those varied viewpoints? If we have been given life by the will of our Creator, doesn't the will of our Creator also command the final transition of our life through death? These are the varied and seemingly conflicting thoughts that came to mind again and again and again. And still nothing that I could think or do could change the reality of what my son did to himself.

During the summer prior to his death Scott began to realise he couldn't depend on his mind. Friends were telling him some of the things he had done while he had been ill, and he had forgotten them. That wasn't what he would normally have done. How awful and frightening it must have been to feel unable to rely on his own mind. Although he had always had an ability to detach, cut off and move on to the next phase, how could he cut off from his family, especially from his children?

I noticed in that summer several things that seemed different with Scott. One was that he seemed unusually quiet at times when he was in company. Another was that he seemed to respond to the death of Princess Diana that August with an intense sadness that surprised me. I, too, was sad about the loss of such an interesting woman, but I wasn't as sad as he seemed to be. I phoned him on the morning when news of her death had just emerged, and he was crying. Never before had I seen him regard anyone's death as that painful. He was not then in a manic phase, but his response to Princess Diana's death made me wonder only vaguely if he might be heading towards a depression. Otherwise I thought he might be feeling a degree of paranoia because once or twice he said something to me that indicated he was afraid.

As I came to terms with his mental illness, I realised that he had experienced a manic phase in the previous spring when he had been hospitalised. He had also experienced a depressive phase the previous autumn before we were aware of his bi-polar diagnosis. Thus, if he had been moving towards another depressive phase, he may have decided that he wasn't willing to endure that again.

These are simply a mother's wonderings about a few things that may have indicated that Scott was moving towards suicide, but they are rather vague and could hardly be said to offer a definitive explanation. I do feel that he didn't kill himself out of genuine depression because he dressed himself up in his best clothes as if preparing to meet his God. I would like to think that Scott somehow understood that he had messed up his mind with drugs and wasn't prepared to inflict on himself or others the long term and gradually deteriorating results of that.

I don't think it was his psychosis that killed him, rather I believe it was in response to a more healthy part of his mind that recognised the psychosis, and its increasing hold on him.

I remember as he left me at the door of my home, the last time that I saw him, he said, "I feel completely disconnected from everything". That didn't sound like a feeling that Scott had willed in himself, and maybe I should have taken that as a sign. Looking back on it, I think maybe it was a sign, but I didn't know what to do with that information, so I was unable to respond to him and to that statement.

And so I was left with all kinds of unanswered questions, with a broken heart, and unable to function. I had to hold onto something about my really deep acceptance of the spiritual world, life after death, meaning and purpose, and the horror of my son's suicide, a violent and murderous act, and I was left to hold these two seemingly incompatible realities for the rest of my life. I didn't know if I could make myself big enough to contain all that. I also held within myself a real sense of privilege at being able to make a home on this earth for this incredible person who had to be known to be appreciated.

I sometimes think to myself that if he had lived for a long time, I probably would have really been sorry that he had experimented with drugs because they might have damaged him in some way that would have become apparent in the long term. However, since he didn't live a long life, I had to admire him for trying everything he could while he was here. This is in no way to suggest that I would either encourage or approve of his use of drugs. If anything I feared what they could do to anyone, but he was old enough to make his own decisions, and I was unable to influence him. I just had to accept that there were endless questions that I would never be able to answer. I had to deal with my grief, my rage, my anger, my hurt and sit with others experiencing those emotions.

I know that I sometimes have felt tremendous guilt about a lot of things, large and small, and I thought about my guilt over his death, but I don't know in what way I might have contributed to it. I do know that I always did what I could to encourage him and support him insofar as my limited resources would allow, and I also know that there may have been things that I did that were harmful. I just didn't know what they were.

I recognise that there is an area that I cannot touch, another wisdom, other reasons, a law beyond what I can understand. In a way I was grateful that there was nobody I could blame for this hugely traumatic event because

Darkest Night

Scott chose to murder himself. He didn't have an accident, and nobody else murdered him. Therefore I didn't have to feel angry at some living soul about his death. However, I have always said that when I get there to the next life after my death, I am going to have words with Scott, and God, for that matter! If I had been like some Irish mothers, I might have boxed Scott's ears as a young child, and I feel as if I would like to do that now, but how could I? I also know that I still love him and miss having him around.

I must say this, I know Scott well enough to know that he would absolutely love the fact that I could shock people by telling them that my son, Scott, had hung himself at age 30. He died like the rock star that he was. He simply wasn't well enough known at the time. He was so musical and creative. He had a wonderful ability to be able to talk with anyone and get onto a very deep level right away.

Also, Scott was the most honest person I have ever met. He put his heart into whatever he did or felt, and I always knew where I stood with him. When he was about six years old, we had an American friend come to stay with us for several weeks. When she first arrived at the door from the airport, I opened the door to welcome her, and he looked at her and said, "I don't like you, Mary Lou." I tried to cover that up, but how could I? She then replied, "Well, I'm not so crazy about you either!" For the whole time she was with us, he never changed and never became friendly.

One day, a friend who had taken over the health food store that we had started in Dublin came to deliver some things from the shop to me at home. Scott came to me and said he had a few pennies, and he wanted to give them to this friend. I asked why he wanted to do so. Scott told me that the last time we had been in the shop, he had taken some beans from one of the open sacks on the floor, and he felt he ought to pay for them. I was really touched by his concern with being open and honest about it, so I praised him and said that I was sure my friend would be really pleased that he would do that.

Scott's English teacher from secondary school in Dublin said that he didn't remember students usually because so many of them passed through his classes, but he never forgot Scott. He said that Scott was like a life force, and this world couldn't contain him. Another friend said that from his short association with Scott he knew that the world had much to learn from him and that he felt he would be spreading his light in a much more receptive place now. Another friend has called Scott a force of nature and said that it is very difficult to live in this world as a force of nature.

A friend of mine once said that no one dies before his time. He suggested that no matter where Scott would have been, he would have died and maybe there would have been an accident.

He was suggesting that suicide is a fated event as much as an accident is. I want to believe that suicide is a fated event in that way, but maybe it is simply an unnatural event that flies in the face of fate.

There is still something in me that says it is just not good enough that my son died by his own hand so young. It is not OK. This isn't all right. My son didn't die as he was supposed to die, at the right time. There is something terribly unnatural or anti-nature about this whole experience of a mother burying her son who is gifted, intelligent, and talented with his whole life ahead of him. Scott was a musician and a poet. Now, when I see such events as the Queen's Jubilee and the Live8 Concert, I wish that Scott were participating in those with his band because I know that he had the talent and ability to do just that. Then I think, maybe he is behind the scenes in the next life assisting those here to do their job. That may very well be the case, but it still doesn't feel right to me that Scott is not here himself where I can see him and throw my arms around him and hug him.

What I remember mostly when I think of what might have caused him to seek entrance to the next reality was that when I was pregnant with him, Philip and I had gone on our first pilgrimage to the Bahá'í World Centre in Haifa, Israel. That mightn't seem too remarkable today, except that in 1966 only a few pilgrims went at any one time, and we were invited to spend two nights in the mansion of Bahjí. It was there that Bahá'u'lláh, Founder of the Bahá'í Faith, had lived and died. We slept in a room that was near to what had been His room, which is still maintained in the same way now as it was then. Because I was pregnant, I got up in the night to go to the loo. On the second night I remember that I was moved to go into Bahá'u'lláh's room to say a prayer. I knelt facing His bed, which was a mattress on the floor and read softly aloud a most beautiful prayer called, The Tablet of Ahmad [1]. I felt the majesty and magic of being close to God in a way that I don't think I could possibly have felt if I weren't pregnant with my firstborn and so devoted to wanting to raise him in a very spiritual and special way. The energy in that room was palpable at the time. I was sure that the baby felt it too. I could only imagine that after having experienced that level of heaven even while in the uterus, Scott would never have found anything on earth to compare with it.

Scott and I had a conversation in the early 1990s when in a kind of reverie he spoke to me about his death. This was long before I thought there was any chance that I would be aware of his death because I expected him to die after me in the usual course of events. He had this to say:

> After I die, I want them to say about me that I believed in something, I stood for something, and I gave of myself. I keep going through the fact that I never arrived and what I want is unattainable. I'm doing something that I love to do that comes from within, and the human consciousness will relate to it and benefit from it. I want to create worth not wealth, value. I want to grow as an individual, and I want to share that growth with others. I don't want to help life's parasites. I want to make it difficult to be a parasite. I just want to be at peace with myself, and I can't unless I have quality time at work, at home, with myself. I have within me an essence, soul or spirit that is capable of creating circumstances to bring out what I have just articulated. Living at peace means striving to do what I might believe at any time cannot be done. In my music, I want to put people in touch with who they are by showing them who I am. My life and who I am is so highly valid that it can be a force in this society. In imaging that force within me, I saw an Aztec statue of a huge man with a staff wearing a sort of raven or bird of prey's headdress. His qualities are strength, solidity, peace. When I put him in my heart, I feel protected, valued, loved, respected. (From a conversation I had with Scott probably in the summer of 1994)

To some, that statement may seem to be full of contradictions because he hasn't lived.

Alternatively perhaps he felt that he had lived that reality to the full. That is part of the pain of those left behind who are left wondering if he felt unable to live his purpose, or if his death was part of that purpose.

---

1   See Appendix A

Somehow I had to hold the horror of Scott's choice to leave this life, and the pain of not even being able to sit down with him and ask all the endless and huge questions that were still hanging in the air. What if I had done this or hadn't said that? To ask him what it is that had so disappointed him that life was not worth continuing? I couldn't do any of that because he was dead and gone, and he had, by his choice, completely removed the option of consultation, negotiation, help or assistance. How could he leave his wife, daughter, son, and us? How could I deal with their pain, my pain, his pain?

In retrospect I can reflect on the possibility that Scott had to go on, that he had done what he needed to do in this life, and he had to leave this life, and it was his time to leave. I felt in some ways perhaps that it was a spiritual step for him that came from a tacit awareness of the next realm, but it left us in so much pain. And yet, he had been married twice and had one son and one daughter. I know he adored his family and I couldn't imagine how he could have left them all behind. I had to wonder what might have been meaningful for Scott about this horrific, self-murder. There were and still are enormous questions about what purpose it served? Was this an inevitable step arising from a longing to go home or was it an inhuman psychotic distortion? I guess I could say it is both.

Suicide is never a productive thing to do, or is it? Even if he longed to go home, it would have been a different thing to recognise that although he was longing to go home, his mind was deeply disturbed at times. He would need to organise a life around himself to care for that disturbance and contain it. It may be that he could have done that, but he didn't.

Scott chose to take his life. Therefore the questions remain: Was Scott's suicide a productive thing for him to do in any respect or was it a really stupid, thoughtless and horrible mistake? Did he benefit from it? How will he deal with its aftermath in terms of his own learning that might arise from it? If we believe as I do that we continue along an evolutionary path all the way through life and beyond death, then he may in some way somehow have to learn to manage himself within the context of whatever situation or circumstance he finds himself in next. I wonder if one can commit suicide from the next life into another next life? What do we do when we hit something that we cannot handle without destroying ourselves or the life we are living at that time?

I could go on and on, but the real question I ask is who killed Scott? Did the healthy part of him kill him because the sick part was getting out of control or did the sick part of him kill him because it believed in a distorted reality? In his most delusional moments did he believe that he was going to go home and sit by the right hand of God because he was Jesus? Could the sick part of him have been fulfilling that desire? He wasn't in a manic state at the time of his suicide to the best of my knowledge, but who knows what was hovering within him? We can only wonder if there would have been more creative ways for Scott to handle the challenges he was facing at the time, and maybe there were not. It may be that it was both the healthy part *and* the sick part of Scott that killed him.

That leads me to further questions about the rest of us. Might we who have been left behind benefit from Scott's suicide? Did he do it out of some amazing altruistic longing to help his loved ones to grow? That would sound hugely grandiose and rather God-like to me, hardly a valid reason to hang himself. And when all is said and done I can't really imagine the answer for him. I can only wonder if I am growing as I struggle to understand. I wonder what kind of positive gift there could be in his act of suicide for we who are left behind.

At some level, Scott might have been saying, "I can't handle the pain any more. It is not meaningful for me to be alive and be in this kind of pain." I am not suggesting that I know what kind of pain he was in, but I do know that something told him that he was not willing to tolerate living in this world. It was as if he didn't feel that he could be free to express himself without censure, that he couldn't carve out a place for himself in the world.

He may have felt worthless because he was failing to find a way to get the recognition he needed both materially and in terms of respect for his very real creativity as a musician and poet. If you feel you have something special and precious, and you are trying and trying to offer it in an unreceptive environment without success, you face a crisis of duality. That means you cannot stand the shortfall between where you feel you could be and believe you should be and where you actually are. That may be the crux of the whole issue and why he killed himself. I wonder why he didn't have the patience and perseverance to keep at it, and maybe that was part of the illness.

Most of us have to hold both a sense of giftedness about those things that we can do well and a sense of ordinariness about the daily mundane pattern of life. If he couldn't tolerate holding life's ordinariness and its disappointments and difficulties, then how much can any of us tolerate? Life continues to throw difficulties at us, and it continues to provide us with a lot of ordinary time spent in ordinary ways, and that can be quite grounding. Some people grow and strengthen through living the ordinary part of their lives and some are defeated by it and shut down. Unable to regain a sense of the joy of life again, some even commit suicide.

Even though Scott was gifted, poetic and interesting, he could sometimes come across as arrogant and even at times grandiose. He might have been saying, "I am so great and fantastic, this world isn't good enough for me any more!" That is the voice of his manic phase, the voice that wanted to speak about his feeling of his specialness in his everyday life. He could be quite penetrating and cutting to others, but when he was in a manic phase this capacity was even more pronounced. His sense of grandiosity may also be an aspect of his choice to leave us all behind. There were times in the year or more before his death that I began to feel that he had gone beyond me. I wasn't sure what that meant, and I never spoke to him about it, but I found him puzzling in a way that he hadn't been before. I wonder if he had experienced a sense of another reality that appealed deeply to him.

In writing about Scott's death now, many years later, I am reminded of some of Hillman's statements in his penetrating book, *Suicide and the Soul*, which I am including here to add to this discussion. They are not necessarily what I believe about suicide. They are simply other and varied ways of looking at it. There haven't been very many books that have been written on this subject, and this book has been very useful to me for this reason.

> The impulse to death need not be conceived as an anti-life movement; it may be a demand for an encounter with absolute reality, a demand for a fuller life through the death experience. (Hillman, 1997, p.63)

> Until we can choose death, we cannot choose life. Until we can say no to life, we have not really said yes to it, but have only been carried along by its collective stream. (Hillman, 1997, pp.63-64)

In reflecting on that last quote, I need to say that one of the impacts of Scott's death on me is that in some way it seems to have forced me to surrender to life in a wilful way. Thus I feel that I have now consciously chosen life, whereas before I did feel myself "carried on by its collective stream". Now, however, I recognise that there is a will beyond mine with which I am attempting to align myself. That feels like a kind of surrendering to what is.

> Suicide is an attempt to move from one realm to another by force through death. (Hillman, 1997, p.68)

> Once the choice is made, ambivalence overcome (as the studies of Ringel and Morgenthaler on suicide notes show), the person is usually deliberate and calm, giving no sign of his intention to kill himself. He has crossed over. (Hillman, 1997, p.69)

> …there is an attempt to achieve another state of being through suicide. There is an attempt at transformation. (Hillman, 1997, p.71)

> Where the death experience insists on a suicidal image, then it is the patient's 'I' and everything he holds to be his 'I' which is coming to its end. The entire network and structure is to be broken, every tie slipped, every bond loosed. The 'I' will be totally and unconditionally released. The life that has been built up is now a cage of commitments to be sprung; for a man it is often with the violence of masculine force and for a woman a dissolution into the soft reception of nature through drowning, asphyxiation, or sleep. What comes next no longer matters in the sense of 'will it be better or worse'; what comes next will for sure be something else, completely, the Wholly Other. What comes next is irrelevant, because it leads away from the death experience and saps it of its effect.
>
> This effect is all that counts. How it comes and when it comes are questions secondary to why it comes. From the evidence which the psyche produces out of itself, the effect of the death experience is to bring home at a critical moment a radical transformation. To step in at this moment with prevention in the name of life's preservation would frustrate the radical transformation. A thorough crisis is a death experience; we cannot have one without the other. (Hillman, 1997, pp.75-76)

> If death is life's goal, then death is more basic than life itself. If a choice must be made between the two, then life must yield to its goal. Physical reality which is limited to life only must yield primacy to psychic reality, since the

reality of the soul includes both life and death. The paradox of the soul is that, in spite of its ancient definition as the vital principle, it is also always on the side of death. (Hillman, 1997, p.107)

These are provocative and interesting perspectives on a rather unexplored topic, and I add them here as food for thought. I realise that for very taboo subjects, there is often what I would describe as a premature closure. In other words, we choose to move away from the subject thinking that it is bad, so it is better to close it down after having expressed the initial grief. Indeed that is what I would have done myself had I allowed myself to.

Instead I have continued to return to what is deeply complex and to stay with tolerating the complexity of it rather than closing it down too soon. If I hadn't been driven for the purposes of writing my memoirs in a meaningful way and of digesting this experience in a way that I can, I could easily have closed the subject myself. However if I had done so, I would have lost a great deal of understanding of what Scott's suicide has meant to me. While in many ways it would have seemed easier for me to close the subject down, I have opened it up again and again to ask more questions. I believe that by doing so I have helped myself to understand better and accept the loss of my first son with more compassion towards him and towards myself.

I have heard, and in many ways I believe, that we are never given more than we can handle. And yet I could not say that is the case for everyone when I had just buried my son by his own choice. I think it is extremely naïve to assume that nobody is defeated by the pain that they experience. I don't think we have to look very far to see people who appear defeated in some ways by difficulties. And maybe it is in that defeat that they have grown to handle the pain?

I might guess that Scott was struggling with being a man in the world, of feeling significant, wondering where his place was and what his contribution would be and wondering if he fit in enough to be seen as valid and worthwhile. He seemed to struggle to try to find a vocation that fed his soul and made material money while gaining him respect. While he had been a creative musician and poet composing his own music and lyrics, he often found himself working as a sound engineer, which he enjoyed and did to make ends meet, and immediately before his suicide selling sound cables for the same reason, which I feel sure he didn't enjoy.

I am guessing that this struggle to make a living in a meaningful and soulful way may be a family pattern. When I look back at family history, I observe that my elder relatives were involved in businesses, and by that involvement were able to satisfy their need to provide for their families and find a place in their community and hence in the world. Because Scott's father was an actor, it was as if the family line had moved from being involved in business to finding a way to work in the arts. Also Philip, Scott's father, was deeply involved in the life of the spirit, and while that didn't support him materially, he was able to find a sense of satisfaction, fulfilment and recognition through it that supported him emotionally. So it seems that there is a kind of creative soul force in our family that struggles painfully with trying to find its place, maintain integrity with and stay in touch with its true essence and be relevant in this concrete world.

This is a very difficult struggle for a man. I believe that a woman can use her creative soulful force in being married, having children, and maintaining family life. She sometimes doesn't have to struggle with this issue in the same way that men do. Many women from my age group have not had to ask themselves the question of what their vocation might be, not having had to choose between work and home life. And yet these days life is different for women, and their choices are more restricted. Many women these days need to work regardless of their opinion of it, simply because they need the income.

Scott didn't see his mother working outside the home, so he probably took on the feeling that making a living was entirely his responsibility, especially after his children were born. In other words he may have asked: how do I make a living for me and the family in a way that is meaningful to me and helpful to people? It may not have occurred to him that he could share that burden with his wife.

It seems as if after Scott came down from the manic phase, there was something lifeless about daily life for him. If he wasn't living at quite a high voltage, life seemed very empty. If nothing was going on externally either to juice him up or keep him excited this Earth may have seemed a really blah place to be. All of which leads me back to something that I may have thought originally, which was that he had done what he needed to do in this life, and he had to go on. That doesn't seem possible to me when I have lived so much longer and still have much that I want to do, and yet that may be what was true for my son.

Coping with his death feels almost like I have had to stretch to the very outskirts of my capacity and beyond to hold a multiplicity of emotions, thoughts, feelings, and experiences all at the same time. As a result I do not simply feel one emotion like anger or sadness. At any given time several are foreground, and I may notice myself feeling deep grief and rage. At another time I may be filled with a profound sense of love and joy and even gratitude. Sometimes I am in deep despair feeling "Who cares? What is the point? Why bother?" Other times I feel inadequate, completely helpless, and at these times I wonder if I can ever integrate such a tremendous shock and horror enough to create a new life for myself. I am sometimes overcome with rage that somebody could do anything that would affect me so deeply, that I could love someone so much that by his or her loss I am thrown into such deep grief. And sometimes I am filled with a deep sense of the privilege of having been able, while in this life, to experience the intensity of such emotions.

Sometimes the sheer horror of Scott's self murder overcomes me. It seems outrageous that I might have given physical life to this person who then turned around and threw it back in my face. How dare he prevent me from being able to protect him from himself and from harm? That is a mother's longing, and with Scott I was unable to do that. I am left with a sense of complete helplessness. I am horrified at anyone, particularly my son, having the audacity to think that he can personally choose when to end his life, and yet that is exactly what is embedded in God's gift of free will to us as human beings. With that free will is also the potential for violation, and it feels like a violation to take a life, anyone's life, even one's own! How frightening is that?

So I am left questioning whose will it is or was that my son is dead, God's or his, and if it is God's will I can feel content with God's will sometimes. At other times I feel angry at God's will. If it is his, I feel conflicted, shocked and ultimately protected from an uncertain future for him in the face of his mental illness, which might have been very difficult, if not impossible for him and for me to manage. Because of his illness and the potential to take drugs again, he may have caused great harm to himself and possibly to others, and I have been saved from having to witness that. All of these thoughts come to me.

I would like to think that we could make a harvest out of anything, which means overcoming even life's most difficult circumstances, but that is not possible unless and until we have fully expressed how difficult it has been, how much we wish it hadn't happened. Those are the immediate and ongoing feelings that cry out for expression. As vital as the expression of painful feelings is for healing from trauma, there is no guarantee that we will reap that harvest after having expressed all that we can. This experience, every day, brings me up against the sharp edge of that reality, of what it means to have had a son who killed himself. I have become more at peace within myself through expressing all my varied feelings in a safe place with a therapist; however the experience is as alive today within me as it was when it happened. It just does not go away.

Often we want to find the cloud's silver lining before we have truly experienced the cloud, in the hopes that we may never have to experience the cloud. People on a spiritual path often feel it is some kind of a failure to admit to the pain, the rage, the grief, the outrage of the death of loved ones by whatever means. They would prefer to say, "I am content with God's will." They would rather explore the joy of such an experience and exclaim that they are so happy for the one who has passed on. When they respond in that way, I often wonder what they do with the "negative" feelings, where they put them, and what is the relationship between the denial of those "negative" feelings and subsequent illness, depression and lack of motivation or energy.

I am here to say that we need to explore both sides of the experience. There is pain, rage, outrage, grief, confusion, anger, depression, for the human being in me, and at the same time my soul rejoices for the person who has crossed over. We are both Divine and human, and we need to hold and honour both experiences and all that means for us while we walk this glorious Earth with all her varied challenges for us. In other words, we have to make ourselves big enough to include all of our experiences and whatever that may mean to us. Sometimes I realise that even when I am in the most intense pain, I am truly alive. Maybe I mean that I feel most alive when I am in the most intense pain or the most intense joy because it is then that I feel most connected with the life force.

The only way out of pain is through it, and going through it can be a very difficult and long lasting experience indeed. Even when we feel that we have come through to the light at the end of the tunnel, we may find that we are suddenly engulfed with another period of darkness that takes us quite by surprise. That pain remains only a breath away from our awareness very often, and that may go on throughout our lives.

It is particularly in the middle of the night that I wake up and lie awake for hours feeling intense feelings of helplessness, inability to cope, fear, and terror. I notice that by staying with these feelings, eventually they move into something else, something new, something refreshing. I guess that is why they are called "emotions" because they are energy in motion. I think we lose sight of the fact that emotions come in waves as part of the grieving process, which means that they move and change, and as dark as I may feel at any given moment, I may again feel hopeful later.

Since my experience of Scott in his manic state, I notice that I sometimes visit my own madness when I feel so down, so unable to function, so bleak and blank that I don't know what keeps me going. There is a way in which I give up in those times. In that state, I notice that I feel as if I am hanging on to a thin, but very strong thread, and I have reached the bottom of it. When I recognise myself still hanging on to that thread, having reached the bottom, I know that if I went down any more I would lose control of myself, and I begin to come up again. I have no intention in this life to abdicate my own responsibility for myself if I can avoid doing so. Therefore, I will go so far into my own depths and no farther. That may be the only thing that differentiates my reality from Scott's because he never noticed the moment when he had gone too far down. Perhaps we all have to manage our madness, which may be an innate part of human nature, and Scott was not able to do that and remain here.

I remember in the past when I would reach that point of feeling myself hanging on by that thin thread, something external would occur that would bring me up and out of that. Now it is more often something within myself that starts my own move upwards.

I notice that with each step I make towards creating a new life for myself, another layer or level of grief and pain emerges. You know, people have spoken of grief and loss and death and the process of grieving the loss of a loved one, but I know of nobody who has actually said that as difficult as the grieving is, the experience of coming back to life is equally difficult. I am reminded of thawing from having been frozen, and how painful it is for the body to feel warmth again after its temperature has decreased significantly. I notice that every time something really positive happens, I am beset by what seems like a bubble or a boil of painful feelings. It is almost as if it is really hard for me to have a good life, want a good life, enjoy life when someone I love is no longer here. It feels like a kind of loyalty to remain in some degree of misery as an expression of my grief. I think that is why so many people seem to remain the same after they have lost loved ones because they cannot face the deeper levels of grief and the re-emergence into life through ever more layers of that grief.

I need to say a few words about friends. Clearly when such a shocking thing happened in my life I became acutely aware of whom my friends really were. People who loved me were there for me in so many different ways. There were other people, whom I might have considered friends, who somehow couldn't take such an experience and quickly faded into the background. To this day, I notice people who seem no longer able to relate to me when once we had been friends. Death in any form seems to separate the true friends from those who are only acquaintances, and suicide seems to do so more ruthlessly. I still have many wonderful close friends, and those whom I have lost are better gone because they weren't friends in the first place.

And so I carry on, and I am changed by this experience. This death is not like any other death: that of a spouse, or of a parent or even of a child by natural causes, and I have experienced them all. This death has been by far the most demanding, the most excruciating, the most challenging. I will carry this experience throughout my life, and it has shaped who I am in the most profound way. It has completely annihilated my life as I had known it. It has put me into a new place in myself where I seem to have ready access to a huge range of feelings and thoughts. These feelings and thoughts stretch from the most primitive cry for survival. They include hatred of the enormity of pain that could cause a gifted and talented young man to end his life. They reach toward the highest calling for spiritual awareness and real joy that my son has gone home and reached his spiritual goal.

On Reflection

Shocking and traumatic experiences are part of life. Even the bursting of a seed from its hard casing is a shock to the seed. It is possible to grow through shock and trauma, but it doesn't happen overnight. Many people who consider themselves to be spiritual or religious may start feeling that everything is all right long before the human physical part of them agrees with that judgement. Particularly for those people, it seems to be a betrayal of their spirituality or religious beliefs to experience grief and anger, pain and despair, and yet these are extremely important emotions that help us to carry on, even though it may not seem so when we are feeling them.

One of the things that we need to do when we have experienced trauma or shock is to batten down the hatches and focus on survival. We are capable of little more than that, and even doing what is necessary to survive often feels like more than we can manage. Grief, pain, and despair cause us to 'give up' for a time, and often that 'giving up' allows us to protect ourselves and just go into a corner and lick our wounds, much like a wounded animal. Whatever our spiritual or religious beliefs are, there is still a physical part of us that responds just like a wounded animal, and that part needs to be protected and nurtured as well. That is why these seemingly negative feelings can be life savers at the time.

The greatest healing comes from allowing the wounded part of us to speak the pain, the grief, the loss, the anger and despair as much as we need to do with some trusted friend, therapist, close relative or just a good listener who is there for us. We often get frozen in time at the moment of trauma, and it is as if the world stops then. That is why it is so hard for us to change our viewpoint about the loss of a loved one, for instance. We remember them often particularly at the traumatic moment, so to move from my loved one who was murdered or died in a horrific accident to my loved one who is in another realm, a spirit world, or whatever way we choose to look at it, is quite a shift, and not something we move towards easily unless and until a good deal of healing has occurred within ourselves.

Gradually we can move toward acceptance of what has occurred, and that takes quite some time, far longer than we would imagine or than well meaning friends and relatives would have us believe. There are some traumas and subsequent losses of people that don't ever go away, but their impact lessens over a great deal of time.

Beginning to engage with life again, to forge a life for ourselves without our loved one is very difficult. We feel disloyal at first, as if it is a sign that they didn't mean as much to us as we felt they did. That is simply not true. Undoubtedly it is sad to move on in life without our loved one, but it is even sadder to allow our lives to stop at the moment of trauma or loss. We are here to live. Life goes by too quickly for us to choose to stop living at any time and for any reason. While we are experiencing the range of feelings that grief includes, we are alive, but if we should decide to shut down to our right to life after the death of a loved one, we are not valuing our self enough.

I would like to invite you to reflect on your experiences and thoughts and feelings about suicide. Wonder if what you have read in this chapter has affected you in any way and made you think or feel differently about the issue of suicide or traumatic loss. If you feel that you have issues about suicide the best place to work on your issues is in therapy. If you are in therapy already that is great and you can take your issues there. If you are not in therapy and you need to explore further, this might be the time to find a good therapist with whom to work. I don't recommend trying to work through these feelings on your own, even with the help of this book.

CHAPTER 18
A Crown of Jewels

Philip O'Brien and I married in the Chicago area in 1965, and we moved to Dublin, Ireland in 1966. All our children were born there. We subsequently moved to London, separated and finally divorced in 1987. We remained in touch frequently through the years, even intending to remarry in the last half of the 1990s. Not long after Scott's death, Philip, who had by then developed prostate cancer, began to deteriorate.

Because Scott's illness and death had taken our attention away from our own lives, we realised that we needed to think about what we wanted from our lives, and in August of 1998 we remarried. This was a simple wedding. I wore a flowered summer dress. Our friend, Dearbhla Molloy, drove Philip there and by that time he walked with a cane. We were first married legally in the registry office in Ealing in front of some family and friends. We then all went to the Bahá'í Centre in Rutland Gate, and had a very simple Bahá'í ceremony with friends and family. That was it. I was thrilled to be married again to the man who was the father of my children and whom I had loved for so long as he had loved me. It felt like the resolution of our differences and a dream come true. At times I had despaired that we might never achieve that desire. I knew that Philip was terminally ill, and I was deeply saddened by that because I had been sure he would live a lot longer.

Gratefully we had a few months together in the final days of Philip's life when his prostate cancer had moved into the bone. One day, I came home from shopping and Philip was lying in bed and he said to me, "I had a wave (he meant a feeling). I don't think I am going to get better." Our eyes filled with tears, and I replied, "Well, then we are going to make it the best we can for what time we have left." Sometime in October, Philip realised that it was the shock of Scott's death that had caused his cancer to escalate and go into the bone, and he thought that by realising that fact, he would be able to reverse it. However, that was not to be.

Philip spent his last couple of months in the hospice with me and Shannon and Brian there every day. As his body weakened, his spirit strengthened, and he was marvellous. I remember that every time I arrived at his bedside, his eyes would light up when he saw me. That was so rewarding especially when it was so hard to watch him losing physical abilities and strength and to see him in pain.

I had been seeing a bereavement counsellor every two weeks to help me to deal with the shock of Scott's death. As if that wasn't hard enough, I realised I was facing yet another bereavement, which made me feel that I had to finish my grieving for Scott before I could deal with grieving for Philip. I remember so much wishing that Philip had more time because I just did not want to go through another period of grieving so soon after the one for Scott.

But my experience of grieving for Philip was very different. In some ways it redeemed some of the shock and horror of Scott's suicide, but it was also traumatising. At least with Philip's death we had some time to prepare, time to be with Philip, to talk about his dying. How different that was to Scott's suicide in which there had been no preparation, no discussion, no progression of life preparing for a natural death, no negotiation. When I began to accept Scott's death, I ended my work with the counsellor because I knew that I simply couldn't carry on dealing with two bereavements at the one time. I have to say here and now that my grieving for Scott's loss was in no way complete at this time, but the imminence of Philip's death was calling for my attention.

I had some very remarkable experiences with respect to Philip's death including a near-death experience of a very different order that I will share with you shortly.

A nurse who worked in the hospice where Philip spent his last couple of months saw spirits. She said to me that every time Philip was in pain or suffering in some way, she saw two spirits whom she went on to describe. One was Scott and the other presented as both a baby and as a young woman of about 25. I told her that was our daughter, Tara, who had died at age four weeks. The nurse said that she couldn't figure it out and didn't know that she belonged with him. She even told her to go away, and that she shouldn't be with Philip. I assured her that Tara did belong with him. When she had described seeing my two children in that way, I would have given anything to have been able to see them myself. She reassured me that there were many ways of knowing, and that "seeing" was just one of those. Some people sense things. Some people hear things. While I knew that she was right, and that I had often had experiences of knowing things that were meaningful and important to me, I couldn't easily let go of that strong desire to be able to "see" my children, who had already passed away, as she did.

I spoke with a friend of mine Arthur Molinary, who is a medium at the London College of Psychic Studies, on several occasions while I was mourning. I just needed some reassurance about my loved ones in the next world. In December of 1998, I saw him. I really needed all the help I could get at this time.

Arthur told me that my son, Scott, would come to me on the day of Philip's death. Later when I told this to the hospice nurse who could see Scott, she said it meant that Scott would wake me up. Arthur said too that when Philip said Scott's name, it meant that he (Scott) was coming to get Philip. He also said that there would still be bits of tinsel around, and somehow that seemed to indicate that it would happen sometime towards the end of December or early January after the Christmas period. At the time, we weren't even sure that Philip would make it to Christmas.

On Friday, the 8th of January 1999, I came home in the evening after having been to the hospice to see Philip, and I was more than usually exhausted. I said to myself that I didn't know how much longer I could keep up the pace. I was visiting Philip every day, and spending hours with him each time. It was so emotionally draining. It wasn't that I didn't enjoy being with him. As always he was entertaining and funny and fun to be with, but there was an intensity in knowing that we never knew how much longer he would be there so I just wanted to spend as much time as possible with him. I spoke to Philip on the telephone that night, and he was looking forward to seeing me the next morning.

The next morning seemed to come earlier than usual. I woke up and looked at the clock. It said 5:19 am. I was thinking about going back to sleep when the phone rang. When this happened, I was sure that it was Scott who had awakened me just in time for this phone call. It was my daughter who said that they had rung from the hospice to say that Philip had taken a turn for the worse. She said that Philip didn't want us (that is Brian and I who were farther away at the time than Shannon was) notified because we had a long distance to travel to get there, so we could come in later, but Shannon wanted Brian and I to know. And, you know, sometimes when you hear something you don't want to hear, you try to change the subject to distance yourself from it? Well after asking her if she was going in, I said, "Are you going to put make up on?" She said she was going in and wasn't going to bother with make up. I said we would go in too.

I went to wake Brian and then I got washed, dressed and put make up on. We were ready to go in about half an hour. We arrived at about 6:30 am. Philip was awake when we arrived, and he asked how we got there. Brian said that we had taken a tube and a taxi. Philip then asked, "Were you scared?" Brian immediately said, "No, I've taken a taxi before!" He was pretty quick with his wit for that hour of the morning.

We let Philip sleep and sat in the waiting room next to his room. We wandered in and out of his room, but he was sleeping most of the time. Our old family friend, Dearbhla, joined us and remained with us throughout. Then we were hungry, and we told the nurses where we were going for lunch and went out making sure they could contact us if there was a need to do so. We enjoyed our food because we really were hungry, but our attention was elsewhere. We made small talk and attempted to be interested in what we were saying, but actually we were ever present to what was going on with Philip. After eating we went back to the hospice with newspapers that we pretended to read. Early in the afternoon, Philip was still sleeping, and we wondered what to do. I went to ask the nurse if we should stay or go and come back later. She said to me, "How would you feel if he died and you weren't here?" I said that I wouldn't like that. She replied, "Stick around." I had said to the nurses all the way along that I wanted to be with Philip when he died, so she let me know that his death was coming. She could read signs that we couldn't.

I had also said several times to Philip that I wanted to be with him when he died. He always replied that he would probably die in the middle of the night. He also said that he would have arranged with the nurses not to phone me until about 9.30 the next morning, so I could have a good night's sleep, and each time, I would say, "No, that is not what I want."

I went into his room and sat beside his bed. I read prayers first aloud and then to myself, and suddenly he opened his eyes and looked at me. He said, like a petulant child, "Good Bye." I replied, "Good Bye." Then I added, "I love you." He said, "I don't care." Then he added, "Go home." I said, "I am here, I am staying, I am not going home." He closed his eyes and drifted off then. I got up and left thinking that I didn't need to listen to any more of that kind of talk! I guess that was a way of saying good bye to me, but I preferred it when later he told me that he loved me. I might have been angry with Philip for being petulant, and indeed I had never experienced him behaving that way before. I was actually more bemused. Looking back I feel sure that he was trying to say goodbye, and it came out in the way it did because the dying process had handicapped his full mental capacity in some way.

I went into the waiting room and sat there trying to rest, look at the television, read the newspapers, and generally pass the time. Then, near 6pm that evening, I went to the kitchen to make a cup of something warm and wet – a cereal coffee. I took my drink with me and went back into the room with Philip who was waking up then. Brian came in too and then Philip said, "Hiven" a pause and then "hiven…hiven". Because his body was shutting down, he was unable to clearly articulate every word, and we knew he meant "heaven". We could feel that something was happening then because he was talking about heaven, so Brian went to get Shannon and Dearbhla. They came in and stood on his left side. Brian and I took up places on his right side.

Philip said, "Mary, here, here Mary, here, here, here. Mary, Mary, here. Lift me up, Get me up, let me go, let me go." Mary was Philip's mom who had passed away many years before. He repeated that sequence a few times.

We raised up the head of his bed when he said, "Lift me up" and put it down after, so we could put it up again when he said it again. Shannon said," You can go, go whenever you want, We are all here, Jane, Brian, Shannon, Dearbhla, and we will be fine, we will take care of each other." Philip said, "Guardian Angels". I am sure that he saw guardian angels. Then he said, "Joan, Joan, here, here, Joan, here Joan, lift me up, get me up, let me go" He repeated that sequence a few times, in his conversation, which was similar in style to that of talking with his mother as I mentioned above.

Joan was his sister who had died of leukaemia at age 35 just in the same way their mother, Mary, had died of leukaemia at the same age. Then he said, "Get me up, get me up, get me up!" Again, he repeated that several times and also said "Let me go" several times as well. He said, "I love you". Then Shannon said, "I am here, we are all here, we love you."

I said several times, "Remember you are safe and you are protected". He said, "The daffodils are beautiful". I gave him healing through his feet to help release the spirit and I said from time to time, It's OK, just relax, release and let go.

"She's fat!" He said suddenly and emphatically. Shannon said, "Tell her, tell her to her face". "You're fat" said he. Then, "There, I told her to her face!" We all laughed together with him. Then he called us all and said, "I love you". Then he said, "Scott, Scott, Scott". He was struggling to form the words almost like a child just learning to talk, but we knew that he was saying "Scott". He went on to say, "here, here, get me up, get me up, get me up". He paused and said, "It's wonderful". Then he again said to us, "Let me go, let me go". He again repeated this a few times and then said, "OK, OK, OK, wait, wait - wait for it". I could tell that he wasn't quite ready, that he had something else to say.

Meanwhile, that clairvoyant nurse walked by me and said, "Scott is standing right behind him". It was so helpful and comforting to hear that. I was so glad that Scott was there and could help his father with the transition. Then Philip said, "Jane, Jane, Jane" I replied, "I'm here, I'm with you, you are fine, you are doing fine. We are all here with you; you can go when you want."

Philip had a habit, when friends were leaving our home after having visited, of saying, "Go, go with God, but go." When he kept saying, "Let me go" during this time, I remember towards the end having heard that a number of times, I said to him at least twice, "Go, go with God, but go".

Finally, he looked at me and said, "I want you to have a crown, a crown of jewels". I can only imagine that he was seeing crowned angels because I know he wouldn't have just thought of such a thing without having seen it.

Then he stopped talking. All we could hear was his breathing, which was louder than normal. The intervals between the breaths were lengthening. At 8.22, we all looked at each other after what we thought was his last breath. Then two minutes later at 8.24 his last breath really did happen. I looked at him and said, "You always did have to prove us wrong, didn't you?"

There was a wonderful fragrance like that of a newborn baby's palm of the hand in the air. It was as if we had participated in his birth into the next world. I felt that we had been a team that had turned him over to a team on the other side, and he had named the people who had made up that team, so we knew who was there waiting for him. I am sure that there were others, but he didn't mention them. It was a most remarkable and uplifting experience that in no way diminishes the grieving that I felt, but it certainly felt like a redemption of Scott's death, a kind of healing experience, healing the emotional pain and trauma of his death. This was a "near-death" experience of a different order. It was as if those of us in this life and those in the next were all gathered around Philip in that hospice bed and participating in a birthing process.

Nurses in the hospice had told us that people continue to hear for an hour or an hour and a half after they die, so we sat there with his body for a while. Then we all went into the waiting room and one by one, we returned to him and said whatever we needed to say before the nurse came to wash his body and remove it from the room. I remember thinking about an hour before he passed over that I was feeling very tired and hoped that the process didn't go into the wee hours of the morning, when Philip had predicted his death would be. I didn't think I could keep up with it.

During the next nine days we took care of arrangements and prepared the funeral, which we wanted to be a celebration of his life. This time I gave the eulogy, and there was standing room only. The chapel was filled with his friends – those who were involved in the theatre and those who were Bahá'ís. Again, people came from other parts of the world for this. There were hundreds at his funeral. My eulogy took longer than we expected, and there was laughter and tears.

I was really exhausted after all the work of preparing the funeral, the experience of his dying, and the months of daily visits to him in the hospice dealing with his pain, and the turns in his condition. I had seen how just as his body deteriorated, his spirit grew stronger. I observed how he enjoyed the people who served him, the nurses, doctors, carers of all different sorts. They used to make a point of calling in to see him because he always had a kind word for them, a smile, and an expression of appreciation. I knew how special the few hours were that I spent with him each day, how they revived our spirits, his and mine, and enabled us to continue through the daily progression of such a vicious illness.

I knew how important it was to me to prepare a eulogy that would be fitting for the occasion. I was asked to speak for about five minutes, and so

A Crown of Jewels

I decided to write a story about Philip, and some of what I considered to be important highlights of his life. I really enjoyed writing it because I so much wanted to emphasise his spirit, his humour, his sharp wit.

When I stood to walk to the front of the chapel to deliver my eulogy, I was thrilled and proud and feeling so moved that Philip had drawn so many people to the celebration of his life. I engaged with the audience very personally, making eye contact with people, who were probably unaware that I was actually doing so. I felt as if I was sharing love from myself and from Philip for all the people seated in the chapel, those standing at the back, and even those who listened outside the door. I was especially pleased at being able to stand up and speak to an audience at all. When I had first met Philip and for many years after that, I was very shy and would not have felt comfortable speaking to a large group of people at all. He was the performer in the family, and I stood behind him. Not so on this day!

I notice the changing moods of the audience, moving from sadness to joy, to laughter, to a kind of awe and appreciation of this man who indeed gave so much of himself to others, whom I loved dearly, and who had been, for so many years, the centre of my life. We were divorced for nearly 11 years, but I have always felt that our divorce was just another part of the marriage.

Although when writing my eulogy, I thought it would fit within the time constraints I was given, indeed I talked far longer than I should have done, and it meant that the other arrangements of people reading, of music and whatever we had planned were delayed. Finally, we got to the stage where the next funeral was knocking on the door wanting to enter the chapel, and we had to make a hurried exit, follow the coffin to the grave site and finish the programme there. There is a Bahá'í burial prayer that had not been said in the chapel as planned, so it was read by the grave, and the rain had just begun. I held my umbrella over the man, a dear friend from Ireland, who was reading the prayer, and I realised after that I think the way I held the umbrella simply allowed the rain drops to fall directly onto his prayer book rather than hitting his head! That wasn't the best way to position the umbrella, but it was all I managed at the time.

When the funeral was over, and people had come up to me and the children to pay their respects, it was time to drive into town to the reception. It was getting dark, and the rain was pouring down, and the journey seemed to take ages, but we finally got there.

The funeral was really a celebration of his life. If it could be said that people enjoyed the funeral, then they did enjoy it. Some said it was the best funeral they have ever attended. The reception afterwards was in one of the bars of a theatre in the West End. Because Philip was a fine actor, the venue seemed fitting, and he had been thrilled when we told him that we had arranged that. I was so pleased that we were able to discuss all this with him before he died. I will enclose some of the material that was read at the funeral.

I want to share my eulogy with you because I felt it was so clear and told his story, much of which is our story, so I include it here. If you would rather not read it now, just turn over the pages and go on to the next part of the book. I guess this is my way of introducing you to my husband!

Hello Friends, on behalf of the O'Brien Family, I would like to welcome you today. It is lovely to see you all here. Thank you for coming. I don't expect that this will take a long time. There are some things I remember. I'd like to tell you a few things about Philip before we proceed with the rest of the programme. He was born in Troy, New York on the 23rd of May 1927 to an Irish Catholic family. His mother is called Mary, and his father was Philip G O'Brien. Philip always wanted to make sure nobody thought of him as a junior. He wouldn't be junior to anyone.

He had a sister, Joan, who was 2 years older than him and a brother, Bob, who was 7 years younger. When he was 8 years old, his mother, Mary, died from leukaemia at the age of 35, and left the children with no mother, so his father, very wisely, asked a woman to come and look after the children while he was at work, and to take care of them and see them to school and do their meals and all the things that a mother would do. Her name was, Kitty, and Philip had endless stories about her, but one of the things that I thought was marvellous, she really adored Philip, was that she called him a "house devil" and a "street angel".

He went to Catholic Central High School in Troy, New York. He finished at 16 because he actually went forward a year, so at 16, he decided he wanted to study medicine, and he went to one of the most progressive universities in America which was a far cry from Catholic High School in Troy, New York.

He studied a year there and decided it wasn't for him, neither medicine nor that particular university and joined the Navy.

He was in the Navy for several years, I don't know quite how long, but he never saw a ship! He was posted in San Diego for one, and I don't remember what other places. He did things like spinal taps because of his year of pre-med. and all sorts of things to do with medicine which anybody who is a doctor would know is rather horrific for a 17 year old to do, but, nevertheless he did them. Not only that, but until he went into the Navy at age 17, he was quite short. I think he was probably about this to me (I point to somewhere mid chest area on me). He grew so much in the first year in the Navy that he had six uniform changes in the year!

After that, he went to New York University and got his Bachelors Degree and Masters Degree in Theatre Studies and Psychology. I think his father was very keen on the idea of his being a doctor, but when it came to going into theatre, his father said, "I want nothing to do with this". And so, Philip had to make his own money and pay for his own education, which he did, enthusiastically, as he always would have done.

After he got his degrees, he worked in New York in and around theatre and television. I guess things were probably a bit slow because he had to sometimes work in a stockbrokers. When he worked in the stockbrokers, he never knew the difference between a stock and a bond, didn't until the day he died and probably doesn't care now and didn't care most of the time anyway. He also worked for Pan Am Airlines for awhile. So, I guess things must have been quiet, and he decided he was going to go out to Los Angeles and live there and try to get some work in television, theatre or whatever, mostly television, I think in Los Angeles, at that time anyway.

He travelled out and he met Keith and Bob Quigley. Bob Quigley had a - I can't remember the name of the production company, but they did things like Hollywood Squares, various quiz shows, things like that, so he worked with them. Through them, he met the Bahá'í Faith. One time, he said, "You know, there are three people in this organisation who drive me crazy because they're so calm and radiant while I am drinking 27 cups of coffee every day and going nuts, basically". He said, "It's you, Bob, Keith and another fellow in the organisation whose name escapes me right now. Bob said "well that's very funny we're all Bahá'ís". So that's how it all started.

In any case, he became a Bahá'í in the summer of 1961. A couple of years later, he decided he really wanted to do something heroic for the Bahá'í Faith, thinking he would go maybe to the Philippine Islands or somewhere, a very far away place that he didn't know anything about. So he sold all his furniture and everything he had. Then he was asked to go to the House of Worship in Wilmette. The Bahá'í House of Worship in Wilmette is near Chicago, and it's a wonderful building. It looks something like the Taj Mahal, a building that looks like concrete lace with a dome. He was co-ordinator, and he would deal with talks and groups and organising tours because it is a major tourist attraction.

So that was 1963, that was the year when I became a Bahá'í. In that summer, hang about; I better check my dates so I know. 1964 it was actually, I wrote to him in the early part of the year, and I said that I really wanted to come and volunteer at the House of Worship to help out with guiding the tours and so on and so forth. I thought I loved the House of Worship so much, and I loved the Faith so much that I'd even be willing to clean the dome with a toothbrush if that were necessary. He said he didn't think that would be necessary really. He said my work (as a guide showing visitors around) would be appreciated by the people in over 150 countries, islands, territories in the world where Bahá'ís resided.

That was enough for me, and I went up there. Well, little did I know! We worked together all that summer, and conveniently I had transferred to a university near the Temple at that time, Northwestern University, and I started there in the autumn, so there I was, present in the same area that he was, so our friendship continued. Basically, we decided to marry, but up until the time we actually got engaged which was February of '65, I had no idea that he was even interested in marrying me, and when I heard that he was, it was like, "I don't believe this". We were such close friends, you know, and I thought that was it. I've been in shock ever since!

In any case, we were married on May 23rd 1965, and that was his birthday, so, guess what, I was his birthday present! Wow!

In the summer of 1966, we moved to Dublin. There were several reasons, and one was that we could help with the Bahá'í Community there. There were very few Bahá'ís in Ireland at that stage. The other was that Philip could work as an actor without a work permit. The other was we wanted to get out of Chicago. We didn't want to live in a big city and raise our children in a big city. Dublin, to us, was a small city.

We got there in August, and very shortly after we arrived we found a house to rent. It cost us £500 a year, a four-bedroom house. Anyway, we went to the Irish Authorities. Of course, one had to go to the authorities when one was moving in to a place, to ask for some kind of residence visa. They were so shocked that anyone would want to move into Ireland when most of the population was moving out they gave us permanent residence visas.

We had four children in the first six and a half years we were there. I didn't believe in wasting any time because Philip was 16 ½ years older than me, so there was no time to be wasted. Our first son was Scott who was born 6 months to the day after our arrival in Ireland. Not only was he born on that day, but our dogs came out of quarantine on that day.

Our daughter, Shannon, was born about a year and a half later. Our daughter, Tara, was born on Philip's birthday in 1971. He had said before we got married that he would like everything to happen on his birthday. I thought, forget it! I couldn't quite oblige with all of them, but we did manage Tara. However, sadly, she passed away 4 weeks after she was born. That was quite a shock, but then, to save the day, Brian arrived in 1973. At that stage, they would have said, in Ireland, "Sure, they've only the three!"

Life was never dull, living with Philip. He had a marvellous sense of humour; he was loving and generous with a strong sense of justice and a razor sharp mind, which enabled him to win just about every argument.

There is a really good story about his razor sharp mind, and this dates back to when we were living in America when we were first married. He was working at the Bahá'í House of Worship at that stage before moving to Ireland. He was invited by a local pastor to come and give a talk about the Bahá'í Faith. Somebody who was in the area of the Bahá'í House of Worship, and the talk was to be given to students. Philip was up there giving his talk explaining about Bahá'í principles, the oneness of God, the oneness of humanity and all this sort of thing. The pastor was sitting at the back of the room rattling his keys going, Ho, hum, ha ho, during the whole talk. I don't know how long it took Philip, but I reckon it didn't take him very long. After he had given the gist of his talk, he stopped, and he looked at the pastor and he said, "You know, I didn't force you to ask me to come and give a talk today. I am here because you invited me, and the whole time I'm talking, you're rattling your keys and laughing." Then Philip said, "I'm here to tell you that your Lord has walked the face of this earth just over 100 years ago, what are you going to do about it?" He fumbled and said, "Er, um, Jesus Christ said that he would return at the end of the world." And Philip looked at him and he said, "Who'd need Him then!" Bahá'u'lláh claimed to be the Return of Christ.[1]

He was deeply shy which many people here probably would never know. He hated going to places and parties where he didn't know everyone. I witnessed that many times.

He loved and cared for many people in his life. He was always generous and giving. He was a pure soul; he is a pure soul. I don't believe that his story has stopped, he is with us today and God knows he must be helping me with this speech.

He is a pure soul whose generosity abounded. He liked nothing better than giving things to people and especially if somebody said to him, "Gosh, I like that". He would say, "It's yours". We used to wonder because it was always the thing that he loved the best. He said, "But I love to give away things that I love." We had another episode which happened frequently in our lives and it was that when he'd buy a birthday present for me, he would come home with it in his pocket or whatever way he would carry it whether it was a pot or a ring or whatever it was, and he would say, "I got your birthday present today." I would say, "Oh that's nice." I liked to wait to the day, you see. He said, "Aren't you curious, wouldn't you like to kind of know something about it?" and "I could give you a couple of hints, like you wear them in your ears." And then little by little, I would give up. He would get such joy out of seeing people's delight and pleasure in his gifts that I couldn't refuse him and I'd say, "That's wonderful."

So that's it. I think what I would like to leave you with, with all the laughter and all the fun, what I would like to convey to you today is that Philip had a very, very deep sense, a very, very deep well of spirituality at the core of his being. He chose as a container for that well, the Bahá'í Faith, and his

---

1   (Bahá'u'lláh, 1992, p.234)

love for Bahá'u'lláh, for His teachings, His writings informed him at all times, nourished and supported him, and it is from that that he made his choices.

Even recently when he was in the hospice, he managed to say his prayers regularly every day. I remember one time when he had gotten behind by 4 days - and that was a lot. I have his prayer book at home, and it has all turned-over pages for all the prayers that he would say every day, so it took him some time, and as he was getting weaker and so on, that must have been harder for him because he had to take so much time for everything else, much more so. So he had fallen behind for these four days, and he actually worked quite hard to catch up on those prayers, saying, you know, several lots in a day. It took him a few days, but by God, he did it.

What most of us had loved in him rather than being simply a characteristic or an aspect of his personality arose out of that deep well which is within him, that deep well of spirituality, and that's what we all loved so much. His devotion to and his steadfastness in the Bahá'í Faith has been exemplary.

He lived a great life until his last breath, through his last breath because we could experience what was going on. He was two months in the hospice, and he was cared for beautifully there. He was tremendously happy. He loved every nurse. Sometimes he could see visitors and sometimes he couldn't, but whatever, the nurses loved him, and he loved them. He took an interest in each and every one of them. They would visit him frequently just to chat, like bees drawn to honey. His actual death process, which was shared by all the family, was a very, very uplifting experience. I couldn't go away from that feeling any sense of, what's the word, lack or regret, there are no regrets over the whole period from the time that we got married to the time when he passed away, we made the best we could of everything that there was, and he enjoyed it thoroughly. He died peacefully and with joy. He was surrounded by those people he loved most and being received on the other side by those people who loved him the most on that side. It was as if we were like a team and we were passing him over to another team on the other side. And so I thank you for listening and for coming. I thank him for his life and the gift of his death which he shared with us all, and his life will continue on for all of us because I don't know any of us here who probably don't have a whole lot of jokes and sayings that came from him.

Here is a piece from an actor, Ron Berglas, which he shared at the funeral:

> On Saturday, the 9th of January, we took a walk on Hampstead Heath. It was cold, cold on the Heath, cold indoors. I realised I hadn't phoned Philip yet but that I would later on. But when we got home I thought he might be asleep so I left it. Then, just after 9pm, Brian phoned and told me Philip had passed away.
>
> If ever there was a holy trinity, then Jane, Brian and Shannon are it: Their devotion to Philip, especially during these last few months has been miraculous. I admire them, I love them and I will always be there for them.
>
> The sky was uncertain that day on the Heath. The competition between the sun and clouds was fierce. Sometimes the rain would blind us; sometimes the sun and sometimes they would hover together over the tops of the hills, framing the trees, silhouetting the people against the majesty of their indecision. It seems nature could not make up its mind about Philip either. Although he knew long ago that he was ill, he "made 'em wait for it". The late Sir Ralph Richardson once said that an actor had to earn the right to pause. Philip has earned the right to pause. Ralph would have admired Philip. They would have had something to talk about. They both had that special gleam in their eyes that never let you know what they were going to do next.
>
> Philip was, in the best sense of the word, a dangerous actor. You never knew what was coming until he floored you with it. For me, who had the great good fortune to work with him on several occasions, I saw how incredible he could be. As soon as I knew we would be working together again, life and the business became much more bearable. And when I saw him work, my blood would race, and my heart would pound because I knew I would have to keep on my toes. This was acting with quality. He did not suffer fools, and if one crossed his path, he would do that thing with his eyes that instantly consigned them to the second-rate bin.
>
> The beauty of his performances was in his never seeming to take any of them seriously. In fact, the opposite was closer to the truth. He took them into himself and made them him, effortlessly, peerlessly, and totally convincingly.
>
> This was how I knew him. Not his life story, that must be left to others, but rather as a colleague, a fantastic actor and the most loyal of friends. As a man he seemed to rise above trivialities and aspire to something deeper, richer and funnier. He was WONDERFUL.
>
> Telling you this now is one thing. Knowing at that time what he was going through with his illness and the loss of Scott was quite another. Last

August, after we'd done the first of two play readings together, I felt I had to let him know what I felt about him. I wrote him a letter, which I will read to you now. You may question my judgement in reading you a letter that I sent to Philip. I can only say in my defence that Philip loved this letter so much he told me he was going to have it made into wallpaper. I read it to you now and I suspect these are sentiments that, in our various different ways, we may all share.

And here is his letter to Philip:

Dear Philip,

You're such a mensch! Nobody could have gone through what you've gone through recently and come up with such a perfect performance yesterday. When you were working I just sat there and gawped. I have such a variety of feelings about you.

First of all I love you. I think you're one of the nicest, most generous, most giving actors I've ever worked with. Nothing's ever too much trouble for you. Where someone else might think about it – you give. You are unstinting in your praise, your support, and your love. Sometimes we might take people like you for granted. I don't. I appreciate the fact that I have been given the opportunity, not once but several times, of working with one of the most talented actors I've ever met.

I admire you. The courage you showed yesterday. I don't know how you did it. Not only did you give another masterly performance, but you did it with your proverbial shoelaces tied together. In other words, the pain you gave us onstage was nothing to the pain you must have been feeling inside. And I know you used it as we all have to. So I watched and I learned and I practised what I learned. And it works.

I trust you. It doesn't matter what I do on stage - you'll be there. I'm not worried about you upstaging me because it doesn't matter. Nobody takes their eyes off you anyway. So we ski in your wake and enjoy the breeze. I know you'd never give a duff performance but rather you make the sun shine through any cloud of a script.

And it's such a lot of fun. Nobody makes me laugh like you do. Not while I'm working. Never.

I appreciate you. Your extraordinary kindness and generosity when my mother was ill. That was like falling into the arms of an angel.

And one more thing. You don't need to respond to this letter. Allow me the privilege of praising the Master without you having to do anything other than enjoy what is due.

All my love

PS: Here's talking at you, Philip

Here is one more letter that we shared at the funeral from Philip's niece, Becky, age 12:

Dear Uncle Philip

I know you hate to be called Uncle, but I've always done it and I couldn't help myself. I'm writing to you on blue paper because it is my favorite color and black ink because well black shows up the best. When I recently heard about your condition, I couldn't help myself, I cried. But since I hate crying in front of people I went to my room. I just can't grasp the fact that I will never see you again. You're such a wonderful person to be never seen by me again. Uncle Philip you are an inspiration to me. The fact that you went to NYU [New York University – ed.] and became an actor and a father and accomplished your dreams gives me hope towards my future. I hope to follow in your footsteps…go to NYU become an actress, start a family and publish some of my poetry, though I don't think you have ever done that I want to do it just the same. I wish you could see me now, my braces are off, my hair is beautiful, and I no longer mumble. My voice is getting much stronger now and I'm beginning to expand my talent. I wish I could talk to you about your life but I guess I can ask my mom. You have always played a big role in my life and I love you very much. I remember when I was younger how you would go outside and make weird faces on the glass. I also recollect one Christmas when you were here and you joked the entire morning. I have always looked at you and thought how much I would like to be like you. I know I will never be able to see you again but I can always pop in the Batman video and you'll be there. Some of my happiest moments are with you, Uncle Philip and I'd like to say thank you. You have played a major role in my play entitled, Becky's Life, so I guess this is just one of my tragedy scenes. Uncle Philip, to get to the point – I love you! I love you so much. Love Becky

And so within a very short time, just over a year and three months, I had met two completely different experiences of death.

Scott's death was a violent, murderous shock that left me reeling and spinning. Internally I felt as if someone had torn me to shreds, leaving me broken and not able to be fixed. Externally, his death created huge tension between those of us who were left behind. Sitting together to arrange his funeral was fraught with tension, anger, upset, and that tension did not quieten down for a very long time. The fact that we, as a family, managed to remain speaking with each other was nothing short of miraculous. We were all so hurt and therefore defensive, ready to hit out at each other verbally or to remain silent and not communicate at all. It was an experience of the effect of a violent death. I suspect that any violent death, including murder, being blown up in a bomb, hit by a train or a car, leaves behind a degree of tearing or dissonance creating conflict that continues to ripple out into the environment for quite some time.

I do not know a reason for violence in the world, and it may have its own purpose, but it does not feel as if it produces unity. It would seem as if any form of violence, even being violent with oneself, has a particular kind of impact that leads to disunity. Thus, if we are living consciously, we need to be aware of the effect that our actions have on our world. Scott seemed unable to make that transition, to move beyond himself to a place of considering the impact of his suicide. How much of that was his soul's evolutionary journey and how much was his illness, we just don't know. It would be easy for me to assume that his death was simply a result of his illness, and therefore I could think that he had a terminal illness, and that was it. However, not everyone with manic depression commits suicide. Some people manage that illness and live very productive lives with it, so the issue is not as simple as that. Even now I am wondering about it all.

I contrast the experience of Scott's suicide with that of Philip's process of dying, and it is like the difference between night and day. With Philip, we knew that he was dying, even though we hoped against hope that a miracle would happen and one day he would just sit up and be well. We were able to participate in the whole process. We were with him as he deteriorated physically and grew spiritually. We were lucky enough to be able to plan his funeral with him and to talk him through his final moments, to be present and to have some kind of conversation with him as the veil began to grow ever thinner for him between this world and the next. The experience of Philip's death left us exhausted but uplifted, sad but enriched, and it created community rather than breaking people up. After it was over, while planning his funeral, I felt a sense of unity amongst those of us who did that. The actual organisation of the funeral took place in a more peaceful atmosphere than did that of organising Scott's funeral. Those of us who were left behind remained in a state of wholeness rather than fracture. We were still sad, and we still miss him, but we were not broken by his natural death. In both cases we created very moving and interesting funerals, but internally the experiences of those two deaths were very different.

On Reflection

We experience losses throughout our lives, the loss of people we love, the passing of a phase or stage of our lives, and we do not always honour that passing and say good bye properly. At those times when we move on to the next stage without grieving the loss of the one before, we are often unable to create a proper ending to the relationship. I believe there is an art to ending something that has been important to us. Endings involve recognising what has been good, noticing what we would have liked to have been different and then grieving the loss.

The feelings involved in grieving include sadness, anger and despair among others, and they are big feelings. We can be afraid that we will be overwhelmed by them or that we will drown in them. People are afraid of feeling the pain. We don't enjoy pain, and often we will do anything to avoid it. However, it is true that the only way out of the pain is through it. We are amazing beings, and it is astounding how we grieve in small pieces. I often say to people that grieving comes in waves, and we can feel pretty normal for a time, but suddenly we experience an aspect of the grief that can sometimes stop us in our tracks. Even when we feel most engulfed by grief, anger or despair, or any other feelings evoked by a particular loss, those feelings eventually stop. The depth of feeling overwhelmed and the struggle to fully come to terms with and accept the finality of that loss do not persist forever. We do actually find a new sense of normality eventually. But that does not lessen the value of sticking with the painful parts of the process. The important thing is that we allow ourselves to feel our feelings as we adjust to the loss.

If we carry unexpressed grief within us, it continues to affect us. It particularly affects our body, our physical health and our attitudes towards other people we love and towards life itself. Grieving is an important tool to help us move through the pain of a loss, so that we can come back into life again after having accepted the loss. If we do not grieve, all those unexpressed feelings continue to work on and through us and are not at all helpful. People can become embittered and cynical and generally angry and unpleasant if they have not allowed themselves to mourn their losses. It often takes far longer to express the grief that we have for the loss of a person, a pet or a stage of life than we imagine it should or than other people insist it should. Very often I hear of people in grief who's 'friends' are saying, "Aren't you over this by now?" There are some losses that we never overcome, but we learn to live with them, and that is the way life is. Those are the losses that take a very long time to learn to accept.

Often, we avoid grieving by throwing ourselves into our work or our family situation or because we find ourselves overwhelmed with responsibilities either at work or at home in the absence of the departed person. We also may inwardly feel that we should be strong and get over it. Our families may criticise us for indulging or accuse us of 'wallowing' or feeling sorry for ourselves. We may feel this way about ourselves too and feel that we are not living up to our own expectations. We may even feel selfish for feeling sadness. All of these responses show how difficult it is for us to really experience grief, sorrow and pain.

There is another aspect of grieving that is less often discussed. After the initial period of grieving has been completed, we reach a time when we don't wake up in the morning feeling terrible. We regain our sense of optimism about life and begin focusing on other things. Often when we think we have done our grieving, we may be surprised to suddenly feel guilty or sad because we miss the person again. Important events that do not include our loved one, especially celebrations like a wedding or the birth of a child or even going on holiday, are poignant because we are aware of who is missing. We seem to expect that grieving is something that we should complete, and once we are feeling better, we won't feel that particular grief again. However when we have lost someone whom we really love, they stay with us all our lives even though we can no longer see them nor throw our arms around them and hug them.

We can choose to see this as a gift. We can still talk about them and include them in our own way.

Loss is not just about grief. Experiencing death often brings more clarity and focus to life for those left behind. There may even be a sense of relief particularly if the person who has died has been very ill and in pain. It is very difficult to watch anyone suffer, especially someone we love. From a more self-interested perspective, there can be enormous relief if they have been extremely difficult and demanding. If that was the case, it is often hard to go back to remembering them as the person we loved before their illness took over. We may feel very angry and resentful of the time and effort we had to spend looking after them, and yet, when they are gone, we still feel emptiness and perhaps guilt, or that we are selfish to feel relieved that they are gone.

In some ways the death of someone close can cause us to rethink and redefine the purpose of our life, why we are here, who we are and what we want. For example when a parent dies, your identity as a daughter or a son can go through a radical change. There can be a degree of liberation from an old role. The loss of an authority figure in our lives can be quite liberating because we no longer have to play the child to someone else. We don't need to obey someone else's rules and regulations, and we can come into being our own authority living life the way we choose to do. It doesn't have to be a parent. If we are in a relationship with someone who is a bit older, that person can carry an aspect of authority for us.

Being close to someone who is dying can make us wonder about how we will die and what may happen to us when we do. More importantly we may decide to live life as fully as possible for the rest of the time we have We may also wonder how we would like to prepare for our own death and decide not to wait until the end to think about it. If we don't consider now how we are living life in preparation for our death, when will we do it? Death may come upon us without warning, and we may not be able to think or change anything when it does.

I have often wondered if death is like a graduation. We may imagine that when we die we will have achieved what we came into this life to do. We may fantasise that when we make that final transition, we will be met by loved ones who have already died, cheering and welcoming us and praising us for what we have made of our life. Images of a joyous reunion and a real sense of arriving home can flood our consciousness. We might also imagine observing our funeral and seeing how family and friends really felt about us. We can consider how we would want them to feel about us. Writing our own obituary, we could think about what we might wish people to say about us after we pass on. We might think about whether we are being that person now, the person whom others will remember in a particular way. That could be both rewarding and surprising. Death is the final frontier and the one place where we will have to let go of controlling our world. It may well be a grand reunion that is ahead of us when we die.

If the idea appeals to you (and I appreciate that it may not, since this can be such a difficult subject to process that you may not feel up to it). If the idea appeals to you, consider writing your own obituary. Take it lightly; what would you want others to say about you? If you read your notes back to yourself, ask yourself if you are living that life now. If you aren't, what one small thing can you do right now to start moving in the right direction? It could be something very small, like giving your child or your parent a hug, sending a text to someone to say you appreciate them, or making a cup of tea for someone. It doesn't matter so much what you do, rather that you make a start today and start living the life you want to be remembered as having lived.

CHAPTER 19
Typhoid Janie?

You may think that my experience with death would be over now, but just wait, there is more! By this time, I had been close to so many people who had died in such a short time that I was beginning to feel a little like "Typhoid Mary". I began to wonder if my job really was to bring the kiss of death to people I loved! As I look at that statement now, I see a kind of black humour in it, but at the time, I was really rather concerned that I seemed to have been so much in demand to assist at loved one's deaths. I wondered if there would ever be a stage of life again for me that wasn't filled with death.

I had only just finished clearing Philip's clothing from our flat when my sister phoned me from California to say that she needed some help with our father. My dear father was nearly 91 years old in 1999, and he too had become quite unwell. He suffered from Parkinson's disease and was wheelchair bound. He had loved good food as a younger man and was quite European in his tastes. He loved French food best. By this time, however, he didn't enjoy food at all and was hardly able to eat. He had pneumonia. He died on the 17th of May when my sister and my niece and I were upstairs watching a television programme called "Seventh Heaven".

We had been with him that day and the day before when he had told us that he had really enjoyed his life despite his disabilities, which had stopped him from playing golf some years before. That had really broken his heart because he loved to play golf. As we spoke in the weeks leading up to his death, I began to feel that one of the things I could give my father was to help him to be less afraid of dying. I said to him, "I am sure that when you get to the next world, you will be able to play golf." He said, "It must be so because it wouldn't be heaven if I couldn't!" I was pleased with his response because he seemed to take what I said as a kind of reassurance.

One day during his illness we took him to see a doctor and during his chest examination he suddenly got a look of tremendous fear on his face and seemed to be watching something high up on his right. We all thought he was dying. I put my hand on his chest and said, "Yá-Bahá'u'l-Abhá," which is a Bahá'í invocation to God. He turned and looked at me in anger, and that emotion seemed to almost bring him back from the dead, but he was clearly back with us again. I was rather amused because people looked at me rather strangely after that.

My father was taken immediately into hospital, where he remained in a coma for 36 hours. My older sister, Marianne, and I were sitting with him one morning toward the end of that time and I decided to read a prayer at his bedside. I took out my prayer book, and she looked at me in some kind of horror and said, "Don't! If he sees that, he will think you are giving him the last rites!" I said, "It is just a short prayer for healing." I prayed, and within about half an hour, he opened his eyes and began asking for steak!

Even though he was having trouble eating generally, my father enjoyed that steak. We were delighted to see him back in the world again, and he said he had made a conscious choice not to be roused for all that time, but we wondered if that were so?

He went home for a couple of weeks and died peacefully exactly two months before his 91st birthday, which would have been on the 17th of July. He had chosen to have his body cremated, so we scattered the ashes at sea in a small family ceremony and held a memorial for him the next day. He had outlived my son and my husband and had led a most interesting and productive life.

So I found myself in the summer of 1999, after having experienced the deaths of my son, my husband and my father, trying to make sense of all that had happened. In just over 1½ years I had lost three men in my life who were so close to me. I had lost my baby girl, Tara, years before and by this time, it all just felt too much. I spent the next few years grieving, adjusting, and just about getting by. I would wake up in the morning and have no idea what to do, or what it was all about. I couldn't concentrate on things that had to be done. I just couldn't function beyond the minimum. I would have a burst of energy and get something done, and then I would just fade, lie on my bed, look at the ceiling, and wonder.

During that time of depression and grief, I was diagnosed with pernicious anaemia, which meant I had to have regular Vitamin B12 injections because my body doesn't have the enzyme necessary to absorb Vitamin B12 from food. I also found that I had trouble with one of the parathyroid glands, which affected the strength in my muscles because it regulates calcium in the blood, and when there is a malfunction, there is too much calcium in the system. I had difficulty getting up from a seated position and walking. The long years of stress and loss and trauma had taken their toll on my body but I was still here, breathing. I was wounded but not dead yet.

In my usual style, I attempted to find my way through the parathyroid difficulty and find a solution through complementary methods, so I chose spiritual healing. I was unwilling in late 1999 to have an operation to remove the faulty parathyroid gland even though the consultant, John Lynn, who was marvellous, suggested to me that if my calcium level rose much higher my heart would stop. I was shattered emotionally, and I feared that if I submitted to an operation then I might use that as an opportunity to check out of life, and some small but very strong part of me didn't want to do that. I just felt I couldn't sustain any kind of assault on any of my systems at that time. I could see that the healing helped, but it didn't solve the problem, so in September 2000 I was able to have the operation, but I had really needed that time before I agreed to it to just be with my feelings.

My walking did improve, but I continued to struggle for many years with legs that just didn't work well. In April of 2009 I had a really bad case of sciatica that nearly stopped me walking entirely. I spent months focusing on healing through acupuncture, cranial osteopathy, McTimoney chiropractor treatments as well as Rolfing and shiatsu.

It was during a shiatsu session that I finally began to understand what had happened to me as a result of the enormous financial pressure I had been under and the emotional pressure I felt following the deaths of some of the men in my family. The shiatsu practitioner explained a Chinese Medicine view of impact of trauma, which is that it severs the energetic connection between the heart and the kidneys and it makes you feel as if the top of your body is not connected with the lower limbs, and that is exactly what I felt.

Gradually and through all these treatments as well as yoga and Pilates and power plate, I realised that I had been using my body incorrectly and it had been as if those traumatic events had punched me in my gut again and again and it was there that I collapsed. Now, thanks to the NHS in the UK and all the treatments that I can find and provide for myself, I have hope that I can regain an ability to walk more normally and properly. I am certainly working hard to make that happen. Another issue that I understand now is that I felt I was a failure as a woman to some degree. It is the feminine aspect within us that is supposed to nurture and protect and I surely hadn't managed that with my husband or my son. I realise now that I punished myself for this failing by closing down the nurturing side of me and did not allow myself to nurture my body with healthy food. It is only now in 2010 that I have begun to realign my own dietary choices, so I am eating more grains, beans and vegetables, and I made miso soup for the first time just recently and have begun to have that regularly. The effect of my dietary realignment shows me that I am once again allowing my own feminine nature to function. That and my regular exercise mean that my body is contracting, getting more toned and really feeling better.

But it has been a long path. For a decade not only did I feel a failure in terms of my feminine energy, but also in my masculine energy because of my financial problems. I chose to focus on the masculine, and I did the one thing that I hoped would help me to find a meaningful life in the future in a way that would take care of me. I got my MA in psychosynthesis psychotherapy. Through the therapy connected with this training, I was able to fully express my feelings and begin to deal with the enormous range of feelings that I was experiencing. I had never taken any medication for depression, but I was in great need of therapy at that time. Having a safe place to express my feelings each week was a lifeline for me, and I began to feel better very very slowly but surely.

My focus in 1999 however was largely emotional and those times were really very difficult. Frequently I felt myself descending into that place that I call "revisiting my madness"; that place within me where I feel as if I am holding on to life by a thin, but extremely strong thread, and I have reached the end of that thread. I see nothing but confusion, despair, and hopelessness. When I recognise myself in that place, I find I begin to come back. I may not have those feelings for a long period of time, but when I do, they feel intense. Since my experience of being around Scott when he was experiencing intense moods, I know that what I experience is not as bad, but it must be similar.

I would often lie awake in the middle of the night feeling helpless, grief stricken, frightened and inadequate. I eventually noticed that if I could stay with those painful feelings and not try to stop them, but just continue to observe them, I would suddenly gain an insight that would enable me to go back to sleep and in the morning I would wake up refreshed and hopeful. I began to consider that these painful feelings might be some kind of portal to a new outlook for me. That still seems to be the case.

At other times in my life I might have been angry with my close relatives for causing me such pain, but this time I found myself angry with God. Even in my anger with God, I always felt that He could take it. Maybe it is part of normal development, just as we may go through a rebellious teenage stage with our parents, perhaps when we grow and mature, we might also go through such a time with God. Once I came to this realisation I accepted that all my feelings were just my feelings, and I needn't condemn myself for having them because they were not wrong. I decided to just feel them because the truest way out of difficult feelings is through them.

It was really hard to take care of daily chores, and I felt as if I were in quicksand. A lot of the time I just didn't care. I didn't want to live, but I wouldn't have had the courage to take my own life, so I guess I was more or less stuck here. I held onto the fact that I still had two wonderful living children and two lovely grandchildren. They kept me going, but sometimes the pain was so great even that was not enough and on those darkest days I felt that I just didn't care.

I was having financial difficulties, so I couldn't just take off and travel or shop until I dropped to block out the pain. I felt as if God were sitting on me, so that I could really experience and deal with my grief, and that is just what I did. It was all that I could do. I couldn't escape or deny what had happened, as I might have done if life was easier, but life was just too hard for too long, and I was certainly not amused.

As time passed I gradually began to take an interest in a few things, even just television programmes, and life began to take on a new pace. Then I noticed that as painful as the grief was, so also was the return to life, if you will, because with each step that I took forward into becoming interested in life, I uncovered another portion of grief and despair. That is something that most textbooks on grief don't mention, and I believe that is why many people spend the rest of their lives identifying themselves as the bereaved; people don't let us know that coming back to life is just as painful as experiencing the death in the first place. So it is no surprise to me that people get stuck.

Many times I couldn't pray or didn't pray. I guess that was part of my anger towards God. "You treat me like that, and see if I pray!" But also it was because life took so much energy, and I felt so slow that I think it took me 48 hours to get through a 24 hour day. Even at this writing, I found it hard to focus and to do what I needed to do. My joyful moments were interspersed with painful and frustrating times, and I wondered where the joy had gone.

I had to keep reminding myself that it was early days still, and while there may have been a new life ahead of me, it had not yet fully formed. Sometimes I felt trusting, hopeful and confident and sometimes I felt frightened and confused. My ability to trust came and went, and I guess what I am describing was very much a kind of dark night of the soul. I did feel "still alive" and somehow whole because I was able to accept and stay with all the feelings that I experienced without condemning myself for having them. However I didn't enjoy my painful feelings when I had them.

This was a period that was so dark that it seemed to take ages for me to emerge from it. I coped with that feeling of a very dark night at the time, but it created such profound questions about the point of life, let alone the meaning of it, that I feel I just barely survived. I might have decided that life was pointless, and if it had a point I didn't care. I haven't decided that, but I did say to God, "Listen You, I am not all that enthralled with being here, but if I have to stay, it had better be good!" In a way it feels as if even that thought was a turning point, small though it may seem, because in thinking "it had better be good" I could see that I was already considering continuing to live, but I had my requirements that things needed to feel better inside me. When I spoke to God that day I was asking for external fulfilment in my external life, as I look at it now, I also understand that I needed to find some peace and acceptance in my inner life.

And so God and I are still in relationship. Along with my anger at God and feeling of being abandoned by God, there is some deeper part of me who recognises that it is only by the grace of God that I have survived such a catalogue of difficulties over such a long period of time. Knowing that I have survived makes me feel that there is a reason for me to be here and that my life still has meaning and purpose. When I couldn't contain the pain of all the loss and didn't think I had any further purpose, God held me, kept me breathing, gave me the help and nurturing that I needed to go to bed at night and wake for another day. Somewhere in my being, I know that I have just been asked to walk beside these people in their lives and their deaths, and believe me I still say that the privilege of being with people in their last hours on this earth is remarkably uplifting.

I continue to walk with God and death, loss and pain, joy and anger, frustration, fear, and sometimes terror. I have slowed down. I have little resilience, and my feelings of security have been growing ever since those experiences. I have had plenty of time to think about life and death and what it all means. I will share with you some of my thoughts.

There is no doubt that death shapes our reality here and now. When a baby is in the womb, it grows limbs and systems and organs. Most of these limbs and systems and organs are primarily for use in this world, not in the womb. It is as if the infant is in a period of preparation for its life on Earth. I believe that the same is true of us in this world; we are in a period of preparation for life in the next reality. It is not physical limbs and organs that we will need, but spiritual or transpersonal qualities, or virtues that we need to develop while we are here. It is not so important what we have accomplished insofar as how much money we have accumulated or how many degrees we have, but rather how much we have loved, how much we have given. Have we lived honestly and truthfully? Are we sincere, and can people trust us? These are the kinds of questions we can ask ourselves. In a way it is as if our bodies are the placenta with respect to the next world because they protect and nurture us as we prepare to move on and it is our bodies that we leave behind just as surely as we leave behind the womb.

It is said that our soul associates with our bodies in this life. That would seem to indicate that our souls live in another reality where they are active even now. What is of benefit to us and to them is the experiences that we have in this world and the way we grow through those experiences. In one way, I would say it doesn't matter what happens to us in this life. What matters is what we do with what happens to us; how we overcome the limitations and hindrances that life imposes upon us.

There is a wonderful quote on this matter by Bahá'u'lláh:

O SON OF MAN!
My calamity is My providence, outwardly it is fire and vengeance, but inwardly it is light and mercy. Hasten thereunto that thou mayest become an eternal light and an immortal spirit. This is my command unto thee, do thou observe it. (Bahá'u'lláh, 1975, pp.16-17)

What I have most desired in my life is to live as fully and dynamically as possible and to do as much as possible what my soul directs me to do, insofar as I can understand that direction, in order to fulfil my purpose here. Therefore I want to die knowing that I have resolved any issues that need resolution, that I have done what I could do, that I have been myself as much as I could because nobody else can be me better than I can. This is the challenge.

I remember a seminar with Bob Proctor, who understands a great deal about living life fully to be of service to people. He was speaking about the acorn, which simply disintegrates over time if it is left on a shelf. If it is put into the right environment, planted and watered, he showed how the energies of life are magnetically and abundantly drawn to it to help it to fulfil itself, so that it can become the oak tree that is its destiny. He also pointed out that in order for this to happen, the acorn is destroyed. I feel that the acorn of who I am has been destroyed, and now I look forward to a life of greater service to others and to myself than I have ever before been able to offer.

On Reflection

Sometimes we are so overwhelmed by responsibilities and having to care for others that we have no time to really think about ourselves. It feels as if we have lost ourselves, and there is nothing left of us at all. When we are in such a whirlwind, the task at hand becomes our reason for being, and even if we find it difficult, painful, and too demanding, we really notice a let down when the requirement is over.

There is something fulfilling about being a carer, and that could apply to mothering, caring for a relative or being with loved ones when they die. When our task is finished, we can begin to think of ourselves again and can wonder, think about and plan what we want to do next. It does feel rather strange in the beginning and as if we have lost one job and not found another one.

Look back at your life and at the times when you have had to care for others. What feelings do you associate with that time? If you are caring for someone now, consider how well you are caring for yourself at the same time. It is really helpful if you can be vigilant about making sure that you have some time to yourself and some time for you to do something for yourself. If your time of caring for others is over or has lessened, allow yourself time to recover and begin to find out who you are again and what is important to you. Don't berate yourself for feeling a bit lost for a while until you find your feet again. That is normal.

Chapter 20

Rags, Riches, Rags...

After having spent so much time with death, dying and loss, it is rather difficult and different to attend to the practicalities of money and earning a living and providing for myself. Anything to do with birth and death felt more compelling, more profoundly meaningful and more spiritual to me than the very physical and material needs of life on Earth.

Money is a complex topic like any of the things that are unavoidable in life, such as birth, death, money, sex, power, and God just to name a few. Those are inescapable, and even if we try to turn our back on them, we have a relationship with them that doesn't go away. Money is sometimes very difficult to understand. It *seems* all very straightforward; we work, and we make money. That provides us with our food, home, necessities and luxuries. But is that the reality?

My experiences with money and my relationship to it couldn't have been more varied and in some ways confusing which is why now I realise the complexity of dealing with money and managing it. I have had times in my life when I was provided with a financial cushion that more than supplied for my needs and the needs of my family. This was a very privileged and fortunate situation and one which is far from everybody's experience. I have also had times when money was a source of terrible anxiety, and the lack of it – or rather the lack of control over it – left me feeling very vulnerable and helpless. Nevertheless, the best way for me to examine money and what it means to any of us is to draw from my varied experience and to reflect on what that has meant to me throughout my life.

I remember my early experiences with money as a child and my thrill when I was first given what we called 'an allowance' which might also be called 'spending money.' I felt like this was my introduction into the world of the adults around me, and it made me feel as if I was growing up and allowed to take on responsibility. My mother would give me this allowance on

Saturday each week, and it was for very little really. I remember the figure of one dollar which bought far more in the late 1940s and early 50s than it might do now. Nevertheless for anything that I might have wanted, aside from some chocolates or sweets, I would have to save my money. I am sure that this process was meant to introduce me to managing money myself and to help me understand the value of money. My parents used to say to me, 'Money doesn't grow on trees.' I am sure that 'enlightened' statement was meant to make me feel guilty for wanting something that was deemed by them to be beyond what they might provide.

It meant a great deal to me to have my own money and to be able to choose how I would use that money. I remember saving money to buy presents for my mom and dad for their birthdays. I felt so excited and grown up when I was able to go to the nearby shop myself to find something to give to them. One thing that I remember I bought for my mother when I was very young was a plastic set of tongs for a salad. I am sure it didn't cost very much, but I know that I felt so proud of myself to have found such a useful present and to have bought it all by myself and to have hidden it where she wouldn't find it and then to be able to give it to her for her birthday.

I also remember buying a tie for my father once. He kept it and never gave it away or got rid of it. I found it many years later amongst his belongings. In fact he gave it to me. I have no idea where it is now, but when I found it much later on I could see how flawed my sense of taste was as a little girl and how little I understood of what my dad might be interested in wearing. What I remember today in writing this is that the colours in the tie were purple and orange among others, and in my child's mind, they were so beautiful. I don't remember the design, but as pure and generous as my intention was, my father would never have worn it except at home to show me that he appreciated my gift and loved me for giving it.

Very early on I remember what pleasure I felt when I could buy a present, give it to someone and feel how much they enjoyed having received it. I loved giving. I also loved receiving things, but I think I tended to enjoy giving even more than receiving. I loved to be able to do something for someone else. Equally I really enjoyed saving and planning to buy things that I wanted. I used to want records, and I would go to the nearby record shop and ask them to put aside some records for me, and I would save my money and go buy them later when I had enough. That was so exciting for me.

When I was just starting secondary school, I used to go to stay overnight with my very good friend, Cynthia. We would go to the local movie theatre to see the latest movie, and while there, I would use whatever money my mother had given me to buy refreshments for us both. One time I went home with little or no money left, and she said to me, 'you spend all my money just as long as it isn't yours in the first place.' This money wasn't part of my allowance, but her words really hurt me because I thought it was a good quality to be giving and generous, but I believe that what she said was a variation on the theme of 'money doesn't grow on trees.' I thought my mother gave me the money to use for going to the movies and offering something to people who had invited me to their home. I never thought my mother would have given me the money if it had represented a real hardship for her. One time, however, quite a long time later, I went to stay overnight at my friend's, and I had my own money – savings from my allowance – with me. I noticed that again I spent my own money and did what I always did, pay for the refreshments at the cinema. I don't think I said that to my mother, but I remember thinking to myself, "there, see, you spend your own money too. It is not just that you are generous only with someone else's money." I felt good about that, but nothing made me forget what my mother had said to me.

Later in secondary school, I found that we were invited to go on some outings that had to do with possible career choices. At the time I thought I might be interested in some kind of interior design work, so I was invited to visit an interior design company. I found that experience extremely interesting, but after having made the visit, I wondered to myself how I could really know at that early stage of my life what I might want to do for my career. I couldn't understand how anyone in their teenage years could make a genuine choice about what to do for a career. I was curious about many things. Many things appealed to me, and I thought well maybe as time goes on I will find that something becomes really interesting for me.

At the time and throughout secondary school I was extremely good at maths. I was very much encouraged and found that I might indeed have a real capacity to work in that field. But maths wasn't what made my heart sing.

At a deeper level than thoughts about having a career, it was clear to me that women who were married and had children just didn't do that.

I planned to marry and have children, and I felt sure that I would marry someone who would be more than capable of looking after me and our family financially. None of the woman amongst my immediate relatives worked outside the home. The only one who did was my mother, and that was because she was divorced and we needed the money. I thought that must be a rare incident, and I was sure that I would make 'the right' decisions and I wouldn't be burdened with the task of looking after our money. That didn't seem to be the way the world worked; at least as I saw it in those days. I observed that for both my grandmother and my mother, one or other of my two uncles would come to their home once a week and write checks and pay bills, so neither of them had to deal with such things.

Even as a schoolgirl I was quite conflicted already about this whole idea of my having a career and what to do about it because I really loved the freedom and sense of independence that having my own money gave me, whether I were married or not. I really wanted to create my own life, something that fit me and wasn't just a copy of what everybody around me considered correct. In fact I so much wanted to get out of St Louis and create my own life that from age 17 I did just that. First it was to go away to university.

While in university I found myself thinking of several possible career choices. The first possibility was maths, which is what I focused on in my first year. Then I saw that I seemed unable to imagine three dimensional space and work with mathematical co-ordinates in that respect. I also felt that I didn't want to spend my days confined to a large air conditioned room which housed computers as they were then. I wanted more interaction with people. Once I made that decision I chose to explore journalism and advertising.

I changed universities because the one I was attending didn't have a journalism department and because my current boyfriend was also moving on to the same university that interested me. Wasn't that curious and convenient? Still there was the dilemma: would it be relationship, marriage and family or career that I would choose to provide me with the financial security and backup that I needed? It didn't seem possible that I could do both together.

After some time at the second university, I had already decided to change universities again because the next one had a better journalism department or so I felt. After deciding to do so, my mother and my grandmother both died within four months of each other. Suddenly I was going to inherit money. I had no idea how much, but anything would have been more than I had then. I had no idea when or how it would all happen, but something inside me felt as if I now had a foundation, backup, and that was something that I had never before felt in that way. I heaved a sigh of relief and felt that I could now trust that my physical life would be supported. I still held on to that dilemma of career or relationship and since there wasn't currently a relationship that seemed to be leading to marriage, I carried on in university pursuing a career path in journalism. I had managed to get out of my home town and was living in the Chicago area, and I could imagine a life building for me there.

Through all of this, I was attempting to build for myself a financial foundation which would be something on which I would rely to support me in whatever direction I might wish to go in the future. It felt like building a system of backup that might replace what my parents had originally given to me. Many of us seek such backup through career and some of us do so through marriage – these days both women and men. We make such effort which in our tiny minds makes us feel supported and as if our physical survival is thereby assured.

Still I wanted marriage and a family, and suddenly that opportunity presented itself. I felt charmed really because not only did I know that I had and would have money available to me, I also felt sure that my husband would be very successful in his work. Didn't it all seem perfect?

It didn't take long before Philip and I were married. Interestingly I remember Philip questioning me before we got married and wondering why I would want to get married at all when I could have quite a nice life with money coming to me and being able to make my own choices. I felt that none of it was all that great unless I could share it with people I loved. Since he was the primary one of those people, I chose to marry him. Then it wasn't long after that we were living in Dublin with our three children who were, along with Philip, the people I loved most in the world, and I would share anything that I had with them.

I was so grateful that I could rest in my trust that Philip and I and our children would be protected financially because of the nest egg that my mother and grandmother had provided for us. I felt so grateful and yet I also felt guilty because I could see that I had more than most people, and I had it through absolutely no effort of my own. It felt unfair to me that others did not have the same advantage. I determined to use my resources carefully and meaningfully.

I kept my vision of taking good care of my resources, but I was so busy in the early years of my children's lives that I didn't have the time, energy or capacity to pay much attention to our financial situation. I still saw us as having backup and that backup made me feel safe at least for a time.

As the children were growing older I saw that Philip did not work regularly as an actor, and when he did work in theatre in Dublin, he was paid £5 a week for rehearsal – not really the stuff that supports a growing family. We had three houses in Dublin: one for our family and two for investment. We had just sold one of our investment houses when Philip had to go away to work. It was my belief that the money we received from that sale needed to be re-invested so as not to lose capital, but I was left on my own at home with the children and no other money coming in, so I had to use the money from the proceeds of that sale to care for the family. I felt my foundation becoming very rocky because it felt like that house dissolved in front of my eyes. My feeling of financial security began to wobble and my childlike trust felt hollow and rather filled with holes. I feared that I couldn't be sure that we would be supported if Philip did not work regularly. Suddenly what seemed like a potential lucrative career for my husband seemed hugely flawed because there was no certainty of a regular monthly check arriving to pay for his services.

This felt like the first prick bursting a bubble of naiveté that I had regarding money. Looking back I realise that I also had a belief that as long as you were a good person living an ethical life that you would be rewarded in some way. I looked around and saw that people weren't always looked after. Good people were struggling, and I was deeply saddened by that. I was also frightened because I felt very helpless without having developed a solid profession. I was learning not to be naïve enough to think that our little family was secure materially. I knew that investments sometimes failed, and Philip's work was hardly secure, so I was beginning to challenge my own assumptions and beliefs. My backup seemed to be less supportive than I would have wished.

Then what seemed to me like a solution presented itself in the form of opening a natural food store, the first one in Dublin. My interests in food and macrobiotics had begun to develop and eventually I was offered space for a food store underneath a newly established vegetarian restaurant. I envisioned having a family business to provide a regular income while Philip's acting work could add the extras that a growing family needs. I could see a possible foundation which would give our family the backup I sought.

Someone came along who was able to manage the shop, so everything looked great. Then the man, on whom we were relying to manage the business, decided to return to the USA where he eventually set up a very successful group of natural food stores in Boston. Afterwards an American couple wanted to join us in the food business, only to be told that one of their parents was not well, so they decided to return to the USA. Finally I had become pregnant once again, and I just let go of the idea of developing the shop because I knew that I would have enough to do with three young children. The shop continued for many years but without us involved. When that attempt to begin a natural food business failed for us even though someone else was benefiting from it, I was still concerned about what I might do if I had to work to support my three children on my own. I felt handicapped and frightened without real qualifications or a profession.

These days it is sometimes hard for women to know whether to have children before a career or early in a career when they are young and fertile or whether to leave it till after a career is established. If they leave it till later, they may be just a little bit too old for it, or worse, they may no longer be fertile enough to even become pregnant. That must be really terrifying for women today. When I was 21 years old, I had jumped into marrying the man whom I loved, longing for children, thoroughly convinced that a mother's best work is to look after her children herself, but I had neglected to prepare for a possible loss of financial support, which was becoming very frightening for me.

Looking back I am glad I stayed with my children and was there for them when they were growing up because I think having one parent with them regularly gives children the best possible start. But I would have felt a lot more comfortable if I could have been sure of a steady growing family business as well. I noticed that Philip didn't seem to be as concerned with all of that as I was. I don't think I ever did understand why he appeared not to be worried about the family's future, and I suspect that he kept that worry to himself. Also once he started to work as an actor, producer and director he may have been more sure of himself and his ability to provide for a growing family than I was.

Still wanting to be able to rely on myself, I decided I had better qualify for something that would be practical in which I might be able to work should the need arise. So, I did a two year full-time course in dress designing. I could only do it in a part time manner because I was so busy with the family, and even in that way, I managed to complete it and qualify in one and a half years. I had that in place, and I was then equipped to work in the rag trade if necessary, and of course I could use my skills at home with the family. By this time Philip was working a lot around Dublin, so it was enough for me to know that I had at least one qualification, and I simply decided to stop worrying about money so much.

While I contented myself to trust my foundations and my feeling of backup, the universe was designing another experience for me. In late 1979 I found that once again the backup that I sought had actually also sought me. As part of my investments, I had a stock that was in a private company that owned a lot of forestland in the southern part of the USA. This had been an investment that my maternal grandfather had bought when he had extra money due to his successful lumber business and when he died I inherited it along with others. It provided a tiny annual income of a few thousand dollars that was below poverty level in the USA, so what I received from it was really like pocket money. I was happy to have shares in that company at the time, and I imagined my grandfather going to Texas to meet the company directors, perhaps even knowing them as good friends from some other connection. It was part of my heritage, so I just held on to it.

That company was sold in 1979, and I received $1.5 million. By the time I paid taxes etc., I was left with approximately a million dollars. I went to the USA to see my father and get his help to invest it. It was a tricky situation because the tax consequences of receiving such a lot of money in one year were pretty awful unless the money were tax sheltered. I vaguely remember being told that I might have lost 80% of the money to US taxes if I had simply put it into the bank. I invested the money in various ways according to the advice of stock brokers and business men that minimised my tax consequences, but some of those investments ultimately yielded enormous losses.

It felt quite odd to have such a lot of money land in my lap and there were times when I had some kind of philosophical wondering why that money had come to me. I remembered that there had been a television programme in the USA in the 1950s about a man who would give, tax free, a million dollars to someone every week. The programme would then show how that money changed the people's lives. I took it all in as a child, and I thought to myself that I would be able to handle it if such a thing happened to me, and it seemed as if that thought somehow got buried in my subconscious mind, only to bloom later when the time was right. I could only imagine that there was some guardian angel working for me who had decided that I could do with more money. I was over the moon about this windfall, feeling as if finally I no longer had to worry about my children's and our future.

My father said that I was a wealthy woman, and although that was a nice thought, deep down it felt as if my wealth was a bit of a sham. I had always wanted to show my father that I could make it in life, but in this case I could only feel that I had succeeded just because I had received that amount of money. That was a hollow victory, and I knew that I had not actually earned this money myself. I would have been far happier making my father proud of me/us if Philip had landed a great movie job yielding lots of money or I had done some amazing business or property deal that had made a lot of money. I wanted him to know, and indeed *I* wanted to know that I was capable of making money myself even though I had chosen to devote myself to my family when the children were young.

This second burst of money from what seemed like nowhere was really quite hard for me to compute. It seemed completely outrageous. How could I even imagine what £1.5 million looks like? Could I put it into a suitcase if I had it in cash? It felt like numbers on a page, and they just didn't seem real. People everywhere seemed to regard money and finances as extremely serious business. I just felt confused, wondering how to take it seriously and what to do about it all. I didn't know what my relationship with money really was. This whole experience was one of the most confusing times of my life.

Part of me was running a belief that you are looked after if you do the right thing in life. Another part of me was feeling that nobody was looking after me, wondering who is in charge and not feeling safe. The money felt like mine but not mine. Receiving money out of the blue in this way did not really attend to that self-regard that comes from earning it. These days everybody thinks that if they receive a lot of money or win a lot of money, they'll be fine. Few people look at the experience of those who do receive large amounts of money unexpectedly to see how many of them have any of it left ten years down the line. Few people look at the enormous guilt that is sometimes felt by those who inherit money or their inability to accomplish much for themselves in life because of it.

What I realised from my own experience, and I am sure that not everyone really wants to deal with this, is that I needed to have an experience of making money for myself. Simply getting it, much as it was lovely, fundamentally didn't touch that sense of my own genuine security because there was always this feeling that if it all went suddenly that I couldn't be sure I could look after myself. Also something in me must have known that I wasn't fully involved in life. It was like living in a tower instead of walking amongst people. I needed to create my own financial support system so that I would know my own abilities and feel that I had a right to my place in the world.

Survival is such a huge part of people's lives. Money is a sort of forum for spirit, an arena in which we can live our spirituality or not as the case may be. Money, how we get it, what we do with it, how we regard it is quite a spiritual theme because it gets us into life, directly involved with the day to day working world. It brings us up against the truth of our beliefs, stamina, courage, self-belief, trust, everything. Very often people on a spiritual path think that money issues are not part of living spiritually. I think that is ridiculous because we have to eat, drink, live in a place, and clothe ourselves. How could we do that without attending to money? How could people have taken me seriously as a wise woman if I had not really confronted my fears in this way as well? Now nobody can ever say that I haven't had a difficult life or that I am speaking just from a position of privilege. I had privilege at one time, and I lost it all.

Partly because this enormous amount of money seemed so outrageous, I felt even more strongly that it was an illusion – a fantasy that couldn't possibly last unless I was wise enough to find ways either to invest it or to provide myself with a profession. Having had the experience of some study of psychosynthesis I determined that my way forward would be to train as a counsellor. I had been able to have a book published, but I was not ready to write more, so being an author didn't seem to be possible at that time. Because I had the illusory backup of the million dollars, I felt confident to move to London to train as a counsellor.

My financial ease wasn't due to last, and when I moved to London in 1986 I sold some of my property investments and took a penalty loss in selling them early according to their terms. They gave me a down payment for a house, but certainly not the full purchase price and I no longer had the comfort of knowing they would mature later and provide me with money when I would have needed it.

You might wonder why I did not have the full purchase price for a house in London in 1986 only seven years after having received a million dollars in 1979. I look back now, and I see that there were a number of reasons.

After receiving that money, a number of the investments failed. Where I might have put $150,000 into an investment, it yielded nothing, not even its original purchase price, and that would make me wonder if there had been some scam or creaming off that could have gone on by unscrupulous people. Much later my father said that if we had money we would have sued on this basis. Several of the investments had yielded "return of capital" on a monthly basis, making them tax shelter investments, so when that money stopped coming in, I had effectively gotten my original investment back, but in the absence of other income the family had to live on that money. I had planned whatever I could in terms of investing for long term gains rather than immediate income, based on the fact that Philip was working regularly, but he was out of work for three years, and we had three teenage children to clothe, house, feed and school.

All in all, and as I had expected, that money disappeared faster than I could have imagined, and I had to live with the failure of my experience. I felt worthless and was wracked with guilt for years over my "failure" to deal with money in a way that would support me and my family for life, but fortunately I was eventually able to let go of that guilt. One of the things that really helped me do so was a communication that I had with a friend, Karen Dubois, who is an accountant. I explained to her what had happened when I had received the $1.5 million, and asked for her viewpoint. Among the very interesting things that she said to me was this:

> You know the old saying, hindsight is 20/20.? I try hard to educate my women clients about this stuff. Remember when you were going through all of this, the old school was saying that the man made the decisions? Men always tried to confuse women with investments. Today, it's different. If you get another $1,000,000, let me know, we will have lots to discuss.

I felt so relieved when I read that because she could see so quickly what I had been wrestling with for years.

At the times when I most felt that I was deeply bad inside or wrong or worthless, I would remember Bahá'u'lláh's writings:

> O SON OF SPIRIT!
> I created thee rich, why dost thou bring thyself down to poverty? Noble I made thee, wherewith dost thou abase thyself? Out of the essence of knowledge I gave thee being, why seekest thou enlightenment from anyone beside Me? Out of the clay of love I molded thee, how dost thou busy thyself with another? Turn thy sight unto thyself, that thou mayest find Me standing within thee, mighty, powerful and self-subsisting. (Bahá'u'lláh, 1975, p.8)

Thus I knew my feeling of inner worthlessness was not right because it was in direct contradiction with what Bahá'u'lláh had said, so I knew that I was not worthless even though I felt very deeply that I was. Despite this, sometimes when I got into that feeling I didn't really know how to get out of it very quickly. I learned to be patient, and to sit with the feeling, as gradually the feeling would just subside, especially if I read some inspirational material.

In 1989 my mortgage repayments tripled, and it wasn't long before I was heading down the road toward repossession despite trying in every way to get work that would support me. I knew that my cash was running out, but I really didn't know what to do about it. In the winter of 1992 I tried to sell my house. I thought I would be able to move to a smaller place, and all would be well. The market was down at that time, and the mortgage company said that the purchase price was not high enough, so they wouldn't accept the sale. I was trapped, and I didn't know where to turn or what to do. On paper I couldn't sell the house, and I couldn't leave it. I couldn't have rented it out to pay the mortgage because the payments were too high. Rent would not have covered them, and I hadn't a bean to redecorate even a little, which would have made a rental more likely. I was deeply saddened at the deteriorating state of the decoration, especially after I had put money into creating a really lovely house after I had first moved in. It was a lovely warm cottage style home, and I had decorated it in that style but in 1992 no matter where I turned I couldn't find a solution.

I was able to get housing benefit, but that paid only part of the mortgage, and that scenario continued for five years until in 1996 the house was repossessed. I was completely lost. I felt as if the earth wouldn't even have me and there was nowhere that I belonged. Nowhere felt safe to me, and I seriously questioned my right to even exist. I felt as if I had tried so hard to make my life work, and I had failed. I felt more worthless than ever. I really was completely and utterly helpless in a way that I couldn't remember ever having been before.

The last few months living in that house were awful. I had wanted so much to keep the house because I loved it. It was a real home where there was love and generosity. I couldn't imagine how, with no money, I would find another place to live. A friend suggested I phone a particular estate agent, and I did. That led me to another lovely little house where I could take my dogs and cats and live in peace with my youngest son – it was a rented house. I arranged to move. This was probably my first experience of the backup that I seemed to have by just living in the moment and following whatever leads present themselves day by day. But that came only after several months of discomfort as I prepared to leave my old home behind.

I attended the court for the repossession hearing, and the mortgage company gave me a good deal thanks to a wonderful group of solicitors that I had. They agreed a purchase price, which they would put into my account as soon as the house was sold, no matter at what price it was sold. In the end, the house was sold for less than the purchase price that I had for it in 1992 even though the housing market was quite buoyant at the time. I felt that if they had left me there to sell it, I would have gotten a much better price for it. I had also taken a second mortgage on the house when I had borrowed £8,800 from a loan company. I had paid back about £11,000 before I could no longer make payments. At the time of the repossession, they presented me with a letter claiming that I owed them a further £12,000. I couldn't believe it, and I certainly had no way to pay it.

I was given two months to leave the house. I arranged when the time came that I would move to the new rental property on the 26th of the month. Then the court contacted me on Monday 18th and said that the bailiffs were due to come to the house on the following day. I panicked. I went to the court and appealed. I told them I would be leaving on the 26th. After going to the court to ask for an appeal which was set for the next morning, I came home. Scott was away, but Shannon and Brian were there, and we all looked at each other and said we had better get as much as we can out of the house in case we don't win the appeal. I rang friends and asked for help. We rented a van and friends came to help. I had already packed quite a lot when I found out the next day that I had won the appeal.

That evening there must have been 15 or more people in and out of the house. Vans were loaded and reloaded and we all worked like crazy packing and moving. By 2.30 am on the 19th, we had cleared out 80% of our things to friends' living rooms, garages, etc. Just as I fell into bed, after all that work, the phone rang and it was someone ringing in reply to my ad for the sale of my gorgeous Yamaha upright piano. It was an obscene phone call. I normally would have been quite upset about it, but I must say after all that work, I couldn't care less, and I just hung the phone up. The fellow phoned back, and Brian answered it, so the man gave up. Brian and I ended up camping out in the place for the next week. In the end I had to sell the piano for less than I wanted to one of the music stores in London. If the bailiffs had come on the 19th as they threatened, I don't know what I would have done with it.

I had been through such a terrible time and really felt how cruel the world could be, but there was an enormous amount of healing that came from the support and loving help from friends. I began to feel then that after all there is good in everything! This was another experience of the backup that does not exist through a career path, money in the bank or a relationship, but rather it had to do with dear friends who loved and appreciated me.

When I got to the new home, I felt like 1996 was my lucky year and I was so relieved. I had to sell extra bits of furniture and loan and give away some to people as well because I had too much. I thought my life would start properly from then. I was so enthusiastic, thinking that I had landed on my feet, and it was just a matter of time before I would develop a counselling practise and life would flow as I had always wanted it to do.

Little did I know that in 1997 Scott would hang himself, in 1998 I would remarry Philip, in 1999 he and my father would both die. There was another move at that time when I remarried Philip, but it wasn't until after he had died that Brian and I made a final move into the flat that Philip and I had shared. Really that was the last straw of it all. I had joined my husband in our flat after we married. Because of his illness, I just left many of my belongings in the home that I had with my son, taking with me only what I needed at the time to look after Philip. I would stay with him four nights a week, and our children would stay the other nights. I would then return to the little rented house that Brian and I shared just to recover a bit. There is no way that any of us would have had the energy for a full-scale move when Philip was terminally ill. After Philip's death, I couldn't bear to be there without him, so I spent some time away from the flat. Some months later, Brian and I moved with all our belongings into the flat I had shared with Philip.

At that time, and after much correspondence with the landlord's agent, I was told that I wasn't eligible to succeed my husband's tenancy because I hadn't changed my bank accounts to the address where Philip and I lived during those months after our marriage. I also hadn't put the gas bill and the electric bill into joint names, so in their terms, I had no proof of my residency there with him. I will let you imagine how utterly shocking and painful that was for me. I can assure you that with the rapid escalation of his cancer, the last thing on my mind was a joint bank account or both our names on the electricity bill. My husband and I had gotten this flat together in the early 1980s. Naturally we separated at the time of the divorce. After our remarriage, however, I wanted to remain as a protected tenant in the flat that I knew as my home with Philip.

Philip and I spoke often about how much we loved our flat, and we had put a lot of money into it to refurbish it when we first got it. Philip designed and had installed American style wardrobes in both bedrooms beautifully handcrafted from piranha pine and a whole new kitchen and bathroom. He also added central heating and rewired the whole flat. When we got it, the flat was really just four walls, floor and ceiling with a lovely view. When Philip knew he was dying, he said that his dearest wish was that I would remain in the flat and that the family would be able to use it. His wish was like a contract for me, which gave me the strength to fight for my flat. After all, our children had grown up here, and it was our long-term home. You know even though Philip and I were divorced, it was as if the divorce were part of the marriage, and we spoke to each other every day. So for all those years, even when I lived away, our flat was like my real home.

The landlord's agents were not so keen on fulfilling my dying husband's wishes, so at Christmas time just less than a year after he had died, and about six weeks after I had moved permanently into the flat, I got a repossession notice from them. That was a real blow and one that I really didn't need just at that time. If I hadn't had the support of my family and my wonderful friends, and the various agencies in Britain for these things, I wouldn't have had the strength to fight it. I was feeling so very down and lost. Also if I hadn't been so sure of how much Philip wanted me to keep the flat, I don't know that I could have fought it as I did. It took two years before I was recognised as a tenant succeeding my husband's tenancy. I know that it would have been to the advantage of the landlords and their agents to get me out and raise the rent to market prices. In their repossession notice, they mentioned that I would owe them for 'dilapidations' (what a wonderful word). I thought they could forget their dilapidations when we put so much money into making the flat gorgeous.

I remembered years before, Scott and a friend were in Camden attending some musical event, and they came upon an old woman defecating in a doorway. Scott spoke with her, and she told them that her home had been repossessed, and he said adamantly that nobody should take a home away from an old woman. He had a great social conscience, and he was right. The only thing that I know is that we are all responsible for our actions, and we will have to face what we have done at some time either in this life or in the next. We all make mistakes, and mistakes are OK because we can feel remorse and ask for forgiveness and eventually forgive ourselves, but if we consciously hurt another human being or cheat them or take advantage of them, that is saddest for those who do it. Whatever action any of us takes is like dropping a pebble into a pond. The ripples go out, and then they come back to the centre with greater force. Put another way, energy always returns to its source of origin. So our acts have their greatest effect on us, be it bad or good.

When I look back at my experience of money coming and going I can see that when I had a relatively whole sense of self esteem, which I had in the early days of my marriage, money came to me very willingly. When I seriously lost my sense of self worth after discovering that I had suffered sexual abuse as a child, I felt so worthless that money flew in the other direction. After my mom and my grandmother died, I felt perfectly justified in receiving the money from both of them because I had survived a difficult life filled with lots of illness, taking care of my mom as I watched her deteriorate before my eyes when I was in secondary school. I didn't resent doing it, but I found it so very painful, and I felt so alone. If my father had been there, it would have been so much easier, but he wasn't. I really felt that I deserved the money I got, and I was using it for good purposes, so it was fine. As soon as I lost my sense of self worth and of having value as a human being, I started to lose money and continued to do so.

Money isn't of itself either good or bad. It is what we do with the money that is important. Bahá'u'lláh says:

> Should a man wish to adorn himself with the ornaments of the earth, to wear its apparels, or partake of the benefits it can bestow, no harm can befall him, if he alloweth nothing whatever to intervene between him and God, for God hath ordained every good thing, whether created in the heavens or in the earth, for such of His servants as truly believe in Him. Eat ye, O people, of the good things which God hath allowed you, and deprive not yourselves from His wondrous bounties. Render thanks and praise unto Him, and be of them that are truly thankful. (Bahá'u'lláh, 1976, p.276)

In 2001 I attended some Bob Proctor seminars which came at just the right time for me. I found them particularly enlightening and helpful because the theories he describes are aligned with my own theories of what happens to enable us to receive money. I had lost touch with those when I lost confidence in myself. After finding that material I was in a kind of state of shock. It is a good shock, and indeed I have never been so impressed with programmes on understanding the right use of money and the right use of wealth as those of Bob Proctor. He has been researching issues of wealth for nearly 40 years. Bob says in his seminars that when he was 26 years old, he was making $4,000 a year and owed $6,000. He said that someone gave him a new understanding of money; he got a hold of a record by Earl Nightingale and listened to it non-stop at every opportunity. Within a year he was making $175,000 a year, and soon it became $1,000,000 a year. He always speaks about how much more a person can be of service to people when they are wealthy and have resources to enable them to be of service beyond what they can offer personally. I trained to facilitate his programme, *The Science of Getting Rich*.

There is a statement entitled *The Prosperity of Humankind* (Bahá'í international Community, 1995) that is well worth reading on this subject. The prosperity of humankind is a global aim that will facilitate much better health in every way for the people of the world.

I think that there is an amount of magical thinking that is sold as spiritual wisdom in our culture today that is not the whole story. It is the idea that if we are good then we will get what we want. Neither God nor the universe is Santa Claus. Having money is not a reward and not having money is not a punishment. We can develop a mature adult kind of co-creativity with life that realises that money is not going to fall from the sky. Regardless of my financial situation I always knew it was important for me to train, qualify, advertise, work hard and show up even when I was tired and didn't feel like it. Within that I could find my purpose and what inspired me in the way of a profession.

That is the work of a human being: creating a way of earning a living from what makes sense, is meaningful, and is of service. I would have expected that by putting my work in and not just hoping for the best, there would be some mutuality in the process, and then the opportunities that I might generate for myself would hopefully be met, grow and be amplified. There is a very subtle difference between just reacting to the unexpected arrival of money by having faith in the reward and punishment of that and actually working hard to enable money to come for value given, while feeling a sense of faith that is grounded in work.

I have been taking a very complex journey through magical thinking, spiritual wisdom, and creating a profession that is grounded in the day to day world. What was most confusing for me at the time I was rebuilding my faith in money was my experience of having trained, qualified, advertised and been willing to work hard, only to see that my counselling practice remained insufficient for my needs. Not only that, but despite my efforts I was unable to find other work that would take up the slack. I couldn't understand that, and it certainly didn't seem right or fair after all the work that I put into developing my profession and seeking work. I was deeply disappointed, saddened and aggrieved about that.

At some stage I decided to look at my experience philosophically. I saw that having a busy counselling practice, which would have kept me in the home that I loved and lost, would have made me unavailable at the time of the deaths of my son, my husband and my father. Thus my apparent failure as a professional actually served what I would have considered to be a higher purpose, that of assisting my loved ones in their final transition out of this world and into the next, insofar as I could. Obviously Scott made his own choice, which was presented to me as a *fait accompli* to which I could only react in horror and then learn to accept. Yet even then I would have been unable to take the necessary time to come to a complete halt, to grieve and to gradually recreate my life in a new way after his death.

Additionally, if I were to add faith to my philosophical musings, I would also see that possibly I needed to undergo all of those experiences for my further development even though I wouldn't have wished for any of them. At another level, I could point to a gradual break down of my world, as I perceived it, and an equally gradual rebuilding of it that happened much later and all in a deep process that took over thirty years. Whatever I may tell myself, my relationship with money has probably been more confusing than my relationship with sex, death, loss, grief, and ill health because it was so enormously complex.

Dr Elisabeth Kübler-Ross, in her workshop, said that when someone is in pain you cannot talk to them about spiritual issues. She was referring to patients who were terminally ill. I believe that statement also applies to people who are having financial difficulties. How can we think about spiritual issues if we are really struggling just to survive? I am not saying that people don't do it, but it is really hard. This has been a difficult chapter for me to write because I have experienced so many difficulties dealing with money. Now, I feel I can move on and grow through those difficulties without holding on to them.

Mostly what I have learned about money coming and going is that I had been wanting to create something that would permanently take care of me here on Earth in a very practical and physical way. For quite a long time I was being cared for practically and physically but not because I created that situation. It was absolutely lovely to have money arriving in a bank account with my name on it regardless of what I did with my days, but it was foolish to feel certain that my backup would always be there whatever its source.

Apparent safe backup can go at any time, and that applies to anything that we might have in place; a job, a relationship or money in the bank. Often what appeared safe becomes no longer safe. There is nothing that is set in stone, safe and secure for us for all the time except our own relationship with ourselves, our creator and our inner resources. Those are the kind of things that cannot be taken away from us. Anything that is physical can be taken from us. And what we thought would always be there very often disappears before our eyes.

We are going through a period of our lives in the world where that is evident. What appeared safe is no longer safe. What we thought would always be there for us is no longer there for us. We face dwindling resources in so many ways. There is uncertainty about the future of the planet, and even the professions that we once thought were secure are no longer so. We haven't yet found our way through these experiences.

It is an illusion to think that we've got backup in the way of security of any kind except what we have within ourselves. All we've really got is today and the things that matter and mean something to us, the things we really care about. When making a decision about our lives, it is important to ask questions: am I choosing this from an illusory place of backup or am I choosing this relationship, this job, this path because it actually has heart for me? Those are profound spiritual questions.

On Reflection

Money, like sex, is used as a way of measuring a person's success or failure in the world. We often believe that if we make a lot of money and have a lot of money in the bank, then we are successful people. Alternatively if we haven't found ways of making money, that means we have failed. The challenge is to recognise that there are many more elements to our success or failure than our financial story. What is much more important is how much we have loved, and served ourselves and others, what qualities we have developed in our lives. Can people trust our word? What about honesty, courtesy, kindness, forgiveness, justice which are some of the qualities that we can develop in this life?

Money and sex are the currencies of relationship. Most couples argue and have enormous power struggles over one or both. We somehow feel we have to have all the answers, and if we don't, we are not valid human beings. Let's be kinder to ourselves and to others. Let's look after ourselves and each other in our vulnerability as well as in our strength. What would we be like if we no longer had to be good at everything and have it all working all of the time? What if we were kinder to ourselves and to our partners? We are often kinder to our friends and those people whom we admire, but to ourselves and to those closest to us, we can be extremely harsh.

We need to be willing to admit that money is not always in our control. Money comes and money goes at the best and worst of times. With the best will in the world, we can lose it as fast as we can earn it or receive it. None of those events make us good or bad people.

There are some destructive relationships that we have with money, like being in debt, or being a compulsive spender or gambler. These can be addictive behaviours that do a great deal of harm to the person concerned and to anyone for whom they may have responsibility. Often the most difficult part of any problem is admitting that we have a problem, especially with addictive behaviours. It takes a lot of courage to face ourselves and say that we need help and then to follow through and seek help. We need to be discriminating enough to know whether or not the methods we have tried are working. If they are not, we may need to discontinue them and try again. It can be a real trial and error process, finding what works for us, but it is well worth continuing.

There are people who get money for nothing by stealing, embezzling, or divorcing for the purpose of getting money. These behaviours involve other people who become victims of our need and greed. There is a great deal of hurt and pain caused by thieves and people who use others without regard to their feelings. This kind of behaviour requires a hard cold look and an ability to face both the behaviour and ourselves. As difficult as it is to be a victim of this behaviour, it may be equally difficult to be the perpetrator. Even if the perpetrator is never caught nor punished, the burden of consequences may be intolerable.

We have a very intimate relationship with money that is often very secretive, and there is a lot of shame attached to it. In this world, money is our survival mechanism, and because of that, we do feel very close to it. If we didn't have money, it could actually kill us because we could not provide ourselves with food, shelter and warmth. That makes it really important to us, but we carry its importance further than a lifesaving resource and imbue it with the ability to maintain our position in society, enabling us to thrive and feel good about ourselves. People sometimes wield or attempt to wield power with money and hope to control others because they have money. That is where we may find ourselves engaging in a destructive relationship with money.

The way we relate to money reflects how we interact with the world and get our needs met. As important as that is, what is far more important is that our relationship with money and our ability to survive in the physical world has an enormous impact on our sense of self. Many people in the therapeutic world might suggest that our sense of self should be independent from our financial situation, but the truth is that we are inextricably connected to our capacity to manifest our value in the world. There are those who may choose to live in a monastery as a way of moving beyond the need to be working in the world, and that is their choice, but otherwise I don't think that we can fundamentally escape our own deep need to manifest our value in the world as a way of knowing our value and having it mirrored back to us.

We are not meant to be here trying to transcend the physical world. We are meant to be here learning to manifest our values, our ideas, our worth, our capacities, our talents and gifts in it. We are meant to do that work. When we aren't doing that, it hurts, and it affects our sense of cohesion. Receiving money for our work, which is our worldly contribution, is a clear and very concrete indication to us that we have value and that our value is being received and appreciated by the world around us. When we are not experiencing that, we may not feel fully grounded in a genuine appreciation of ourselves and our intrinsic value. The physical world is a physical world for a reason and we are part of that physical world to get to know ourselves as physical beings with value. Not having our value mirrored back to us has a great impact on our own sense of ourselves, and most profoundly so when our value is not mirrored in physical form.

Regardless of our financial situation, we need to take care of any issues that we have with money, so that we can take care of ourselves and our loved ones better. Any shame or dishonesty with ourselves and others that we may have is an indication that we need to look more closely at our relationship with money. The only shame is in not dealing with something that requires our attention. As long as we are working towards finding a way forward and are willing to learn how to take care of our money, we will be making some progress.

From a spiritual perspective, everything in creation is spiritual, money no less so than prayer. Money is simply one of the many forms of energy that are part of creation, and it is a convenient mechanism of exchange. Any other values we apply to it come from us, and we can change them and change how we feel about money. We are in this life and on Earth, so that we can participate in creation and enjoy, love, appreciate and involve ourselves with the physical world around us. Many people on spiritual paths seem to spend a good deal of time trying to get out of the world and separate themselves from some of the most glorious physical experiences that we can only enjoy in this life because we have the body to do so. We need money to feed, clothe and house our bodies, which are our vehicles for our soul as long as we live, so they need to be cared for lovingly and with respect and reverence.

The more money we have, the more generous we can be. The more money we have, the more we can also be of service to the world around us. Physical things are here for us to enjoy, and money is a means to enable us to enjoy them and to be able to share our enjoyment with others. One of the qualities that I admire most in people is what I call generosity of spirit. How enthusiastic are we about the good fortune that we have or that others around us have? Can we be truly pleased when a friend tells us about something good that has come to them? Do we share the good fortune that has come to us with the same kind of generosity with which it has been given?

Think about your relationship with money and the physical things of this life. Wonder when and where you may be able to enjoy these things if not whilst you are on Earth. Also consider being gentler with yourself and forgiving of the times when you feel you have not been able to take good enough care of your physical world, but at the same time be as clear with yourself as you can, so that you do not ignore a problem if you have one. Ask yourself what it means emotionally and spiritually for you to have money and to not have money? What are the themes that come up when you ask yourself "where is my backup?" What is that a teacher of and about for you?

CHAPTER 21
I Still Remember the Smell of the Lilacs

What does this title mean? To me, it means that I can go back through my memory banks and recall fun times and interesting happenings with my family and friends. You know I have had so much to appreciate through all these experiences. One of the things I have learned in life is that through all the tragedies, pain and suffering, learning to find things to appreciate, even the tiniest of things on some days, is really important to maintain sanity. So here is my chapter of acknowledgements and gratitude because there has been much to appreciate as well as much to be grieved in my life.

I was born and lived in St Louis, Missouri from age 7 to 17. That was 10 years of my life, and until I moved to Dublin, it was the longest time I had spent in any one place. From birth to age 7, I lived in New York, New Jersey, St Louis, Chicago, Detroit, Montreal, Canada and back and forth between them.

When I lived in Montreal in the 1950s I remember that daily milk was still being delivered by horse drawn carriages. That was great because the children in the neighbourhood would all get little rides on the back of the carriage. I moved so much because before my parents were divorced, my father changed jobs frequently always going to a better one. I got used to changing schools, losing old friends and making new ones. It created a kind of flexibility in life that has served me well over many years. I remember that my mom would frequently take me back to St Louis to be with her mom and see her brothers and their families, so from very early on, I was travelling by plane from other cities to and from St Louis.

What do I remember about St Louis particularly? Well I remember the really hot summers when the temperature and the humidity would soar. I would always get burned at least once during the summer and be in agony because of my fair skin. And I do remember the smell of the lilacs because they smelled so gorgeous, the combination of heat and moisture in the air

355

must have been just right for them. There were some wild lilacs near the streetcar that my mom and I took on some Sundays to church. It was one of the few remaining streetcars, and it was really fun to ride. I always buried my nose in the wild lilacs when they were in bloom because they smell so utterly heavenly and delicious.

I also remember the lightening bugs, or fireflies, in the summer nights. When it got dark, we would look around and see little lights coming on and going off in the garden all over the place. They were the lightening bugs. They were probably the size of a bee or a wasp, and they would light up for a second and then go dark and repeat that procedure frequently. Because they moved slowly, we would catch them in jars for a time just to watch them as they lit up, and then release them.

I remember the colour of the leaves in the autumn, the brilliant reds and oranges and yellows and how beautiful the trees looked just as they were losing their leaves. I also remember the shades of green of the trees in the heat of the summer. There are a lot of trees around St Louis, and it is wonderful to be in a big city with so many trees. I used to love the winter days when it had rained and then the temperature had dropped below freezing, so the trees were coated in ice, and the whole place looked like a fairy land. I lived very near to the Mississippi River, so I am probably one of the few people in the world who really knows how to spell it. I certainly didn't see it often, and when I did it was to drive across it. I was very much aware of the river as a child, even though it wasn't something I saw often.

It was as if that mighty river flowed somewhere in the background of my consciousness, and I used to always marvel at the thought of that great and powerful river not far away from me. That image of the river reminded me of the image that I have of my own life force. For me that river continues to symbolise the life force that characterised the city of St Louis. There is a wonderful arch and park on the riverbank entrance to St Louis.

The arch was built after I left St Louis. I have never seen it nor been up in it. Now it has been over 40 years since I have lived there. I looked it up though, when I was doing my research for this book, and I was reminded of the significance of St Louis' history, of the pioneers who travelled through that bustling city, of Dred Scott who sued for his freedom in the Old

Courthouse. I closed my eyes and imagined Thomas Jefferson's inspired vision of the spread of freedom and democracy from "sea to shining sea".[1]

Still just as St Louis was the gateway to the West, it was my gateway to the world. To this day I often think of the place and especially that great and mighty river, that old man river, the Mississippi River that just keeps rolling along.

I so much wanted to ride horses when I was in St Louis, and I dreamed of having my own horse. I think that had a lot to do with my older sister who loved horses and was an expert horsewoman. I just never did much riding. I went with my mom to a ranch in Colorado called the Bent X Ranch, I think. I spent a couple of weeks there riding every day. There was one moonlight ride in the mountains, and I was thrilled. I was quite young, maybe 11 years old. It was the best holiday and probably about the only holiday that we had together. I loved Westerns on television - we had only black and white television at the time, and much of it was live. There was a soap opera on every day called *As the World Turns*, and I loved that title. I don't think I was able to watch it much, but I did watch it when I was at home, sick.

When I was in primary school, the 3D movies came out first. I remember I had a boyfriend at the time, and we would go to the movies. One week, I would pay for the tickets in, and he would pay for the candy, and the next week, we would change roles. His mom would drive us and pick us up. It was so romantic! One of the 3D movies was *It Came from Outer Space*. Of course, I thought that all that outer space stuff was actually happening at the time. I just believed it, and I loved it as well. I wanted to have friends from other planets and get to know more beings. It seemed so exciting, a kind of magical world.

I remember one of the programs on television was *The Howdy Doody Show* with Mr Bluster and Princess Summerfall Winterspring. Of course Howdy Doody was the star!! There was also *Buster Brown*. Television was

---

1   The Gateway Arch reflects St. Louis' role in the Westward Expansion of the United States during the nineteenth century. The park is a memorial to Thomas Jefferson's role in opening the West, to the pioneers who helped shape its history, and to Dred Scott who sued for his freedom in the Old Courthouse. Thomas Jefferson's vision of the spread of freedom and democracy from "sea to shining sea" inspired Eero Saarinen's masterpiece of modern design. The 630 foot stainless steel Gateway Arch reflects St. Louis' role as the gateway to the West. (National Park Service, 2011)

so new, and it was a real miracle to be able to watch as well as listen. I did remember listening regularly, like every Sunday evening, to a radio show that was called *O Henry*. That must have been in about 1950.

There was a magazine for girls called *Calling All Girls*, and it gave instructions on how to start a club with the same name. I gathered together a group of girls from my school, and we had the club. We would meet every once in awhile in each other's homes. I don't remember if we did anything of any note; it was a start.

One of my favourite things to do in St Louis was to go to the St Louis Municipal Opera. It was outdoors in Forest Park under the stars. In the summer it got dark around 8pm, so on a clear night, the stars were brilliant overhead. There were usually operettas being performed like *The Mikado* by Gilbert and Sullivan. I loved theatre in any form, especially musicals, and this had the added delight of being outside. I also loved having to run to our car when the heavens would break open, and the rain would pelt down and look as if it were going to stay. Sometimes, it would be just a shower, and we could go back to our seats, and often it would be pouring to stay, so we just went home. You know the rain in St Louis was so different from the usual light and gentle rain in England and Ireland. When I went there from Dublin for a visit with my children in 1979, a dear friend of my mother's, whom I referred to as Aunt Skiddy, took us to a dinner and show on a riverboat on the Mississippi. During the show, it rained so hard that I had to take my children outside to look at the rain. Having been raised in Dublin, they had never seen rain like that. As much as they loved the show, the rain was a phenomenon not to be missed.

When I was in John Burroughs School, a co-educational secondary school in St Louis, I remember being painfully shy and sadly unable to communicate with boys especially and also with some girls. I felt as if I got on better with older people than with people my own age, so I often found it easier to speak with teachers than with boys certainly. Of course it depended on the teacher. Because I was especially good at mathematics, I got on very well with the mathematics teacher, Mr Montgomery. I also got on well with my English teacher, Mr Acker.

I lived on my own with my mom, so it was helpful to me to befriend some of the teachers because of the fact that I had very little male energy

I Still Remember the Smell of the Lilacs

around without my father. In fact I was friends with Jack Acker and his wife Ginny until their deaths many years later. They visited me in Dublin in the 1970s and in London in 1995, and after Ginny passed away in October 2002. Jack had learned to use the computer and was able to send me emails. We emailed each other frequently until he passed away in June 2004. He wrote the best letters and emails of anyone with whom I have ever corresponded. I miss them both tremendously because they were such long-term friends. I had some very good girl friends at school, and I have still maintained a little contact with the school and some of the people that I met there.

There was a time when I felt that many of the class didn't like me much, and I was going to transfer to a girl's school, Mary Institute, where my mother had gone. She had really wanted me to go there, but I knew that I needed to be around fellows in a co-educational setting in some way after having been raised mostly by her and my grandmother. I never actually did transfer to her school because I got sick and missed out the one full year at school, which would have been the year of my transfer. During that year, I found that the people in my class did care for me because they kept in touch with me, and they all wanted to get together and give me a television to have in the hospital where I was for six weeks. I was so astounded and felt so appreciated by my whole class that I just didn't then feel right about making the change. And so I carried on and completed secondary school at John Burroughs. When I was in my last year, my mom was diagnosed as being terminally ill although I didn't really understand it in that way at the time. I had a dear friend, John, who was always there for me during the stress filled days of looking after her. He was a rock, and just helped me to feel a kind of stability that I didn't have in any other way. It was a hard time, but with such a good friend beside me, I was able to get through it.

When I left St Louis at age 17 first to attend Lake Forest College, I was not aware that I would never return to St Louis to live there again. I certainly didn't want to spend much time there because there were other places to which I wanted to travel and where I wanted to live. I spent the summer with my father and his family in Switzerland, and really loved being in another culture. I experimented with new foods and a new language – French. I got to know people who were friends of my dad's, and I grew to understand his work. At that time, he had just begun to work for Boyden, an American company that deals with Management Consulting.

My father had brought the company to Europe and had opened offices for the company in Paris, London, Frankfurt, and Geneva to name a few. He loved his work because he was helping people to move into the job that was just right for them and helping employers to find people who were just right for them. He was dealing much of the time with presidents and vice presidents of companies all through Europe. He was a great judge of character and most helpful to others.

I loved the idea of helping people, all sorts of people, and determined to do that when I got older. Spending time in Europe was a real blessing for me at the time. I was one of the first in my class and in my school to actually venture out of America at that time. People didn't travel as readily then as they do now. Travelling by plane was a joy, and the food was great. I remember the summer after I graduated from John Burroughs, I asked my dad if I could travel to Europe by boat rather than by plane, and he let me travel over on *The France*, a fairly new ocean liner. It was a five day crossing, and I was exhausted because of my exams and with looking after my mom. What a way to go, however!!

My first choice of a place to live outside St Louis was Chicago. I liked the windy city, so being in Lake Forest, just north of Chicago, for that first year of university was great. I still maintain contact with a very dear friend of mine, Lynn, who was one of my best friends there. In fact, she was in London on the day that Philip died. I saw her during her visit here, and it was just wonderful to renew our friendship after all those years.

I did keep in touch with an ex-boyfriend, Ken, whom I first met at Lake Forest College and who transferred to the University of Illinois for the second year of University studies as did I. He died a few years ago. He was only 50 years old when he died. He and I were friends for a long time. He had even met my family in St Louis because he had come down to visit there sometimes. I remember a strange thing happened. He phoned me in the summer before he died, and I was saying that I was having trouble about money. He offered to send me some money just to buy some groceries if that would help. I said no, thank you, it is all right. Anyway several months later, I got a letter from a company that was in Skokie, Illinois in which I had held some stock some years before. They said that a check they had sent to me about eight years previously had not been cashed. The check was for about $1100. They enclosed a form for me to sign and return to them before they could send me the check. Wow, I sure needed the money, and I was a bit surprised that they would still have a record of a check not cashed for such a long time. I was also surprised that they would contact me about it. Just about a month after that I received a letter from Ken's family to say that he had died, and it turned out that he had passed away only just before someone in that company in Skokie, Illinois had written to me with news of the check. I was stunned because Ken was from Skokie, Illinois! Now, you can say what you like, but I like to think that he helped to get me that money.

I spent one and a half school years at the University of Illinois. I got my first car during that time. I can tell you now the story of that. Ken and I were good friends, and we decided that I would write to my Dad to ask him to help me buy a car. I felt I needed a car to go to my mom in St Louis when necessary because she was by then in a nursing home. I just wanted a car really badly then. I was 19 years old, and transport to and from Champaign/Urbana where the University of Illinois is to St Louis or to Chicago was difficult without a car. In fact, it was well nigh impossible. Anyway, Dad, in his wisdom said that he would pay for half the car and I would have to repay him for half even though he would advance me all the money to pay for the car. He asked that I check out a price on the lowest model new car – Ford or Chevrolet type. I went to a local dealer and decided on a Chevrolet in metallic red. I told my father the price of the car, and left that to him. This was probably in January of 1963.

Of course, I thought that Dad had only to write a cheque. I didn't know anything about investments and having money committed here and there. He looked as if he had plenty of money to me, and that was fine. I didn't hear from him and didn't hear from him and didn't hear from him but I knew I could count on him. His word was law, and I knew he would send the money once he had said that he would. My sister always said, "You could go to the bank with his word." I could always count on him to fulfil his promises. I could really trust him.

Well that was all well and good, but Ken and I were getting impatient, and we had time to think while we were waiting. Ken suggested that we might try a Chevrolet dealer in Chicago because we might find that a bigger dealer would have cheaper prices, so I might be able to get even a better model car for the same price as the lower model was quoted in the small university town. So, when we went to Chicago, we stayed at his family home and we went to a Chevrolet dealer called Nicky Chevrolet. Sure enough we were able to find a mid-range Chevrolet at the same price, and that appealed to us much more than the lower-range car. In fact the whole idea of having a car was really getting too attractive for us to wait much longer.

I thought of an idea. I had some jewellery – a couple of diamond rings and a diamond bracelet. I don't remember what I put together for this. I asked them if they would consider allowing me to take the car while holding the jewellery as collateral until I received the check from my Dad. They agreed, so I turned over my jewels, and they gave me the car. Wow, we did it, we had the car. It was in my name, and my uncle in St Louis arranged to have it insured. All was well. I waited, and I waited, and I waited. I didn't think I could phone Dad because if I did, then it might annoy him. I certainly couldn't tell him the deal that I had made with this Chevrolet dealer. I realised that I might never see my jewellery again. We were getting so nervous that we went to the post office in the mornings before 8am because we were so keen to get that letter with the check. Finally the day came; the check arrived. The next weekend, we drove to Chicago, reclaimed my jewellery which I did get back and paid for the car. Whew! It was touch and go for a while, and we were so nervous, but it worked. I had the car early. I did repay my Dad for the car, and he never knew the story. I don't remember if I ever told him. I am sure that he knows it now as I write this. I feel sure he is encouraging me as are all the other members of my family who are in the other realm.

When I lived in Dublin I made some wonderful friends there who have been supportive of me all the way along. As well as my friends, I also really appreciated the children's teachers at school who were so helpful. I remember one time when it was near Christmas and a teacher was speaking about Jesus Christ in that connection. Scott made a comment saying something like, "you must remember that there are others aside from Christ like Krishna, Moses, Muhammad, Bahá'u'lláh." She is reputed to have said, "That will be enough out of you, Scott!" I thought that was very funny. There is a wonderful Bahá'í community in Ireland, and we were fortunate to have lived in Dublin during the years when that community developed and grew. I loved being in Dublin and being part of life there. When the time came to move to London, it was a great sadness to me to leave my dear friends behind in Ireland, and what I discovered, of course, was that I didn't leave them behind, but I carried them with me. Ireland is not so far away, nor is the USA, and I am still in touch with many people in America too whom I met all those years ago when I lived there, and also with many whom I meet as my life goes on.

In the summer of 1981 I travelled to America with my children. It happened that my two half sisters, Marianne, who is older than me, and Susie, who is younger, and I were all visiting our father in his mobile home in Carpinteria, California, one day. I am sure that all three of us sisters had not been together with our dad for well over 20 years. This was something to celebrate. Well, on this occasion, Dad brought out the family tree. It was a rolled up, taped together document, handwritten in pencil, which he had kept for years. He had two aunts who spent 25 years of their lives researching our ancestry and making sure that what they wrote was accurate. Dad said he had the document and wondered what we wanted to do with it. Nobody said much for a while. Then I suggested that I could take it back to Dublin and to the National Gallery there where I could find someone who could restore it and fix it in a way that it might keep. I also offered to get copies of it for my sisters and for my children. Problem solved. Now I have this enormous document which traces our family back for over 3,000 years. The genealogy was ratified by the Magna Charta Society; highlights of it were published in Philadelphia in Volume VI of Magna Charta, American Families of Royal Descent. I understand that the genealogy also would make me and my sisters eligible for the Daughters of the American Revolution, Daughters of 1812 and the Colonial Dames. I have never been very much interested in genealogy but I was really impressed by the love and dedication shown by my father's two aunts who spent all that time, energy and work to research their own history, which was also my history.

I am proud of my ancestral association with some of the people who had the foresight to produce the Magna Charta and to ensure our freedom and the need for everyone to abide by the law through it.

The Magna Charta resulted from the peace made between King John of England and about sixty of his rebelling barons in 1215. After preliminary negotiations with the barons through the Archbishop of Canterbury, Stephen Langton, as go-between, the King and his party met the barons on 15 June in a meadow known as Runnemede next to the Thames River. After several days of face-off discussions on the 19th the document language was agreed upon and the barons elected 25 of their number to be "Sureties", holding title to a few of the King's properties, including the Tower of London, to guarantee the King's compliance with the laws and liberties of the Magna Charta.

Thus began the long legal process of putting limits on kingly (and hence, by later extension, governmental) authority and of granting explicit rights to the ruled. From the time of its issue, the Magna Charta became a symbol of freedom to the barons and people alike, and kings during succeeding centuries were expected to affirm it.

This compact, originally just between the king and his discontented barons, has been invested by time and later interpretation with real and mythological power far beyond its original intent and far beyond any other single document in English law.

The Magna Charta led to the English and later the United States Constitutions. More precisely it gave protection to the rights of the nobles and common citizens alike to be free of arbitrary actions against their persons or property by their sovereign. It has come to be recognised as the first cornerstone of liberty and justice in the western world.

It is the well-spring of modern concepts of free speech, free association, the right to petition the government for redress of grievances, the right of due process according to the law of the land, to the public and impartial trial at the hands of our peers, the right to travel freely in the time of peace, and perhaps most important of all, the recognition that even the sovereign is subject to the law of the land. The Constitution of the United States of America refers specifically to the Magna Charta in section nine, amendments one, five, six, and eight, and implication is made in both documents to "No taxation without representation". (Baronial Order of Magna Charta, 2009)

While the genealogy produced by these two devoted sisters speaks of ancestors such as Julius Caesar, Shakespeare, Henry VIII, Anne Boleyn, Queen Elizabeth, Mrs Thomas Jefferson and Daniel Boone, for me it is the association of my ancestors with documents that ensure freedom and justice that most interests me. It also interests me that I somehow came to live in London.

Fairly recently I discovered that my father's parents who were both Americans had gotten married in 1906 in a church in South London. I also knew that at various times my father's mother had lived in London and other parts of England. As a teenager, my father had gone to Brighton College for a while. That gave me a real sense of destiny and a feeling of coming home when I knew that I had unwittingly returned to live in a country which had that distant connection with my family. Actually it was not just me. It was as if Philip and I had come full circle in returning to the origins of our families – he had ancestors from Ireland and I had ancestors from Ireland and England.

On Reflection

Reminiscing and having a sense of connection to our story and history is important because it gives us a sense of who we are. When I look at my history, my story, I begin to see answers to such questions as: When I look at my history, I can ask myself who is this person who lived that history and what can I tell about myself from exploring how I have lived the story of my life? I can particularly get a sense of my qualities and then I can decide if I like the qualities I have expressed in living my life. I can ask myself what has been the truth? What experiences have I had? What makes me unique from the journey I have taken?

We know ourselves as a collection of the stories we tell ourselves about our lives and about our relationships with people, with things, with events, and with all our experiences. Exploring my own story tells me who I believe myself to be, and it helps me to see whether what I have done is what I have wanted to do. Do I value the choices I have made along the way? Can I admit that what I have chosen to do seemed like the best idea at the time or that in some instances I was foolish? What would I have done differently? My story helps me to see where I might have made different choices and to wonder what might have happened if I had done so. It helps me to see whether I have been happy with the results of my choices and to fantasise about the possible results of other choices I could have made. Very often I managed to do something which turned out to be very valuable indeed, but at the time I could have made a different, often easier, choice. I could so easily not have done the very thing that turned out to be so valuable, and when I see that I can then be thankful that I took the decision I did.

Looking at where I am in my story at the present time enables me to make changes that I might want to make before I continue on. It is a bit like going back to the drawing board and seeing which things I wish to continue as they are and which things I wish to change. If we are not attentive and do not account for what we are doing and why we are doing so, we can often lose track of our values. If I just let life happen to me, I may ultimately not be very happy with the results. If, on the other hand, I do monitor my progress and my achievements or lack thereof, I can turn my life in a different direction if I so desire.

Exploring our history is a sort of an audit where you get an overview, an evaluation, and a valuation because I can see my own value as I tell my story. I notice my strengths as I see the struggles I have endured in my life, and I notice my limitations as I see where I might not have dealt well with what has happened to me. I can see what has been meaningful and important to me just by seeing what I have done and how I have spent my energy. I can even begin to understand myself through younger parts of me who behaved in the ways they did at the time. I may also be able to begin to forgive those younger parts of me for their inability to have all the answers.

When I look at my story I may also find that some of my memories and my interpretation of them are quite accurate whilst others may not be so. I can then change my viewpoint about aspects of my story. One of the results of therapy is that I can learn to value events in my life differently and perhaps to see my strength through someone who can witness what I have endured. Even without therapy, connecting to my story and my history in some way embraces and ties together the different aspects of my journey. It connects me to my roots and returns me to belonging to my tribe with all its joys and pains but at least to that real sense of being part of something bigger than myself. Often we want to escape our past and our history, but it is only when we look at it more closely, evaluate it, see what it has given us, and what we have discarded from it that we can feel whole. We don't have to like it, but we do need to see what we have learned from it.

My story gives me a feeling of belonging to a people, a tribe, a time, a place, and it also gives me a sense of being part of the passage of time on this earth. My story connects me to my environment, my surroundings, my culture, my heritage, my nation, my world. Without an understanding of my story, I can feel somewhat adrift, not rooted or anchored in my life.

There are different ways of connecting to our story. We can simply tell the story as we remember it, and/or we can enhance the story by using our senses to evoke memories that we might otherwise forget. For example, fragrances are a very important part of our lives. They can tell a story in a way that may be subtly different or sometimes very different from the story you may simply reconstruct from memories. Did you ever encounter a fragrance that brought back to you a whole memory? Even the subtle fragrances, the smell of the central heating in winter, the smell of the summer barbecue, and many more give us a world of experiences aside from the memories themselves. How tasty would food be, if there were no fragrance? Can you identify a fragrance that means something to you?

Some fragrances connect to pleasurable experiences, the fragrance of someone we love or of a new baby or puppy or kitten? Other fragrances bring us to most unpleasant experiences, the fragrance of fear or of rage or of people who evoke those feelings within us. The fragrance of dampness in a building or stale cooking orders can be most unpleasant. Look back over your life and remember fragrances that have been important to you and with those fragrances look at the memories that they bring to mind and write your own story based on your memory of fragrances. You can include both the pleasurable ones, and the ones that are not so pleasant, and see what kind of a tale you can tell.

It is not just fragrances, but sounds as well, memories connected to pieces of music or sounds of life. Notice how replaying a song that you heard many years ago can put you back into that time and those feelings in an instant. We live in a world of sound and fragrance as much as in the world of memory and experiences. Look at what the thoughts of different music bring to you.

Also sensations, did you ever feel a coldness or a warmth on meeting someone and let that feeling lead you to a sense of the person's character? Sensations and feelings guide us in so many ways. Sometimes we experience a body sensation connected to feelings and sometimes it is just a sense of knowing that can be uncannily accurate. All these sensory experiences make up our memories of our relationships with the physical world.

Taste is another important sense that is often overlooked. What is the flavour of a person or an event? Taste also connects us to a quality, sweet or tart, pungent or bitter. What is the role that taste has had in your life? What different tastes can you remember as being meaningful and significant?

So do connect to your story, and write what has been important to you. Tell your story as you remember it. Then explore your relationship with your senses and see what kind of story about your life emerges. It may be no different from the usual story you might write or tell, but it may have more unusual detail. We tend to predominantly rely on our visual memories. The other senses like fragrance, sensations, taste, and sound are the more unusual and often overlooked portals that evoke aspects of your story; they are actually just as powerful as our visual memories in terms of connecting us to the past and our feelings about our experiences.

Another way of looking at your story is to imagine an image or symbol of your life, draw the symbol and then write your story from that symbol. You can focus on a symbol for your whole life or you can imagine a symbol for aspects of your life, for instance childhood, teenage years, maturity or work, relationships, spirituality. Whatever you do, explore your story in whatever ways you can. It will help you to make meaning of your life and to see the threads that connect various events in it. It will help you to see that you have been a valuable asset to this world and to see the contribution that you have made and continue to make.

Another way of connecting to your story is to keep a journal. This is a way of not just connecting to the past but also to feel more in touch with your current story. Don't make this a journal about what you have done in the day. Make this a journal about what mattered to you, what lingered with you, what was evoked. Write down smells, sensations, sounds and tastes. Make it a more sensual account. Also make it more internal, considering what occurred inside of you in terms of your feelings, sensations, thoughts, noticing how your belief systems might have been evoked and how you felt about the experiences that evoked them and your responses. For instance, if you believe that you are not worth much, and somebody complimented you, were you able to graciously accept the compliment and say, thank you, or did you throw it away, deny it or dismiss it rather clumsily without really appreciating the gift the other person had given to you? If you had such an experience, you might notice it and decide that you would rather receive such compliments and respond with grace and appreciation. Then you can begin to monitor your behaviour as you go along. Each time you receive a compliment, you might watch yourself to see if you respond with appreciation or if you persist in your habit of dismissing it. Gradually you will be able to make a choice about how you respond. It takes time to change habitual behaviour, but it is possible to do it. The best ally in all this is for you to become your own observer, so you can both be involved in your behaviour whilst at the same time noticing what you are doing. When you can do that, then change is possible in many habits.

Remember this is your life to make with it what you will. There are many choices you don't have and will never have, but there are also many choices you do have along the way in each and every day. The more you are able to make those choices willingly without relying on habitual responses, the more you will feel in command of your life, and the more your life will feel like your own. Also remember that life goes by in a flash, and when the time comes for your life to be over, you will want to know that you have lived it well with enthusiasm and passion and that you have done what you meant to do whilst here on earth.

CHAPTER 22
Epilogue: The Conclusion is not The End!

I first began writing my autobiography after the deaths of my son, my husband and my father because I believed that I would be the next to die, and I wanted my family and friends to have an idea of what I had experienced in my life. Then as time went on, and I experienced more psychotherapy to help me deal with the losses, I realised that my experiences might be meaningful to many other people who are seeking answers to some of life's deep questions. Therefore I set about making my book more accessible and I added discussion about the issues that were the subject of each chapter as well as a special part at the end of each chapter called 'On Reflection', which included thoughts and feelings that you, dear reader, might use to look at your own life. The issues addressed, such as life threatening illness, spiritual quests, health and healing, marriage, parenting, death in its many forms, money, sex, pleasure and pain are all universal issues that occupy our time on this beautiful earth. How we relate to ourselves, to our many issues and to all of life makes us who we are.

We live in a sparkling universe filled with all kinds of life as well as all kinds of other matter or non matter. Our earth spins around on its axis once a day at a speed of something like 1000 miles an hour whilst at the same time travelling around the sun at a speed of 67,000 miles per hour. That is an impressive piece of engineering and not something any of us might design or emulate as far as I can imagine. We have a limited time on this planet to enjoy its beauty, to taste its fruits, to contribute to the betterment of life and to be ourselves. When we are young, we look ahead to a life of about 70–95 years, and some of us will make it that far whilst others won't. We have no real control over our deaths, and there are many limitations to our choices in life depending upon where and when we were born, to whom and in what culture.

Epilogue: The Conclusion is not The End!

We can, if we so desire, work to improve our lives and those of others around us by simple things like a smile to another human being whom we pass on the street or caring for those who are nearest and dearest or coming up with some remarkable system that can heal many ills for the people who are our friends and neighbours on this planet. One of the ways in which we can be most helpful to the world is by bringing ourselves to account each day, evaluating our own behaviour and noticing where we feel we have lived according to our intention, and where we have fallen short. We need to notice what behaviour makes us feel right with ourselves and what behaviour causes disappointment or even shame. We cannot align our behaviour with how we see ourselves and how we wish to be unless we are aware of what we are doing.

We sometimes fail to honour and connect with our own wisdom, and that is a deep loss for us and for those around us. If I could wish anything for you, dear reader, I would wish that you would really believe in yourself, work to get to know yourself and to be true to yourself, treat yourself, your friends, family, animals and nature with love and respect and live your lives with as much consideration and seriousness as you can, so that when you get to the end of your life, you can look back and say, I did it, and I did it well!

The engineer who designed our universe and untold other universes is as beyond our comprehension as the painter is beyond the comprehension of the painting. That there is order and intelligence to the universe and that there is much more to life than what we see and feel and think we know seems to be rather clear if we can see beyond our own noses. A friend and colleague once told me that life is the result of an ongoing mating game between Grandfather Sun and Grandmother Earth. I loved that image, and I thought of the sun beaming its rays continually on to the earth and of the earth twirling, so those warm life-giving rays can reach every nook and cranny of her surface while at the same time she spends her days circling her beloved sun. That is quite an image and quite a relationship. This earth is our home, and we are its caretakers. In some ways we have lost touch with her needs and we sometimes seem to have not enough respect for her wisdom.

As for me, I am still working as a therapist, and loving my work. I am deeply involved in the Baháʼí Faith and Psychosynthesis and I also continue to benefit from many of the other approaches mentioned in this book as well as new ones because I love finding disciplines that enhance my quality of life and that of my friends, family, colleagues and clients. I am now considering working with people to help them to improve their intuitive connection to their inner wisdom and as I learn more I will also want to share new things that I learn.

I love life, the change of seasons, the beauty that surrounds us that is nature in all its glory, the fact that the sun comes up each day and goes down each evening, and I have a roof over my head, clothes on my back, food in my belly and wonderful family and friends whom I love dearly. I know that one day I will no longer be in this world, and there is a feeling of sadness about that because, for all its difficulties, I love life and feel privileged to have been able to spend so much quality time here. Nevertheless there will be that inevitable transition one day, and when I do make it, and meet Philip and Scott and Tara and the baby whom I lost in a miscarriage as well as many other family members and close friends, I am sure we will have a lot to talk about. What a day that will be!

Bibliography

'Abdu'l-Bahá (1923) The Covenant of God. In Holley, H. ed. *Bahá'í Scriptures*. New York: Brentano's. pp. 265-555.

'Abdu'l-Bahá (1982) *'Abdu'l-Bahá in London*. London: Bahá'í Publishing Trust.

Assagioli M.D., R. (2000) *Psychosynthesis: A Collection of Basic Writings*. Amherst, Massachusetts: The Synthesis Center Inc.

Bahá'u'lláh (1975) *The Hidden Words*. Wilmette, Illinois: Bahá'í Publishing Trust.

Bahá'u'lláh (1976) *Gleanings from the Writings of Bahá'u'lláh*. 2nd ed. Wilmette: Bahá'í Publishing Trust.

Bahá'u'lláh (1991a) *Bahá'í Prayers*. Wilmette, Illinois: Bahá'í Publishing Trust.

Bahá'u'lláh (1991b) *The Seven Valleys and the Four Valleys*. Wilmette, Illinois: Bahá'í Publishing Trust.

Bahá'u'lláh (1992) *The Kitáb-i-Aqdas*. Haifa: The Universal House of Justice.

Bahá'í International Community (1995) *The Prosperity of Humankind*. London: Bahá'í Publishing Trust.

Baronial Order of Magna Charta (2009) *Magna Charta*. http://www.magnacharta.com/ [accessed 15 June 2011].

Browne, E.G. (2004) Introduction. In 'Abdu'l-Bahá *A Traveller's Narrative*. Los Angeles: Kalimat Press. pp. vii-liii.

Browning, E.B. (1954) *Sonnets from the Portugese and other Love Poems*. Garden City: Hanover House.

Chang, J. (1991) *The Tao of Love and Sex*. New York: Penguin.

Davis, A. (1954) *Let's Eat Right to Keep Fit*. San Diego: Harcourt Brace.

Doheny, K. (2010) *10 Surprising Health Benefits of Sex*. http://www.webmd.boots.com/sex-relationships/guide/10-surprising-health-benefits-of-sex [Accessed 24 April 2012]

Dossey, L. (1993.) *Healing Words: The Power of Prayer and the Practice of Medicine*. New York, N. Y.: Harper San Francisco, a Division of HarperCollins Publishers.

Duffell, N. & Løvendal, H. (2002) *Sex, Love and the Dangers of Intimacy*. London: Thorsons.

Dürckheim, K.G. (1980) *The Way of Transformation: Daily Life as Spiritual Exercise*. London: Unwin Paperbacks.

Esslemont, J. (2006) *Bahá'u'lláh and the New Era*. Wilmette, Illinois: Bahá'í Publishing Trust.

Ferrucci, P. (1982) *What We May Be: The Visions and Techniques of Psychosynthesis*. Wellingborough, Northamptonshire: Turnstone Press.

Gibran, K. (1992) *The Prophet*. London: Arkana, Penguin Books.

Hillman, J. (1997) *Suicide and the Soul*. 2nd ed. Woodstock, Connecticut: Spring Publications Inc.

Moore, C.C. (1823) The Night before Christmas. *Troy, New York, Sentinel,*.

Shoghi Effendi (1956) *God Passes By*. Wilmette, Illinois: Bahá'í Publishing Trust.

Shoghi Effendi (1968) *Bahá'í Administration* Wilmette, Illinois: Bahá'í Publishing Trust.

Universal House of Justice (2001) Letter to the author.

Appendix A
Prayer of Bahá'u'lláh – Tablet of Ahmad

"These daily obligatory prayers, together with a few other specific ones, such as the Healing Prayer, the Tablet of Ahmad, have been invested by Bahá'u'lláh with a special potency and significance, and should therefore be accepted as such and be recited by the believers with unquestioning faith and confidence, that through them they may enter into a much closer communion with God, and identify themselves more fully with His laws and precepts." – From a letter written on behalf of Shoghi Effendi

He is the King, the All-Knowing, the Wise! Lo the Nightingale of Paradise singeth upon the twigs of the Tree of Eternity, with holy and sweet melodies, proclaiming to the sincere ones the glad tidings of the nearness of God, calling the believers in the Divine Unity to the court of the Presence of the Generous One, informing the severed ones of the message which hath been revealed by God, the King, the Glorious, the Peerless, guiding the lovers to the seat of sanctity and to this resplendent Beauty.

Verily this is that Most Great Beauty, foretold in the Books of the Messengers, through whom truth shall be distinguished from error and the wisdom of every command shall be tested. Verily He is the Tree of Life that bringeth forth the fruits of God, the Exalted, the Powerful, the Great.

O Ahmad! Bear thou witness that verily He is God and there is no God but Him, the King, the Protector, the Incomparable, the Omnipotent. And that the One Whom He hat sent forth by the name of Ali (The Báb) was the true One from God to Whose commands we are all conforming.

Say: O People be obedient to the ordinances of God, which have been enjoined in the Bayán by the Glorious, the Wise One. Verily He is the King of the Messengers and His Book is the Mother Book did ye but know.

Thus doth the Nightingale utter His call unto you from this prison. He hath but to deliver this clear message. Whosoever desireth, let him turn aside from this counsel and whosoever desireth let him choose the path to his Lord.

O people, if ye deny these verses, by what proof have ye believed in God? Produce it, O assemblage of false ones.

Nay, by the One in Whose hand is my soul, they are not and never shall be able to do this, even should they combine to assist one another.

Oh Ahmad! Forget not My bounties while I am absent. Remember My days during thy days, and My distress and banishment in this remote prison. And be thou so steadfast in My love that thy heart shall not waver, even if the swords of the enemies rain blows upon thee and all the heavens and the earth arise against thee.

Be thou as a flame of fire to My enemies and a river of life eternal to My loved ones, and be not of those who doubt.

And if thou art overtaken by affliction in my path, or degradation for My sake, be not thou troubled thereby.

Rely upon God, thy God and the Lord of thy fathers. For the people are wandering in the paths of delusion, bereft of discernment to see God with their own eyes, or hear His Melody with their own ears. Thus have We found them, as thou also dost witness.

Thus have their superstitions become veils between them and their own hearts and kept them from the path of God, the Exalted the Great.

Be thou assured in thyself that verily, he who turns away from this Beauty hath also turned away from the Messengers of the past and showeth pride towards God from all eternity to all eternity.

Learn well this Tablet, O Ahmad. Chant it during thy days and withhold not thyself therefrom. For verily, God hath ordained for the one who chants it, the reward of a hundred martyrs and a service in both worlds. These favors have We bestowed upon thee as a bounty on Our part and a mercy from Our presence, that thou mayest be of those who are grateful.

By God! Should one who is in affliction or grief read this Tablet with absolute sincerity, God will dispel his sadness, solve his difficulties and remove his afflictions.

Verily, He is the Merciful, the Compassionate. Praise be to God, the Lord of all the worlds.

Bahá'u'lláh (1991a) The Tablet of Ahmad. In *Bahá'í Prayers*. Wilmette, Illinois: Bahá'í Publishing Trust. pp. 209-213.

Appendix B
Prayer of Bahá'u'lláh – From the Sweet-Scented Streams

From the sweet-scented streams of Thine eternity give me to drink, O my God, and of the fruits of the tree of Thy being enable me to taste, O my Hope! From the crystal springs of Thy love, suffer me to quaff, O my Glory, and beneath the shadow of Thine everlasting providence let me abide, O my Light! Within the meadows of Thy nearness, before Thy presence, make me able to roam, O my Beloved, and at the right hand of the throne of Thy mercy, seat me, O my Desire! From the fragrant breezes of Thy joy let a breath pass over me, O my Goal, and into the heights of the paradise of Thy reality let me gain admission, O my Adored One! To the melodies of the dove of Thy oneness suffer me to hearken, O resplendent One, and through the spirit of Thy power and Thy might quicken me, O my Provider! In the spirit of Thy love keep me steadfast, O my Succorer, and in the path of Thy good pleasure set firm my steps, O my Maker! Within the garden of Thine immortality, before Thy countenance, let me abide for ever, O Thou Who are merciful unto me, and upon the seat of Thy glory stablish me, O Thou Who art my Possessor! To the heaven of Thy loving-kindness life me up, O my Quickener, and unto the Daystar of Thy guidance lead me, O Thou my Attractor! Before the revelation of Thine invisible spirit summon me to be present, O Thou Who art my Origin and my Highest Wish, and unto the essence of the fragrance of Thy beauty, which Thou wilt manifest, cause me to return, O Thou Who art my God!

Potent art Thou to do what pleaseth Thee. Thou art, verily, the Most Exalted, the All-Glorious, the All-Highest.

Bahá'u'lláh (1991a) *Bahá'í Prayers*. Wilmette, Illinois: Bahá'í Publishing Trust. pp. 141-142.

www.ingramcontent.com/pod-product-compliance
Lightning Source LLC
Chambersburg PA
CBHW021958160426
43197CB00007B/173